TIMOTHY HYMAN is well known both as a writer on art and a painter. He was elected a Royal Academician in 2011 and is an honorary research fellow at University College London. He has exhibited widely and his work is in many public collections, including the British Museum, the Los Angeles County Museum of Art and the Deutsche Bank Collection. He was lead curator of Tate's major Stanley Spencer retrospective exhibition and has written a pioneering monograph on Bhupen Khakhar. His articles have appeared in the *Times Literary Supplement* and the *London Magazine*, and he is the author of *Bonnard* and *Sienese Painting*, both published by Thames & Hudson.

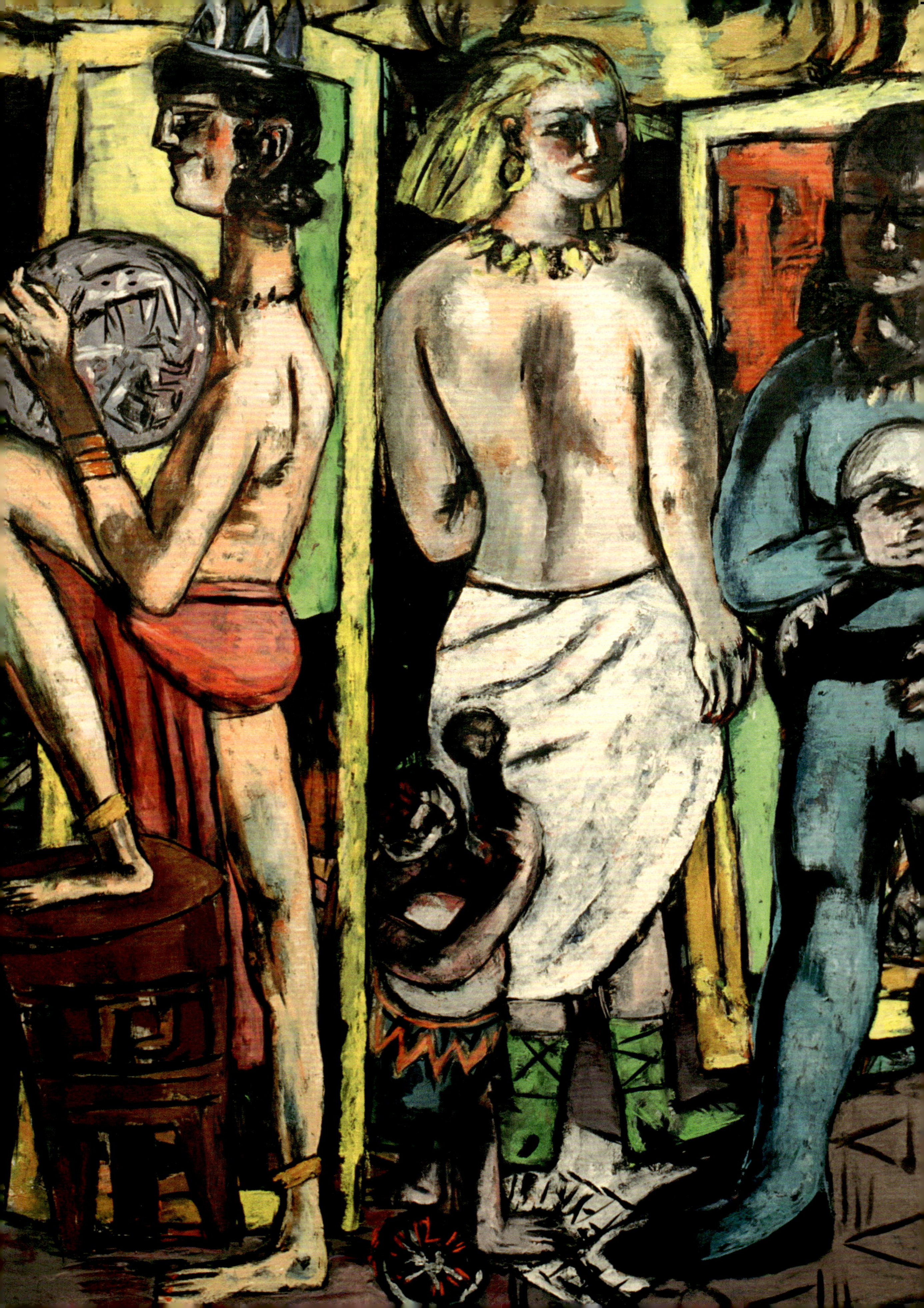

Timothy Hyman

THE WORLD NEW MADE

Figurative Painting in the Twentieth Century

With 158 illustrations

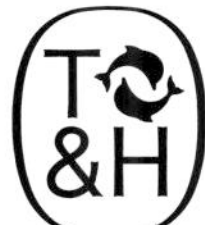

Dedicated to
EVA AND JEFF SKELLEY
Brave Comrades in Art and Life

Cover:

MARSDEN HARTLEY
Adelard the Drowned,
Master of 'The Phantom'
1938–39
(detail, see p. 48)

Frontispiece:

MAX BECKMANN
Acrobats
1937–39
(detail, see p. 155)

First published in the United Kingdom in 2016 by
Thames & Hudson Ltd, 181A High Holborn, London WC1V 7QX

First published in the United States of America in 2016 by
Thames & Hudson Inc., 500 Fifth Avenue, New York, New York 10110

First paperback edition 2022

The World New Made © 2016 Thames & Hudson Ltd, London
Text © 2016 Timothy Hyman

British Library Cataloguing-in-Publication Data
A catalogue record for this book is available from the British Library

Library of Congress Control Number 2015959507

ISBN 978-0-500-29653-0

Printed in China by Shenzhen Reliance Printing Co. Ltd

Be the first to know about our new releases,
exclusive content and author events by visiting
thamesandhudson.com
thamesandhudsonusa.com
thamesandhudson.com.au

CONTENTS

Painting and Experience in the Twentieth Century

To put a line around a form; to embody a vision in colour and tone; to re-create experience across a surface, equivalent to the depth and charged emotion of a lived life – for thousands of years such pictorial representations have engaged humankind. Yet in the twentieth century 'figurative painting' became an activity fraught with difficulty.

The history of twentieth-century art has often been told as a shift away from the illusionistic or representational towards the 'pure' and abstracted, structured in terms of an evolutionary sequence of 'movements': Cézanne passes the baton to Cubism, Cubism to Mondrian, Mondrian to American Painting... But that linear account of what we now call modernism no longer rings true. Abstract painting was just one of the ways by which, in the face of existential uncertainty, artists renewed pictorial language. In this book I will be concentrating on those twentieth-century painters who took a contrary path, towards a new kind of figuration.

MODERNISM AS LIBERTY

When the means of expression have become so refined, so attenuated that their power of expression wears thin, it is necessary to return to the essential principles which made human language.... This is the starting-point of Fauvism: the courage to return to the purity of the means.

HENRI MATISSE, 1936

In his huge canvas *The Dance* (1909–10) [illustration pp. 8–9] Henri Matisse (1869–1954) imagines a community reborn in naked primal liberty; an icon of earthly joy, whose antecedents are in Gauguin's Tahiti and Cézanne's bathers, in the 'primitive' worlds evoked by African tribal sculpture, but also in Greek and Roman literature. The perennial myth of a Golden Age – a time before hierarchy,

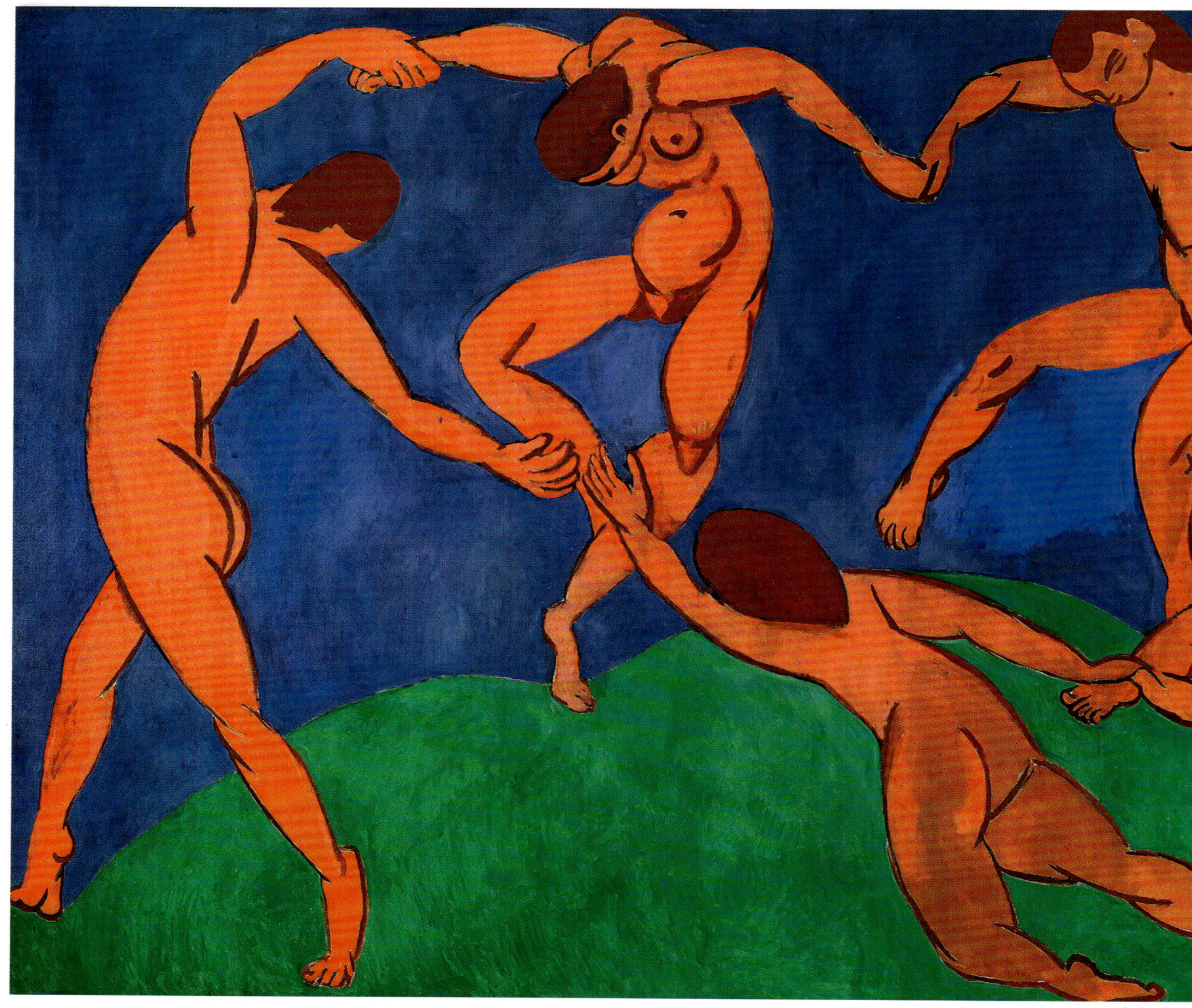

Commissioned for the first landing of the stairs at the Moscow Mansion of Sergei Schukin, *The Dance* was conceived as a functioning public image. 'I imagine the visitor coming in from the outside. There is the first floor. One must summon up energy, give a feeling of lightness.' Hence the springing rhythm that becomes emblematic of unbound liberty.

class, nation, gender, religion or race divided humankind – took on new potency in France around 1900, when Matisse became closely linked to older *Age d'Or* Anarchist painters such as Paul Signac, and Van Gogh's friend John Peter Russell on Belle-Île.

Ever since *Le Bonheur de Vivre* (The Enjoyment of Life) in 1905–6, Matisse had sought a pictorial language equivalent to that elemental vision; *Bathers with a Turtle* (1907–8) is another epic-scale affirmation. In *The Dance* he achieves a vernacular of utter directness: painting unburdened by aristocratic or bourgeois tradition, available to all. With its vast expanses of flat colour – the linear rhythm of the red dancers set within what he called an 'absolute' blue – Matisse shows how simplicity of means need not be impoverishment. Compositions of languorous nudes in a paradisal landscape had long been a staple of academy and salon – even Ingres had painted *The Golden Age* in 1862. Yet Matisse's version of the Age of Gold is too exhilarating to signify mere nostalgia. Encountering *The Dance* today, at the

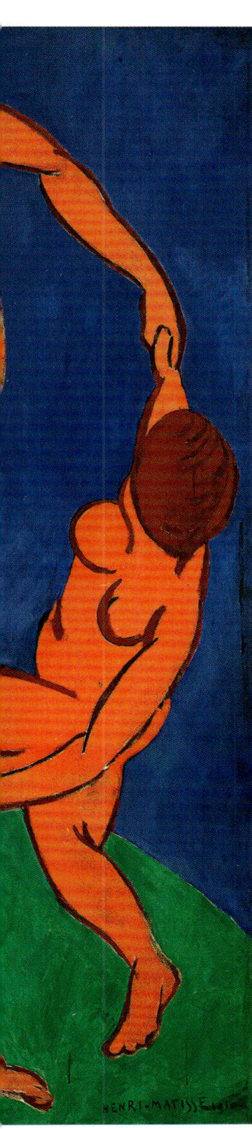

Hermitage in St Petersburg, it registers as a public image of liberation, prophetic of future revolution.

I have placed this image at the outset of this book to stand for the cleansing of pictorial language in the early twentieth century. That moment of joyful liberty can be felt also in several of Matisse's contemporaries in the first rooms of the Museum of Modern Art in New York, but as Cubism becomes a 'movement', a sense of restriction and exclusion, of an oppressive stylistic imperative, sets in. Matisse himself would acknowledge having been painfully 'grazed' by Cubism [see p. 18]. The full impact of art as imprisoning ideology is felt after 1920, as the modernist canon is first contested. During the 1930s both Nazi Germany and Stalinist Russia adopted variants of academic realism, and suppressed modernism; in the 1950s, the CIA in turn invested heavily in abstract painting as cultural propaganda of the Cold War.

The Dominance of Abstraction

Abstraction is the major mode of expression
in our time; any other mode is necessarily minor.

CLEMENT GREENBERG, 1954

Across the past hundred years abstract painting has carried many meanings, but the primary rationale has always remained: that the material, observed world is less significant than the metaphysical. Hegel had written of 'spirit...liberating itself from nature'; the theosophical underpinnings of Mondrian, Malevich and Kandinsky gave an explicitly evolutionary thrust to their art. By the mid-1920s there was a loose network, centred on the Bauhaus, united in the belief that humankind's continuing progress was embodied in 'non-objective' art. Abstraction was seen as more spiritually evolved, more advanced, than figuration, which was regarded as retrograde. Geometric abstraction, especially, appeared to be aligned to modern science and engineering; the anarchist, poet and critic Herbert Read, as early as 1935, saw abstraction as 'the art of the new classless society [...] all the artists of any intellectual force belong to this movement'. At its height – for some thirty years, roughly 1952 to 1982 – the triumph of abstraction seemed so evident that many believed painting was moving inexorably towards the non-representational. 'It is no longer possible', wrote the critic–painter Andrew Forge in 1968, 'to imagine figurative painting as an alternative tradition.' Modern art and abstraction had become almost synonymous.

A few years later, beginning in the mid-1970s, a parallel account had painting itself withering away in favour of other media (video and installation, interventions and stagings) – grouped together as 'conceptual', 'third area' or 'the expanded field'. In both these versions of twentieth-century art history, figurative painters were cast as backward children, conservative throwbacks, outdated survivors.

An alternative formulation would be to see the artists in this book as a kind of 'Resistance', responding first to Cubism, then to other varieties of abstraction, but never losing their concern for a core of experience – physical, social, psychological – that could not be reduced or schematized.

PEOPLING THE VOID: EPISODES FROM AN ALTERNATIVE HISTORY

*Man would prefer to make the void his
object than be devoid of objects.*

FRIEDRICH NIETZSCHE, 1887

A sense of unreality in objects was shared by representational as well as abstract painters. The kinds of figuration I will be celebrating in this book emerged from that same existential experience, often referred to by the artists themselves as 'The Void'; as when Picasso writes in 1932: 'Each time I take up a picture I have the sensation of throwing myself into the void.' Max Beckmann invokes 'this infinite space, the foreground of which one must constantly pile up with any kind of junk so that one will not see behind it to the terrible depth.' Expressionists experienced this Void, Dadaists and Surrealists made a thesis of it, Abstract Expressionists a metaphysic. In the opening chapter of this book, Fernand Léger follows the path into The Void – but then re-emerges, able to affirm a reality in objects. Léger's art has to pass through the purgatory of abstraction in order to be liberated for a renewed, revalidated figuration. He wrote in 1937:

> It was the Impressionists who made the breakthrough, especially Cézanne.
> The Moderns have followed by accentuating this liberation. We have freed
> colour and geometric form. [...] It *is* possible for us to create and realize a new
> collective social art. We are merely waiting for social evolution to permit it.

It might seem a violation to construct any common cause out of such wayward individuals as Max Beckmann and R. B. Kitaj, Charlotte Salomon and Philip Guston, Alice Neel and Ken Kiff, Balthus and Bhupen Khakhar, Leon Golub and Stanley Spencer, yet in their different contexts each was linked by their 'resistance'. These artists should not be confused with academic diehards; their art was nourished by the same concern for a renewal of pictorial language that fed their abstract counterparts. There is a shared trait of the *emphatic* in several of these painters – in the exaggerated black contours of Léger, Beckmann, Hartley and Guston, for example – that evidences their difficulty in resisting the dematerializing Void, as if they needed to *insist* on The Real.

Even so apparently unwavering a figurative painter as Beckmann viewed 'positive tangible reality' as an illusion. 'I hardly need to abstract things, for each object is unreal enough already, so unreal that I can only make it real by means of painting.' This could be applied to most of my cast here. Their figuration acknowledges the Void, even if they rebound from it. They are aware of the claims of abstraction – as a transcendence, as a purification, as an autonomous pictorial language – and it affects their art. Abstraction, both in its salutary stringency and in its oppression, becomes midwife to a newborn figuration.

In this book I am not attempting any comprehensive survey; the field is too large, too crowded with the most diverse individual artists. I have conceived it, rather, as an archipelago – with each painter as an island on which to touch down, however briefly, almost as a picaresque episode, before flying on to the next. Several will be represented only by a single painting; each stands for some much wider hinterland.

My first decision was to cut back on the two painters I recognize as by far the most influential: Picasso and Matisse. Throughout the chapters that follow, these two will be felt as giant, but mostly hidden, presences. This allows me to focus on artists whose development may be less familiar (for example Hartley, Salomon, Kiff, Neel, Khakhar) and to give space to those most central to my project (including Léger, Beckmann, Balthus, Chagall, Spencer, Kitaj and Guston). My bias throughout is evident: I am less concerned with 'straight realism' than with artists who create narratives and microcosms.

Although early in the century artists such as Paula Modersohn-Becker and Frida Kahlo exemplify that new flowering of women painters prophesied by the poet Rainer Maria Rilke (see p. 121), in practice an exaggeratedly masculinist painting-culture became dominant. The women figurative painters discussed here are the exception. Eventually, a range of prominent artists who happened to be both figurative painters and women (Mamma Andersson, Marlene Dumas, Nicole Eisenman, Rosa Loy, Nilima Sheikh and Dana Schutz among them) did emerge, but their achievement has mostly been recognized after 2000.

One spur for writing was the exclusion from current narratives of twentieth-century art of so many of the paintings I have loved most. Thus within the 700 dense pages of the quasi-canonical *Art Since 1900* (written by Rosalind Krauss, Yve-Alain Bois, Benjamin Buchloh and Hal Foster, published in 2004) there is almost no overlap with my own cast: no early Chagall, no Rousseau, no late Léger; no mention of Balthus or Spencer; no Beckmann triptych or late Bonnard self-portrait; no Charlotte Salomon or Alice Neel; no late Guston or Henry Darger. So this 'alternative' account is both corrective and refutation – a recognition of diversity.

Perhaps this book is best understood as the history of a collective *retrieval*. All across the world, isolated artists found an idiom for human-centred painting in the midst of modern life. Both anthology and hagiology, my book sets out to assemble those free spirits. Together they offer a counter-argument to Western formalism, as well as a promise, and even a foundation, for the figurative painters of the twenty-first century.

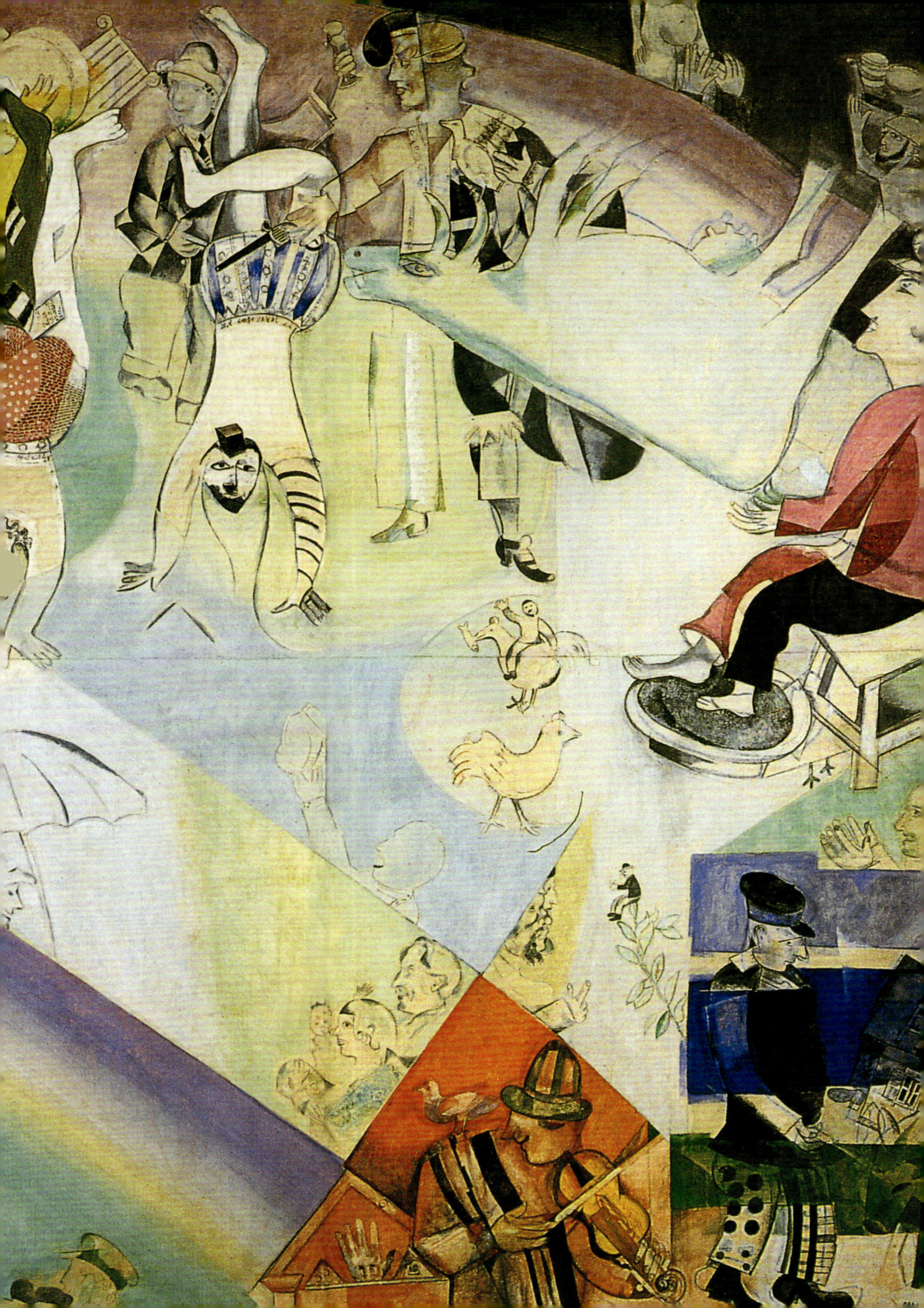

CHAPTER ONE

After Cubism: Reinventing the Language of Representation

To set Picasso's monumental *Seated Man with Glass* of 1914 [illustration p. 14] alongside Léger's three-metre canvas of 1954 *The Campers* [illustration p. 15], is to recognize the expansion of pictorial language that Cubism opened up for modern figuration. Pablo Picasso (1881–1973) is just emerging from the monochrome, bare linearity of early Cubism, into exuberant painterliness. *Seated Man* remains cryptic – an invitation to a riddle we will never entirely solve. Piecing together the clues, I take him to be a black-clad drinker on a stool at the corner of a bar, napkin on lap. His head is a kind of white helmet seen in profile, while two other mask-like heads may indicate his drinking companions. Most evident is the contrast between the central black shape of leg and torso (in which the zigzag lapel is especially telling) and the profusion of little dots that bubble tipsily all around him, out of the pale green field; including, on the right, a dotted French Tricolour.

Across this huge, sustained *jeu d'esprit*, the figure is being retrieved piece by piece, almost as a series of 'part-objects'. We might look ahead, to Philip Guston for example (see pp. 197–98, 216–19), and imagine what is entailed when an artist rebuilds the figured world after abstraction. Was Picasso's post-Cubist turn towards figuration, as some have argued, a failure of nerve, an apostasy? Rather, at the moment of *Seated Man*, there seems an entirely new possibility in representation; from this springboard, painting can go anywhere.

In Léger's *Campers*, forty years and two world wars later, the problematic and broken world of Cubism appears to have receded. Under close scrutiny the image proves to be full of tensions and ambiguities: how, for example, does the tentpole come to have both ends visible? This is a long way from literal depiction. The Picasso of 1914 offers primarily an enjoyment of visual language; the Léger of 1954 (discussed in detail, pp. 25–26), the conviction of a reimagined reality, of wholeness.

For figurative painting, Cubism marked a new beginning, both a cleansing and a reactivation. Painters such as Mondrian and Malevich (see pp. 36–37) saw Cubism as opening the path to an art entirely free of reference to the objective

MARC CHAGALL

Introduction to the Yiddish Theatre

1920

(detail, see pp. 38–39)

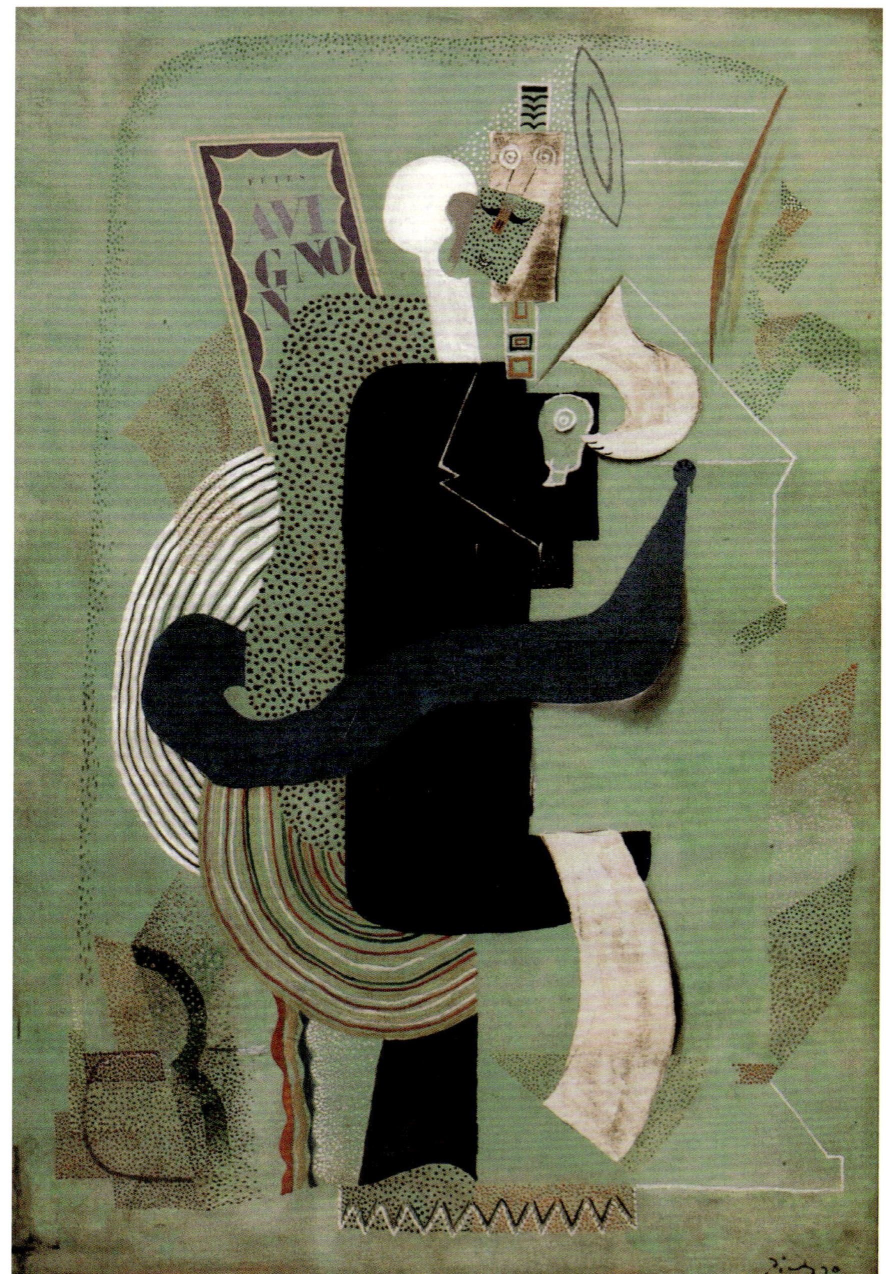

world, a stepping-stone to abstraction. Yet Cubism could also be defined as a kind
of realism – a break with mere naturalism, in order to make a free investigation of
the true essence of things.

The Cubist paintings of Picasso and Braque in 1910–11 had been as restricted
in scale as they were in colour and subject-matter: mostly small still lifes, with a
scattering of 'portraits' and depthless 'landscapes'. The ambition of the French
nineteenth-century *grandes machines* – those public-scale, complex easel pictures,
secular heirs to altarpiece and fresco, from Géricault's *Raft of the Medusa* (1818–19)
to Seurat's *A Sunday Afternoon on the Island of La Grande-Jatte* (1884–86) – seemed

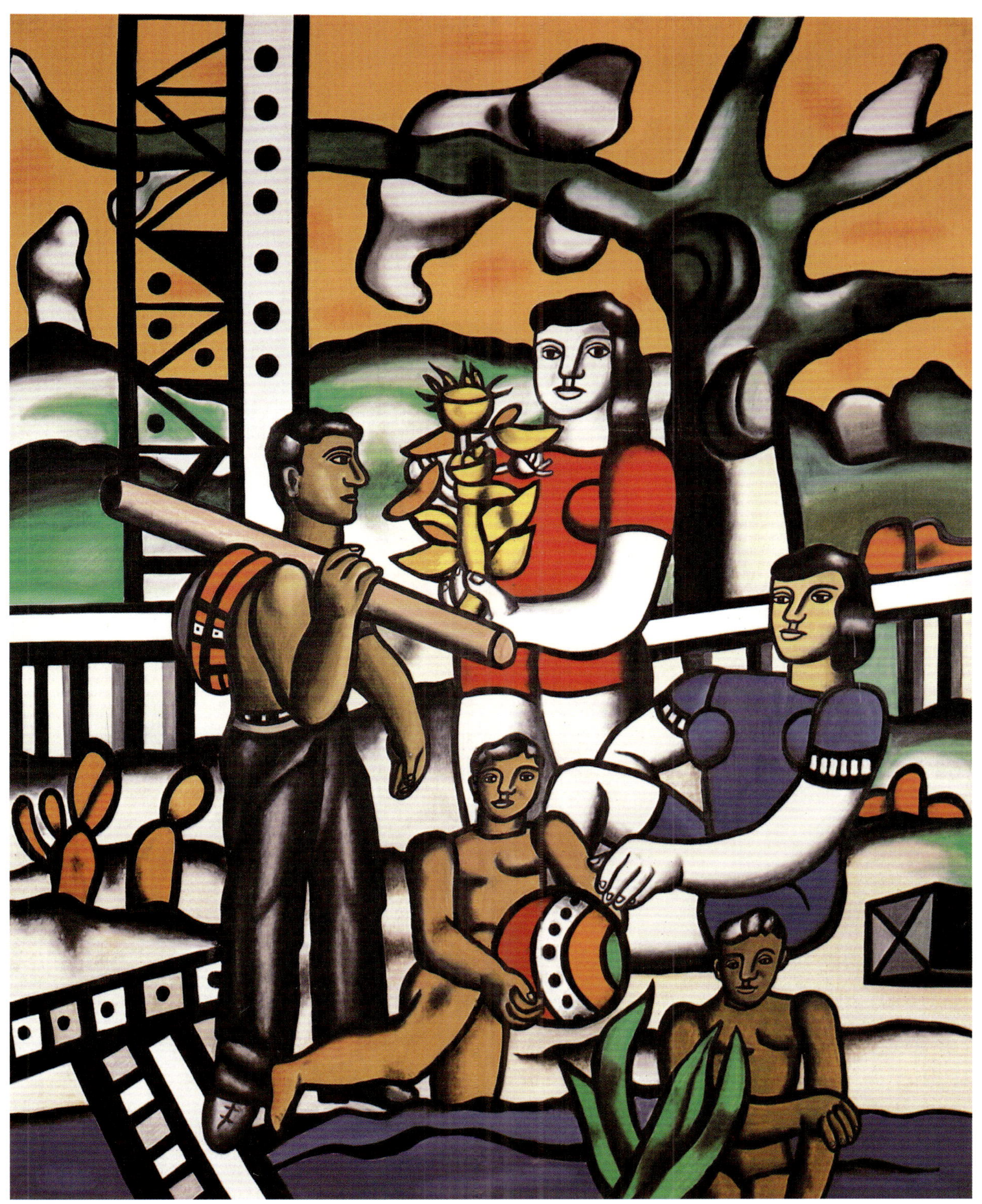

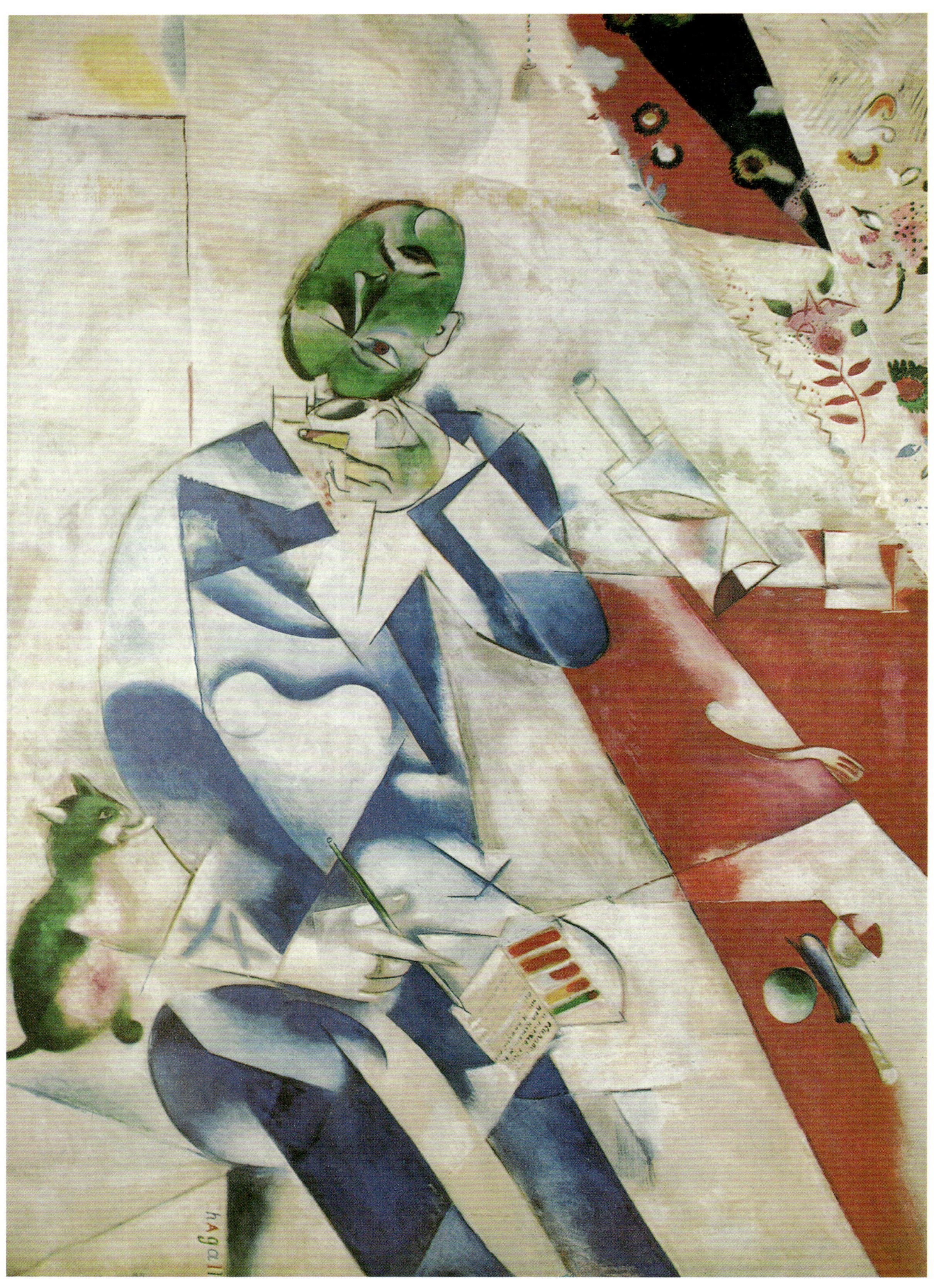

to have been jettisoned. But that aspiration would resurface, not least in Picasso himself. In Léger, it became paramount; and *The Campers* may best be understood as a mid-twentieth-century *machine*, realized in a post-Cubist vernacular.

The quest for that new 'vernacular' idiom will be a central theme throughout this book. All the painters in this chapter started out steeped in Cézanne and Cubism but found they needed a more demotic pictorial language – less stylized, less insistently broken – if they were to convey the fluid continuity of everyday experience. Although some later interpretations of Cubism, such as Alice Neel's 'the human race torn in pieces' (see Ch 2 pp. 104–9), might seem naïve, the reconstruction and healing of the shattered image will be a shared project for most of the painters in this book.

CHAGALL'S *HALF PAST THREE (THE POET)*, (1911)

I was alone in my studio in front of my oil lamp.
Two or three in the morning.... Dawn is breaking....
I used to sit up like that all night long.
My lamp burned, and I with it.

MARC CHAGALL, *c.* 1920

Half Past Three (The Poet) [illustration opposite] registers the impact of the Cubist counterculture on the twenty-four-year-old Moyshe Shagal (1887–1985), who had arrived in Paris two years earlier from Vitebsk. He was now based in *'La Ruche'* (The Beehive) – the art-phalanstery at the slaughterhouse-edge of Montparnasse, where Léger rented the next-door studio, and Amedeo Modigliani and Chaim Soutine would eventually become fellow lodgers (see Ch 3 pp. 134–35). Befriended by Robert Delaunay, and by the poet Blaise Cendrars (a lifelong comrade of Léger), the reinvented 'Marc Chagall' flowered, painting his first enduring masterpieces in a fractured, ecstatic idiom that fuses Cubism with El Greco (whose work had become familiar after his Salon d'Automne retrospective in 1908).

The more-than-lifesize Poet pauses from writing, and as he drinks, encouraged by his affectionate cat, his head spins off into planetary, topsy-turvy realms. Chagall had already been criticized by hard-line Cubists (he called them 'formalists') for being too literary. *Half Past Three* is both riposte and manifesto – a declaration that Cubist language should serve not just The Real, but the poetic imagination also. 'Painting', wrote Chagall, 'seemed to me a window through which I could take flight into another world.' In Chagall's later works that sense of euphoric floating can wear thin. But in *Half Past Three* his lyricism is given an edge by the astringency of Cubist syntax – linearity, slants, flatness, geometry – which would still inflect his mural-scale *Introduction to the Yiddish Theatre* [see illustration pp. 38–39] nearly a decade later. By the time of his greatest achievement as a graphic artist, the *Dead Souls* etchings of 1924–25 [see pp. 33–41, illustrations pp. 34–35], Chagall would discover a liberty of language beyond all Cubist stylization.

MARC CHAGALL
Half Past Three (The Poet)
1911–12

Alongside the fracturing of Cubism, Chagall's art was fed by the parallel, kaleidoscopic verse of his friends Apollinaire and Cendrars and the similarly broken syntax of Russian poets such as Mayakovsky and Khlebnikov. The actual Cyrillic text is a poem by Aleksandr Blok. Left behind in Berlin in 1914, *Half Past Three* was one of three key pictures at last returned to Chagall in 1926. Purchased by Christian Zervos (a close associate of Picasso who had just begun his editorship of *Cahiers d'Art*), it was sold on – by Marcel Duchamp as agent – to the great collectors, the Arensbergs.

MATISSE'S *VIEW OF NÔTRE DAME* (1914)

*The period when Cubism was occupying the forefront
of the art scene was a difficult one for me...I was
virtually alone in not participating in Cubism.*

HENRI MATISSE, 1952

Late in life, Matisse admitted to having been 'grazed' by Cubism. He knew that his deepest aspirations – to pleasure, to serenity, to the affirmation of an earthly paradise – were being mocked by the young Picasso and his gang: 'How they made me suffer!' He'd seen André Derain, his closest disciple and co-founder of Fauvism, go over to the 'other side'. The aesthetic of Cubism was skeletal, a puristic stripping of colour, of the natural fleshiness of oil paint, in order to reveal the bare bones.

By 1914, and then throughout the First World War, Matisse's imagery also became stark, harsh, reduced. *The Moroccans* (1916) is his large-scale masterpiece from that conflicted period; Pierre Schneider has called it 'a tragic formulation of happiness'. *Bathers by a River*, begun in 1909 alongside *The Dance* [illustration pp. 8–9] on a canvas of exactly the same vast dimensions (and partly a homage to the little Cézanne *Bathers* he had bought from the gallerist Ambroise Vollard in 1899), finally emerges in 1917 as the closest to Cubism of all Matisse's Golden-Age *machines*.

Both these epic works have been richly explored in recent writing. I want here to focus on a picture rather more modest in scale, the *View of Nôtre Dame* (1914) [illustration opposite]: about five feet high – that is, roughly twice the size of a typical Impressionist view. Matisse had been painting the cathedral from his studio window on the Quai Saint Michel ever since 1895; that view had remained one of the most stable presences in his life. But in 1914 every aspect of this seeing was thrown into question. The canvas records the processes by which the image has come into being. He watches himself. We are allowed to see all the procedures – scrapings, erasures, surgeries – by which the cathedral is made to shift and swell so uncertainly; and we are made to feel the mystery and strangeness of spatial representation. He tests his own reactions to the marks he has made. And eventually, out of the blue matrix, these traces and signs coalesce fully to become a monumental pictorial statement.

Matisse would never again approach so close to the image-annihilating Void. As in the *Portrait of Madame Matisse* of the previous year the subject, made up of half-eradicated vestiges, just barely survives – a truth emerging from all the potential lies of conventional academic representation. Matisse wrote in this period of each painting as an 'ensemble of signs' and his *View of Nôtre Dame* becomes even more poignant when set beside his total life's work, as the near-monochrome of a great colourist. Cubism's bitter aseptic had cleansed his art of all facile lyricism. What resulted was a kind of *tabula rasa* from which, in 1920s Nice, Matisse could set out once again to describe, to elaborate and even to embellish.

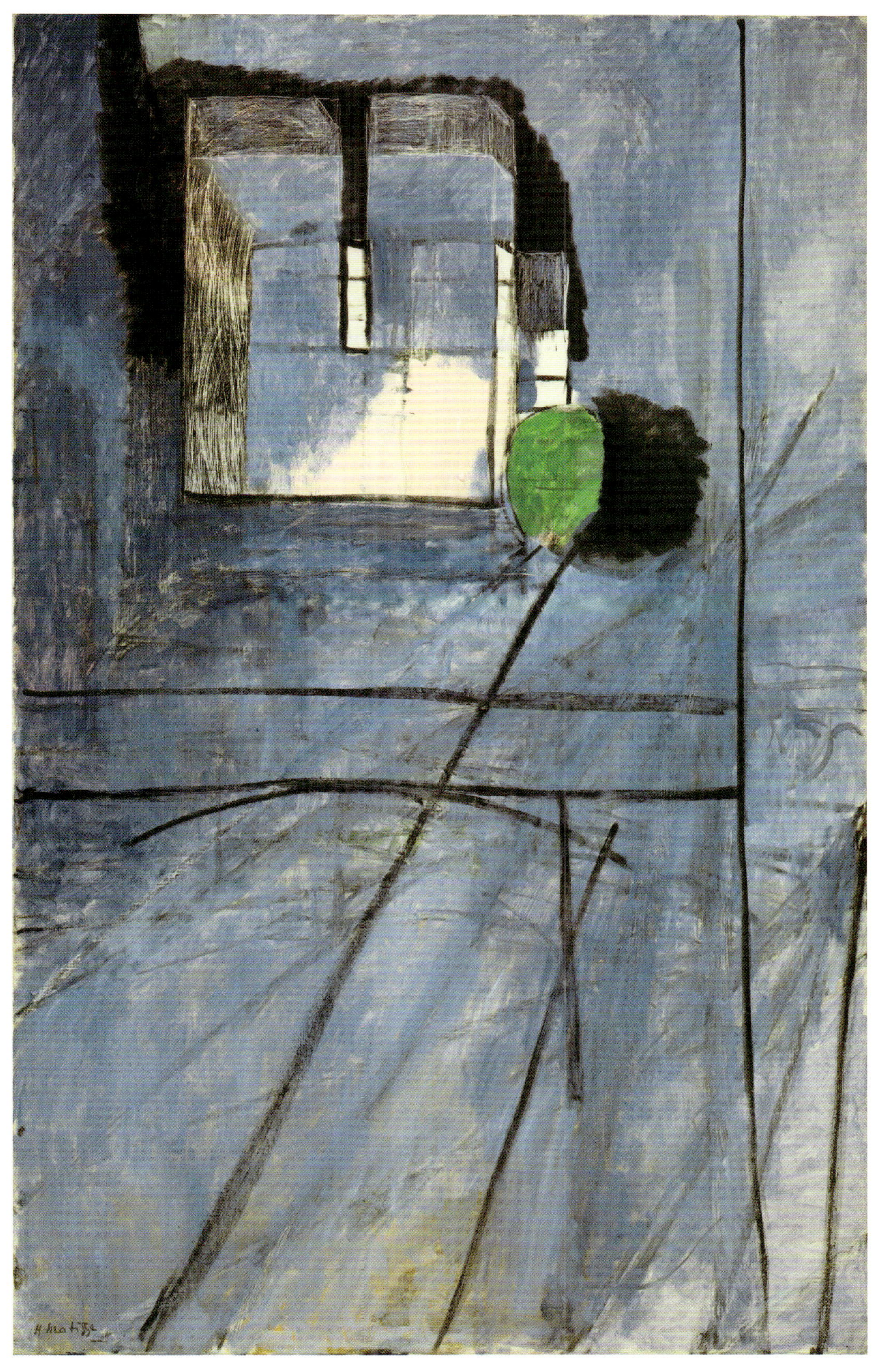

LÉGER, ROUSSEAU AND THE 'RETURN TO "GREAT SUBJECTS"' (1918–54)

*A return to 'great subjects'. That, it seems to me,
is the normal logical direction for the contemporary
evolution of easel painting, after the whole gamut of
explorations that has been made since Impressionism.*

FERNAND LÉGER, 1952

I want to return to Léger, and trace the long journey that led him to *The Campers*
of 1954 [illustration p. 15], partly in the artist's own words. He arrived in Paris aged
nineteen, in the first year of the new century, after apprenticeship in Normandy
as an architectural draughtsman. His writings cover the period from 1913 to 1955,
the year of his death; through them, we can relive afresh the narrative of painting
in the early twentieth century.

Fundamental to his own development was his changing attitude towards the
object. In the imagery of the *fin-de-siècle*, whether *Symboliste* or Impressionist,
the world of objects had begun to appear spectral, weightless, dissolved. 'I
sometimes wonder', Léger wrote later, 'what would have happened to painting
without Cézanne.' For his generation, the impact of the 1907 Cézanne memorial
retrospective at the Salon d'Automne had been transforming. Yet Cézanne had
returned painting to the object, only to assert that 'the relations between objects
are more important than the objects themselves'. And it was chiefly from Cézanne
that Braque and Picasso would derive the language of Cubism, an art made up *only*
of 'relations', where the object was once again dematerialized. As Léger recalled:

> It took me three years to discard Cézanne's influence. His hold on
> me was so strong that I had to go right into abstraction to throw it off.

A fundamental 'contrast' underlying reality first occurred to Léger in 1910, as he
watched smoke rising above the rooftops from Montparnasse station: curved against
angular, soft against hard. From that point onwards that same vertical structure
appeared repeatedly, as *Houses in the Trees* (1913), for example, or more enigmatically
in his seven-foot canvas *The Wedding* (1911), where little faceted, urban males clamber
over the pale, smoky curves of a gigantic female nude. By 1913, he was rendering the
metaphor more starkly, in a long sequence of quasi-abstract images, painted very
rapidly in impasto on rough canvas, entitled *Contrasts of Forms*.

Soon after the outbreak of the First World War, Léger went into the trenches, first
as a sapper, later as a stretcher-bearer. In 1917 he was gassed at Verdun, and invalided
out. He wrote in 1949:

> During those four war years I was abruptly thrust into a reality which was
> both blinding and new. This was enough to make me forget the abstract art
> of 1912–13. A complete revelation to me both as a man and as a painter.
> Suddenly, and without any break, I found myself on an equal footing with

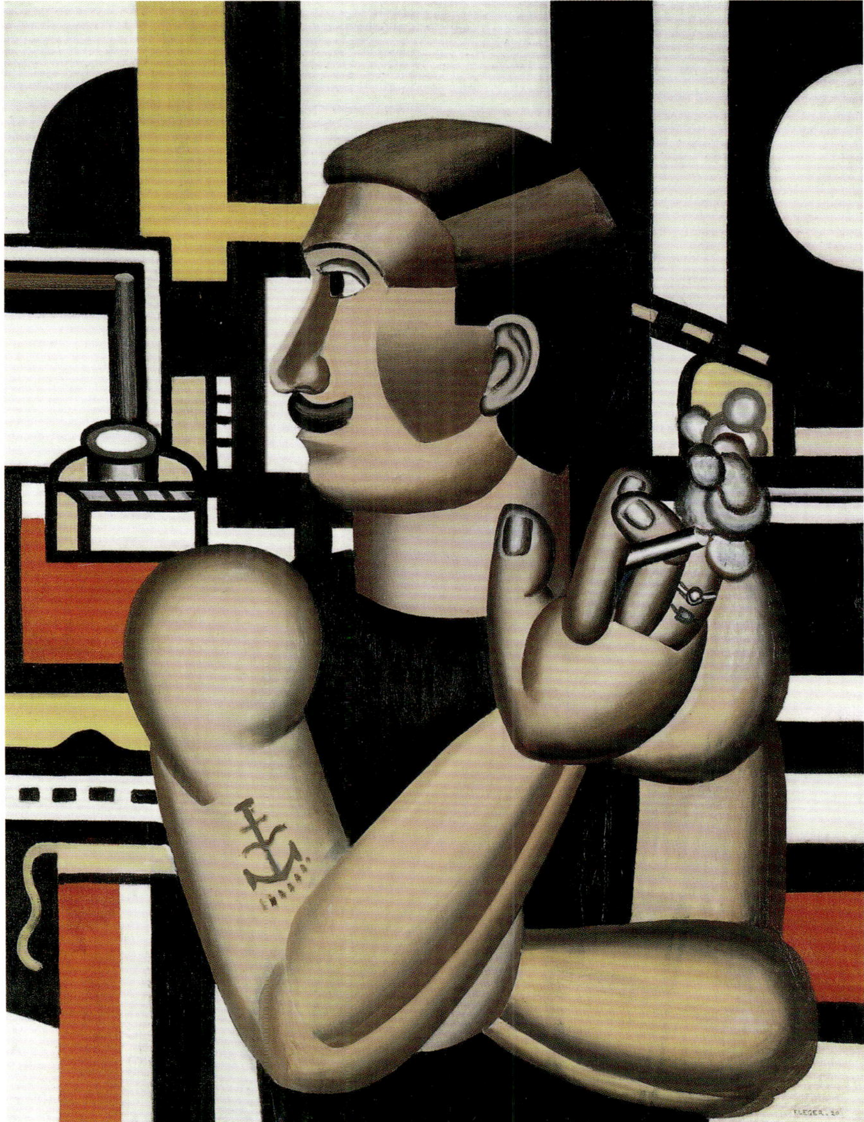

FERNAND LÉGER

The Mechanic

1920

As is evident from *The Mechanic*'s abstracted setting, Léger was stimulated by his contact with the Dutch movement *de Stijl*. He wrote an admiring essay on Mondrian in 1931: 'this path is dominated by that same desire for perfection and total liberation which produces saints, madmen and heroes.'

the whole French people.... Once I had got my teeth into that sort of reality, I never let go of objects again.

The Mechanic (1920) [illustration above] is the first uncompromising icon of Léger's affirmation of the figure. We no longer grope our way through a Cézannian 'reference' to objects; by the force of the image, we come near to grasping the object directly. Seeking a new way of painting the human figure, substantial yet uncorrupted by historical style, Léger enlisted the much older painter he'd come to know just before his death, Henri Rousseau (1844–1910). *The Mechanic*'s huge cigarette-toting hand is a near-quotation from Rousseau's 1891 *Portrait of Pierre Loti*. The innocence of Rousseau enters not only Léger's art, but much of modern figuration, recovering a primal truth in painting. Rousseau's majestic single figures, such as *Child with Doll* (1904–5) [illustration p. 22], affirm a world new-made, with all the power and intensity of a child's vision.

Rousseau was a painter's painter: Picasso owned four, Kandinsky two, Robert Delaunay at least twenty. In this book, artists as various as Beckmann and Carrà, Stanley Spencer and Bhupen Khakhar, will all at some point look to Henri Rousseau as exemplar for a renewal of figural language, reborn in the image of childhood.

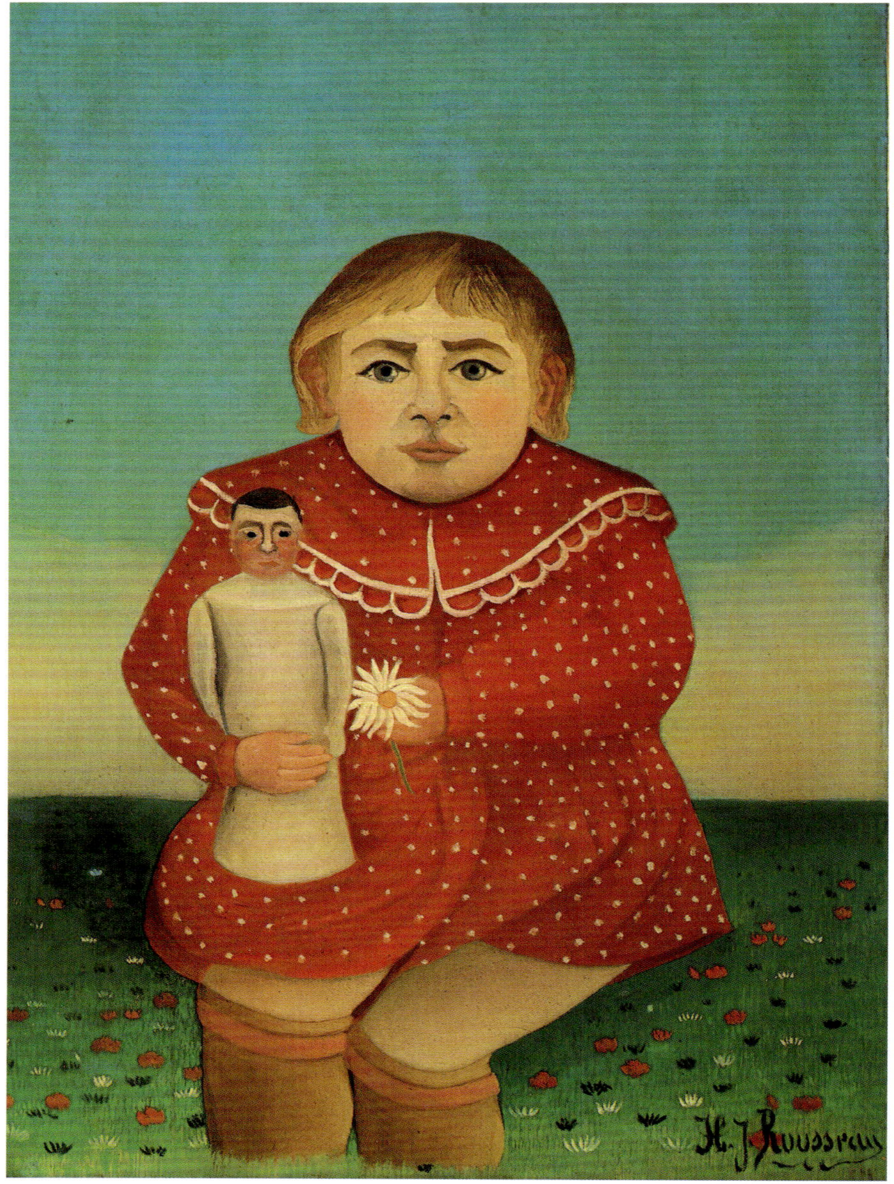

Léger saw Henri Rousseau as reaching back to a freedom lost ever since the Renaissance: 'I was attracted to Romanesque sculptures, to the completely reinvented figures, the freedom with which the Romanesque artist constructed them.... The whole question is there, one invents or one does not; the Renaissance copies, the pre-Renaissance invents, Rousseau invents.' The new generation's admiration for Rousseau was as much ethical as formal. 'Such a love, such personal generosity, such a gift of his naked heart, such absence of falsehood', wrote Robert Delaunay (supporter not only of Rousseau but also of the young Chagall). As Léger recalled in 1955:

I came straight from a milieu of intellectuals to find myself among peasants, labourers and bargemen.... I wanted my work as a painter to be as tough as their slang... I thought back again to my first abstract studies, and a quite different idea concerning the means, the use and application of abstract art took root in my mind.

The Mechanic is building the new post-war world: Léger embeds his rounded forms within an abstract grid, borrowed from his friend Mondrian. That 'contrast' of human and machine, of figurative and abstract, could be seen as visual equivalent to dialectical materialism. Léger was already in his mid-thirties when the 1917 Bolshevik Revolution transformed the European Left, and his social ideas were rooted in syndicalism, a devolution of power to collectivized trade unions. When the French Communist Party was founded in 1920, he didn't become a member, and in the 1930s he would often clash with Party hardliners. Alongside his architect friend Le Corbusier (a lifelong syndicalist, who he first met in 1920) Léger strove to create an imagery of utopian community; but in Léger's case that aspiration was essentially libertarian. From *Speaking of Cinema*, 1933:

> Cinema is thirty years old; it is young, modern, free, and has no
> traditions. This is its strength. It sprouts in every corner of the district....
> It is on an equal footing with the street, with life.... It is in shirtsleeves.
> Mass-produced, ready-made, it is collective.

The Syphon (1924) [illustration p. 25] presents a 'close-up', an everyday object rendered monumental. Léger painted it while completing his avant-garde film, *Ballet mécanique* (Mechanical Ballet) – the opening and closing of a human eye juxtaposed with the repeated motion of a piston. Yet what is most striking in *The Syphon* is its fixity; despite his cinematic espousal of the dynamism of modern life, in his painting Léger becomes an artist of closed, complete, stable forms: hand and lever are an affirmation only of stillness and permanence.

In *The Syphon* and in figure-icons such as *Nude on a Red Background* (1927) [illustration p. 25], Léger can be affiliated with that conscious renewal of the classical, manifested in so many European painters after 1918. The mood of post-war reconstruction seemed to demand an idiom less fractured than Cubism. Unlike Picasso, however, Léger never invoked classical tradition in the spirit of parody; and in contrast to his fellow-northerner Matisse, his classicism took on no 'Mediterranean' overtones. From 1923 onwards, he set out to reimagine a classical figure for the machine age. *Nude on a Red Background* is single-breasted, something of an Amazon; beside the nudes of Matisse or Picasso, she presents herself without erotic charge. She is a new genus, almost science fiction. Yet she is not robotic: the impassive, fearless gaze of Léger's faces always preserves the warmth and vulnerability of a human presence.

He remained discontented with the social function of the painter as creator of trophies or commodities for the rich. 'You are fortunate', he wrote to the Russian film director Sergei Eisenstein in 1932, 'in belonging to a profession which is socially oriented to the masses. We are isolated by the fact that our public is an exclusive one.' Eisenstein told Léger he'd often had *Ballet mécanique* in mind while making the montages of *Battleship Potemkin* (1925). But in the mid-1920s Léger was still committed, both in his cinema, and in painting, to an avant-garde modernism that refused all narrative.

Many twentieth-century painters had seemed content to see their role shrink, allowing cinema to annex all that was most loved in the art of the past: narrative, human presence and even eventually, the image itself. By contrast, Léger came to admire cinema as an exemplar that could lead him to a new kind of painting – more fully popular, more human, richer in imagery. But the screen never can fulfil the serenely architectural functions of a monumental painting; cinema can fling imagery around, it can simulate dreams, it can create a rhythm, but it cannot become part of the stillness of a wall.

> My architect friends, we should be able to get together about this wall. You want to forget that painters are brought into this world to destroy dead surfaces, to make them liveable, to spare us from overly extreme architectural solutions.… Out of pride, you haven't wanted to call in the painter, who is waiting at the foot of the stairs…he is waiting for your decisions.…

Léger was reproaching architects at a conference in 1933: he believed the re-integration of the painter in society was bound up with a renewal of mural-painting. Like so many painters before and since, he recognized the majesty of the mural tradition; the sense that easel painting was a diminishment, not just in scale, but in aspiration – as when an Impressionist landscape is set beside, say, Giotto's Arena Chapel of *c.* 1305. Part of the attraction was functional: the mural lifts painting out of the market, where it ceases to be a commodity, and also provides a true atelier role for assistants (as Léger's Montparnasse associate Diego Rivera demonstrated in Mexico during the 1920s [see pp. 41–45]). Léger came to feel modernist architects had broken the 'contract' that should exist between 'the wall – the architect – the painter': 'The modern architect has *gone too far* in his magnificent attempts to cleanse through emptiness.'

His own architectural collaborations were, in practice, disappointing – whether with Le Corbusier, on *Le Pavillon de l'esprit nouveau* (Pavilion of the New Spirit) of 1925; in his dialogue with Alvar Aalto; or his contact in America with Buckminster Fuller. During the 1930s, more politically engaged than most painters, Léger became a frequent speaker at the anti-fascist and *Front populaire* rallies, and his atelier students assisted him in carrying out several huge, but always semi-abstract, hoardings. Although he spoke of a 'return to "great subjects"', in the murals he still held back from any large-scale human depiction. Perhaps that would have brought him too close to his enemies: to salon academics, to Soviet realists, to the overscaled posturings of fascist figuration.

By the 1930s, Léger had become famous in America and when France fell under occupation he crossed the Atlantic into exile. Still in New York in 1945, he at last joined the French Communist Party, though aware this would bar him from future re-entry into the USA. His next, final decade would be centred on a sequence of wall-sized easel paintings, never explicitly political, but each a warmly humorous celebration of some collective endeavour: a victorious bicycle team; an acrobatic feat, brought off together by the clowns and circus-people of *The Great Parade* (1954); and *The Constructors* (1951), assembled on the scaffolding of the

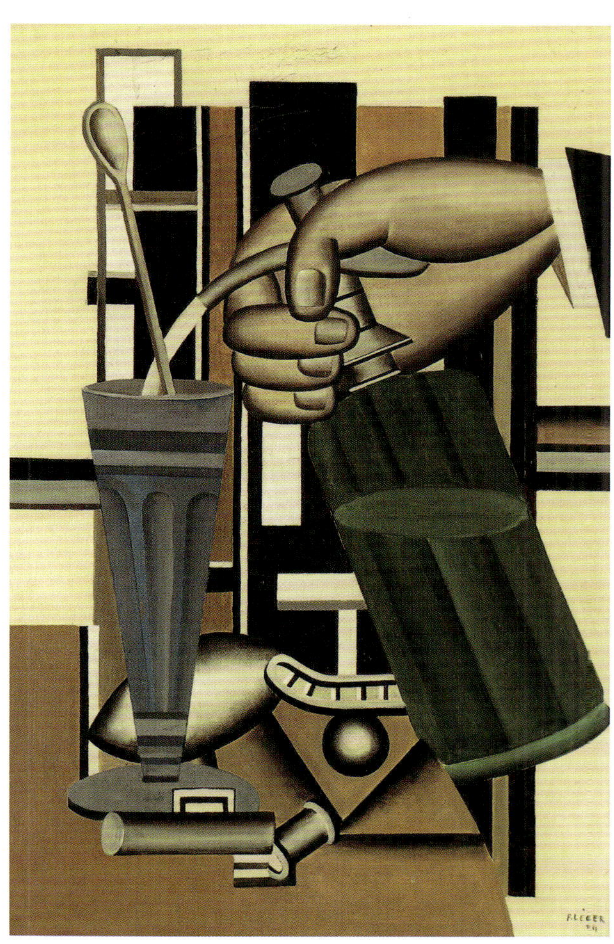 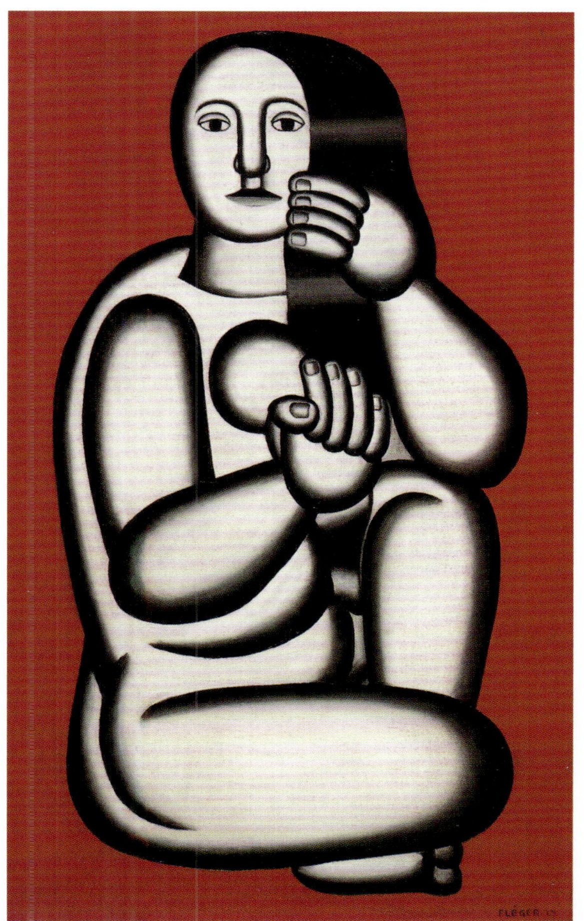

tall building they have created. The aggressive straining for modernity that was so much a part of Léger's earlier art gave way to a more humanistic depiction. As he admitted, 'each artist possesses an offensive weapon, that allows him to intimidate tradition. In the search for vividness and intensity, I made use of the machine.' By the 1950s, that weapon was no longer needed. In his late pictures, Léger removed the armoured structure of his figures, and what is heroic in *The Campers* [illustration p. 15] is partly the unlearning entailed in becoming so direct.

Les Campeurs – the title may have more of a ring to it in French – was first conceived in 1943, in wartime New York. Some of the early studies bear the inscription '*Le Bonheur*' (Happiness, Pleasure, Joy), that perennial theme explored by Seurat, Bonnard and Matisse: the vision of mankind freed from servitude, and experiencing '*le bonheur de vivre*' (see Introduction pp. 7–9). Léger's landscape setting reprises his series of *Paysages animés* (Animated Landscapes) of the 1920s, in which (aided by Le Corbusier) he depicted the emerging industrial scene – affirming a unity of nature and man, and man's constructions. Here, as before, the pylon meets with cloud and tree, the girder reaches into the river. Their 'contrast' is stark, but the serene well-being of the figures affirms the harmony; most of all, the central Earth Mother, cradling her plant, resplendent in her red bathing-costume. The horizontal bands of colour – blue, white, green – rise up to the hot yellow sky. Everything is reconciled in its illumination: a new Golden Age has returned.

In *The Campers* Léger arrives at a pictorial language 'in shirtsleeves' (see p. 23), allowing a candour and directness denied to almost all modern painting, and certainly to Cubism. There's a deliberate exclusion of psychology, of personal emotion; allied to this, a willed dryness of paint-handling, without obvious 'touch' or gestural mark. Many of those hard-won freedoms of modernist painting which will recur throughout this book – licence to remain unfinished, to retain the evidence of process and making, to conjure up suggestion and ambiguity – are discarded in Léger's aesthetic. His late figure-compositions have been variously misinterpreted as a betrayal of modernism and as a surrender to Communist Party directives. Yet the underlying thrust is always libertarian. In 1953, two years before his death, he designed a mass-distribution lithograph, a visual setting of Paul Éluard's 1942 Resistance poem, with its repeated refrain, *'Liberté, j'écris ton nom'* (Liberty, I write your name); to write LIBERTY on a French wall, under the German occupation, had been to risk execution.

Léger's stance in his final works called into question most of the underlying suppositions of the art of his time. He saw the situation of the easel-painter as unsatisfactory. Facing up to the sense of impotence and superfluity that has afflicted most modern painters, he called for a more public function and role, connected to architecture: for mural painters to join with architects as part of the 'teamwork towards more or less social goals'. To those who saw abstraction as an imperative that led inexorably beyond painting to an art of idea and concept, those late compositions of figures were bound to seem an irrelevance. Yet what is admirable in Léger is his readiness to enter into the intellectual developments of his time, to harness his creativity to societal, as well as personal concerns – to lead the artist out of isolation, to give painting a function.

CLASSICISM AFTER FUTURISM: CARRÀ AND SIRONI (1921–22)

*The dissolving forces of pessimism must be
overtaken again by the candour of a new faith.*

CARLO CARRÀ, 1920

Carlo Carrà (1881–1966) began to make his transition towards a renewed, post-Cubist figuration in the middle of the First World War, watching his own movements closely, and, like Léger, leaving an essay or two at every turn in his path. When, already into his forties, Carrà completed his two most compelling images – *The Pine Tree by the Sea* (1921) [illustration opposite] and *The House of Love* (1922) [illustration p. 28] – he achieved a new kind of 'classic art', fresher and more heartfelt than the neo-classicism of Picasso and his French counterparts.

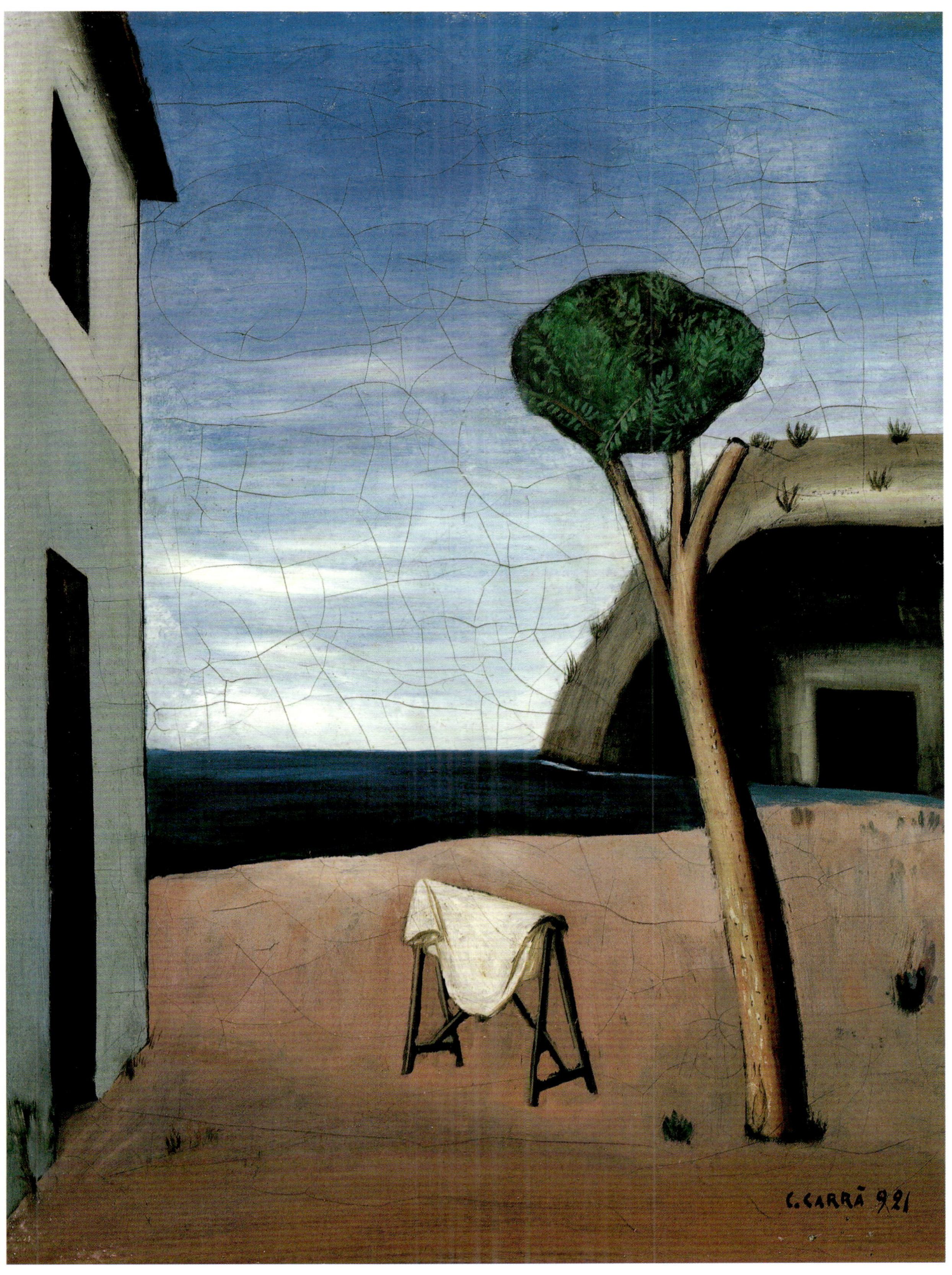

C. CARRÀ 9 21

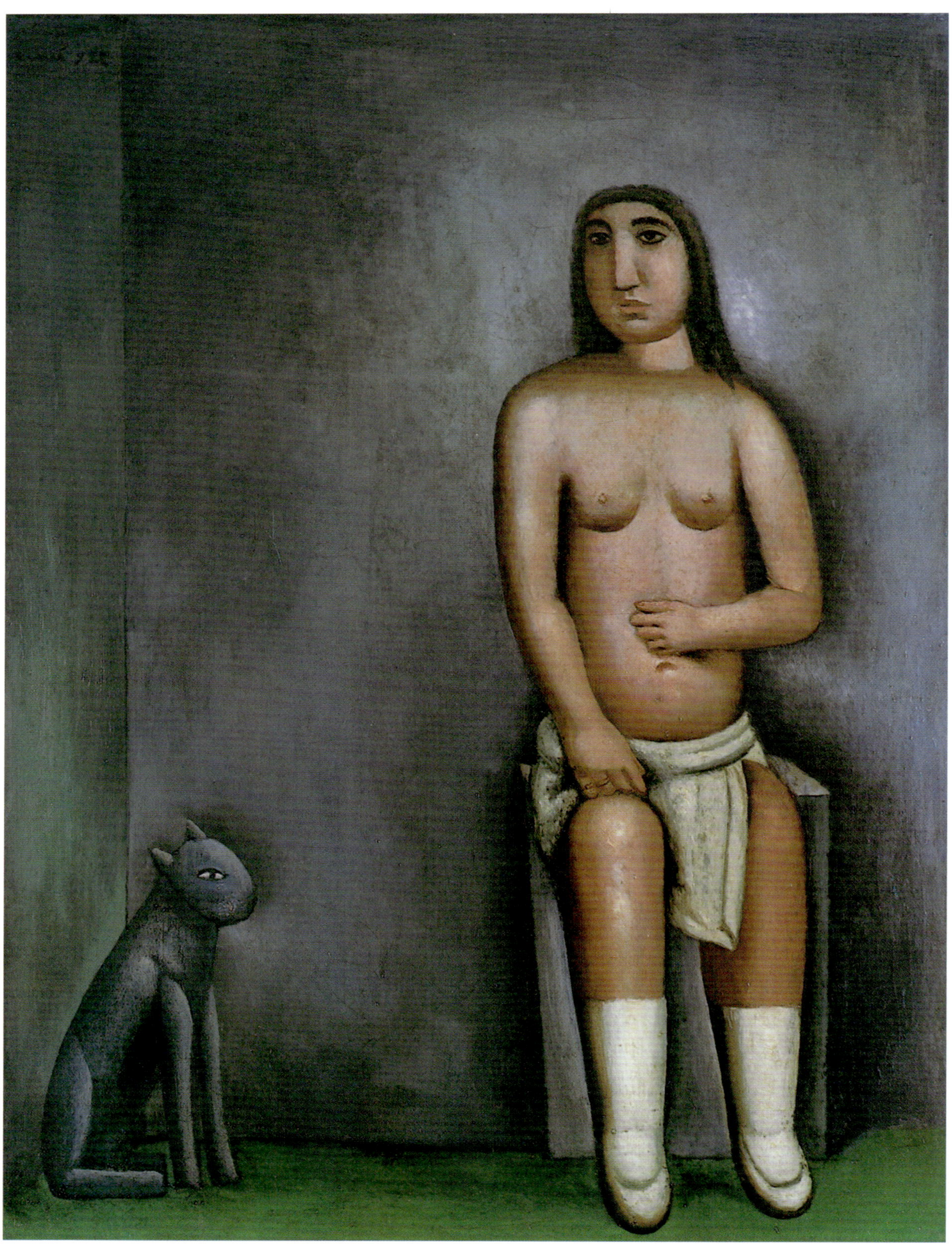

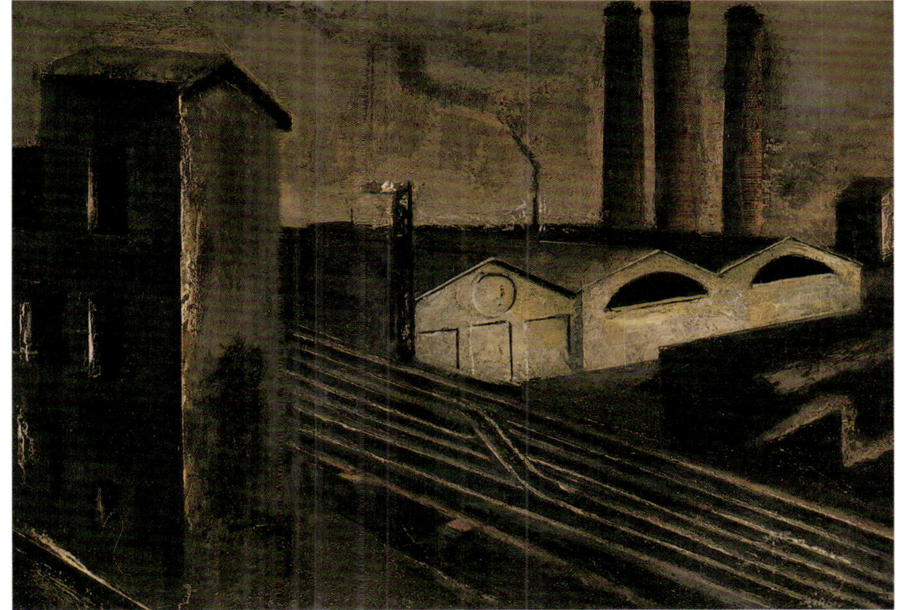

In 1900 he'd spent six important months in London, living among the Italian anarchist community in Clerkenwell, studying Marx and Bakunin. His first major painting was *The Funeral of the Anarchist Galli*, an epic-scale *grand machine*, first conceived in that symbolist/divisionist idiom common to most of his fellow Futurists, but later reworked after their group visit to Paris in 1911. What the Futurists discovered in Cubist faceting was a potential for kaleidoscopic disruption – a rhetoric of fragmentation that dissolved the physical world and for a few years became far more influential across Europe than Cubism itself. But in 1916, with the Futurists dispersed by military service, Carrà experienced a kind of conversion.

He found himself painting a sequence of frontal, doll-like figures and heads; it was as though, in order to reconstitute the world of objects, he had to re-enter the world of the child. Like Léger, he too looked towards Henri Rousseau, but also, more intimately, to the pre-Renaissance. He wrote of his aspiration towards the 'magical silence' of Giotto, 'eternal, peaceful, reassuring'.

Later, lying in a military hospital in Ferrara, Carrà became close friends with the more severely wounded Giorgio de Chirico (1888–1978), seven years his junior, but with most of his 'metaphysical' paintings already behind him. Carrà was critical of this imagery: 'a cold, literary rationalization'. Nevertheless, having recovered first, Carrà plagiarized de Chirico's melancholy mannequins, establishing himself as the founder of a new *pittura metafisica*.

Between 1918 and 1920, Carrà was once again questioning everything, completing barely four or five paintings. In the journal *Valori plastici* (Formal Values) he defines his own aesthetic against the neo-classical parodies that had become so prevalent after the war. He warns against irony, 'this subtle malady which in our time consumes the finest creative forces'. He conceives Giotto as a 'Constructor', and himself an 'Engineer'. And then, in 1921, with *The Pine Tree by the Sea* [illustration p. 27], he arrives at an image that truly does embody something of Giotto's

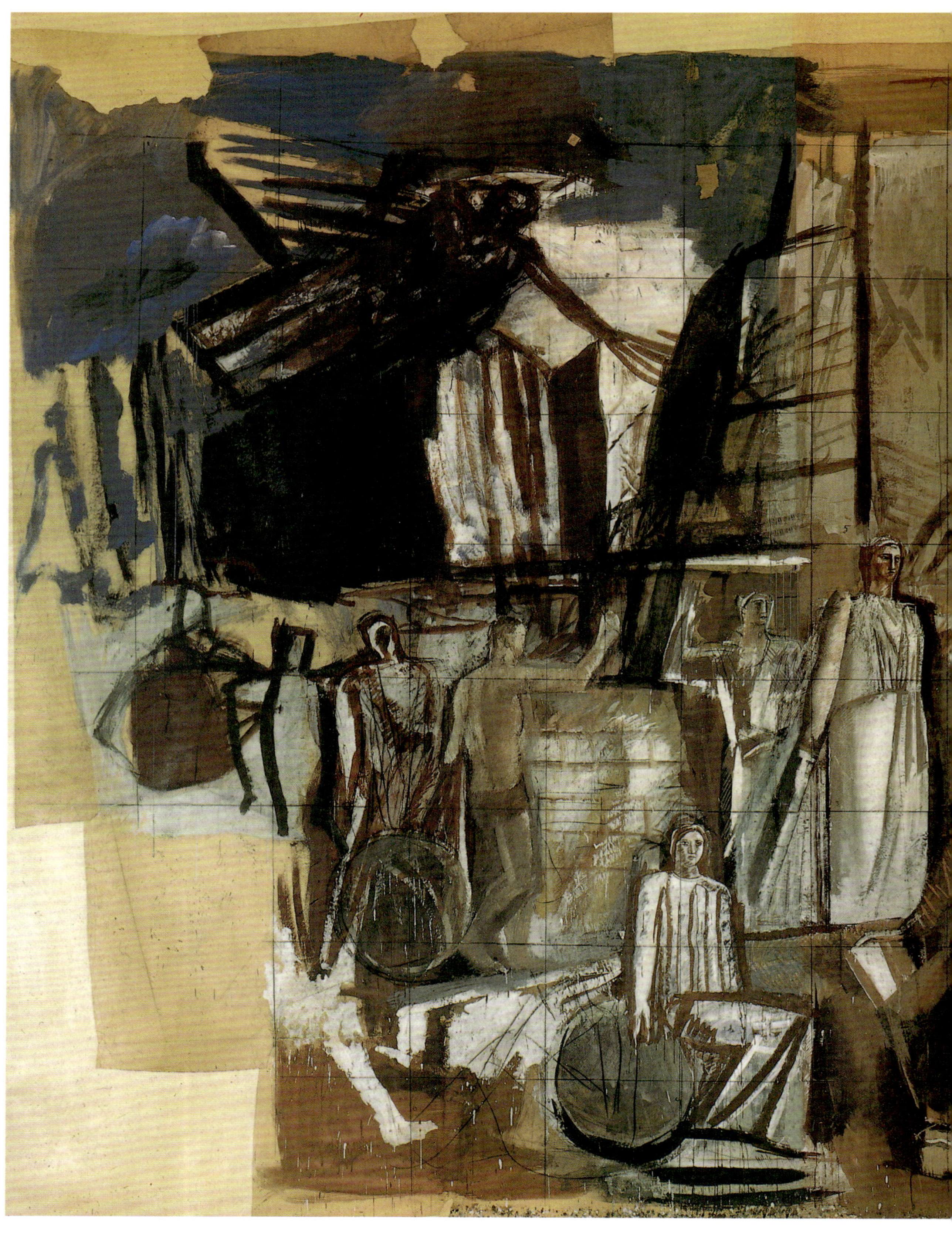

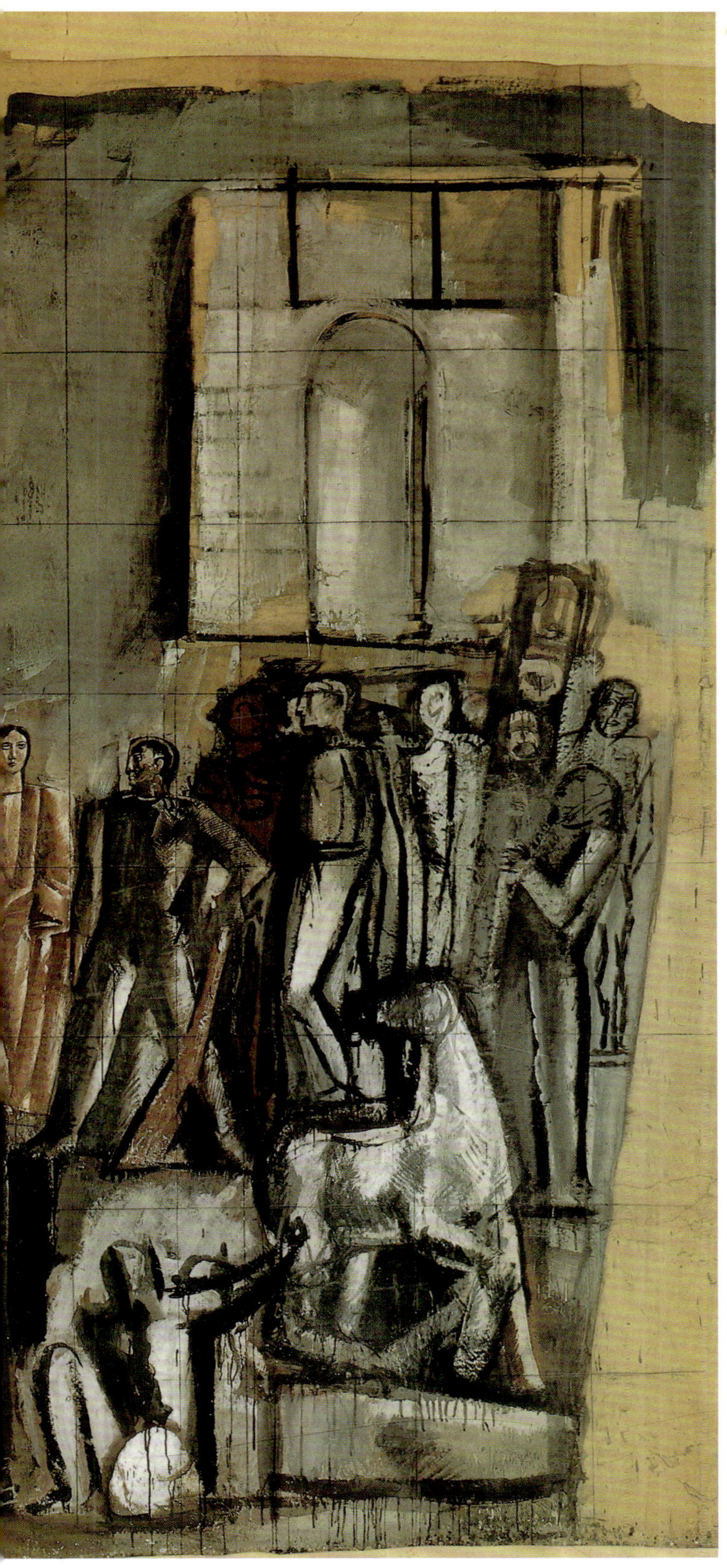

MARIO SIRONI
Study for *Italy Between the Arts and the Sciences*
1935

A less-than-half-scale preparatory image, towards the even more colossal (but much inferior) mosaic mural in the Aula Magna of Rome's University 'La Sapienza'. The sense is of a classical frieze being *disrupted* by the flying figure in the vast emptiness above. Sironi was a committed fascist, joining Mussolini in his puppet-court at Salò in 1943, and becoming after the war an unmentionable, dying in poverty and neglect.

'magical silence'. Carrà wrote later of his intention 'to represent the mythical in Nature': it is a Tree to stand for all trees, a lonely presence, cut back to a single frond. And, similarly, the House, the Sea and the Cliff are conceived as archetypes, existing outside of time. After his long search, Carrà has achieved an unforced depiction. The art historian Wilhelm Worringer stumbled across the image in reproduction four years after it was painted, and wrote about it in a famous essay, admiring this pictorial language as 'laconic'; that pruned-down stump held the promise of a new flowering.

The figure in *The House of Love* (1922) [illustration p. 28] is also reduced to her essence; seated in a box-like cell, her squat, earthy presence is entirely free of irony. The subtlety of colour (the tender harmonies of grey and green against the brick-hued flesh) and the extreme delicacy of touch (especially in the hand on the belly) establish an unexpected fragility and evanescence. The achievement of Carrà is to have conjured the soul back into the body. She is among the most affirmative of all twentieth-century painted figures, to be placed beside Léger's 1927 *Nude* [illustration p. 25]. For inter-war artists, from George Grosz to Balthus (see pp. 70–73, 93–102), Carrà's new archetypal figuration proved fertile ground.

In those same months, the thirty-six--year-old Mario Sironi (1885–1961) was working on the powerful, brooding images of the industrial suburbs, or *periferie*, of Milan that remain his greatest achievement. Sironi had served his apprenticeship in the studio of the Futurist Giacomo Balla in Rome, but he followed Carrà into the new Giotto-inspired language, creating dense, planar surfaces. Images such as *Urban Landscape with Chimneys* (1921) [illustration p. 29] seem simple in construction. Yet the perspectives of these slab-like factory walls and empty tramlines create a mood of thought, of enigma; Sironi has been called a 'metropolitan metaphysical'. Where de Chirico and Carrà are melancholy, Sironi is angry. One remembers these 'black paintings' for their unforgiving glare, their metallic colour, their characteristically sluggish paint. The otherworldly promise of Carrà's poetic realism is lost: this is an evocation of a blighted society, sullenly waiting for revolution.

It was a kind of prophecy. In Italy 1920–22 had been the 'Red Years', with socialists and anarcho-syndicalists initiating strikes – broken by the state's use of Blackshirts, activists of the rapidly growing National Fascist Party. In October 1922 the March on Rome by 25,000 Blackshirts was the prelude to Mussolini's dictatorship. The previous year Carrà had written of fascism as 'more an opiate than an elixir'. But Sironi (under the tutelage of Margherita Sarfatti, Mussolini's mistress) became the leader of the classicizing group *Novecento* (Twentieth Century). Soon he was engaged mostly in public works – mosaics, stained-glass, frescoes. Sironi wrote in his essay 'On Mural Painting', 1932:

> Easel painting is too weak, too incapable of capturing attention,
> in our epoch of mighty myths and fantastic shocks

A year later, his Muralist Manifesto was signed also by Carrà. Sironi's completed murals could be disappointingly suave, but his huge 1935 preliminary cartoon for *Italy Between the Arts and Sciences* [illustration pp. 30–31] retained the farouche, cross-grained rawness of his earlier pictures. Involuntarily, Sironi had created a tragic allegory: the white figure of Italy threatened by dark forces.

Fascism made a lie of Carrà's modernist classicism. After re-energizing a generation of Italian painters around 1920 – including the young Giorgio Morandi – it had been all too easily subverted; its 'timelessness' endowing a spurious authority to *Il Duce*'s imperium. Yet the mythic realism of *Novecento* did contribute to the great post-war flowering of Italian cinema: fifteen years later, the long final shot of Visconti's *Rocco and His Brothers* (1960) still carried echoes of Sironi's *periferie*. Carrà's project – to reinvent the classical figure, without irony, for ambitious modern painting – still has resonance for artists today.

TOWARDS THE CHAGALL OF *DEAD SOULS* (1920-25)

The grotesque in Gogol is…a negation of abstract,
immobile norms that claim to be absolute and eternal.

MIKHAIL BAKHTIN, 1940

Chagall's ninety-six etchings to Gogol's *Dead Souls* (1924–25) are the highpoint of his graphic art, assembled together in the greatest illustrated book of the twentieth century. The first sixty images include most of the finest [illustrations pp. 34–35], and in them, Chagall makes a transition from what was still a tight, spiky post-Cubist stylization, towards a comic–grotesque idiom, equivalent to Gogol's narrative: unfolding the picaresque journey made by the fraud Chichikov among scoundrels and fools. There is a real affinity between the artist of the 1920s and the author of the 1842 novel (Gogol called it a 'poem'): both are addressing Mother Russia from the vantage point of exile. Gogol wrote *Dead Souls* in Paris and Rome; Chagall was now back in Paris, twelve years after his youthful flowering in Cubist-inflected images such as *Half Past Three (The Poet)* [illustration p. 16].

The comic laughter of Chagall's *Dead Souls* etchings can be seen as a weapon with which to refute all doctrinaire notions of art. I want here to set Chagall/Gogol against the classicizing inherent in Léger and Carrà; and even more, against the Cubist-inspired geometric abstraction that would emerge in revolutionary Russia with the force of a new gospel.

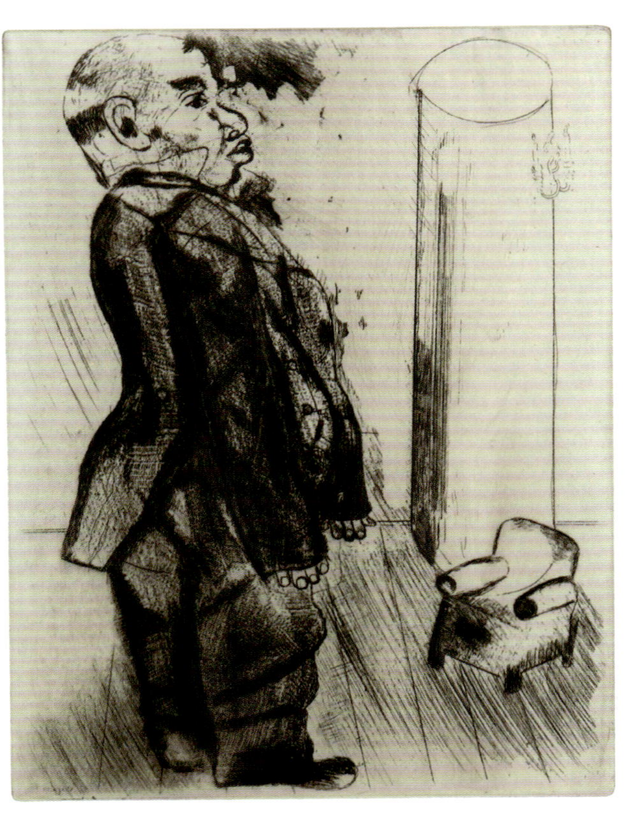

MARC CHAGALL

Sobakevich in front of the Armchair (illustration to *Gogol's Dead Souls*)

1924–25

In an image that most would identify as 'German' in its grotesque humour, Chagall makes a wonderful parallel to Gogol's description of a monstrous serf owner: 'The table, the armchairs, all of them were of the most heavy and uncomfortable shape, in short, every object, every chair, seemed to be saying "I'm a Sobakevich too!" or "I, too, am very like Sobakevich!"'

MARC CHAGALL

The Garden Beyond Plyushkin's House (illustration to *Gogol's Dead Souls*)

1924–25

Gogol's beautiful description of the neglected garden that epitomizes Russia would have had a special appeal to the newly exiled Chagall: 'The extensive old garden that stretched behind the house and came out behind the village before, overgrown and neglected, it lost itself in the fields, appeared the sole feature of this large village that possessed any life, that was truly picturesque in its wild beauty…. On one side at the very edge of the garden a few aspens, far taller than the other trees, lifted up their enormous crows' nests into their quivering crowns…. Everything was better than either nature or art could have devised separately.'

MARC CHAGALL

The Volga Barge-Haulers (illustration to *Gogol's Dead Souls*)

1924–25

For Chagall, as a supporter of the 1917 revolution, Gogol's barge-haulers became emblematic of a community of free workers: 'Have you ended up on the Volga and joined the barge-haulers? […] The endless fleet which will move off in single file when spring melts the ice…. Then you barge-haulers…will get down to the toil and sweat, pulling the ropes to one and the same song, as endless as Russia itself.'

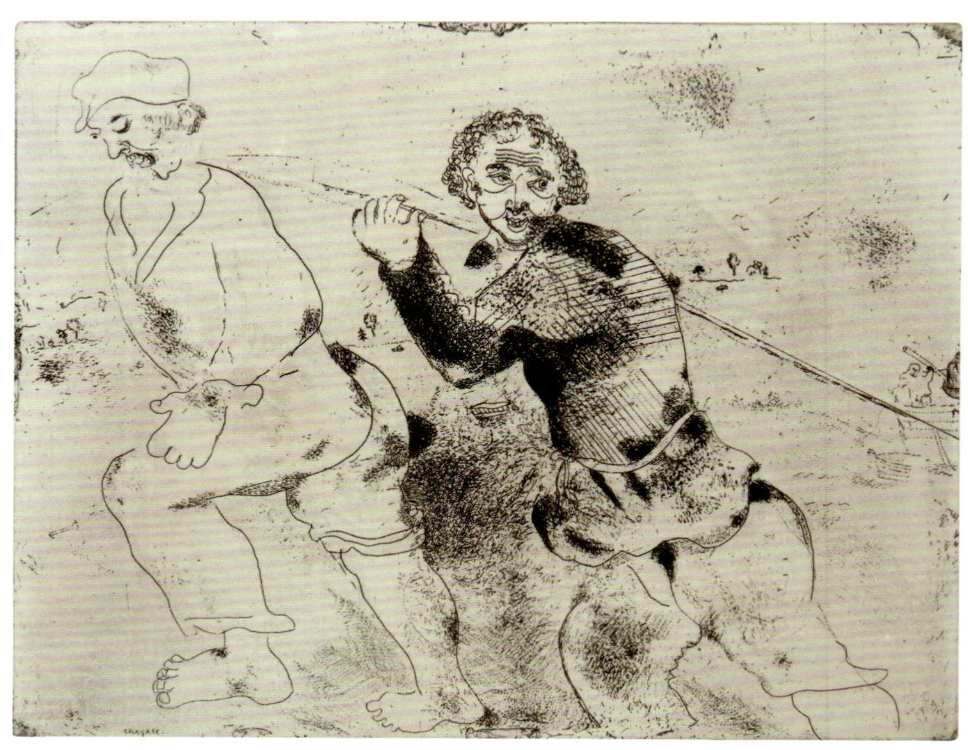

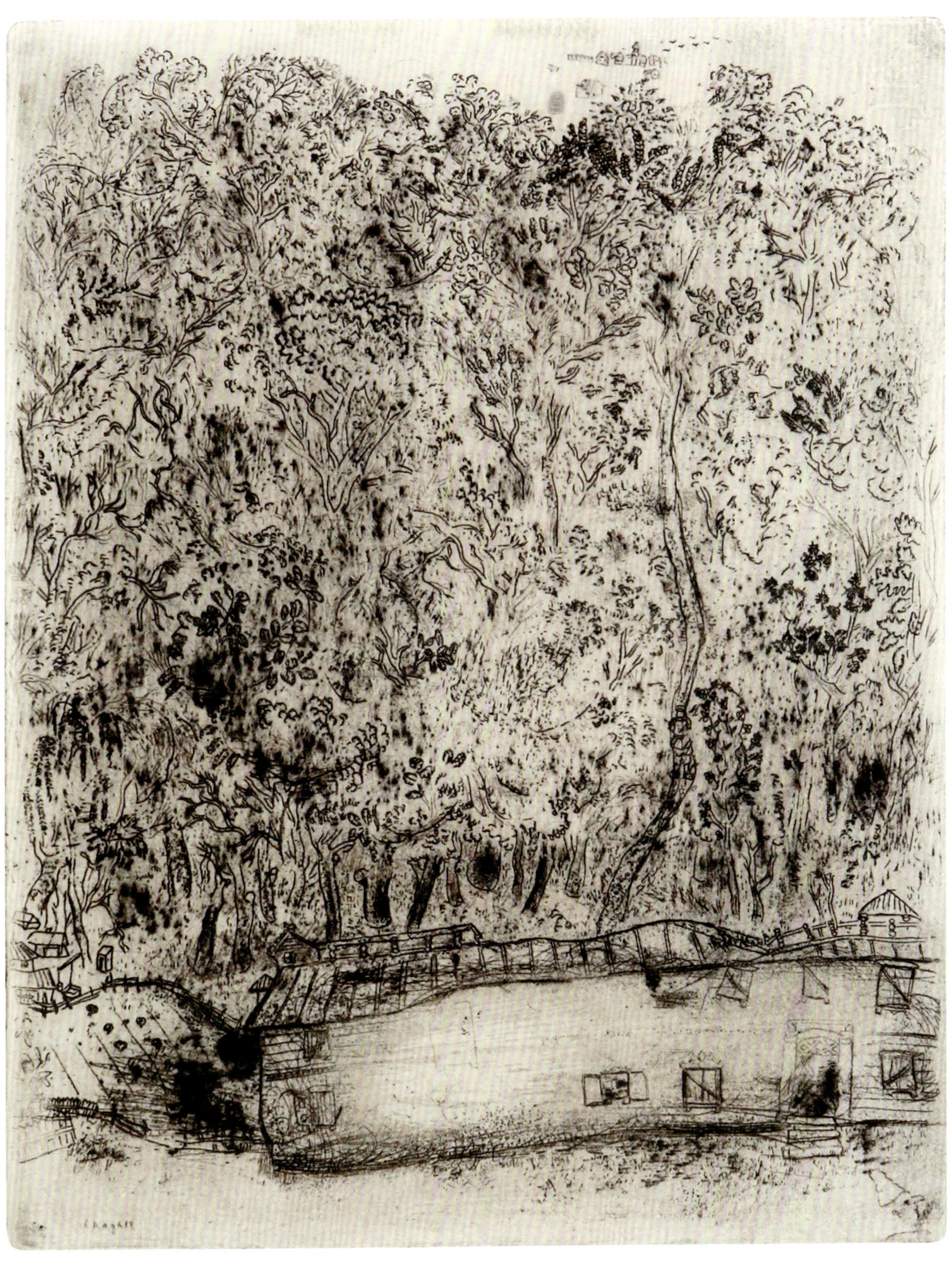

Chagall and Malevich: The Vitebsk Renaissance (1918–20)

SERGEI EISENSTEIN, 1940

In the summer of 1914 Chagall transported forty of his Parisian canvases
(along with 160 drawings and gouaches) to be exhibited in the offices of Berlin's
leading avant-garde journal, *Der Stürm* (The Storm). A month after the opening
he made the long journey east to Vitebsk, intending to fetch his fiancée Bella.
But war broke out, and the borders closed. Thus two hundred Chagall images,
including *Half Past Three*, remained stranded for several years in an exceptionally
prominent Berlin location. In 1915, Raoul Hausmann wrote to fellow-Dadaist
Hannah Höch after seeing at *Der Sturm* 'some wondrously beautiful Chagalls…
a great master'; and the new generation – Otto Dix, George Grosz and Max
Beckmann – found in Chagall fresh resources for their own anti-authoritarian art
(see pp. 63–80).

The newly-weds moved to Petrograd, where Chagall was an enthusiastic
witness to the 1917 Revolution. In 1918 the art-critic-turned-politician Anatoly
Lunacharsky appointed him Commissar of Plastic Arts for the Vitebsk Region;
Chagall invited El Lissitzky and other avant-garde artists to join him as teachers at
his newly founded People's Art College. (The College was one component of what
has come to be known as 'The Vitebsk Renaissance'.) During these years of civil war
and ferment, Chagall came into contact with a brilliant literary circle that included
the charismatic young lecturer Mikhail Bakhtin, already formulating his history of
laughter (in which the humour of Gogol always had a central place). The Vitebsk-
based *TEREVSAT* (*Teatr revoliutsionnoi satiry*, Theatre of Revolutionary Satire)
flourished, with Chagall contributing designs for sets and costumes.

At the College, he was no longer on speaking terms with his former disciple
Lissitzky, who in 1919 recruited Russia's leading artist, Kazimir Malevich (1879–
1935), nine years Chagall's senior, and in the full flood of Messianic aesthetic
prophecy. Like Chagall, Malevich in his earlier work had drawn inspiration first
from Russian folk-imagery, then from Cubo-Futurism. But in 1915 his *Black
Square* initiated the ultimate geometric abstraction of Suprematism. He wrote
in a manifesto of casting aside 'art-ideas, concepts, images' in order to reach a
'desert in which nothing can be perceived except feeling'; he equated the Black
Square with feeling, and the white field as 'the void beyond' (see Introduction
pp. 10–11). The works that resulted (many of them now at the Stedelijk Museum
in Amsterdam, where they can be seen alongside several wondrous early Chagalls)
are among the most beautiful and rewarding of all abstract paintings.

Yet the Malevich who arrived in Vitebsk five years later was now opposed to painting *per se*, as counter-revolutionary; he likened individual artists to 'landlords and owners of their own personal systems'. Painting was, he asserted 'done-for long ago'. From 1918 onwards, he'd enacted a series of *Paintings in Dissolution*, in which geometrical forms literally fade away at the edges. With Lissitzky as henchman, he set out to redefine the fledgling Vitebsk People's Art College as a collective, UNOVIS (*Utverditeli novogo iskusstva*, Champions of the New Art), where students wore black squares stitched to their sleeves, and adopted the slogan 'Art Into Life'.

Chagall tried to see Malevich as a comrade: 'Both of us are striving towards the leftist domain of art, nevertheless we see its means and goals differently.' They attempted collaboration in decorating the Vitebsk streets, but here, as at the art school, Malevich emerged triumphant, as the bemused Eisenstein found shortly after.

The Vitebsk encounter has been seen as prefiguring painting's future difficulties – the Duchampian 'anti-art' postures that took over many art schools in the later twentieth century, and came close to killing off painting altogether. In the midst of a revolutionary society Chagall's clinging to his childhood vision – his recreation of it through painting – could all too easily be condemned as solipsism. Malevich's aspiration to overcome the self, the ego, was admirable; but it soon led beyond geometric abstraction, to the devaluation and discarding of painting altogether.

The Yiddish Theatre (1920)

I have been thinking endlessly about the destiny of art (especially of my kind) in Russia. Does what I did…have any meaning for anybody? Who needs it? [...] For it seems there is nothing on earth more 'individualistic' (despicable word) than I versus the 'collective'…

MARC CHAGALL, letter to Lunacharsky, 1921

Chagall followed his resignation from the public role of Commissar at Vitebsk with one more attempt to place his vision at the service of the collective. In 1920 he joined the newly formed Moscow Yiddish Chamber Theatre, not only designing the young troupe's sets and costumes, but transforming every inch of their small auditorium into what came to be known as 'Chagall's Box', a space dominated by an almost twenty-seven-foot-long painted frieze.

Introduction to the Yiddish Theatre [illustration pp. 38–39, detail p. 12] incorporates elements of Cubism and of Malevich's Suprematist geometric idiom within its overall design. As in *The Poet* of 1911 [illustration p. 16] Chagall here assimilates an abstract pictorial language, onto which he unfolds an essentially autobiographical, figurative narrative. Many of the figures incorporate visual breaks – a head slightly out-of-sync with its body, for example (the effect is akin to

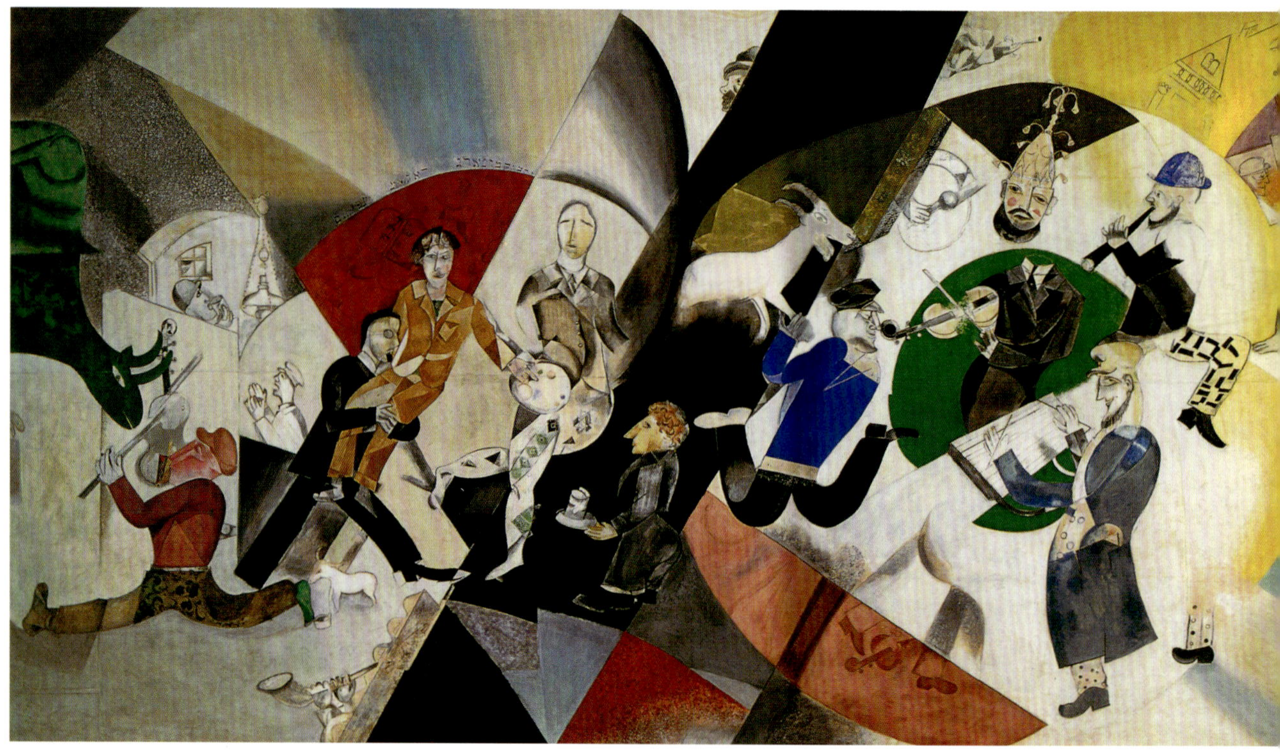

The ninety-seat theatre was adapted from the salon of a requisitioned Jewish mansion. In the winter of 1920 Chagall worked 'virtually day and night' for six weeks to complete its decoration, including this long wall. The artist himself is carried in the arms of his friend Efros towards the aloof figure of The Director. The troupe's lead actor, Solomon Mikhoels, is represented twice (see also detail, p. 12).

stop-motion animation). This alters our sense of 'reality': we perceive the painted world as a construct, as having been first broken, then put together again. There are sly, linear marginalia: hands reach up to a naked torso; a figure rides astride a cock, with a fish in its mouth; one man sits high in a tree, another urinates on a pig. These carnivalesque elements peep out from behind the geometric structures – defacing their radiant purity.

Surrounded by this mural scheme, in which Jewish cultural tradition is explicitly roped together with the revolutionary avant-garde, the troupe developed their repertory in a new acrobatic–grotesque performance style. Yet, for Chagall, this episode too ended badly. He fell out with the director, and never received payment. He found himself demoted to a lower category of art-worker within the Soviet system, teaching Jewish war-orphans one hundred kilometres from Moscow, on a third-class food ration that barely fed his wife and young daughter. It seemed the Revolution had no role for him as a painter, though he would remain a Leftist all his long life (one with a substantial FBI file – he was refused a US visa from 1951 to 1957). Like his compatriot Wassily Kandinsky, he felt rejected by the new Russian dispensation and its doctrinaire constructivism, which regarded the very activity of painting as futile. Both Chagall and Kandinsky were now seen as tainted by their years in the West. For both, Lunacharsky procured passports.

Chagall returned to Berlin in 1922, a penniless exile. At *Der Sturm*, those two hundred works had disappeared into private collections, any proceeds rendered valueless by the hyperinflation that overtook the Weimar Republic 1921–24 (see

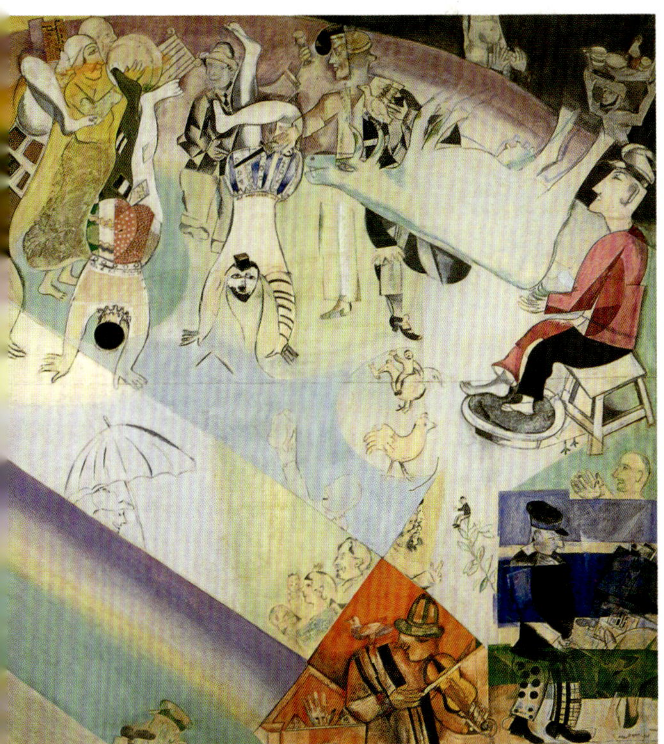

Ch 2 pp. 59–62). It was graphic work that saved him. First, the art dealer Paul Cassirer commissioned illustrations for Chagall's already half-written Yiddish autobiography, published in translation as *Mein Leben* (My Life). This entailed learning to etch: Chagall recreated his Vitebsk childhood in dry-points of great intensity, simultaneously modernist and infantile. (They would be much admired by the Surrealists.) But then, called to Paris by another gallerist, Ambroise Vollard, he chose a more ambitious project.

Dead Souls (1924-25)

Marc sits there like a cobbler hammering away on his copper plates…. His wife reads the chapter aloud to him. They keep on laughing.

YVAN GOLL

Gogol's visionary comedy had provided a leitmotif for Chagall throughout the difficult years in Vitebsk and Moscow. In Russia it was almost a sacred text. Aleksandr Herzen, reading *Dead Souls* just after its publication, saw its revolutionary implications: the Russian provincial serf-owners are 'the true dead souls, and we meet them at every turn'. Bakhtin describes the novel as 'a merry carnival journey through the land of death'.

Chagall's great sequence of etchings enters into Gogol's narrative at a level of interpretation far deeper than the merely illustrational. This he achieves partly through his extraordinary sympathy with the medium, his sensitivity to the possibilities inherent in small scratched and separate marks, and the intimacy of surface that can be created when inking an acid-bitten copper plate. While the dry-points of *Mein Leben* have the stark black-and-white clarity of Soviet poster-design, the lines of the *Dead Souls* etchings are broken and discontinuous, and from the deep yellowish plate-tone there blooms what I would describe as a 'controlled foul-bite' – a mildew or mouldiness marvellously at one with Gogol's torpid world. This smirched effect, sometimes in conjunction with areas of aquatint, and clusters of tiny, bitten marks, becomes a new expressive means that undermines any too lucid design.

When in 2008 the illustrations were set within the narrative of a new English translation, by Donald Rayfield, anglophone readers could at last appreciate the complex interaction of text and image. For example, it has always been recognized that Gogol's loving and lengthy description of the garden behind the serf-owner Plyushkin's house is emblematic of Russia itself, both in its decay and in its 'wild beauty'. In the foreground of Chagall's etching [illustration p. 35] the house totters 'like an invalid on his last legs', but above and behind it, the whole surface of the plate flowers into an exuberantly lyrical tangle. The artist has created a visual equivalent for Gogol's overgrown paths, for the 'young maple branch', under one of whose leaves 'God knows how, the sun had crept, and suddenly transformed it into a translucent, fiery, wondrously radiant thing...'. Its placement in the narrative, interrupting a sequence of comic–grotesque figures that evoke a stagnant society – the rigid arms of Sobakevich echoed in his tiny armchair [illustration p. 34], for example – allows Chagall's image of the garden to take on a richer significance. Russia, with its monstrous, bureaucratic tyranny, is redeemed by the chaos, the disorderliness that bursts through. 'Nature can give a wondrous warmth to everything that was created in the chill of measured purity and neatness.'

Another break in the narrative, the two pages devoted to a list of 'dead souls' – Stepan-the-Cook, Maksim-the-Cobbler, Gregory-Never-Get-There and so on – engenders in Chagall a sequence of seven full-page plates. The anti-hero Chichikov's musings drift into a fantasy, in which the runaway serf Abakum Furov has joined the outlaw community of the Volga Barge-Haulers [illustration p. 34]. Turning smilingly towards us, Furov becomes emblematic of the Free Worker. The contour-line made by Chagall's needle, wonderfully alive, is supplemented by a dishevelled dry-point scribble (patches of hairiness) while miniscule vignettes of the icy river and its boat-life are touched-in all around.

Gogol's special brand of 'cosmic satire' – as Nabokov pointed out, only a single letter separates the comic from the cosmic – found its perfect match in Chagall. The account by the Alsace–Jewish writer Yvan Goll, of Bella reading *Dead Souls* aloud as the etchings take shape, is significant. The Chagalls' first language was Yiddish, but in Paris the newly exiled artist used the Russian of Gogol as a route back into that Russia-of-the-mind, to which etchings and text make both tribute and reproach.

In 1927 Chagall donated proofs of the ninety-six etchings to the Tretyakov Museum in Moscow 'with all the love of a Russian painter for his homeland' but they would remain unexhibited in Russia for most of his lifetime. Vollard never brought out *Dead Souls* as a book; his successor Tériade created a definitive edition in French – *Les Âmes mortes* – only in 1948, by which time Chagall's disastrous falling-off as a painter had begun to obscure his earlier achievement.

In Paris in 1925 Chagall was already under attack from a new angle – the incipient ideology of socialist realism – when the communist-affiliated journal *Clarté* (Clarity) reviewed his first solo exhibition there. Chagall 'who had led so hard a combat for Abstraction, for Anarchy, for his Self and his navel', is accused of descending into 'petit-bourgeois naturalism'. He has 'found no place among the Bolsheviks, despite his ultra-revolutionary words and acts'. Chagall's art 'signifies objectively a step backwards towards anarchism, and not a step forward towards proletarian realism, towards the organization of reality'.

How an artist 'organizes reality' will be the central debate throughout this book. Fuelled first in 1911 by Cubism and its poetic possibilities – its spliced-together spaces creating multiple or simultaneous realities – Chagall extended those interpenetrations to mural scale (*Introduction to the Yiddish Theatre* [illustration pp. 38–39]). In the *Dead Souls* etchings he dispenses with Cubist fracturing and faceting altogether, while intensifying his relish for the instability of reality: *Plyushkin's Garden* [illustration p. 35] is a celebration of nature untamed, beyond all control, and it speaks of liberty. Gogol led the artist to a sense of poetic freedom and anti-authoritarian comedy that makes the Chagall of *Dead Souls* so ripe for rediscovery by a new generation in the twenty-first century.

MURALISM PART 1: RIVERA'S RETURN TO MEXICO (1921-24)

I stopped painting in the Cubist manner because of the war, the Russian Revolution, and in the belief in the need for a popular and socialized art.

DIEGO RIVERA

The extraordinary flood of fresco-imagery created by Diego Rivera (1886–1957) immediately following his return home to Mexico in 1921, having abandoned Europe at the age of thirty-five, stands as a significant episode, though one that is often omitted from accounts of twentieth-century painting.

Rivera had been part of the Montparnasse Cubist milieu, a close associate of Léger and Chagall around 1913, and, eventually, of Picasso. He'd shared living-quarters with Piet Mondrian (fourteen years older, drawn to Paris and Cubism in order to make his own transition towards a radically purified pictorial language). Soutine recalled Rivera speaking of Cubism as a 'corridor' or 'passage'; for many painters, it afforded a shedding of individual identity. One strikingly awkward image epitomizes this period of Rivera's generic Cubist picture-making: *Zapatista Landscape* (1915), owes much to the beautiful cut-up compositions of Juan Gris, but is violently broken into by an almost life-size naturalistic rifle – emblem of Emiliano Zapata, the peasant-general in Mexico's civil war.

The formalized language of Cubism was in conflict with Rivera's politics. It was hard for him to reconcile revolutionary rhetoric with the production of tame easel paintings for a bourgeois market. Help came from two unexpected sources. He was befriended by the philosopher-of-art Élie Faure, who provided a theoretical basis for Rivera's impulse towards mural-painting (reinforced by discussions with his compatriot the painter David Siqueiros). And in 1920, with Zapata assassinated and the civil war ended, Rivera was summoned home by the new regime. But first, the Mexican ambassador funded a study-tour of Italian fresco-schemes. For nearly a year and a half, Rivera was immersed in Giotto, Lorenzetti, Uccello, Gozzoli, Signorelli, Pinturicchio, Michelangelo.... Those same months coincided with the publication of the ex-Futurist Carlo Carrà's Giotto polemics in *Valori plastici* (see pp. 26–32 and p. 74), which may also have fed into Rivera's post-Cubist synthesis.

By early 1922 Rivera had been assigned two huge arcaded courtyards at the Ministry of Education in Mexico City, embarking with his assistants on a fresco-programme that would entail more than a hundred large murals, and a total painted area of over fifteen thousand square feet. In *The Day of the Dead: City Fiesta* (1923–24) [illustration opposite] Rivera's idiom is consciously popular. These figures are yet further children of Henri Rousseau, born-again 'primitives' (see pp. 21–22), but decidedly non-European; it is the native 'Indian' rather than the Hispanic that Rivera embraces as his rediscovery of Mexico deepens. So the heaving Gozzoli/Pinturicchio crowds of the second courtyard are peopled with utterly unclassical figures – stumpy, rounded, honey-brown – hundred upon hundred of them, with only the occasional freakish paleface. The cumulative sense is of Rivera's flow of compositional invention, so long dammed-up by Parisian modernism, suddenly released by the new mural imperative.

Already in 1922, together with Siqueiros, José Orozco and others, Rivera had signed a manifesto:

> We repudiate all so-called easel painting, and all the art of ultra-intellectual
>
> circles…and we glorify the expression of Monumental Art because it is a
>
> public possession.

The particular contingencies of Mexico – a post-revolutionary regime seeking to instruct a largely illiterate peasantry in their political identity, under the patronage of José Vasconcelos, with his vision of a 'Cosmic Race' in universal harmony – gave these muralists an urgent function in the 1920s. (Though Orozco, often a deeper thinker than Rivera, at first mocked: 'Why paint for the people? The people make their own art.') Painters in Europe and the USA were soon energized by the developments in Mexico; in this book, for instance, both Stanley Spencer and the young Philip Guston (see pp. 80–85 and 197–98). The photographers Edward Weston and Tina Modotti were drawn to Rivera, travelling south in 1923 from their libertarian milieu in California; Modotti remained in Mexico after Weston's departure in 1926, documenting the muralist movement. A debate about the function of art had opened up. Had these painters signed away the liberties of modernism in the service of the state? Even in those first fresco-programmes, Rivera's method – an initial line-drawing, transferred to the wall and filled-in largely by assistants – could lead to mechanical routine and mediocre overproduction.

Nevertheless, by the 1930s, Rivera was among the world's most famous artists; he was chosen in 1931 by the newly founded Museum of Modern Art in New York as the subject for their second retrospective exhibition, following Henri Matisse. In that city two years later, Rivera was at work on a mural for Radio City when he inserted an unscheduled head of Lenin. He refused to back down and his patron, Nelson Rockefeller, under pressure from virulent anti-communists, reluctantly ordered the whole wall erased. The issue split the art world. Matisse, who happened to be in the United States, came out emphatically against, declaring 'Propaganda has no place in art…I do not agree with Mr Rivera…that every art must have its political viewpoint'.

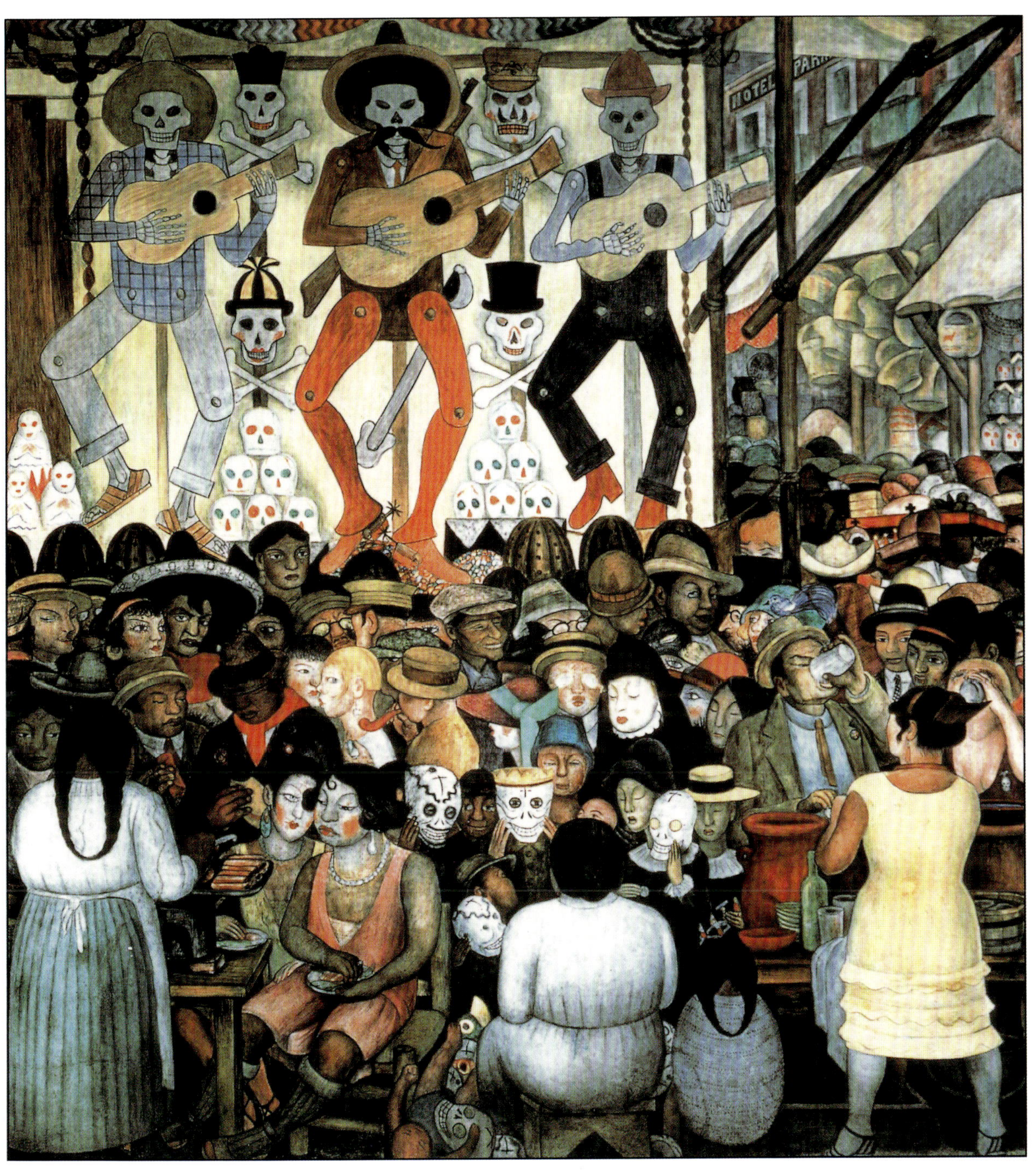

HOTEL PARIS

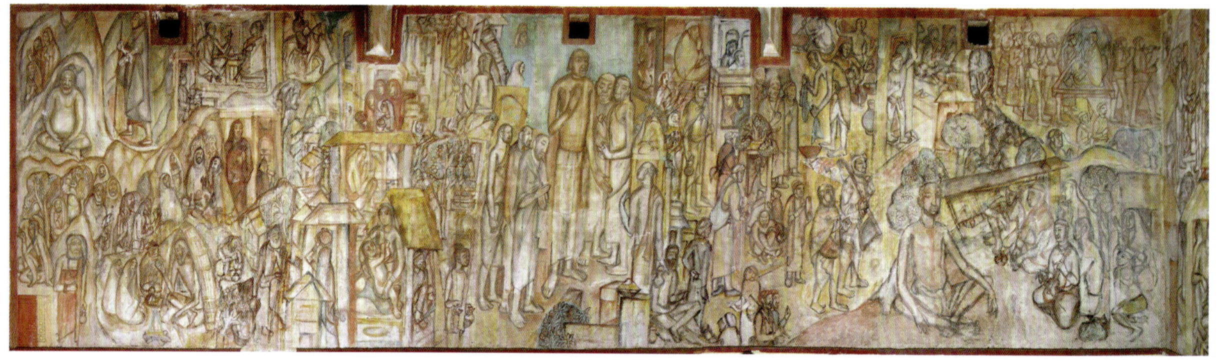

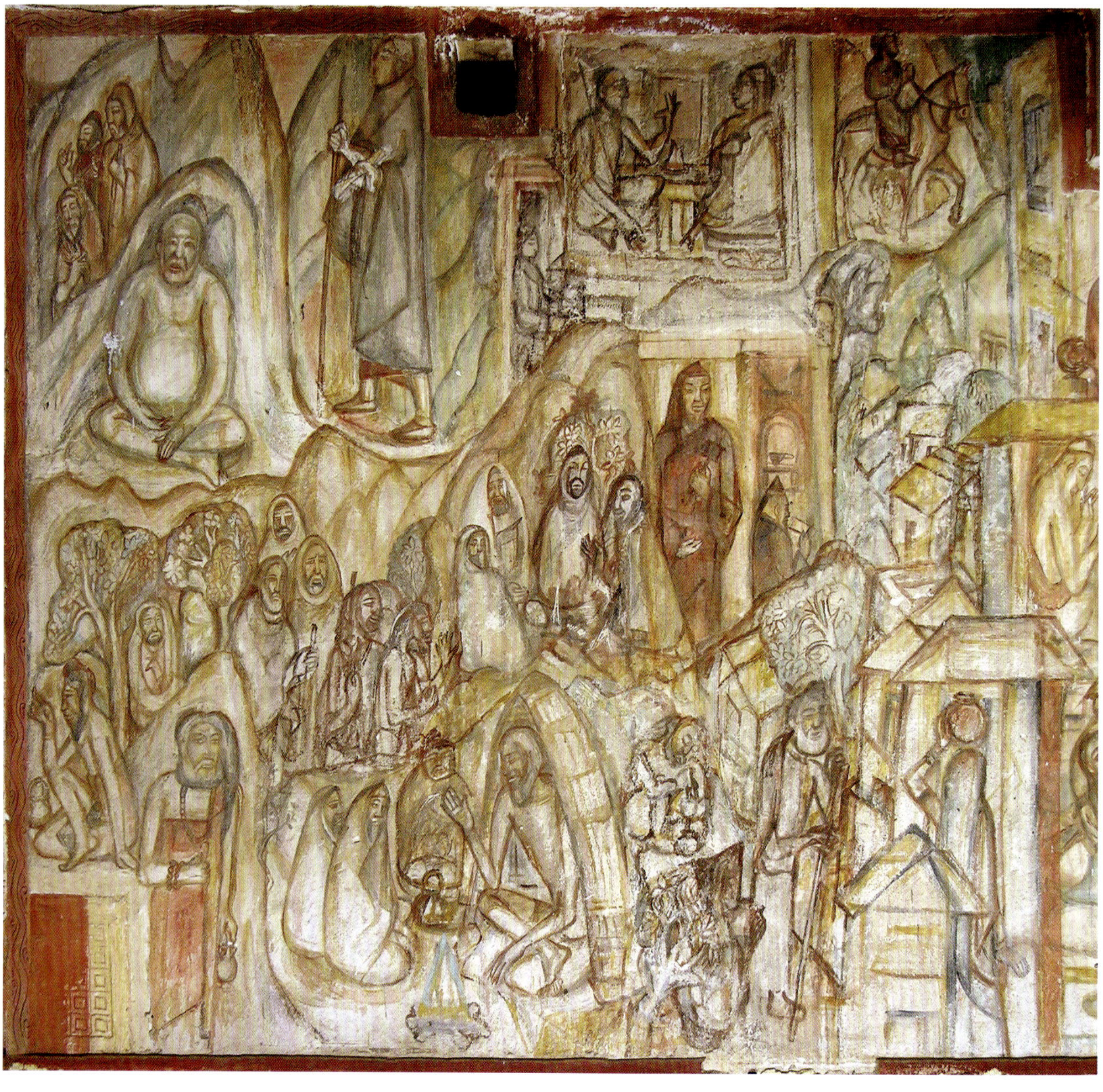

A year earlier, David Siqueiros had completed three murals in Los Angeles (among those watching him at work was the teenage Philip Guston) before being deported in 1932. The Mexican Muralists had an enormous influence on the subsequent development in the USA of the Works Project Administration (see Ch 2 p. 104) and related schemes for public art. But during the Cold War that whole enterprise was largely erased from art-world discourse. In his *Concise History of Modern Painting,* published in 1959, Herbert Read wrote of the Mexicans, 'They have adopted a propagandist programme for their art, which seemed to me to place it outside the stylistic evolution which is my exclusive concern.' The idea of The Mural as synonymous with a crassly populist aesthetic and Leftist politics proved a setback for post-war wall-painting in the West. But the mural always held other possibilities.

MURALISM PART 2: BENODE BEHARI MUKHERJEE'S *THE LIVES OF THE MEDIEVAL INDIAN SAINTS* (1946-47)

*I have endeavoured to work directly on the wall because the spontaneity which went with it appeared to me very valuable....
The artist must animate the wall by a constant creative struggle that is renewed every day.*

BENODE BEHARI MUKHERJEE, 1969

BENODE BEHARI MUKHERJEE

The Lives of the Medieval Indian Saints

1946–47

The first of the three frescoed walls that make up this 'Great Procession'.

In the year leading up to Indian Independence, a very different attempt to fuse modernity with the mural tradition was taking shape at Santiniketan, the 'forest university' founded by the poet–philosopher Rabindranath Tagore, in remote rural Bengal (see Ch 4 pp. 171–73). *The Lives of the Medieval Indian Saints* (1946–47) [illustration opposite] is painted freely and intimately in fresco across three walls, as a continuous seventy-five-foot-long procession. 'The most noble and effective work of art created in India in the twentieth century' was the judgement of the film director Satyajit Ray, writing in the early 1970s. Its painter, Benode Behari Mukherjee (1904–80), had a sophisticated awareness of his complex East/West inheritance: of the Ajanta cave-paintings, but also of Giotto and Lorenzetti; of Cubism; of Kirchner (see pp. 124–27) and Expressionist woodcuts, as well as of Japanese and Chinese scrolls; and certainly of Rivera too, since a young Mexican muralist had made the pilgrimage to Santiniketan in the mid-1930s.

But Benode Behari's mural procedure was radically different from Rivera's poster-like filling-in. He set out each day without any preliminary cartoon, painting almost calligraphically onto the wet plaster with an extraordinarily immediate touch, reminiscent of those sinopia underdrawings found beneath Italian frescoes. No one in the modern West has dared to paint on the wall so directly as this, nor achieved this fusion of a monumental public scale with such a lyrical and tender voice.

In 1917, at only thirteen, Benode Behari had entered Santiniketan, where he would remain more than thirty years, eventually as teacher, and curator of the museum. Early in childhood he'd lost the sight in one eye, while the second was seriously impaired. (Our experience across the mural of a tremulous *closeness*, of a succession of focuses, each fading into a blurred penumbra, may partly result from this.) Tagore's project at Santiniketan was to create a nurturing community, drawing to it international visitors from every field of knowledge, yet without loss of Indian identity. *The Lives of the Medieval Indian Saints* is a late flower of that utopian vision, with overtones also of contemporary Gandhism, above all in its refusal of hierarchy. Painted in the main hall of the Department of Hindi Literature, the ostensible subject was the vernacular tradition of the mystic–poets: the Sufi weaver Kabir (born to a Muslim family); blind Surdas; the Sikh Gobind Singh; the Tamil Ramanuja; and Tulsidas, author of the most popular version of the Ramayana – all from the lower strata of a caste-divided society. They are shown as 'silent revolutionaries rising from within the populace' (in the words of Gulammohammed Sheikh); and that populace, even more than in Rivera's fiesta-crowds, becomes the mural's true theme.

Multiplicity seems especially characteristic of Indian visual tradition, as in the incrustations of the temples – the sense at Ellora or Khajuraho that there are more figures than the mind can possibly hold; the great carved boulder cascading all creation at Mahaballipuram – or the myriad micro-narratives painted by flickering torchlight across the caves of Ajanta. Here too, it is as though the solid plane of the wall has come alive with a mass of bodies. Multiplicity is bound into the subject matter: the plurality of ways for living out religious experience. The crowding is essential for the creation of this hall as a brimming vessel, full to overflowing. Hence perhaps the opening inscription above the door: 'wherever Tulsi goes, with his monk's bowl of karma, he finds it cannot hold a drop more of anything, whether he dips it in river, sea, well, or lake.'

It was as a human river that the young assistant on the mural, the artist/writer K. G. Subramanyan, saw it unfolding. 'From small beginnings in the mountain fastnesses the tradition swells and meanders through the plains, becoming more varied and populous, growing larger and deeper and more expansive before throwing itself finally on the ocean of mankind in the Indian villages.' Benode Behari felt instinctive affinity for the human-centred Franciscan frescoes of Assisi; the verticality of his figures is more Gothic than Indian. Like Tagore, he was brought up in a Brahmo milieu, and all divinities and idols are eliminated from his mural's version of Hindu tradition. At the moment when Partition was about to separate Muslim from Hindu, his mural was an affirmation of the undivided: his aim, 'to present the basic unity between the various traditions and styles'. One might see his refusal of all preliminary design as equivalent to non-violence – as going unarmed into the struggle. Restricting himself to the mild hues of earth pigments, he conjures within the hall an ambience of gentle, loving human assembly.

I see in this feat of improvisation the potential for a new mural culture, with its own utopian ethic – as contrasted to the Mexican as Gandhism is to Marxist-Leninism. Soon after, for complex reasons, Benode Behari left Santiniketan; and in 1957, after a botched operation, found himself entirely without sight. Satyajit Ray's film *The Inner Eye* (1972) documents the blind artist continuing to make images. It also incorporates a superb sequence shot in the Hindi Bhavan at Santiniketan, providing for many their first encounter with the mural. Ray's tribute to his mentor marked the beginning of a slow process of rediscovery, culminating in the magnificent Benode Behari Mukherjee retrospective mounted at Delhi's Museum of Modern Art in 2006–7.

MARSDEN HARTLEY'S 'LATE COURAGE' (1938–40)

Towards the end of the 1930s, at sixty-one, and almost despite himself, Marsden Hartley (1877–1943) became what he had never been before: a painter of the human figure. To register the poignancy of Hartley's final phase, one needs some sense of the long road travelled, the thirty years of cul-de-sacs and wrong turnings. He'd been an associate of *Der Blaue Reiter* (The Blue Rider) group in Munich, but also an unconvincing quasi-Cubist, and, later, a hopelessly derivative follower of Cézanne. He'd been a painter of the Elemental, of mountain and sea; or else of symbolic still lifes dissolving into abstraction. In all these modes, his art had been shaped by a long-held prohibition against any overtly 'personal' or figure-centred subject matter. But in those final few years Hartley broke all his own rules.

Much as I admire his late 'sea-windows' and landscapes, I want here to look only at the figure paintings – mostly unknown before 1980. The phrase 'late courage' comes from an unpublished essay written in 1940 by Hartley's long-standing friend, the poet William Carlos Williams. He defines the new paintings as '...full of late courage and passion, of the sort of love that's not easy to kill, or to understand either, for that matter'. Williams, six years younger than his difficult comrade (who had once declared to him, 'I'm never intimate with anyone'), was responding to the pathos of this large, awkward, helpless painter arriving so late at release and achievement.

In New York at the beginning of 1935, Hartley spent his fifty-eighth birthday destroying a hundred unsold works he could no longer afford to store. He'd lost his once-high reputation in American art, and since 1932 he'd lost the financial and fraternal support of the photographer and gallerist Alfred Stieglitz. (He once likened their relationship to that of Vincent and Theo Van Gogh.) That autumn Hartley's unquenchable wanderlust – which had taken him in the previous few years to Provence and Dresden, Mexico and New England, Cleveland and Hamburg and the Bavarian Alps – drove him northward, beyond his native Maine and into Nova Scotia, until in October 1935 he encountered the Mason family and settled in for several weeks in their remote island house at East Point. He would recall them as 'five magnificent chapters out of an amazing human book, these beautiful human beings, loving, tender, strong, courageous, dutiful, kind...'.

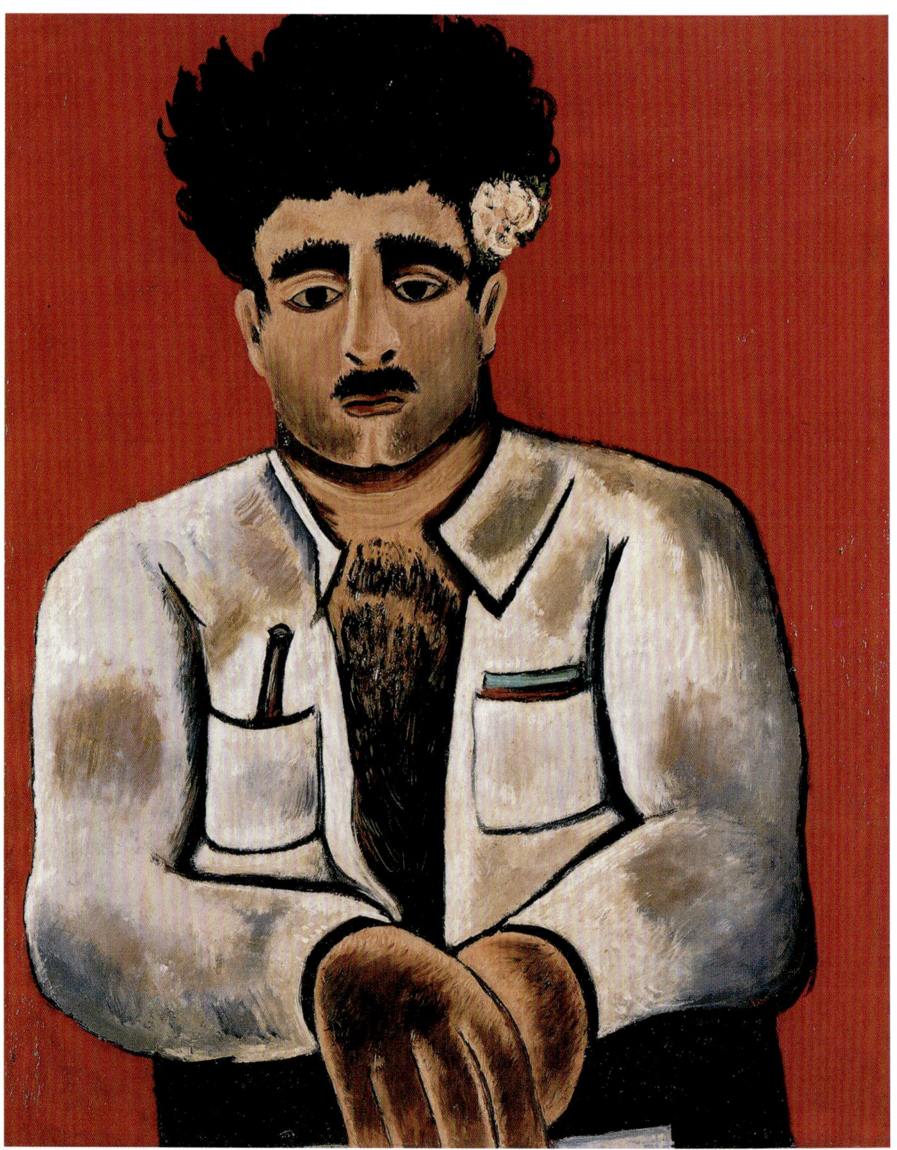

He discovered a second father in Francis Mason, a huge-headed seventy-year-old,
and beloved brothers in the two giant unmarried sons, already into their thirties.
He knew he had found a fertile context; writing to a friend in 1935:

> I could draw such life from it – thereby become more alive myself – therefore
> more attractive to myself and others – therefore more eligible for society.
> I haven't liked myself for some time now.

Returning the following September, Hartley took seriously the Masons'
suggestion that a shack of his own might be built for him on the island. But
then, on the stormy night of 19 September 1936, both Mason boys, together with
a young cousin, were drowned at sea. Joining parents and sister in their grief,
Hartley stayed on, painting several of his most powerful sea pictures. He finally
left for New York in November, never to see the family again.

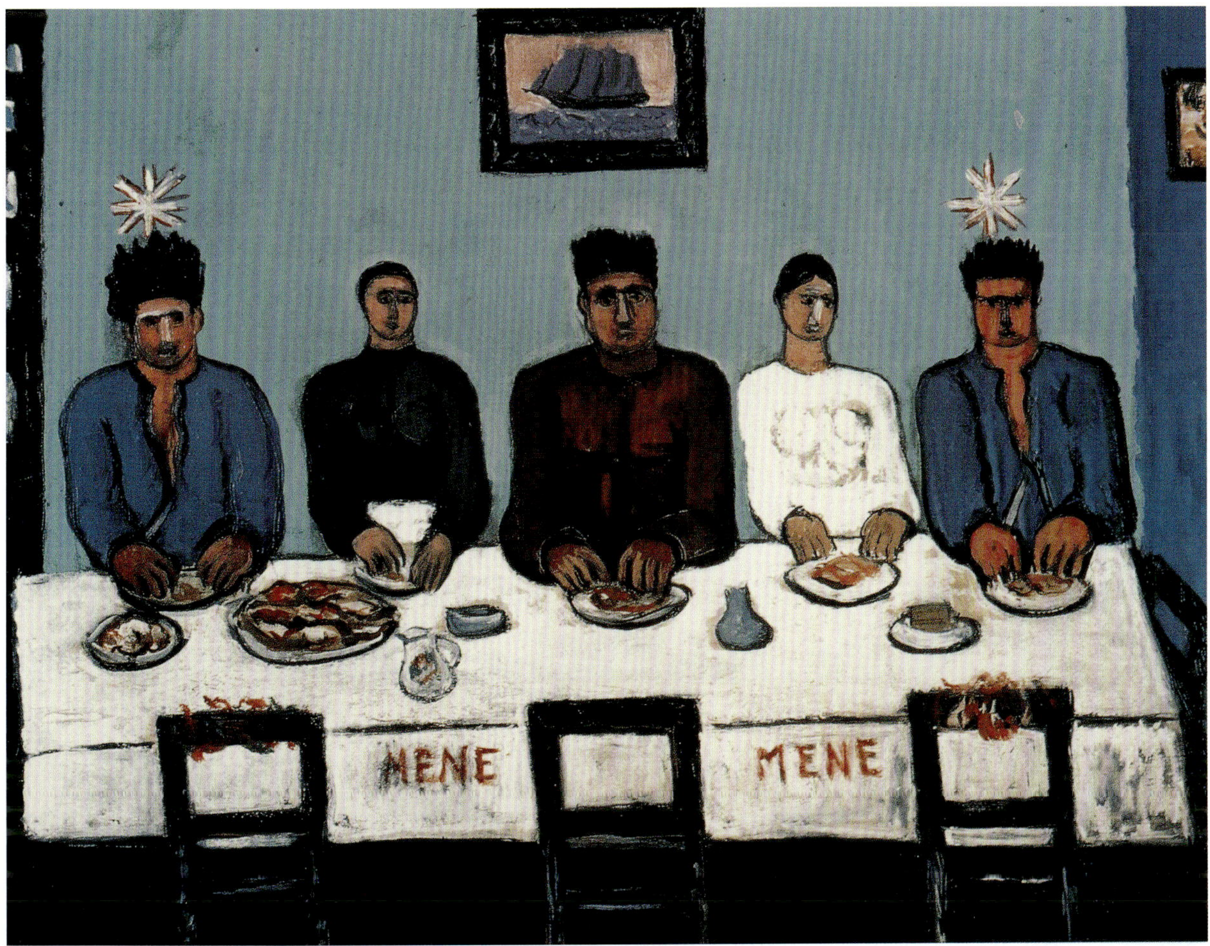

MARSDEN HARTLEY

Fishermen's Last Supper
1938

In this first version, the
tablecloth bears the 'writing
on the wall' from Balshazzar's
Feast – a prophecy of
destruction – while stars
shine above the doomed boys.
Hartley's death-redeeming
ex-voto recalls the Bavarian
Catholic folk imagery he'd
admired in the collection
of Kandinsky and Gabriele
Münter when he visited them in
Bavaria before the First World
War. (In colour and paint-
handling it carries some echo
of Münter's own depictions of
domestic interiors.)

It was only in 1938, on another island (Vinalhaven, off the Maine coast), that he finally began his sequence of 'modern icons' depicting the Masons under fictive names: Cleophas for the father, Adelard for the elder son. In *Adelard the Drowned* (1938–39) [illustration opposite], this massive moustached child-man is set against the deepest cadmium red; bear paws, pipe in breast pocket, hairy torso bursting through, set against a pink rose tucked behind his ear. His shirt with its brown stains is very broadly handled – but is then overlaid in white with the daintiest little feather-light dabs. 'Beneath all his strength,' wrote Hartley of Alty Mason, 'lies a heart as tender and as beautiful as that of a young girl.'

Adelard is recognizably of the same 'family' as the figures of Léger, Beckmann and Guston; artists who've passed through existential demolition and retrieved from the ruins a new human imagery. Popular idioms feed in an inflection of comical innocence, even when their paintings seem most powerfully monumental. The body is emphasized as a massive construction bounded by a black contour; a physicality so exaggerated as to signal an underlying fragility.

Like so many twentieth-century painters, Hartley yearned to give his art a social function. In his most naively Whitmanesque phase he'd conceived panels 'for an arcane library' or 'intended for use as focus motives in a convalescent

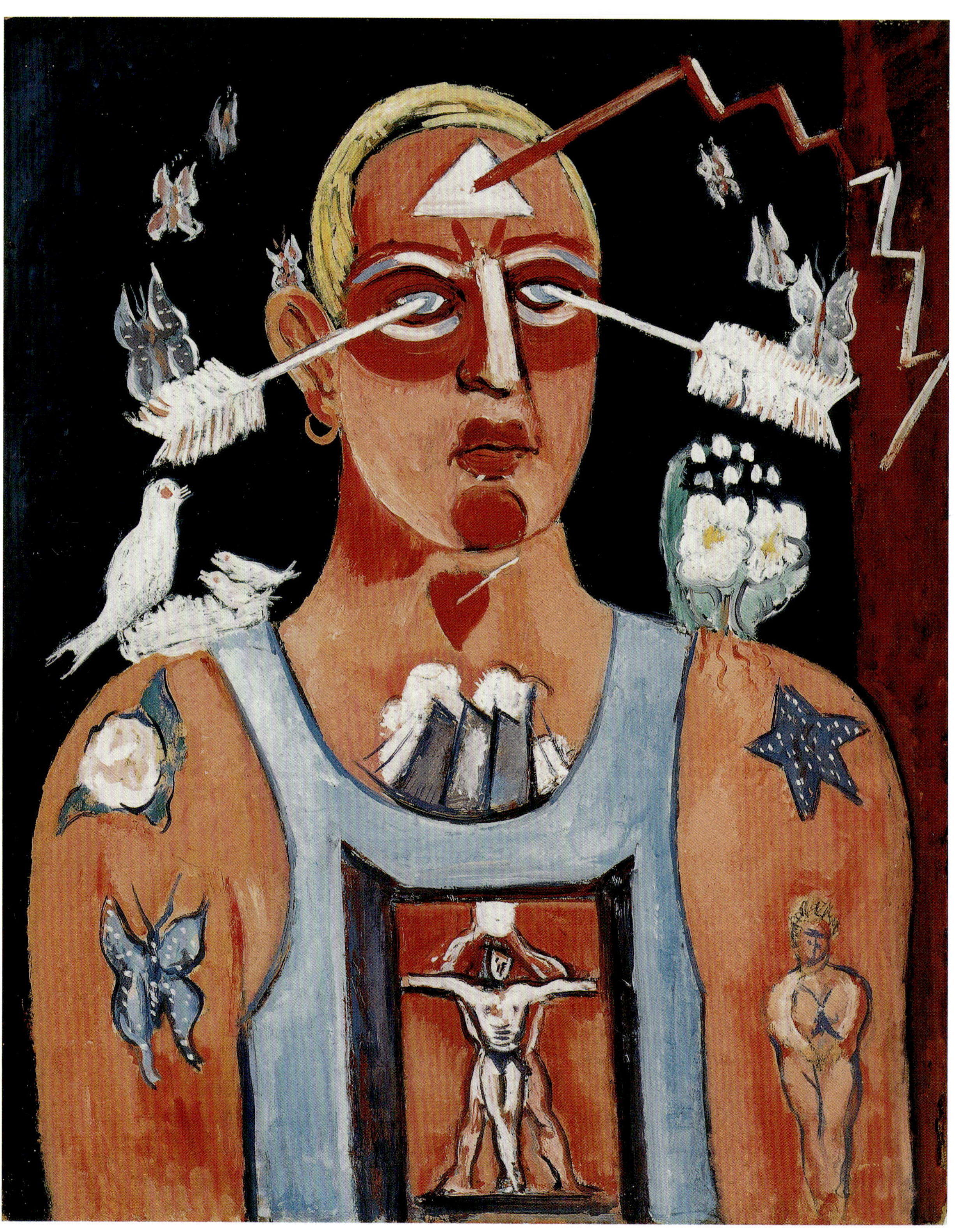

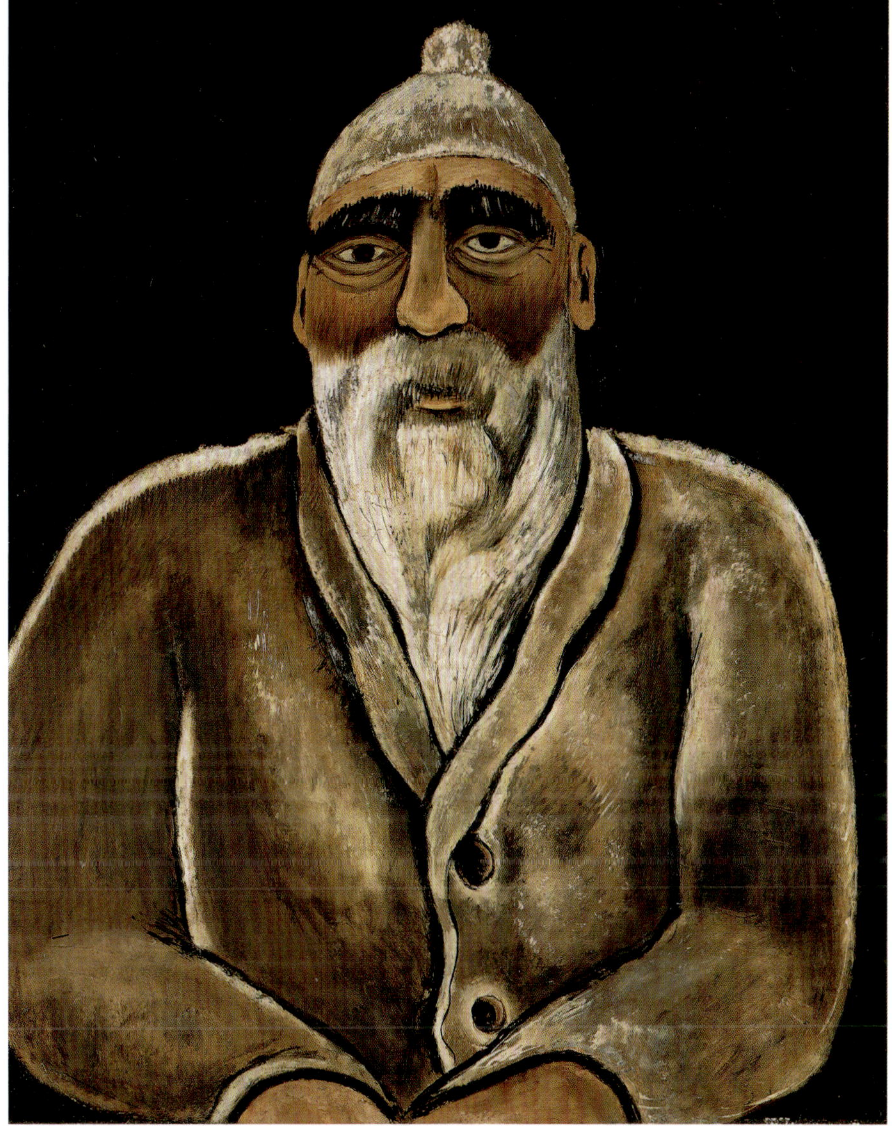

pavilion, mostly neurotic'. Now he dreamed of 'modern icons for a wooden sea-chapel in the bitter north...for a seamen's Bethel...for a fishermen's community-house'. Central to this room, alongside the five Mason portraits, would be the composition he called *Fishermen's Last Supper* [illustration p. 49]; as with Gauguin's Breton 'tribals', his Nova Scotia primitives embody a community of belief in which Hartley participated only vicariously. In the first version, the three colossal young men are set forever at table (two half-sized girls squeezed between). Wreaths and stars spell out the death symbolism, but the Mason dining room (described by Hartley as 'flaming robin's-egg blue') is faithfully conjured. In the larger, second version of 1940–41, the room is a deeper blue, the table further from us, and the whole composition given more of a tilt – suggestive of memory, or perhaps of the heave of the ocean.

On the wall behind is a sailboat of the genre Hartley always loved, most of all when transmuted in the mysterious marines of Albert Pinkham Ryder (1847–1917). He'd seen his first Ryder in 1909:

> It was a picture that so affected me that I, in all truth, was never the same after…it shook the rafters of my being and left me sort of shaking in the force of the wind.

Ryder had long been shipwrecked in his own room, and when Hartley visited his New York studio he was amazed at the 'filth and debris'. But he would sometimes glimpse his hero in the street 'in his woollen jacket and woollen skullcap'. Hartley's own doomed vessels under aureoled clouds are homages to Ryder; and it is Ryder he calls up from the dead alongside the Mason boys in a further 'archaic' portrait [illustration p. 51], invoked as a Maine folk-prophet or fisherman–saint of legend.

The artist must buckle himself with infinite patience…
He must await the season of fruitage without haste,
without worldly ambition, without vexation of spirit.

ALBERT PINKHAM RYDER, 1905

Hartley was the youngest, late child of a working-class English couple, Manchester millhands who had emigrated to the cotton town of Lewiston, Maine, in the 1840s. When he was eight his mother died; from that moment he was 'in psychology an orphan, in consciousness a lone left thing'. The first climacteric of his art was triggered in 1914 by the death in battle of his German officer friend Karl von Freyberg; the second by the drowning of the Mason boys. As the art historian Jonathan Weinberg has observed, 'Hartley seemed capable of making art about love only when the lover was dead.'

Among the few documentary traces of Hartley's homosexual identity, the most vivid is a wartime letter of 1942, a year before he died, to the writer Robert McAlmon, in which he describes 'All the navies in white duck, and the thighs and arses something to tell mother about – simply wonderful.' In the late 1930s, Hartley fused beefcake with religion: a bust of Christ with large red-nippled breasts; a gay *Pietà* (now in the Hirshhorn Collection, Washington, DC) where a tiny-headed Christ lies in the lap of a huge lumberjack, with a whole male community of bare-torsoed, blue-hatted Hulks stacked up behind, perhaps waiting their turn to fondle the man-god. In this vein the weird picture entitled *Sustained Comedy: Portrait of an Object* [illustration p. 50] may be his testament. Painted in New York in 1939, it is usually interpreted as a self-image: a Blond Beast (as Hartley might wish to have been) but so plastered with emblems of self-mockery as to become a clown – or (as the back of the board is inscribed) a 'TRAVESTY'. Against the deep blue of night, an expanse of densely impastoed pink flesh is invaded by butterfly and bird's nest, flower and sailboat, a star as well as a coy, androgynous nude: not so much tattoos as emanations or attributes. Earring, lipstick mouth, and heavy 'slap' complete the mask, while his blue eyes (which Hartley always reckoned his best feature) are pierced with arrows. The pale-blue vest opens at the heart to a crucifix that may also be a buggery.

The 1944 commemorative retrospective at the Museum of Modern Art in New York was limited in scope, excluding nearly all the pictures I've mentioned here. If Hartley surfaced at all over the next thirty-five years, it was usually as the 1914–15 Berlin-based pioneer of abstraction. In 1950, however, his landscapes did arouse an unexpected response from Clement Greenberg:

> I myself value them for their clumsiness and the sincerity of their failures as much as for the rightness of their successes. There are and have been greater painters than Hartley, but few whose *sentiment* I value more. Sentiment is a dangerous term nowadays, but I dare to insist on it as something that means the valuable, very valuable, when referred to an artist as sincere and true as he was.

I think Greenberg touches on an important insight, which applies even more to the figures than to the landscapes. Hartley aspires to an art of massive strength. But he does not have that strength. And the greatness of his paintings lies in their vulnerability, their 'failure'. In Milton Avery's well-known portrait of Hartley, painted in 1943, he appears a tragicomic character, queenly in his purple and gardenia; confirming the special flavour of his art, which I would define as both stoical and hysterical. Hartley proposed for his epitaph: 'Here lived one who did the best he could with what there was, and all in all liked the struggle.' William Carlos Williams understood in 1940 that Hartley was 'painting better today than he ever could have hoped to do formerly'; that mind, body, and spirit had coalesced in his 'late courage': 'drawn gradually together into one life and finally flowering, once.'

The rediscovery of Marsden Hartley in the 1980s was part of a wider reconsideration of twentieth-century painting. Today we can view his figures within a much broader spectrum, not just the black-line 'family' of Léger, Beckmann and Guston, but the wider community of 'lost' artists, from the 1920s onwards, each creating their own individual variant of a 'modern' figure painting, with their backs to the Void. Like Hartley, they carry the scars of negation, even when they attempt affirmation, reillusionment. That is what makes them so moving, and so close to us.

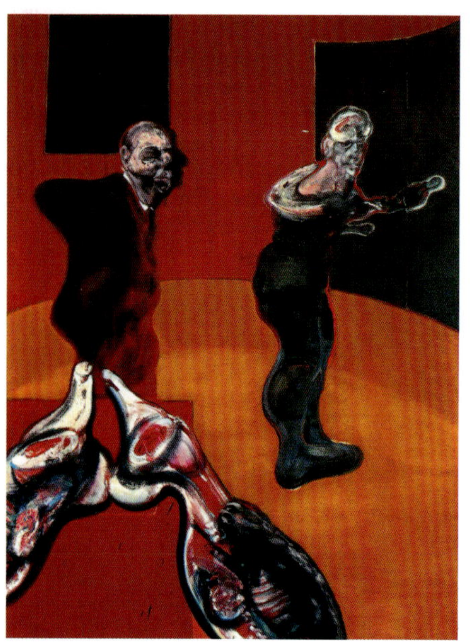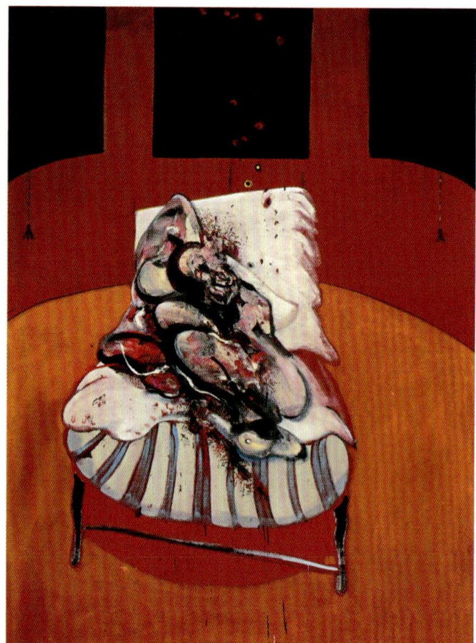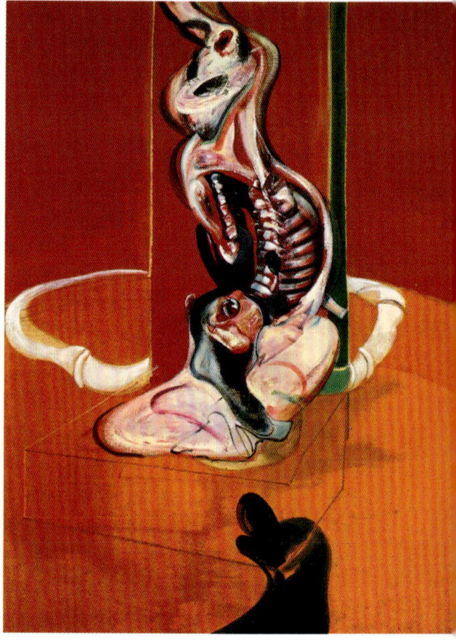

FRANCIS BACON'S *THREE STUDIES FOR A CRUCIFIXION* (1962)

…this image is a kind of tightrope walk between what is called figurative painting and abstraction. It will go right out from abstraction but will really have nothing to do with it. It's an attempt to bring the figurative thing up onto the nervous system more violently and more poignantly.

FRANCIS BACON

Three Studies for a Crucifixion
1962

Shortly after breaking up with his long-term lover, Peter Lacy, and with the Tate retrospective looming, Bacon embarked on his most ambitious picture. As he explained to David Sylvester, 'It was a thing I did in about a fortnight…and I did it under tremendous hangovers and drink; I sometimes hardly knew what I was doing'.

In Bacon's 1962 triptych *Three Studies for a Crucifixion* [illustration above] we seem to be looking down from our own crucifixion at left, into a strange curved room (I think of the decompression chambers of science-fiction films), in which two figures float below us, morphing as they turn in space. In the centre, under the harsh artificial light, a metal bed casts a deep orange shadow; on the striped mattress squirms a pile of gory flesh. Off to the right we see a kind of sculptural installation: a circular base resembling a pipeline made of white bones, supporting a vertical plank; on which is racked a conjunction of carcass and crucifix whose upside-down ribcage ends in a screaming open mouth.

Three Studies for a Crucifixion is the most blatantly infernal of all Bacon's images, heir to the pictorial idiom shared by Van Gogh, Gauguin and Munch, in which areas of strong, flat colour are enclosed within a linear arabesque. Like so much of his work, it creates a visual shock, registering the pain of experience with a transfiguring intensity – the special territory of those earlier, 'Expressionist' painters. Bacon's phrase 'exhilarated despair' could equally be applied to canvases by Munch or Kirchner, for example; among the most impressive of all such paintings by Bacon is the series based on Van Gogh's *The Artist on the Road to Tarascon*.

In contrast to that 'Expressionist' vein is his monochrome imagery of the early 1950s, often painted from black-and-white photographs, on a dark ground. The elegance of Bacon's brushwork here counters the ostensible content – a lone figure screaming from within a cage; two men wrestling on a bed – and arrives at a modernity of a very poetic kind. Neither of these aspects of Bacon might seem to bear any relation to Cubism, except in the sense with which I began this chapter – of Cubism as a necessary cleansing prior to a renewal of representation (not least for Picasso himself). It has become clear, however, from the few surviving works that have emerged from Bacon's youth, that Picasso was utterly dominant in his imagination. A dematerialized *Crucifixion* from 1933 fuses a Picasso-like figure and X-ray photography; in the 1944 *Figures at the Base of a Crucifixion*, Bacon is still manifestly in thrall to Picasso.

According to his biographer Michael Peppiatt, 'in choosing the agony on the cross as his central subject-matter, Bacon was surely driven to express a wound at the core of his being.' Peppiatt goes on to interpret the 1962 triptych as a half-hidden narrative; for example, the left panel may depict Bacon in female underwear, discovered by his father. In *Three Studies For a Crucifixion*, Bacon, almost despite himself, participates in painting's perennial role as a *medium*, as a vehicle of dream, vision, prophecy. His growing international prestige – his images appearing as cultural signposts in such films as Pier Paolo Pasolini's *Theorem* (1968) and Bernardo Bertolucci's *Last Tango in Paris* (1972) – conferred some validation on a new generation of British figurative painters. Within the context of this book, Bacon's 1962 retrospective at the Tate Gallery in London stood against the ever more engulfing tide of American abstract painting (see Ch 5). It coincided also with the sudden emergence of new figurative painters, such as R. B. Kitaj and David Hockney, at the Royal College of Art. Already Bacon had been a mentor to both Lucian Freud and Frank Auerbach. Now a core of 'resistant realists' formed around him as *chef d'école*.

That 'School of London' (see p. 205) tended to emphasize representation over imaginative narrative. The avoidance of narrative is a constant theme in Bacon's conversation as published by his friend, the critic David Sylvester, in 1975. Bacon likes the 'triptych layout' because 'it prevents it having a story': 'The moment there are several figures...the story begins to be elaborated. And the moment the story is elaborated, the boredom sets in.' In parallel, Bacon repeatedly disparages any detailed depiction, which he calls 'illustration', in contrast to 'real painting.' Nearly all the artists in this book will risk being – in Bacon's terms – 'illustrational', or 'narrative' or both at once. Bacon's own achievement is to have walked his 'tightrope' and to have handled paint so magnificently in his best work, as to transcend banal storytelling; but in the overall context of twentieth-century painting his taboos against depiction now appear far too restrictive.

PAULA REGO: *THE BARN* (1994)

I threw everything in there, everything! The perspective was there:
I wanted to see above, and to see across and to see over the other side,
so that you had this feeling of depth…I even put my mother going out
in her dressing gown. And a really sexy melon, bleeding…

PAULA REGO, 2007

Those post-Cubist or 'formalist' taboos lingered almost to the end of the twentieth century. For Paula Rego (b. 1935), cutting up and fragmenting her own images blocked her achievement between the ages of thirty-one and forty-four – the long years of collaging she excluded entirely from her first retrospective. Only in the 1980s did she at last break out, painting very rapidly, with utter graphic candour, usually working on the floor, like a child, in acrylic on paper. Her first animal fables, such as *Wife Cuts Off Red Monkey's Tail*, brought immediate recognition. Many factors contributed to this release. In 1979 she'd encountered the visionary watercolour narratives of the 'outsider' Henry Darger (see Ch 4 pp. 176–80); she'd also seen some of Ken Kiff's acrylic-on-paper *Sequence* (see Ch 4 pp. 184–91). (Both Rego and Kiff were emerging from years of Jungian dream-analysis, with a sophisticated awareness of folk-tales.) More personally, with child-bearing behind her, she was rediscovering sovereignty and freedom, as well as her Portuguese identity, while working mainly in London.

Her art underwent a second fundamental change over the next decade, taking on the ambition of classical figure composition, while retaining that vein of childhood fantasy she had previously identified as 'nursery violence'. *The Barn* [illustration opposite] was triggered by the title story in Joyce Carol Oates' *Haunted: Tales of the Grotesque*, published in early 1994. A twelve-year-old girl, beset by puberty, trespasses into a long-abandoned farm, and suffers an erotically charged beating; in the story, at the hands of the ghostly big farmwife, but in Rego's painting, administered by two miniaturized little girls. What remains only implicit in the story – that the repeated injunction to lie on her stomach and take down her panties may be an internal voice – is rendered explicit in Rego's masturbatory child. Painted over a six-month period this nine-foot-high canvas (its powerful, deep space based on a Tintoretto *Nativity*) became a grand affirmation of early sexual experience, with overtones more comic than tragic. She has climbed the ladder, not into a derelict, dark chamber, but a warm hayloft presided over by a huge cow; the miniature presences all around her – the old woman feeding fowls in a corner, as well as the dolls and bats – are part of this self-created world.

In 1990 Rego had been appointed Associate Artist at London's National Gallery, and she'd sometimes felt oppressed by the assembled masters, 'as if an old man had climbed on her back'. Her thoughts often turned to Henry Darger, creating his own raw masterpieces without reference to tradition. Yet in the subsequent decade she consolidated her commitment to a radically 'factual' pictorial language (taking the later works of Lucian Freud as one exemplar). Although this literalness could sometimes

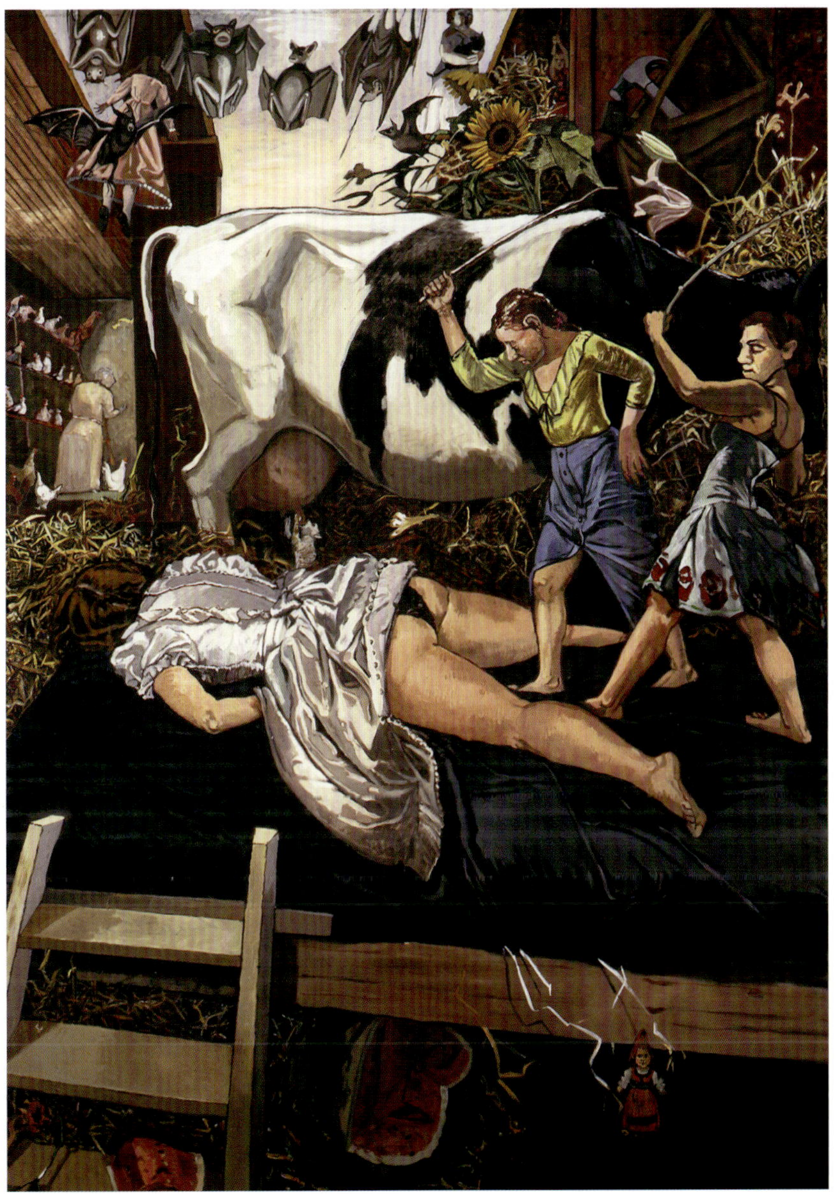

PAULA REGO

The Barn

1994

The Barn's upwards-rushing composition is stronger than in any of her previous works. It was the first painting completed in Rego's newly purchased London studio – a large industrial space, lit only from above.

seem disconcertingly in conflict with her imaginative fantasy, it would prove appropriate to her 1997–99 *Untitled* scenes – single female figures of suffering, the nearest she had ever come to 'straight' depiction, made in pastel at about half life-size. Those images would play a significant part in the campaign to legalize abortion in Portugal. As Rego's life work has become widely exhibited internationally, her special position as a role-model for women painters has come into focus. Many feminists from the 1970s onwards had abandoned painting as an exclusively masculine activity. But Rego defiantly reclaimed the painter's liberty to tell stories, even to 'illustrate', emancipated from what she has called 'that stupid old Fine Art snobbery'. As the end of the century approached we all had, as she put it, 'total freedom to paint exactly as we please.'

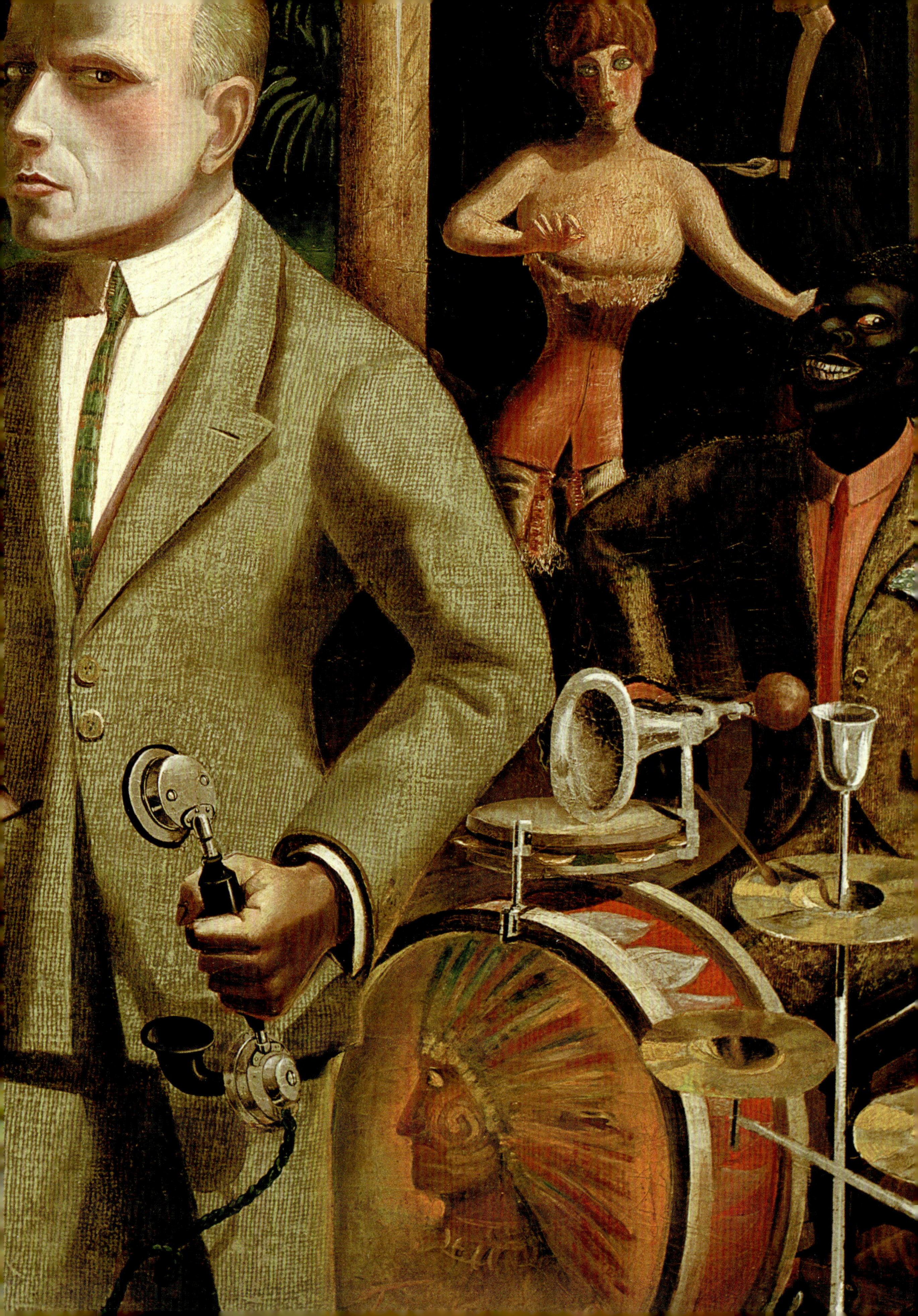

CHAPTER TWO

After Expressionism: 'The New Thingness'

The German phrase '*Neue Sachlichkeit*' remains notoriously resistant to English translation; 'The New Objectivity' or 'The New Sobriety' are two of the more common variants. When the slogan was first used in 1923 it identified 'artists who have retained or regained their fidelity to positive, tangible reality'. A more recent definition is Wieland Schmied's 'a condition in which the reality of objects appears to be the last refuge within an unknown, inexplicable world'. Perhaps the most vivid variant occurs in Elias Canetti's autobiography of 1920s Berlin:

> You moved in a chaos, but it seemed immeasurable…. Things floated like corpses in the chaos, and human beings became things. This was known as *Neue Sachlichkeit* ('New Thingness'). Little else could be possible after the long and drawn-out shrieks of Expressionism…

The many new varieties of 'realism' that emerged in Europe and America after 1918 have yet to be fully re-evaluated, and individual painters are still being rediscovered. If Germany during the Weimar years had by far the richest crop of such 'modernist realists', it was partly because the Cézanne/Cubist lineage was less central to their inheritance. Van Gogh became meshed with the far more blatantly confessional art of Edvard Munch (see also p. 161), whose painting-sequence *The Frieze of Life* toured almost every German city before arriving at the Berlin Secession in 1902; as Emil Nolde (see pp. 60–61) recalled, 'Munch's art acted upon us like an explosion'.

But these were also the years when Germany rediscovered in Grünewald's *Isenheim Altarpiece* of 1515 a realism of suffering that challenged the Italian/French Classical canon. The English painter/critic Roger Fry defined the devotee of Classical painting as 'one who enjoys above all pure art without any rhetorical emphasis'. He wrote from Germany in 1928: 'appalling as their modern art is, it is not so depressingly bad as the medieval art which they show with such pride…. Their artists are so incredibly bad.' And five days later, 'Of course, German art was wrong from the very beginning'.

OTTO DIX

To Beauty

1922

(detail, see p. 69)

Nietzsche and Nolde: *Excited People* (1913)

Our task is to create a second
great period of German art...

EMIL NOLDE, 1908

Like so many Germans of his generation, Emil Nolde (1867–1956) responded to the
gospel of Friedrich Nietzsche. In *The Birth of Tragedy* (1872), Nietzsche took to task
a post-Enlightenment culture too much in thrall to Apollo (who we might picture
as an insipidly 'beautiful' neoclassical marble). If our art was to aspire to the true
spirit of the Greeks, we would need to summon also the contrasted deity, Dionysus
(to whom the tragedies of Aeschylus and Sophocles were dedicated). Dionysus was
'The Liberator', the god of drunkenness and ecstatic states; of sex, of madness; and
of all those realms of the human psyche we now call 'the unconscious'. Nietzsche's
calling-up of 'the Dionysian' has often been seen as an opening of Pandora's box,
but it was also a reform, a version of modernity. Both Freud and Jung were shaped
by their early reading of Nietzsche.

The art we now call Expressionism embraced that Dionysian cult; sometimes
in its psychological intensity and confessionality, as in Munch and Kirchner (see
Ch 3 pp. 124–27); sometimes, as in the imagery of Emil Nolde shortly before the
First World War, in a rediscovery of the mythical and the primitive. In the 1900s
Nolde met Munch and visited James Ensor in Ostend (see Ch 4 pp. 163–68);
became immersed in Grünewald; read Nietzsche; and linked all this to his
experience in Paris of Daumier, Van Gogh and Gauguin. In 1906 he found himself
lionized by Kirchner and *Die Brücke* (The Bridge) in Dresden, at one point even
joining them in their utopian commune. The mask-like heads that appear in his
1909 *Last Supper* are partly an inheritance from Ensor, but here they no longer
signify society's hypocrisy. In Nolde the mask regains the meaning it once had
in the Dionysian theatre – the god who speaks through man at moments of
extreme emotion. The heads that crowd around the masked divinity of *Excited
People* (1913) [illustration opposite] are being taken over by the ecstatic, in a kind
of daemonic contagion.

Nolde always opposed the dematerialization inherent in both Cubism
and Futurism:

> Instead of disintegration I sought after cohesion, instead of the break-up of
> forms I wanted concentration, and in place of taste and technique I searched
> for deepened expression, broad planes and healthy strong colours.

Nolde's primitivism, his appeal to gut emotion, was just one element in the pre-
war flowering of German painting. Nietzsche once defined art as 'the code tapped
out by our nervous systems', and the best imagery of the Expressionists – perhaps
even more in graphic art than in painting – embodies that visceral directness. Each
of these artists found new pictorial language for emotional crisis, for states beyond

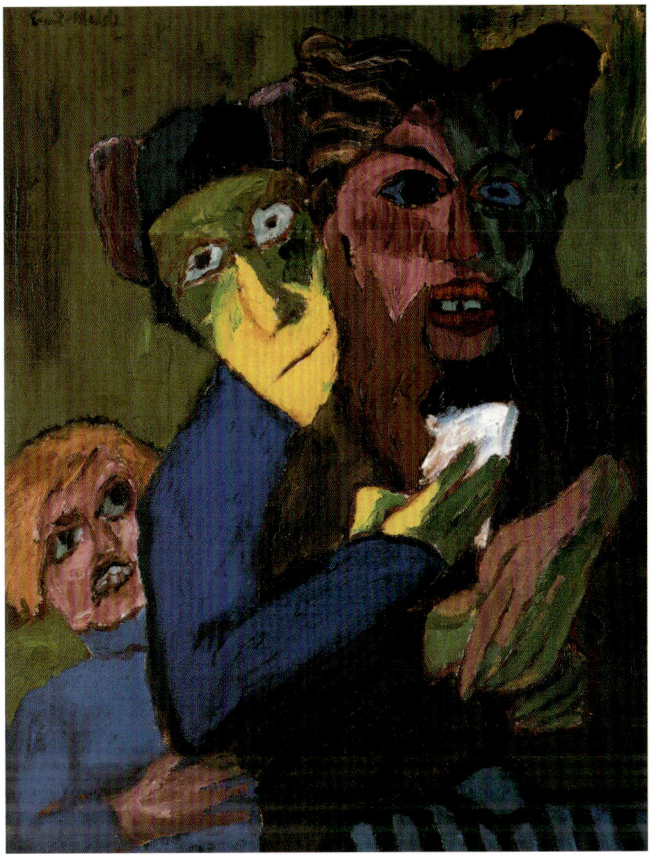

EMIL NOLDE

Excited People

1913

When he painted *Excited People* Nolde was a socialist; as late as 1919, he signed the *Workers' Council for Art* manifesto. In 1922 he wrote 'I'm completely at sea, I don't even know myself whether I should vote for the German Nationalists or the Socialists.' But by 1934 Nolde was a Nazi party member; three years later his work was confiscated from museums and featured in the 'Degenerate Art' exhibition.

the decorum of a more formalized aesthetic. Expressionism was not merely a cult of hysteria and neurosis; often when Munch or Kirchner appear most confessional, they are attempting to speak *for* the deranged, the socially outcast. Nevertheless, the shift after 1918 in artists such as Otto Dix, Max Beckmann and George Grosz, would be away from the concerns of the individual, and towards those of society.

In contrast not only to Nolde, but to his own pre-1914 mode, Beckmann's ugly masterpiece of 1918–19 *The Night* [illustration p. 62] is painted dryly, tightly. Essentially a tinted drawing, it refuses the florid naturalism that had made the young Beckmann famous as 'the German Delacroix'. He wrote in 1918:

> Just now, I feel the need to be in the cities, among my fellow-men. This is
> where our place is. We must take part in the whole misery that is to come.
> We must surrender our heart and our nerves to the dreadful screams of the
> poor disillusioned people…we must give them a picture of their fate.

The Night inherits its shallow stage from the crowded bony scenes of late Gothic wooden altarpieces, fused with the tense, paranoid space developed by Kirchner and other pre-war 'Expressionists'. Its spare, joyless surface marks it as an early manifestation of that new *Sachlichkeit*.

Emerging from the ashes of Expressionism, into the very different cultural climate of Germany's defeat and subsequent civil collapse, this new aesthetic

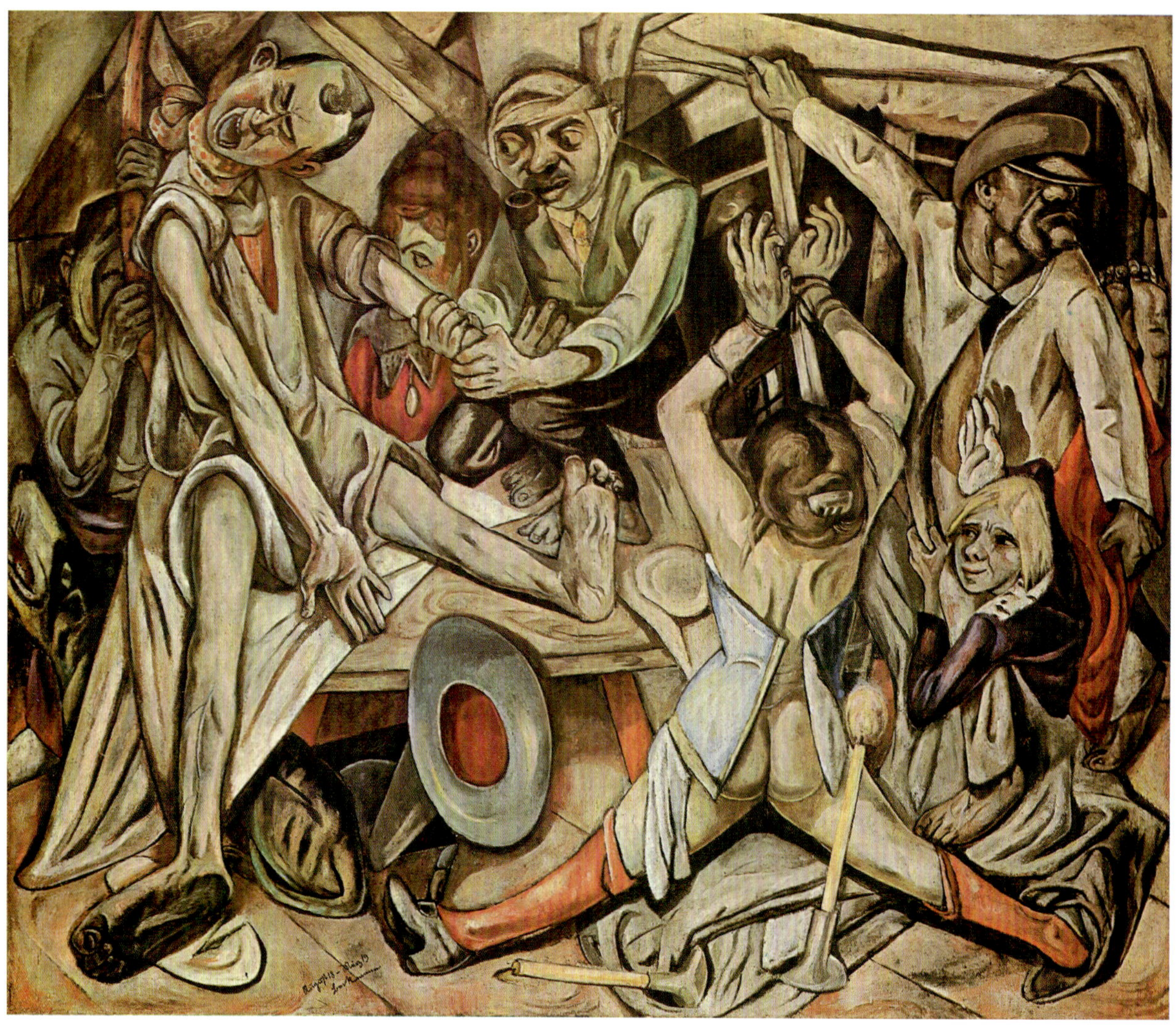

MAX BECKMANN

The Night

1918–19

Beckmann's depiction of meaningless violence – the gang who break into the family's attic, who rape the mother and hang the father – should not be misinterpreted as sadistic fantasy, as 'German grotesquerie'; it reflects an historical moment.

damped down the exuberance, the 'narcotic' intensity of the pre-war generation. The first years of the Weimar Republic were a kind of collective breakdown: civil war, famine, runaway inflation. The realism that developed in Germany after 1918 was associated with disillusionment.

Elsewhere in post-war Europe, as well as in Britain and America, there was a shared sense among painters of a need for reaffirmation of solidity, of 'thingness'. Yet outside Germany any detailed realism (what Léger dubbed *petite réalisme*', little realism, in contrast to his own *grande realism*e') would remain, in most 'advanced' art circles, beyond the pale, almost to the end of the century. The English painter David Bomberg believed detail in painting entailed a 'loss of dignity'. Nevertheless, for many of the painters in this chapter, that loss would be the necessary price for grappling with the real. I will be arguing here for the persistence of a polemically insistent *Sachlichkeit* – an ideology of Thingness – even long after the Second World War. Balthus and Alice Neel, Stanley Spencer and Lucian Freud would all deny input from German painting of the 1920s, but their art tells a different tale.

NOT THE HOW BUT THE WHAT: OTTO DIX AND *THE NEUE SACHLICHKEIT* GENERATION (1917–32)

In *Pragerstrasse*, 'Dedicated to my Contemporaries' (1920) [illustration p. 65] the young Dresden artist Otto Dix (1891–1969) created a manifesto-like response to the condition of both Germany and of painting. In this post-catastrophe world, in the Saxon capital's principal street, the pavements are littered with legless war-cripples, begging under the heels of passers-by, under the noses of dogs. During March 1920, the Kapp Putsch (an attempted right-wing *coup d'état*) had led to several days of street-fighting, with Right butchering Left in Pragerstrasse itself before being vanquished by a centre-Left coalition. Dix seems to have begun work on the canvas shortly after, and the collaged newsprint comes from election pamphlets for the forthcoming June elections. Emerging from the dachshund's snout we can make out the headline '*Juden raus!*' (Jews Out) and elsewhere 'dictatorship of the Right'. In parallel Dix was working on a six-foot frieze of *War Cripples* – his contribution to the '*Erste Internationale Dada-Messe*' (First International Dada Art Fair) held in Berlin in June 1920. A much more schematic image, *War Cripples* would eventually feature prominently in the '*Entartete Kunst*' (Degenerate Art) exhibition that opened in Munich in 1937, hung with an accompanying banner that read 'Painted sabotage of defence'. Like so many of Dix's most scandalous, ambitious and monumental paintings, it is now lost.

In *Pragerstrasse* Dix creates an astonishing jargon of fragmentation, in level upon level of collaged imagery. The shop windows are cluttered not only with corsets and condoms and abortion advertisements, but also prosthetic limbs; behind the miniature ribboned wigs of actual hair (probably ripped from the heads of dolls), tiny photographic 'reflections' have been glued in, including two little photographs of Dix himself in uniform.

Collage can signpost absurdity, disintegration – a world that no longer makes sense. By 1920, Dix was certainly aware of George Grosz, Hannah Höch, and the Berlin Dada Group, all of them employing kaleidoscopic juxtapositions in that absurdist spirit – yet tending to steer away from the 'high' art medium of oil painting, towards graphic imagery and photomontage. Otto Dix experienced that same infantile 'Dada' rage; he couldn't accept the classical premise of painting as a seamless, integrated surface. But he didn't want to abandon oil painting, and his best art came out of that tension. If Germany was broken, then painting must be broken too; the image must be made to *jump out of its skin*.

At fourteen, Dix had been apprenticed to a painter-decorator in a small Thuringian town; he did not see his first old master until he was twenty, when he enrolled in the Commercial Art School in Dresden. The following year, in 1912, he made a plaster bust of Nietzsche; and painted a *Self-Portrait with Carnation*, setting himself (as Cranach set Luther, in 1529) against a sky-blue ground. But the dual impact of first, modernism, and then of the trenches, left him floundering in a helplessly clumsy variant of Futurism. Serving as an NCO, with bayonet and

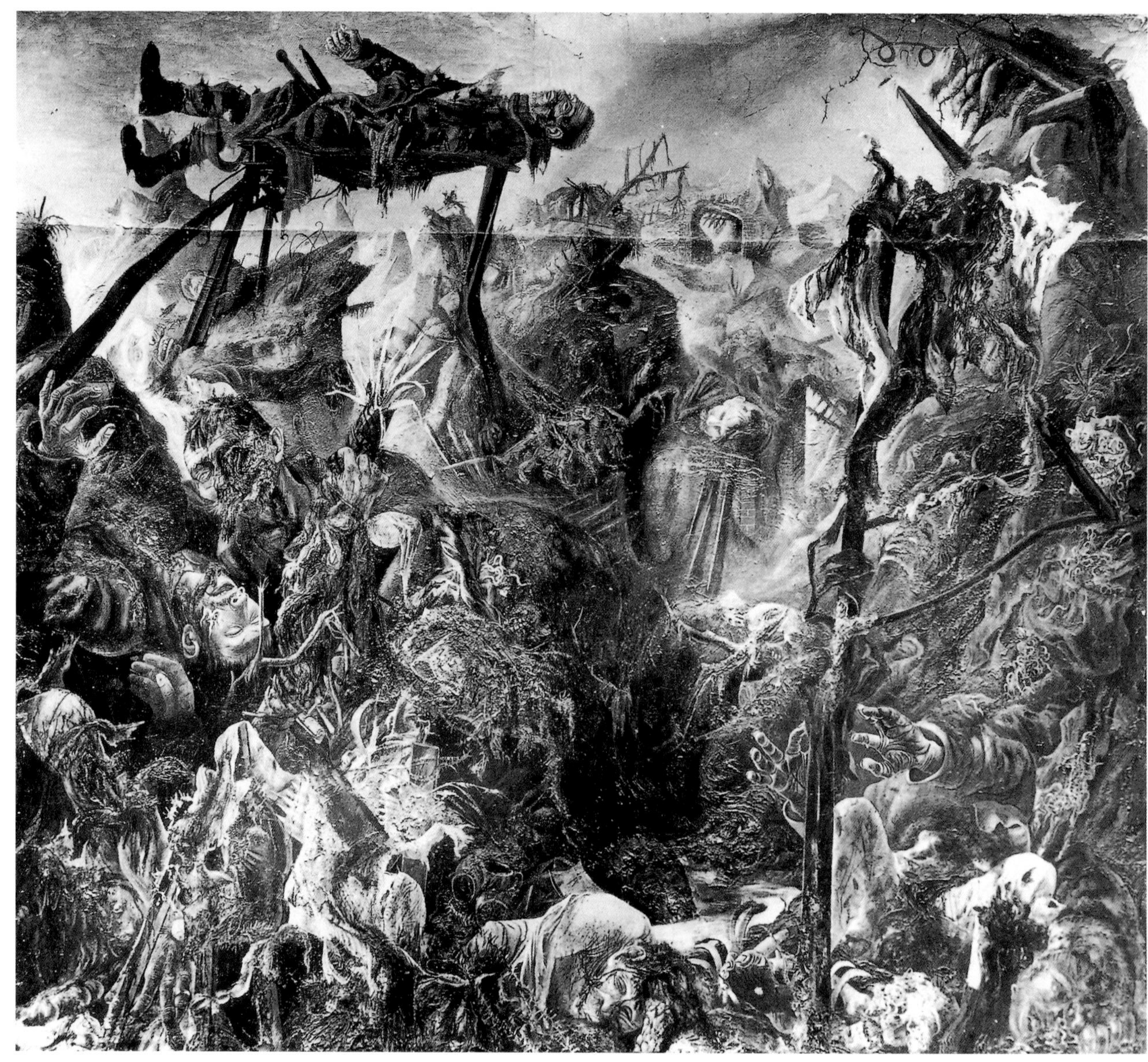

OTTO DIX

The Trench

1920–23

In 1931 Alfred H. Barr, director of the newly-founded Museum of Modern Art in New York, described *The Trench* as 'perhaps the most famous picture painted in post-war Europe'. But subsequent to a starring role in the 'Degenerate Art' exhibition, *The Trench* disappeared. Dix remained in Germany throughout the Nazi years, lying low. After 1945 he was essentially a forgotten figure, his earlier work largely invisible to the international art world until the 1970s.

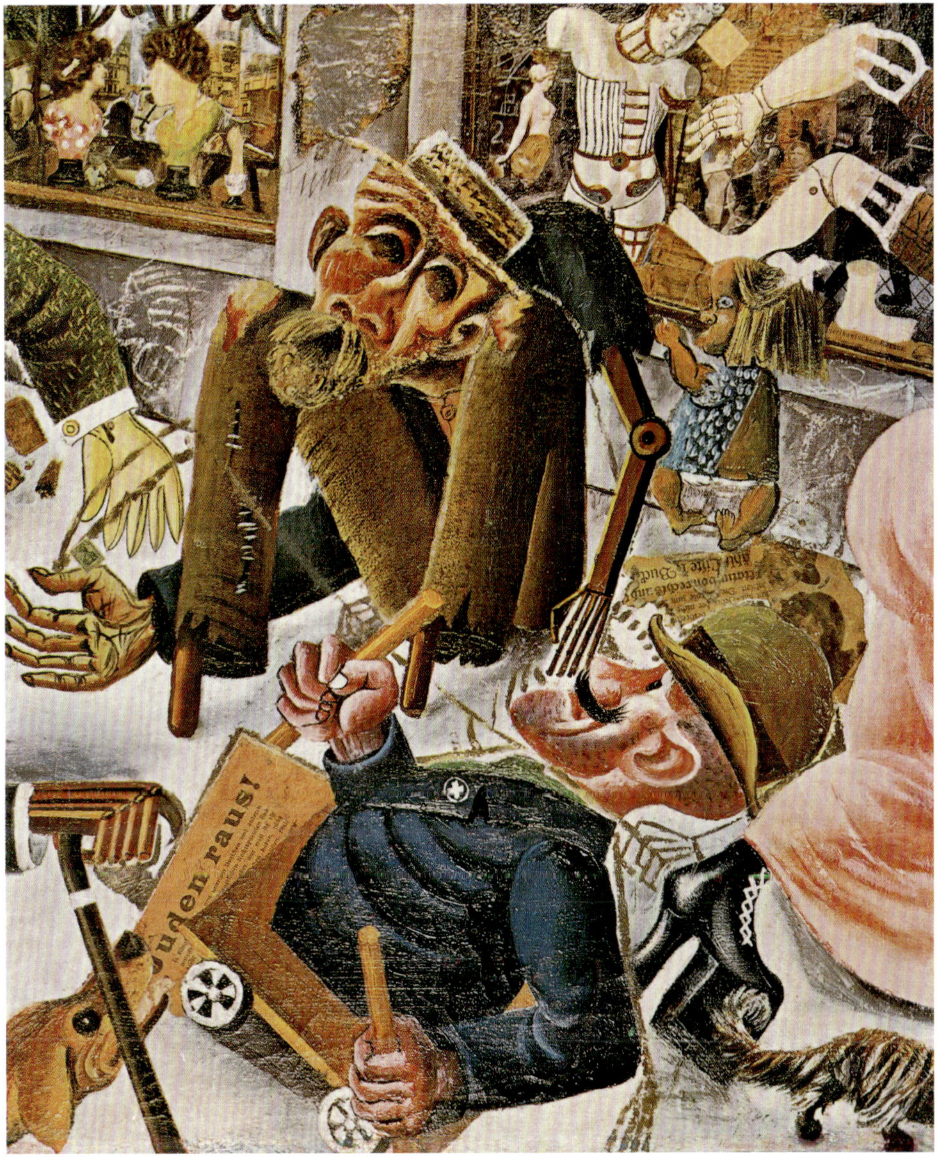

machine gun, he participated in the slaughter on both Western and Eastern fronts.
Like other Germans of his generation, Dix learned from pre-war Chagall (see Ch 1
p. 17) that the Cubo-Futurist idiom could be recreated as a vehicle for fantasy, for
humour and magic realism. Only in 1919, returning to study painting after the war,
at the Dresden Fine Arts Academy, does his imagery suddenly cohere:

> I simply had a lot to tell; I had a subject...I felt that one side of the reality
> had not been depicted at all – ugliness. The war was a hideous affair, but
> nevertheless something powerful. I had to see it all with my own eyes. The
> hunger, the lice, the mud, the shitting in one's own pants with fear.... If you
> want to be a hero, you also have to affirm the shit.

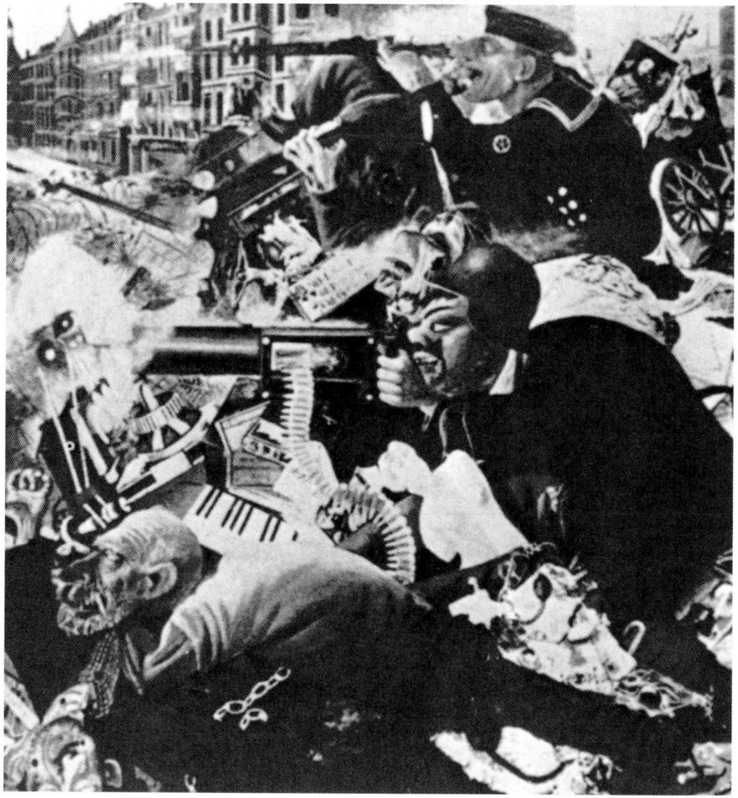

In the year of *Pragerstrasse* Dix was (in the words of his studio-mate Conrad
Felixmüller) 'lonely, desperate and poor'. He began, but couldn't continue, the
eight-foot masterpiece that would make him famous, *The Trench* [illustration
p. 64] (eventually completed in 1923, and lost, perhaps burnt, after 1937). His
rage fuelled a sequence of astonishing satires against a social order that had
made such a catastrophe possible. The dirty-postcard hilarity of *A Souvenir of the
Mirrored Halls in Brussels* (1920) masks a more agonized insight. Those 'mirrors'
are glued-down silver foil. We view the naked prostitute from every angle – upside
down, at the lower edge, even her gaping, hairy vagina – but her client is still in
full uniform, red-faced, shouting; the breakout of the maddened beast on the way
back to the slaughterhouse. In equally transgressive vein, Dix completed his almost
life-size *Self-Portrait as Sex Murderer* (now lost). Dressed in pepper-and-salt suit, the
painter brandishes a bloody knife in one hand, a severed female leg in the other,
body parts flung all around. Dismemberment was the prelude to collage, to the
new construction formed from disparate elements. Just as *The Trench* was partly
built with corpses, to hold the mud in place, so, for *The Barricade* (1920, also lost)
[illustration above], domestic objects – a piano, statue, paintings – construct the
emplacement for the maniacal machine-gunner.

Dix's double-portrait of 1921, *The Artist's Parents I* [illustration opposite]
is without collage, and without irony. Reproductions tend to smooth away the
ruggedness of its awkward surface, in the smeared white patch along the father's

OTTO DIX

The Artist's Parents I

1921

Otto was the eldest son of
Franz Dix (b. 1862) a mould-
maker in an iron foundry and
a committed socialist; and
Louise née Amann (b. 1864),
who worked in a porcelain
factory. The painting was
originally purchased by Joanna
'*Mutter*' (mother) Ey, who would
persuade Dix (nominally still a
'master-pupil' at the Dresden
Academy) to join her stable
of young artists in Dusseldorf,
where she was both art dealer
and landlady.

arm, for example, overlapping his striped shirt. We are made aware of Dix's
struggle, in the spirit of an early German 'primitive', to render solid and real
each separate hand, limb, face – but artlessly, without any trace of academic
illusionism. He sets out to *reconstruct* the body. Rheumy-eyed, balding, with
stubble on his chin, the painter's father stoops inwards, exhausted, stoical; his
mother establishes her own bowed posture and gaze, more intent and alert,
almost sardonic. They are at the end of their working lives and their bared lower
arms lie heavy and inert, the four huge swollen hands realized with a hallucinatory
intensity. Dix had written, in 1927:

'Create new forms of expression!' was the slogan that excited the last
generation of artists. But for myself, I doubt whether that's any longer
possible. The important issue has always been in my case to get as close as
I can to the object I'm representing. Because for me the What comes before
the How (which should follow from the What)...

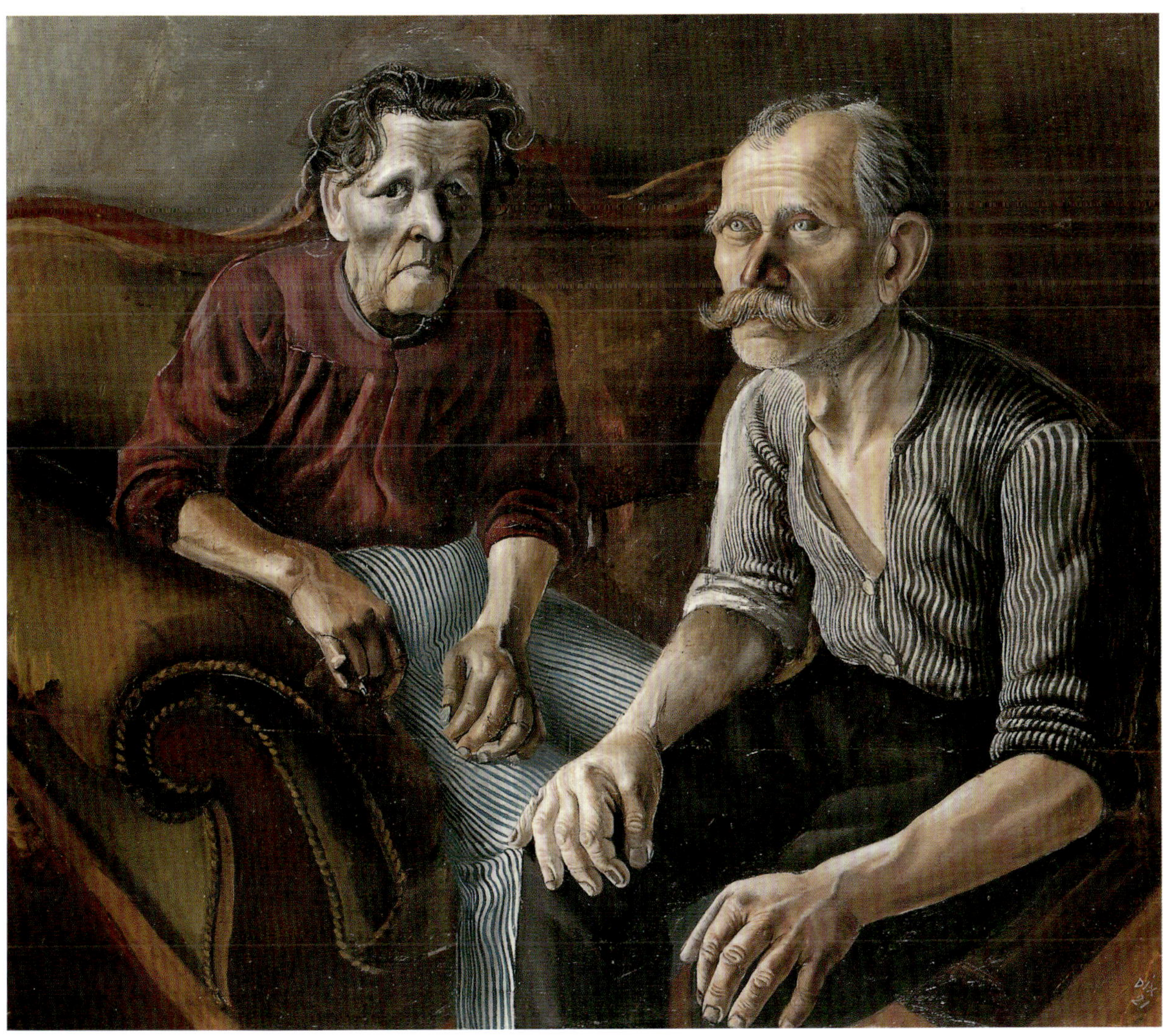

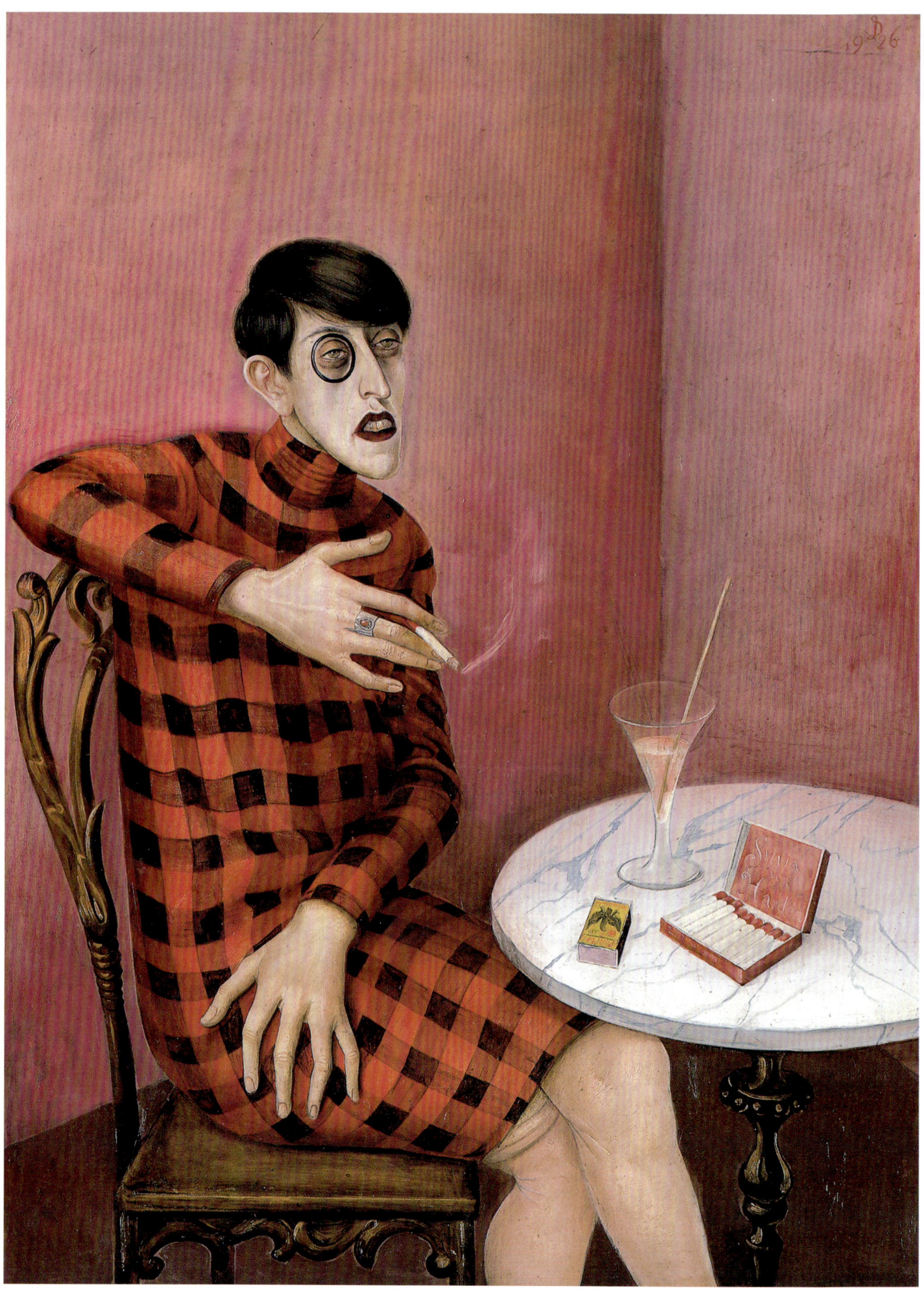

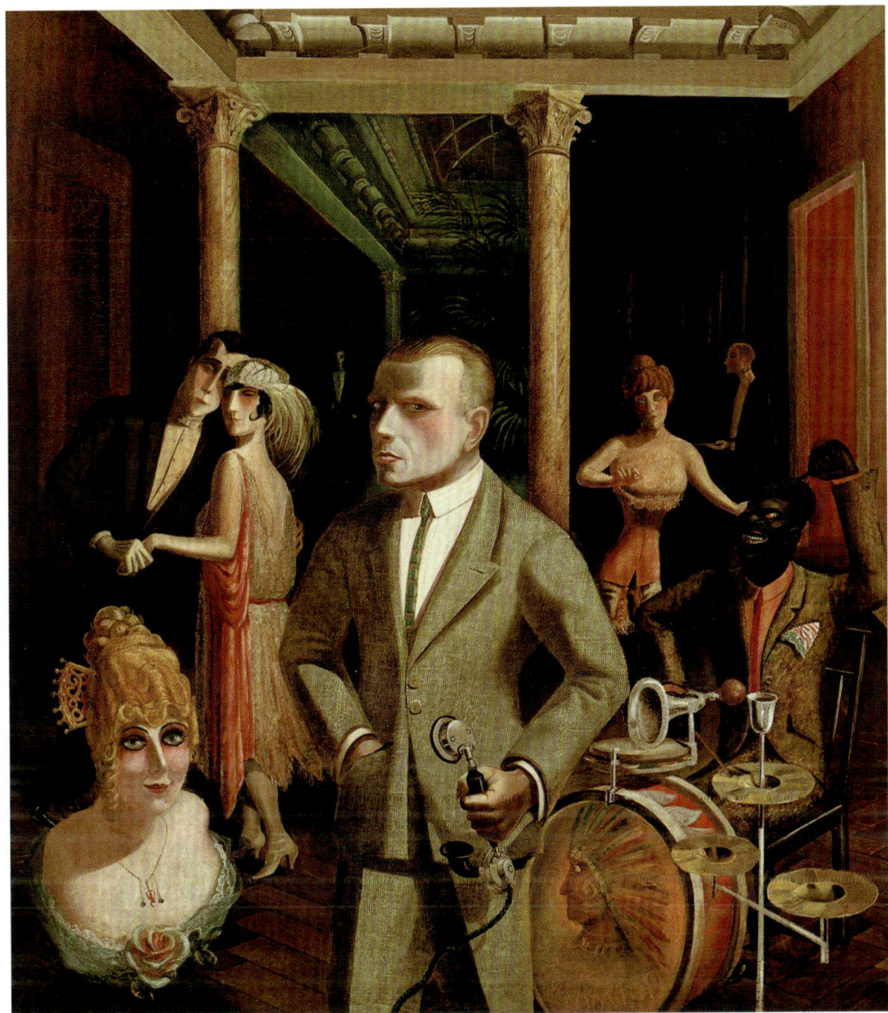

The Artist's Parents I marks Dix's shift towards Thingness – in his own formulation,
'from the How to the What'. That reversal is a challenge to the modernist insistence
on formal language. In his self-portrayal of 1922, *To Beauty* [illustration above, detail
p. 58], Dix casts himself as witness, as truth-painter with a hotline to his epoch;
he clutches that hyperreal telephone – painted on silver foil – as a weapon, to be
wielded against an over-aestheticized modernism, which in practice excluded so
much of the reality of modern life. What Dix embraces is a new 'critical' realism,
which came to be known as 'verism' – truth-telling. His role was well understood by
contemporaries such as Carl Einstein, who wrote in 1923, that Dix 'hands the kitsch
back to the bourgeoisie; he can risk that because he paints so well that his art aborts,
even exterminates, kitsch'; though the same critic would also characterize Dix as 'a
reactionary painter of Left themes' – a paradox that hangs over many of the artists
in this book.

After *The Trench* [illustration p. 64] had been exhibited, Dix abandoned
painting for six months to complete what is arguably his greatest achievement,

the etching-cycle *Der Kreig* (The War). In fifty aquatints (published as five portfolios in 1924) Dix relives every aspect of his wartime experience, using corrosive acid to soil and wound the plate, to replicate the rot of corpses. That winter, travelling for several weeks in Italy, he was excited by Bronzino's high-gloss Medici portraits, in the Mannerist style. By 1925, Dix had become famous, and, at his dealer's insistence, moved to Berlin, where he would paint most of the sequence of 'Weimar portraits' for which he is today best known: portraits that bring each individual character into focus with unsurpassed vividness, while collectively conjuring a doomed society. The journalist Sylvia von Harden, painted in 1926 [illustration p. 68], emerges in contorted elegance from her envelopment in shocking pink, defiantly androgynous in boy's haircut and monocle, the apparition of the new woman as café intellectual. Even the smoke from her pink-tipped cigarette is pink. Painting on wood (tempera under-drawing overlaid by elaborate oil glazing), Dix's technique is not homage but parody: marrying his German forbears with Bronzino, he exaggerates just those elements – their viscous, slimy surfaces, their sick-to-death intensity – that induce revulsion.

George Grosz Abandons the Fractured Image (1917-25)

In those days we were all 'Dadaists'. If that word had any meaning at all, it meant seething discontent, dissatisfaction, resentment.... We were complete, pure nihilists, and our symbol was the vacuum, the void.... This was 1917, when people had stopped believing in anything...I could feel the earth shaking beneath my feet and its tremors were reflected in my drawings...

GEORGE GROSZ, 1955

Grosz invokes Oskar Panizza (1853–1921), a notorious ranter against the German state. Panizza, a former psychiatrist turned anarchist, published a famous play about syphilis, for which he served a prison sentence; he was now in an asylum. In Grosz's 'protest against humanity gone mad' he echoes the sinister carnival imagery of James Ensor (see Ch 4 pp. 163–65).

In 1915 the twenty-two-year-old Georg Grosz had been invalided out of the army before seeing active service; almost immediately, he met (the even younger) Wieland Herzfelde, and his brother Helmut, committed Leftists who would harness Grosz's misanthropic imagery to the revolutionary cause. In pre-war Berlin Grosz had already devised a project for 'a major 3-volume study entitled *The Ugliness of the Germans*'; as he wrote in 1916, 'to be German means always to be tasteless, stupid, ugly, fat, inflexible'. In their disgust for wartime jingoism, both changed their names – Georg adapted his to that of the English King, while Helmut became 'John Heartfield'. George and John shared a studio; Wieland published their drawings and photomontages, often affixing telling captions. All three joined the German Communist Party in 1918.

Grosz's early ink drawings, akin to the spiky graffiti he admired in *pissoirs*, soon became less infantile. The most complex create microcosms, multiple spaces within which buildings, figures and advertising slogans overlay one another, recreating the maelstrom of urban life. He'd seen Italian Futurist

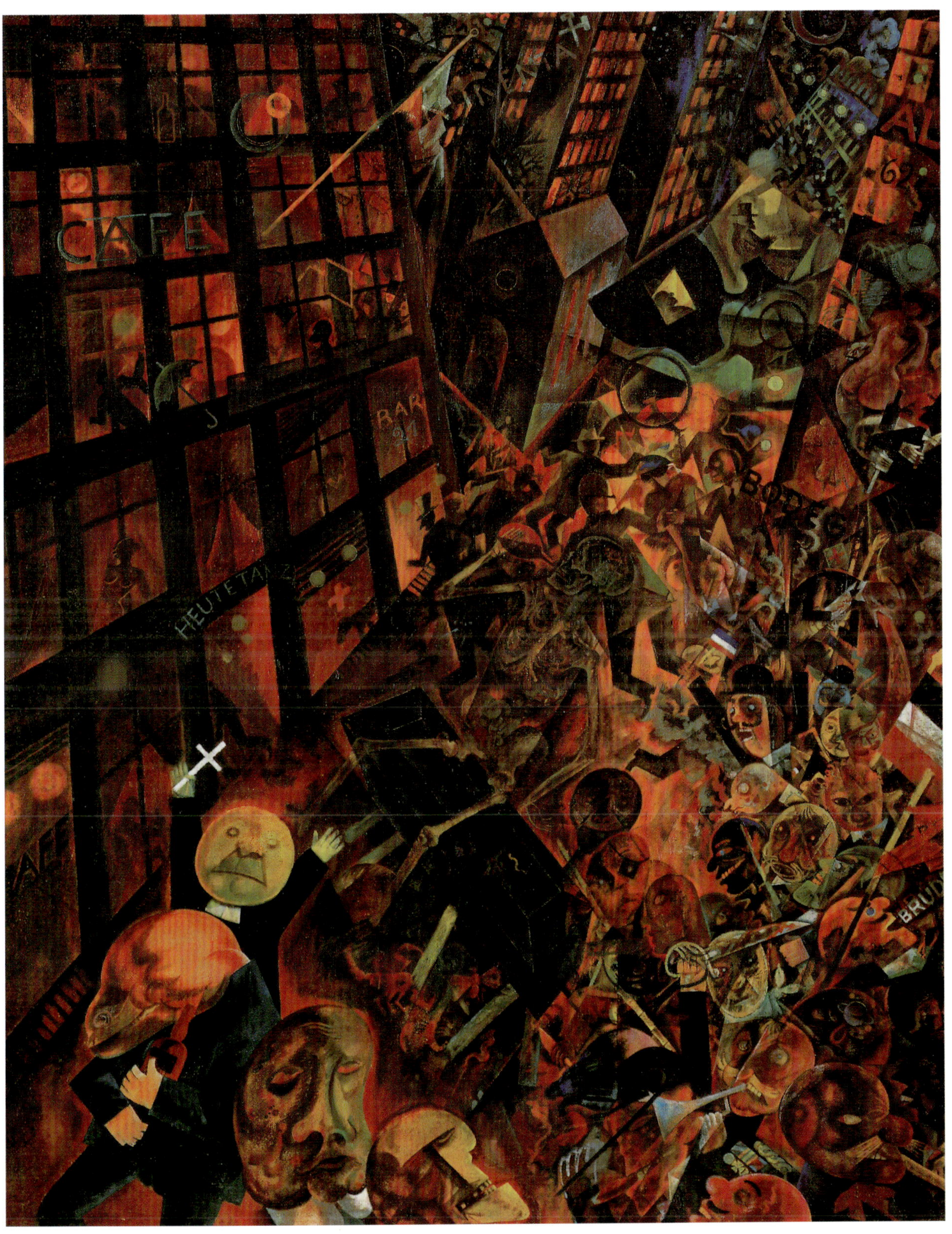

CAFÉ
BAR
HEUTE TANZ

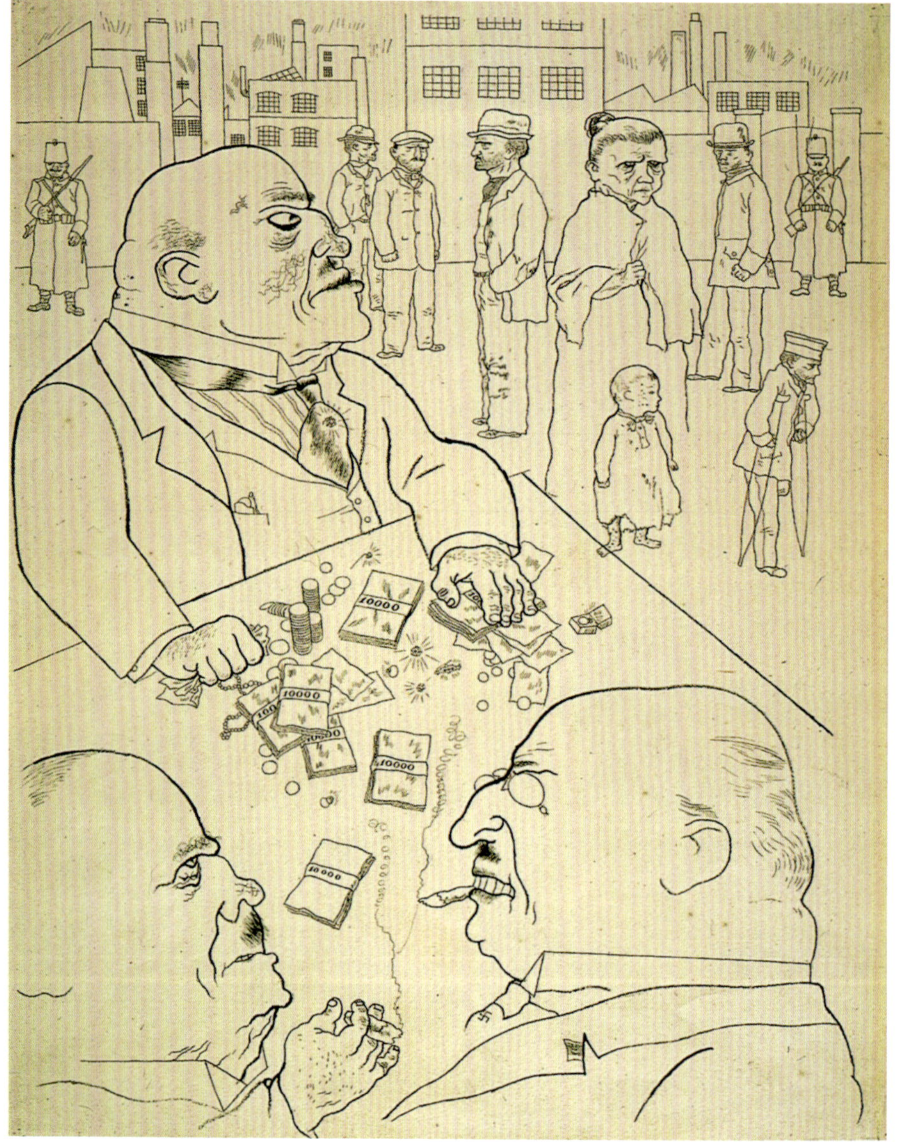

paintings, exhibited at *Der Sturm* before the war, and when he taught himself
to paint in oil, their fracturing provided a language; raw nocturnal scenes
lit by 'the blood-red of my suicidal palette'. On 15 December 1917, Grosz
wrote to the artist Otto Schmalhausen, 'Right now I am working on a large,
infernal picture, a Gin Lane of grotesque corpses and maniacs…. When this
epoch comes crashing to its destruction, you bet I'll be there watching.' *The
Funeral (Dedicated to Oskar Panizza)* of 1917–18 [illustration p. 71] became a
kaleidoscopic procession, a bestial mob (led by 'Alcohol, Syphilis, Pestilence')
flooding between a canyon of office blocks, Death's coffin carried on their
shoulders. It is the funeral of an epoch.

Berlin Dada, with its anarchic cabarets and provocations, was in many ways
a re-run of Futurism, but given a new urgency of political protest by the war. In

1917, Grosz was recalled to the army, only to suffer a breakdown; his attitudes hardened, both against the current social order, and against picture-making. As he recollected in 1923, 'to the extent that high art stood for the beauty of the world, it did not interest me – what interested me was the work of the committed outsiders and moralists of painting: Hogarth, Goya, Daumier.' Yet *The Funeral* retains the many-layered ambiguity of modernist painting, inherently resistant to any instrumental role. For the next three years Grosz turned instead to drawing, creating linear denunciations of capitalist society that could reproduce well in the huge editions published by Wieland Herzfelde's Malik Verlag. *The Seated Toads* [illustration opposite] is drawn with a beautiful calligraphic fluency (closer to that of Japanese master Hokusai than to any European) but it also supplies propaganda as a fractured painting never could. These were the images that established Grosz as the greatest political artist of his time.

After German defeat, after the Russian Revolution, after the street-battles, the right-wing putsches and the workers' republics, questions of the artist's role in society became urgent for German painters of all persuasions. In 1919, Paul Klee wrote to Alfred Kubin (see Ch 4 pp. 168–71):

> Ephemeral though this communist republic seemed from the outset…it was not without its positive consequences. Of course any extreme, individualistic art is not suited for general consumption…. But we should be able to convey the results of our inventive activity to the mass of the people. This new art could then spread into the crafts and bring forth a great flowering…. And so the workers' republic has taught us a great deal.

Klee would become a key teacher at the Bauhaus, where Leftist utopianism became fused with a formalist aesthetic; a purist creed actively combated by Grosz in his 1925 text *Art is in Danger* (written with Wieland Herzfelde). He rebukes his abstract counterparts as 'wanderers into the void'.

> Whether these artists believe their work has no deeper meaning, or whether they impart to it an emotional or metaphysical meaning…they intentionally renounce all the artist's possibilities of ideological influence (in the areas of eroticism, religion, politics, aesthetics, morality, etc.) standing silent and indifferent, that is, irresponsibly.

Max Beckmann and 'Transcendental *Sachlichkeit*' (1917-35)

Those two contrasted views of art offer a stark choice. A room full of Grosz and Dix can induce a sense of overkill, up to our necks in excrement; a room of Bauhaus works might seem a relief from all that verist ugliness, yet an inadequate response to the catastrophic events unfolding around them. It would be the special role of Max Beckmann's art after 1930 to offer pictorial structures that acknowledge both social reality and Void, both Thingness and The Metaphysical,

and thereby to move painting beyond that impasse, in what he himself called
a 'Transcendental *Sachlichkeit*'.

Beckmann was nine years older than Grosz; he had been an acknowledged
young master in pre-war Berlin, with a glamorous wife and young son,
contemptuous of any expressionistic primitivism. His huge canvas of 1912, *The
Sinking of the Titanic*, established him as something of a catastrophe specialist.
But after suffering a breakdown as a stretcher-bearer in the trenches in 1915, he
abandoned both family and careerism. He took refuge in the attic of friends in
Frankfurt, where he discovered the South German *Fastnacht* (carnival), whose
masks would dominate his mature imagery; twice-born Beckmann came to view
his own life as carnivalesque absurdity, an upside-down masquerade. He created
a new, more jagged artistic identity in harsh dry-points such as *Madhouse* and *The
Yawners*, both part of a series originally entitled *Theatre of the World*. His lineage is
clear; writing in 1920 to his print-publisher, Reinhard Piper, Beckmann cites:

> Brueghel, Hogarth, Goya. All three have the metaphysical in the objective.
> That is also my goal.

The Night [illustration p. 62, see pp. 61–62] marks his first re-emergence as a
painter. His renunciation of *belle peinture* releases a vein of cruel caricature, of
mean and repellent forms that bring his imagery into alignment beside Grosz
and Dix. Yet there is also a dream-like, somnambulistic slant of cosmic fantasy
and magic realism that links Beckmann to Chagall. In *The Synagogue* (1919)
[illustration opposite] the space is so discontinuous that we feel our eyes being
constantly yanked about: down the street to the little carnival revellers, then
soaring with the glass globes, and the balloon, high above the advertising column,
to end in a wonky façade.

The quietness of the beautiful little 1922 *Landscape near Frankfurt with Factory*
[illustration opposite] seems like the silence after an earthquake, with chimneys,
trees and apartment blocks leaning in different directions. Beckmann had written
of his hope that 'with the development of the communistic principle, the love
of objects for their own sake will become stronger'. He enters gently into this
miniature world, into each separate allotment, allowing every component an
unforced completeness and *Sachlichkeit*. I'm reminded of Léger's utopian *Paysages
animés* (see Ch 1, pp. 25–26) or of Carrà's striving to reconstruct the world of
objects; standing behind all three is the exemplary figure of Henri Rousseau.

In 1921, Grosz's drawing took a brief and unexpected turn towards the new Italian
figuration published in *Valori plastici* (Formal Values) (see Ch 1 pp. 29–32). He
wrote, in *Concerning my New Paintings*:

> I am trying to give an absolutely realistic image of the world once more....
> In this endeavour to create a clear and simple style, one involuntarily finds
> oneself coming close to Carrà. Nevertheless, everything combines to separate
> me from him, because he seeks to be appreciated in a highly metaphysical way.

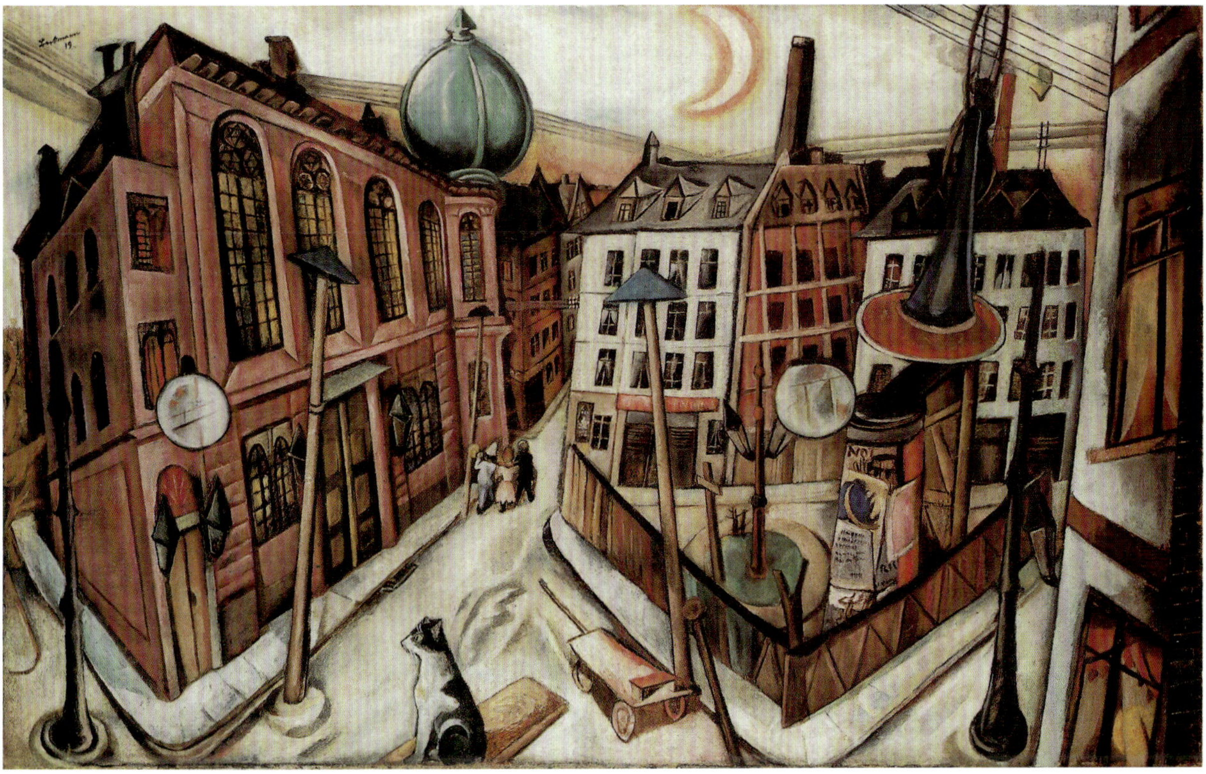

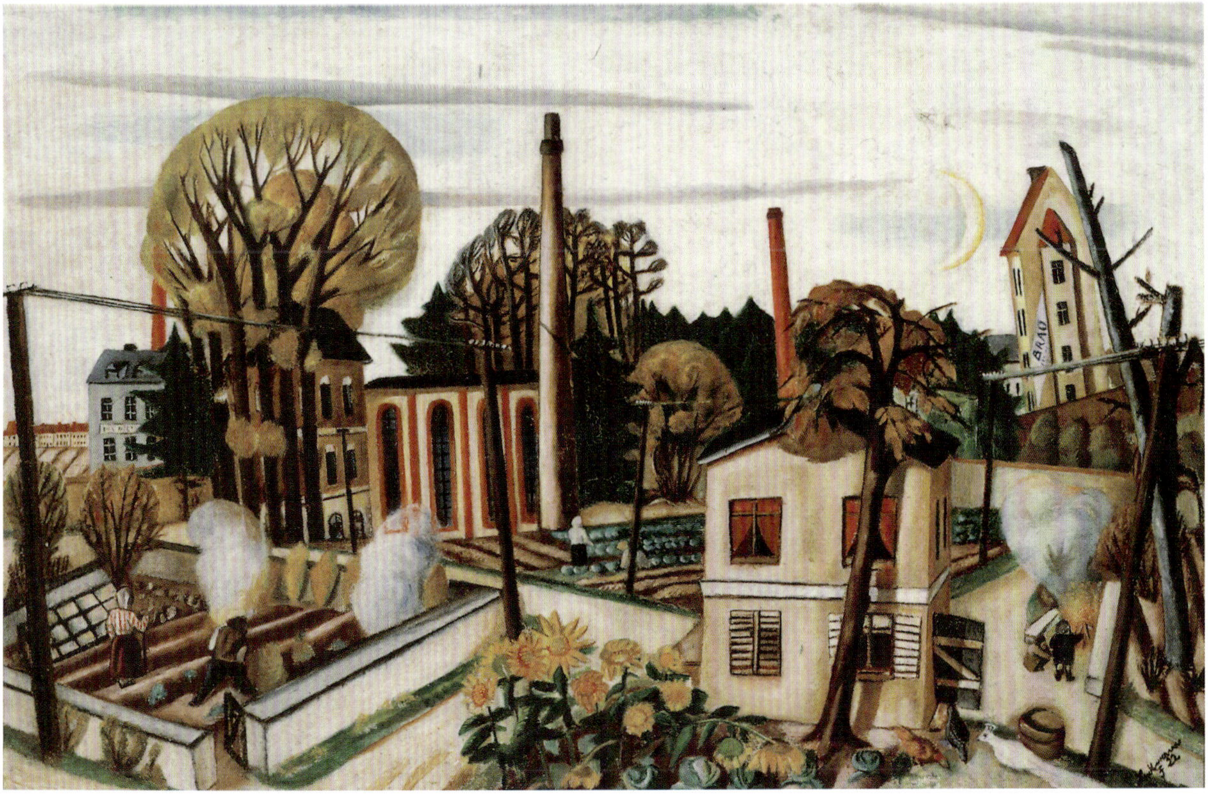

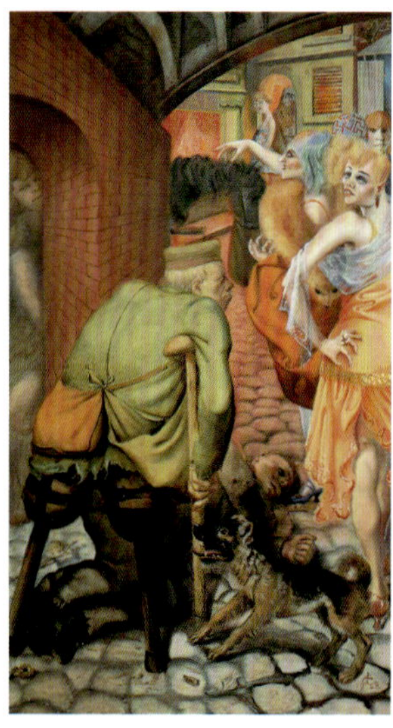
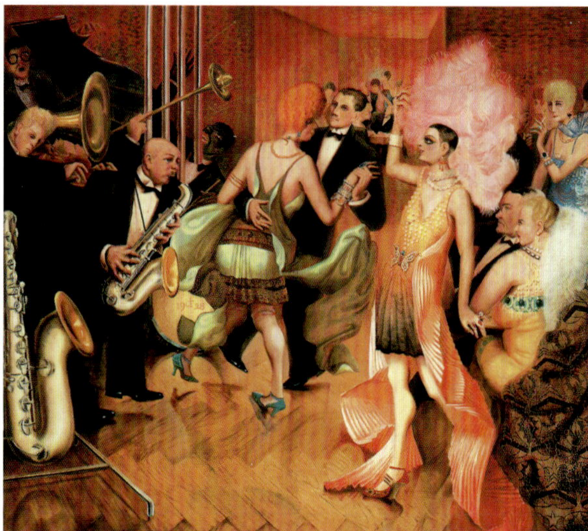
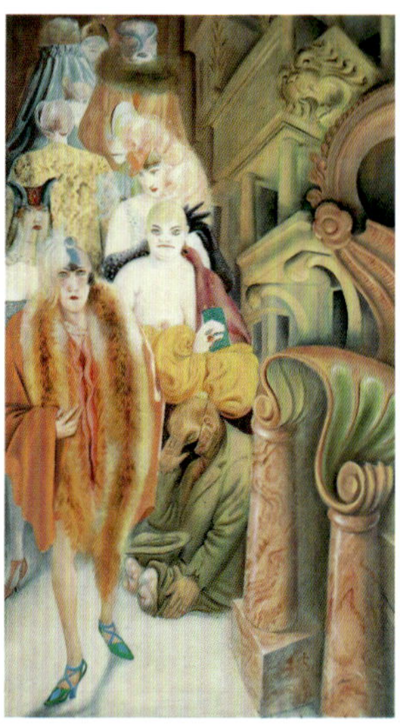

By the mid-1920s his earlier intensity had been overtaken by a more banal
stylization. Meanwhile, Dix too, had begun to lose his edge. Returning to Dresden
in 1927 to take up a professorship at the Academy, he embarked on a summation
of his experience in the Berlin metropolis, the twelve-foot triptych *Grossstadt* (Big
City) [illustration above]. A central nightclub image (the familiar 'decadent' Berlin
of the Roaring Twenties) is flanked by vertical panels crowded with war-cripples
and prostitutes (the lowlife Berlin made no less familiar to us by Brecht and
Döblin). Juxtaposed, their dialectic creates a kind of altarpiece to an unjust society.
Colouristically, the central panel is astonishing; the hot-pink plumes suspended
like candy-floss, the dancers encrusted with lustrous pearls, rubies, emeralds – all
reflected in the shiny orange parquet. On the right, a masque-like procession of
whores is led by a figure (her fur boa fringing a torso of glistening, pink crumpled
satin) who might best be described as a walking vagina.

After 1928 Dix seemed to misunderstand himself. An artist whose strength
lay in the grotesque now made academic life drawings. Several years before
Nazism, both Grosz and Dix had already lost their way. By contrast it was the
'metaphysical' that would save the later art of Max Beckmann. Five years after the
Frankfurt *Landscape* [illustration p. 75], in the strikingly Chagallesque *Chinese
Fireworks*; *Small Dream* of 1927 [illustration opposite], Beckmann has moved
deeper into the territory of inwardness. In several paintings he piles up overt
symbols and archetypes, though always with an edge of irony.

By the late 1920s, in Paris for part of each year – absorbing Léger's black
lines, Matisse's arabesques, Picasso's monumentality – Beckmann discovers in
himself an art of affirmation. The angular has become curved, the forms larger,
more generous, more architectonic. On a dark ground (at first blue or red, but
usually black) Beckmann has learnt to spread buttery paint with a relaxed, almost
off-hand finesse, realizing arm or breast as a wonderfully tangible surface; the
most flesh-like paint of the twentieth century. It was as though the fabled quest
for a synthesis of German and Hellenic might at last be fulfilled.

In 1932 Beckmann began the first of the nine triptychs on which his reputation chiefly rests. The general scheme of *Departure* [illustration pp. 78–79] is clear enough: between two panels depicting suffering, the middle opens into a calm sea. The form of the triptych has allowed him to bring together both the urgent horror of *The Night* and the sensual pleasures of his Parisian works, and to place them in a dialectical relation. One text to set beside *Departure* is Nietzsche's famous passage in *The Birth of Tragedy* (see p. 60), where Raphael's divided *Transfiguration* is made to signify both Dionysian pain, 'the sole ground of being', as well as the Apollonian realm emerging from it, 'a new illusory world, invisible to those enmeshed in the first'. We are shown, writes Nietzsche:

> how there is need for a whole world of torment in order for the individual to produce the redemptive vision and to sit quietly in his rocking rowboat in mid-sea, absorbed in contemplation.

After Beckmann made his departure from Hitler's Germany, some such Nietzschean 'master-thought' would sustain him throughout all the years of his

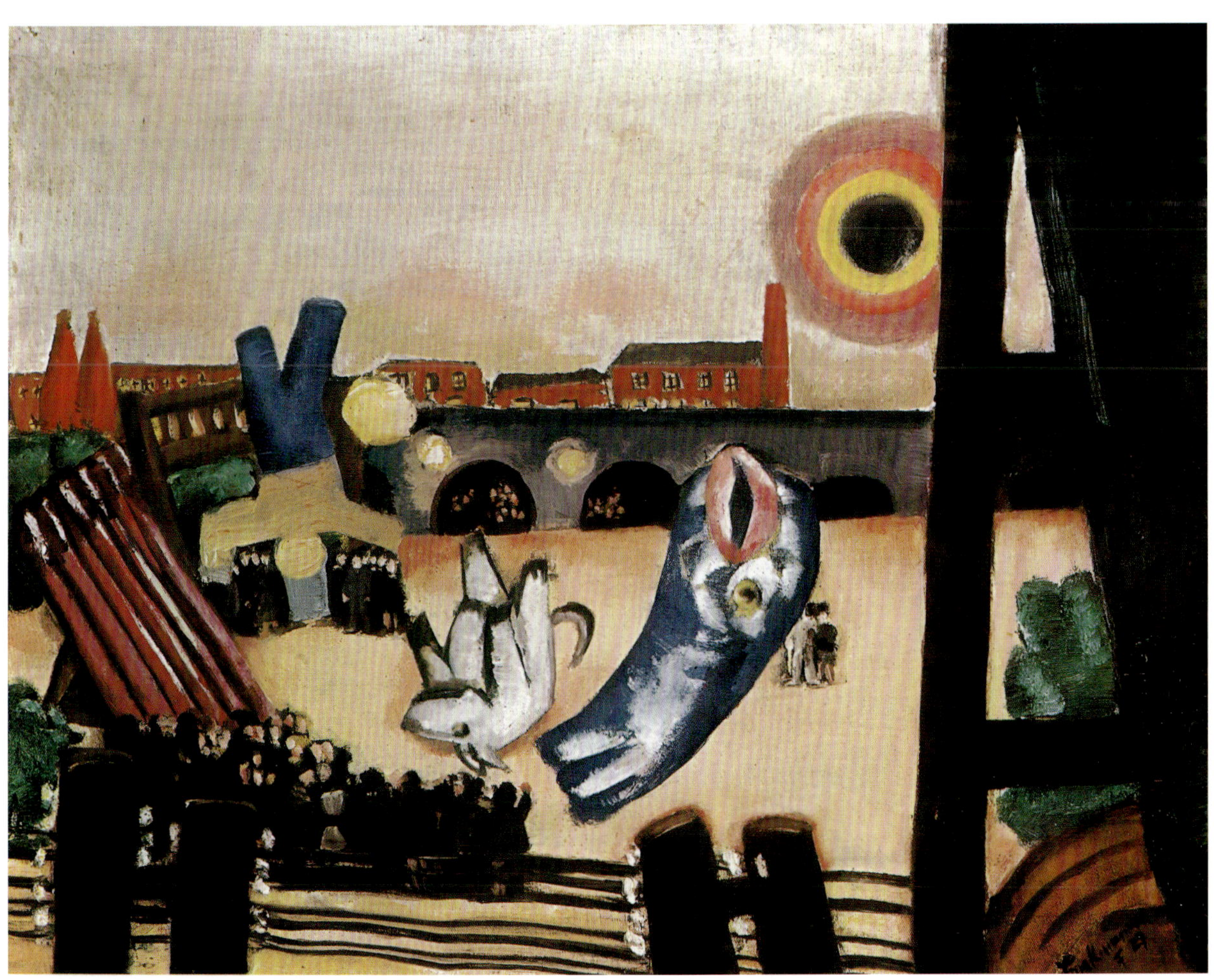

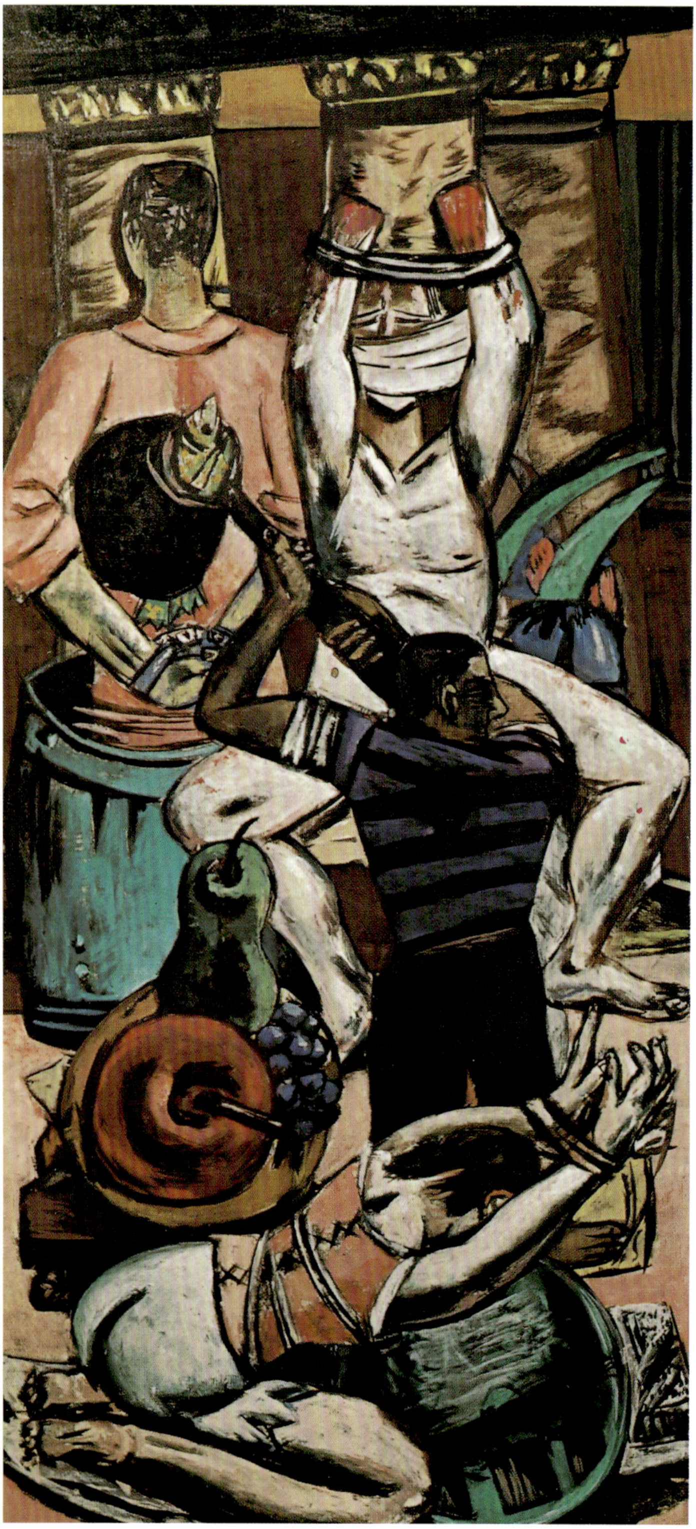

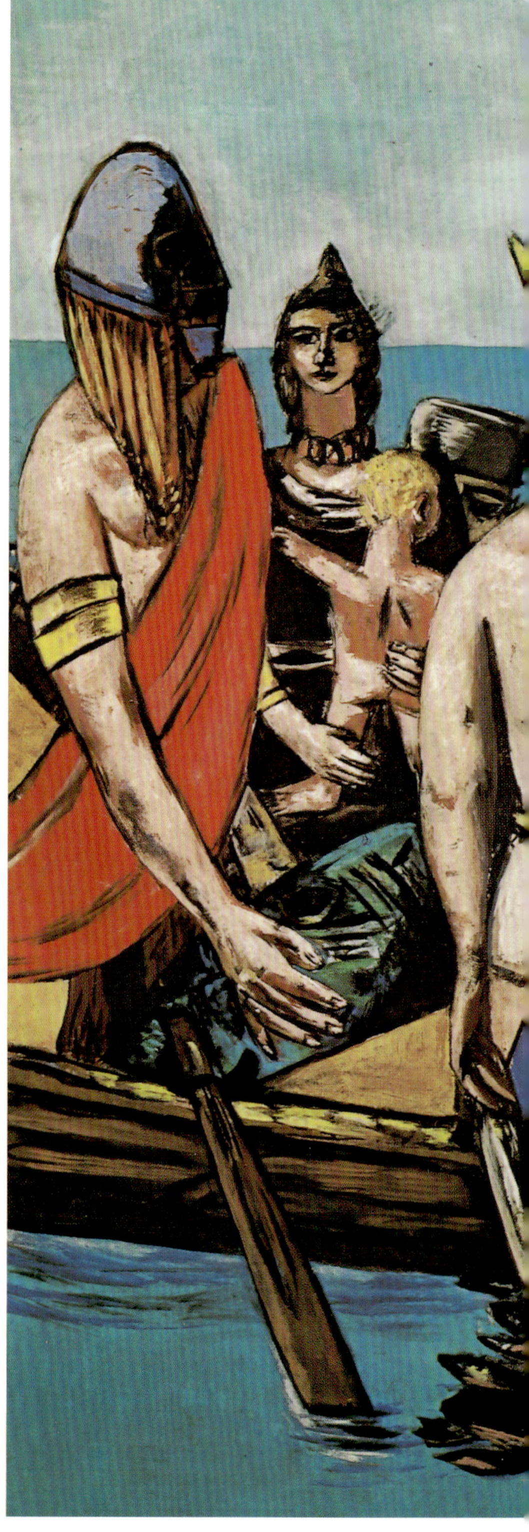

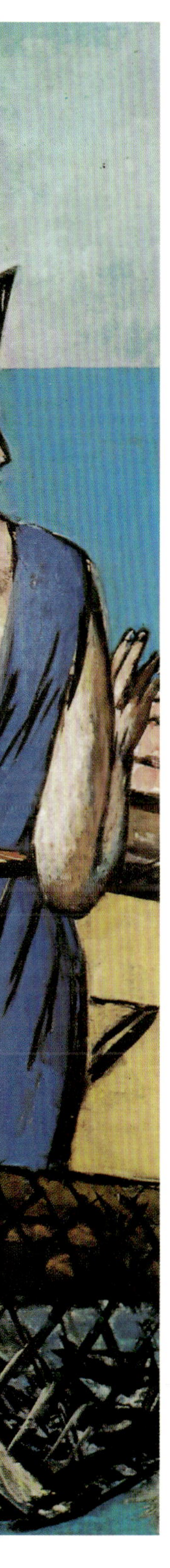

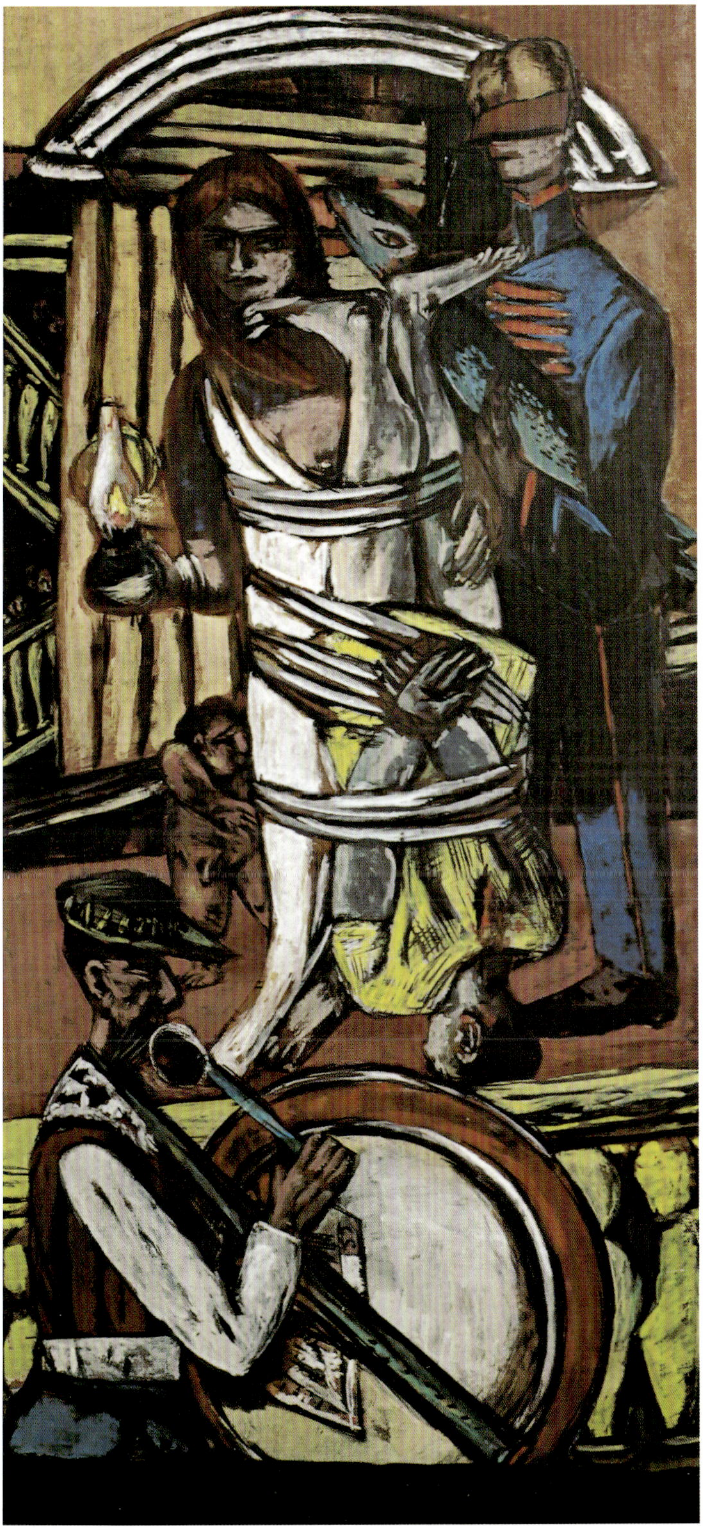

MAX BECKMAN

Departure

1932 and 1933–35

Beckmann was dismissed
from his professorship at
the Fine Art Academy in
Frankfurt as soon as the
National Socialists took power.
He moved to Berlin, taking
Departure with him. Acquired
by MoMA in 1942, and often
shown in sight of Picasso's
Guernica (1937), *Departure*
would come to represent,
for many young American
and European painters, the
continuing possibility of epic-
scale figuration.

Amsterdam exile (see Ch 3 pp. 152–59). In a poem of 1934 Bertolt Brecht would write poignantly of the renunciation demanded by the times. 'Solely because of the increasing disorder/ In our cities of class struggle/ Some of us have now decided/ To speak no more of cities by the sea, snow on roofs, women...'. *Departure* is, in Brechtian terms, a betrayal, with too much 'delight in the contradictions' to carry any social critique. That *one-sidedness* was essential to the verist project; but it would render most Weimar painters helplessly at a loss after 1933, overwhelmed by political events for which a 'realist' language was no longer adequate.

'A NEW SORT OF REALISM': THE WAR AND ITS AFTERMATH IN ENGLISH PAINTING (STANLEY SPENCER, PAUL NASH, WILLIAM ROBERTS AND EDWARD BURRA, 1914-37)

I have seen the most frightful nightmare of a country more conceived by Dante or Poe than by nature...I am no longer an artist interested and curious, I am a messenger...

PAUL NASH, 1917

If these four artists are now beginning to receive the international attention they merit, this is mainly because we can at last situate their work alongside their 'realist' counterparts in post-1918 Europe and America. They no longer appear merely eccentric or provincial. Their shared idiom is not verist or 'critical', nor is it as idealized as Carrà's or Léger's, but it does convey a similarly renewed belief in the object, in Thingness. All would have conceived themselves as modernists, part of a pan-European return to objectivity. Spencer, Nash and Roberts had passed through an exceptionally hard-line drawing regime at the same London art school. But for each, in different ways, the certitudes implicit in academic representation would be shattered.

Stanley Spencer (1891–1959) arrived as a seventeen-year-old at The Slade, and there in 1909 attended the lectures of Roger Fry, preaching his synthesis of Giotto-and-Cézanne as a new gospel of formalism. (Fry was already preparing his first Post-Impressionist exhibition.) In 1910 the even younger William Roberts, then fifteen, joined Spencer and – together with Dora Carrington, Christopher Nevinson and Mark Gertler, with Paul Nash as a further late arrival – formed a Slade grouping known as 'The neo-primitives'. (They looked to Italians of the early Renaissance as well as to Gauguin and his Parisian disciples, such as Maurice Denis.) By 1911, Stanley Spencer was their acknowledged *chef d'école*. His *John Donne Arriving in Heaven* (1911) – blocky white figures on a green ground, fusing Giotto with Denis – was included by Fry in his 'Second Post-Impressionist Exhibition' of 1912.

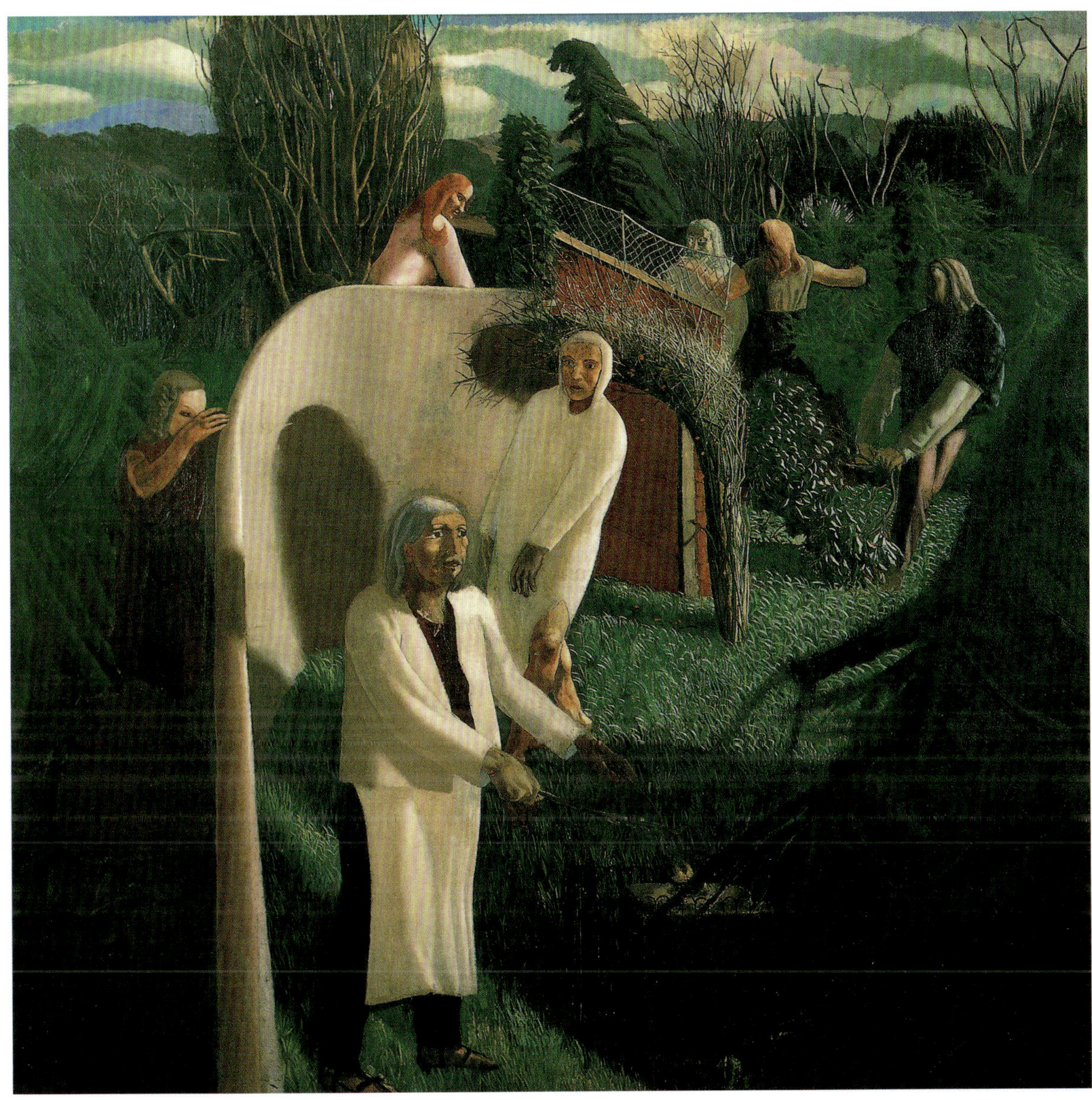

STANLEY SPENCER

Zacharias and Elizabeth

1913–14

Early in Luke's gospel we hear of the infertile
couple, and the Angel's words: 'Fear not
Zacharias, for thy prayer is heard and thy wife
Elizabeth shall bear thee a son' – the future John
the Baptist. In Spencer's post-Slade masterpiece,
painted in Cookham, the saturated, sunlit intensity
of a winter light about to turn to spring, and the
amazing evergreen bursting into the foreground,
are components of an intensely descriptive
landscape; filtered through an understanding of
Derain's trees and Henri Rousseau's clouds.

Every evening Spencer returned from London to his family in the Thameside village of Cookham; so rooted in his home territory that Slade friends wrote to him as 'dear Cookham'. In *Zacharias and Elizabeth* (1913–14) [illustration p.81] meaning resides not in the biblical narrative, but in the mood of trance and ritual Spencer creates in the Cookham landscape, the pictorial architecture, the high, 'exalted' horizon. The figure-action is barely legible. Struck-dumb Zacharias at sacrifice, arms extended like a dowser, his garden-altar ringed with little English-park palings; wingless Gabriel stalking him like some strange sleep-walker; the Christ-like gardener dragging the ivy branch – all these seem emanations of place rather than protagonists. Spencer comes close to the visionary pastoral of 1820s Samuel Palmer, whose early drawings were being rediscovered also by Paul Nash and other contemporaries.

By 1913 his Cookham seclusion had sundered Spencer from his former comrades. William Roberts (1895–1980), meanwhile, had briefly joined Fry's Omega Workshop, and shortly after, the Futurist-influenced breakaway group that would become the nucleus of Vorticism – Wyndham Lewis, David Bomberg, Ezra Pound and Jacob Epstein. Soon Roberts and Bomberg were painting side by side, moving rapidly towards 'English Cubism' and abstraction. In December 1912, the American painter Marsden Hartley (see Ch 1 pp. 47–53) reported to his patron, Alfred Stieglitz: 'I found them in direct revolution against the Roger Fry group – Fry it seems has a terrible power for good and evil there.' A critic in May 1914 commented how Roberts had 'managed to compress the development of a lifetime into six months…but one instance of the general insolvency which has followed an overdose of modernism.' And then, into this ferment of very young artists, there broke the First World War.

Nash was jolted out of his late-Romantic dreamscapes by his experience of the trenches, first as a combatant, then under the British 'official war artists' scheme. After his return from the front – at Passchendaele shortly before the infamous campaign – he began for the first time to paint in oil and immediately found a convincing idiom in images such as *Void* and *The Ypres Salient at Night* (both 1918). But his most visionary and monumental canvas, *The Menin Road* (1919) [illustration opposite] was begun in a Buckinghamshire barn a year after the war ended. Nash's characteristically dry, biscuity surface and formalized design – the slant of searchlights and shadows against the verticals of blasted trees – reinforce the dehumanizing impact of its eleven-foot expanse; within this vast apocalypse the tiny uniformed figures barely register.

From 1919 onwards, as many as ten war-transformed painters would meet informally each week in Hampstead. The group might include Paul Nash and his brother John; William Roberts and Mark Gertler; Stanley and Gilbert Spencer; Christopher Nevinson and Henry Lamb; as well as their Leftist hosts, the Carline family. (Stanley Spencer became engaged to Hilda Carline in 1922.) The aspiration of these erstwhile neo-primitives, to reform figuration, was now renewed in the light of post-war reconstruction. After the smash-up of war, after the fragmentations of 'English Cubism', the wholeness of the image must again

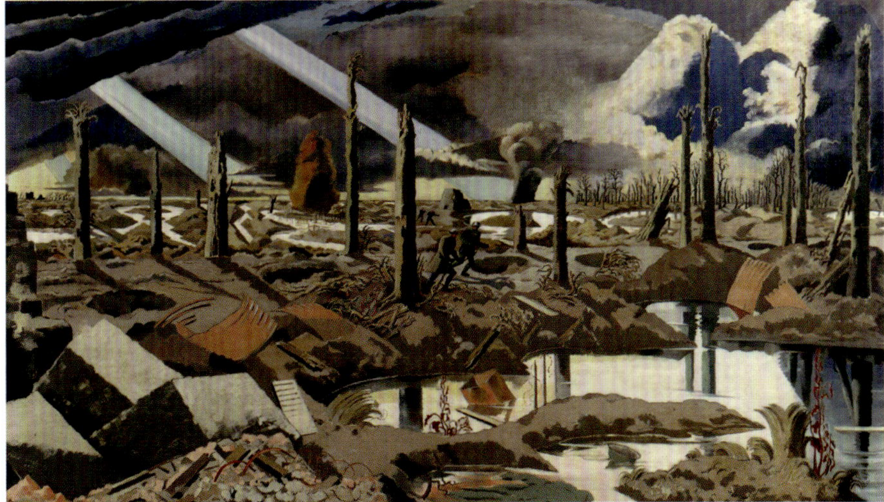

be retrieved. Out of those exchanges emerged a shared language of painting: for example, post-war Spencer sometimes took on the matte handling of Nash, the anonymity of Roberts's figures.

What they all held in common was their commitment to lucid depiction; and linked to this, their refusal to lose the subject, bringing them into sharp conflict with the formalist values associated with Roger Fry. In Fry's own words, 'the esthetic emotion is an emotion about form…a special emotion which does not depend upon the association of the form with anything else whatsoever.' Popularized under the catchphrase 'Significant Form', that doctrine would become after 1920 an orthodoxy among 'advanced' English art-lovers. Fry's later hostility to Spencer – 'I am sick of his muck', he declared in 1932 – as well as to Nash, whose widow wrote of a 'persecution', has been documented.

Yet for each of these painters, the issue of subject matter remained crucial. Paul Nash would later write of the 1920s as 'Struggles of a War-Artist without a War'. That sense of having lost his purpose would be resolved only near the end of his life when, after flirtations both with abstraction and with European Surrealism, his poetic vision re-emerged in landscape-images – both paintings and photographs; a renewal of his earliest impulses, but with a fresh, modernist conviction.

For William Roberts, after years as an artillery gunner on the Western Front, his demobilization released almost immediately a new imagery of everyday London life. *The Cinema* (1920) [illustration p. 84] is still heavily formalized, recording a specifically modern spectacle. There is more than a hint of satire: those different levels of reality, and that play-of-shadows, invoking the 'strange prisoners' of Plato's Cave, eyes absurdly glued to the flickering images on the wall – the cowboys of the sepia screen. Writing in *The Sunday Times* on Group X, which included Roberts alongside former Vorticists, Frank Rutter understood the position of these artists in 1922: 'The real tendency of this exhibition is towards a new sort of realism, evolved by artists who have passed through a phase of abstract experiment.'

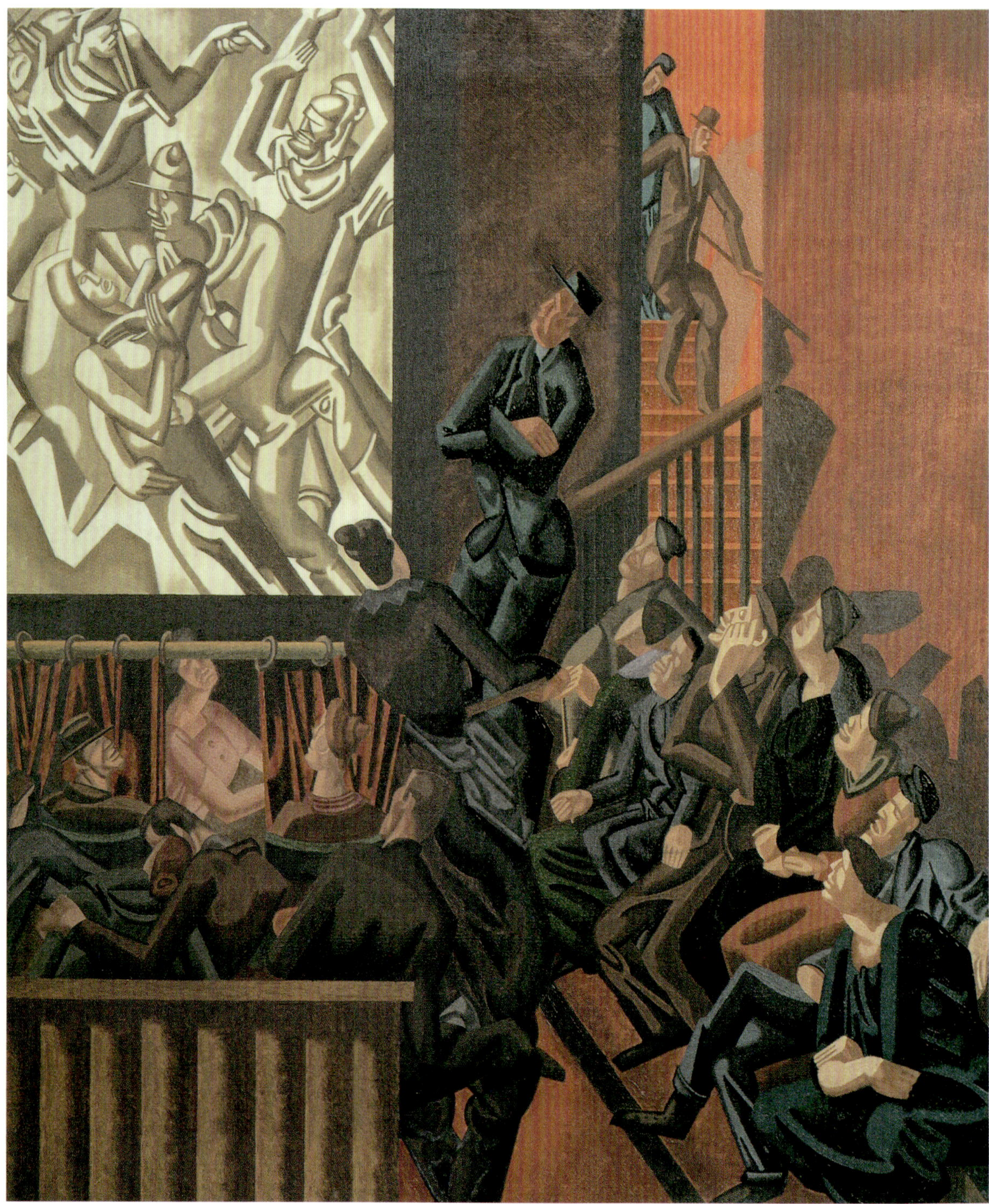

WILLIAM ROBERTS

The Cinema

1920

Roberts's retrieval of the figure, after the years of
Vorticist abstraction and 'English Cubism', is not a
retreat, but a commitment to post-war modern life.

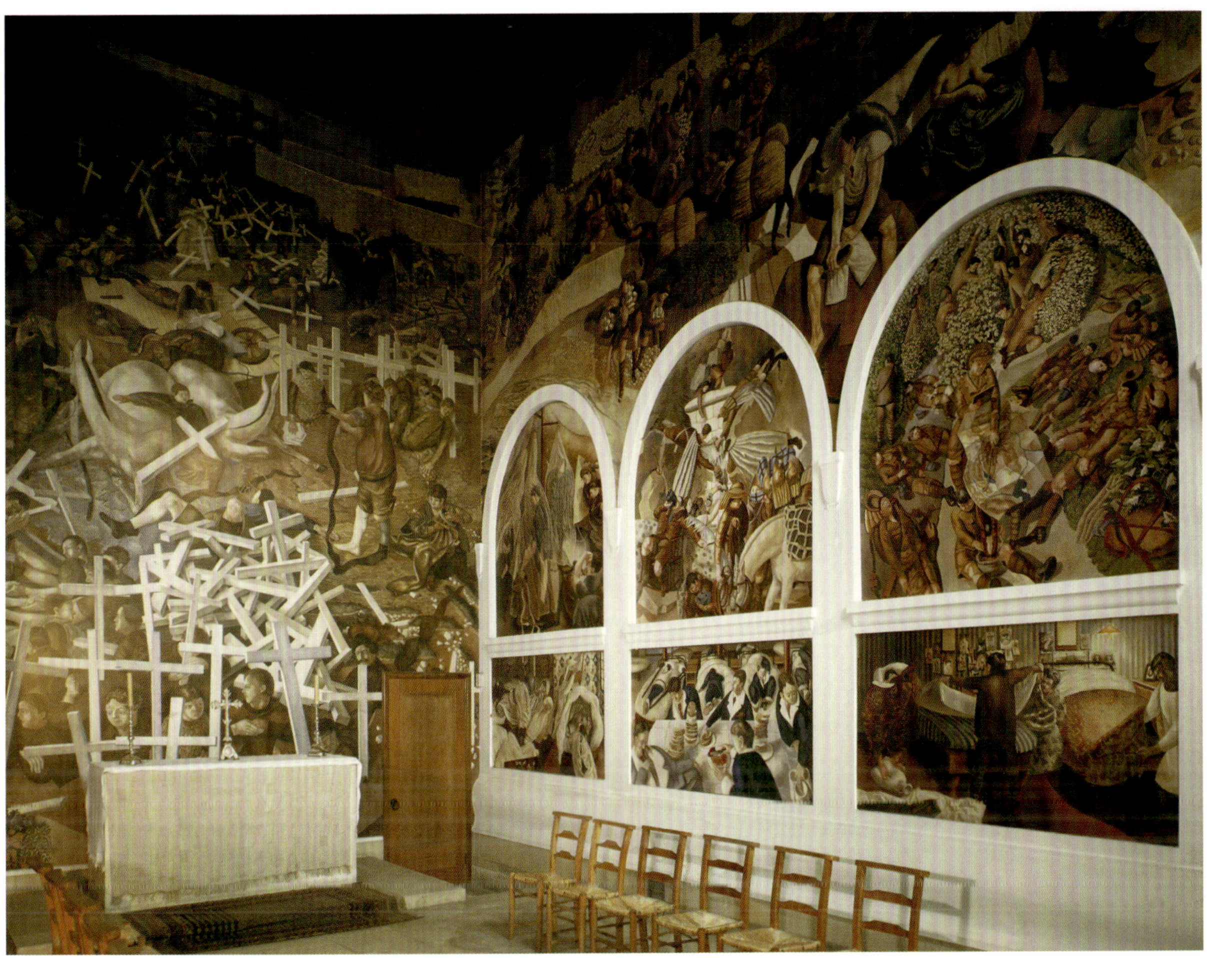

Stanley Spencer at Burghclere

Nothing other than complacence could produce another Zacharias. Anyway, whether he should or should not have done, he felt the all withering and icy blast of the war.

STANLEY SPENCER, 1948

For Stanley Spencer, returning home after almost four full years at war (first as medical orderly in a Bristol hospital, then as an infantryman at the Macedonian Front) that 'new sort of realism' became associated with a 'loss of Eden'. The spell of Cookham had been broken. In the changed climate of 1921, Spencer's religion-and-village vein now appeared to Paul Nash an exasperating anachronism. 'I used to admire him inordinately & believed him to be the real thing...something perfectly his own which caught one by a strange enchantment...I used to pin my faith on him, but,' he concludes, 'it would have been better for him and us if he hadn't been born behind his time.'

All through the war Spencer had nurtured his neo-primitive aspiration
to paint a fresco-cycle, dedicated to his war experiences. In 1923, after several
aborted mural-schemes, he at last sat down to make detailed wash drawings of his
imaginary 'chapel of peace'; only for the project to be immediately set in motion,
sealed by Spencer's cry, 'What ho, Giotto!' During the three years the chapel was
under construction at Burghclere, he completed in Hampstead an eighteen-foot
canvas, *The Resurrection, Cookham*, the last extension of the green-and-white
pastoral of *Zacharias*, but now infiltrated with new, urgently present themes
of sexuality and selfhood. We read this panorama as a long diagonal, from the
crowded riverboat at top left, along the churchyard path, to the figure of Spencer
himself at bottom right, dreamily awakening within two subsided graves that
have become a stone book. For five years Spencer's painting had been flat and
formalized, as he attempted a fresco-like surface, but here white wall and setting
are realized with vivid three-dimensional intensity. In the words of a *Times* review,
'It's as if a pre-Raphaelite had shaken hands with a Cubist.'

Burghclere chapel [illustration p. 85] is the most sustained memorialization
of the First World War in European art. Like Dix, Spencer had waited several years
before he was ready to depict his war; by 1932 he was painting from designs of
1923, about events as far back as 1916. But Spencer doesn't show himself lifting
the dying onto stretchers or digging their graves. Within a sacred space, dedicated
to *All* Souls, the most humdrum activities are exalted. He embraces the Thingness
of mosquito nets, shampoo-lathered heads, jam sandwiches, clusters of barbed
wire, heaps of towels. Burghclere's half-comic inclusiveness undermines any
militaristic hierarchy. From this point on, a central aspect of his art is the raising
up of the ordinary, of what might be described as '*In*significant Forms'. While
the overall scheme pays homage to Giotto's Arena Chapel, the actual mode of
depiction is utterly un-Italian and un-fresco-like; painted in oil, on canvas glued to
the walls, Spencer's impastoed, minutely realized objects are close to the fetishized
telephone of Dix's *To Beauty* (see p.69, illustration p. 69, detail p. 58).

If his turn towards Thingness came out of disillusionment, that detailed
depiction enacted a kind of re-illusionment. 'I no longer have a clear vision of
God; I'm somehow involved in the created. Sometimes I feel as if I were showing
His creations to God.' Burghclere became a monument to the anti-monumental,
especially in the two irregular upper strips (the twenty-eight-foot-long spandrels)
filled with a diffuse imagery of cooking breakfast, collecting litter, shifting
stones – all the unheroic activities of a tented army. In the twenty-one-foot-high
Resurrection, behind the altar, soldiers and mules awaken (one of them, secateurs
in hand, releasing another from the barbed wire); amongst a vast patterning of
repeated white wooden crosses, Christ is a small, white subsidiary figure, barely
visible. Spencer's refusal of rank, of discrimination, became the vehicle of new
religious meaning, to be fulfilled in 'The Church of Me' (see Ch 3 pp. 138–46).

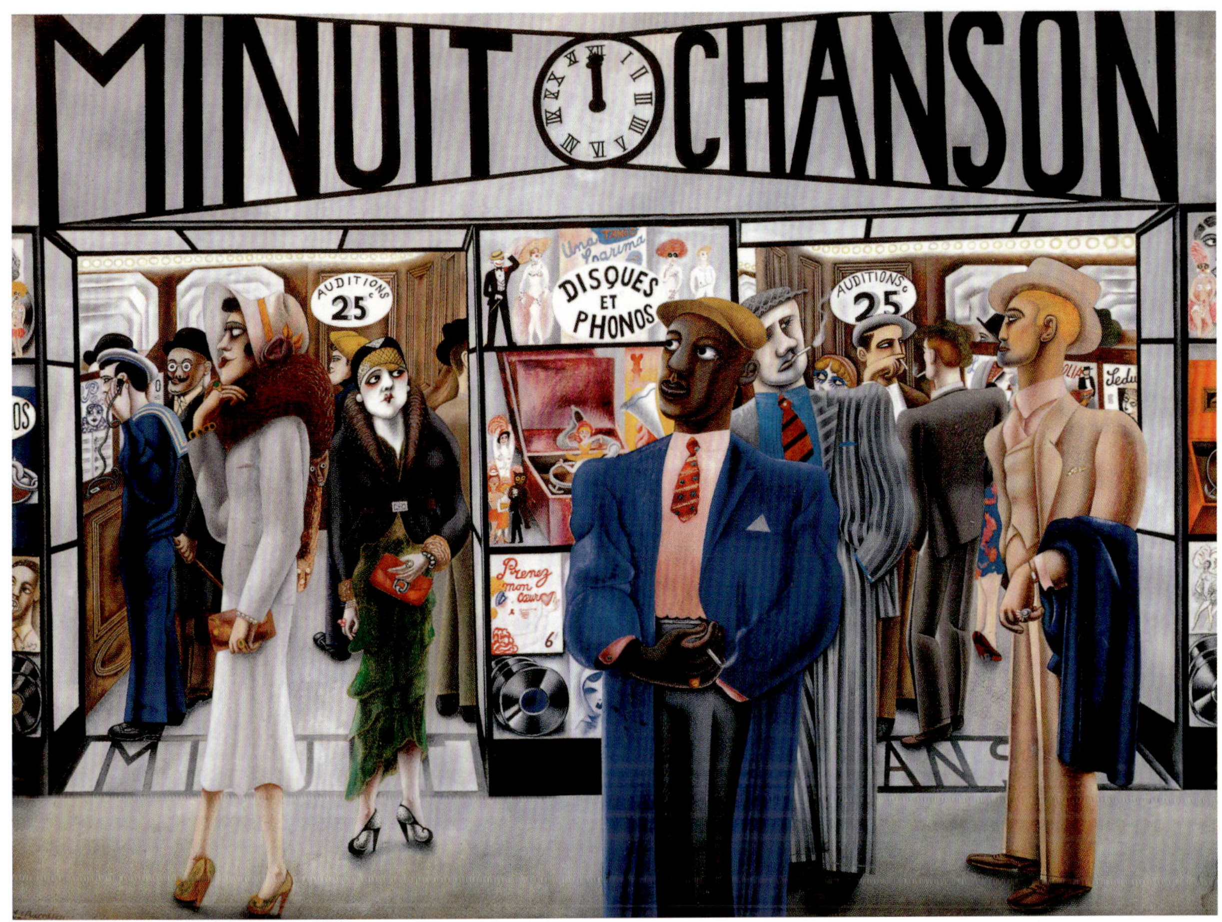

The English '*Sachlichkeit*'

EDWARD BURRA

Minuit Chanson
(Midnight Song)

1931

Burra filters the Parisians of a spring night through a sensibility essentially comic and camp. (He once claimed the only erection he'd ever experienced occurred in the cinema, watching Mae West.) As with Lautrec, infirmity gives a special poignancy to Burra's re-imaginings of nocturnal glamour.

We should not underestimate these English realists' awareness of their European contemporaries. Visiting Cologne, Munich and Vienna in 1922 with the internationally minded Carline family, Spencer may have been exposed not only to a hefty dose of Brueghel and Northern 'primitives', but also, one might speculate, to at least a glimpse of current German painting. William Roberts's knowledge of Léger is unmistakable, his figures becoming steadily more tubular, cogs-in-the-machine.

In 1923 the eighteen-year-old art student Edward Burra (1905–76) chanced across a Roberts exhibition, to lasting effect; but his own rendering of street-life would owe much also to Grosz and Rivera, as well as to Art Deco high-style. He was taken up by Paul Nash, fifteen years his senior, who wrote in 1932 of 'Burra's extraordinary fantasies, perhaps the most original in imagination of any contemporary English artist'. Burra's crowd scenes, in contrast to Roberts's, are nearly always set in faraway societies: Paris, Marseilles, Toulon (visited with Nash); Spain and Mexico (with the writers Malcolm Lowry and Conrad Aiken); above all, New York – more specifically, Harlem. Stricken with rheumatic fever as a schoolboy,

Burra brings the English tradition of street-satire (of Hogarth and Gillray, whose prints adorned the parental home) into the era of international modernism. *Harlem* is rich in detail – for example, the play of red-and-white shirt-stripes and brown jacket-stripes seen through the foreground balustrade. Nevertheless this remains a world reinvented, rather than reported.

WILLIAM ROBERTS

The Vorticists at the Restaurant de la Tour Eiffel: Spring, 1915
1961–62

Roberts's touching and magisterial picture – painted forty-five years after the event – was brought out of obscurity in 1995 as a star in Jean Clair's great exhibition to mark the centenary of the Venice Biennale, 'Identity and Alterity' (see Ch 3 pp. 113). Roberts recalls his nineteen-year-old self, sitting alongside Ezra Pound and Wyndham Lewis, and it affirms his journey – from 'English Cubism' to an uncompromising Thingness. Richard Cork describes it as 'A Vorticist Last Supper, with copies of *BLAST* being passed around like a sacrament'.

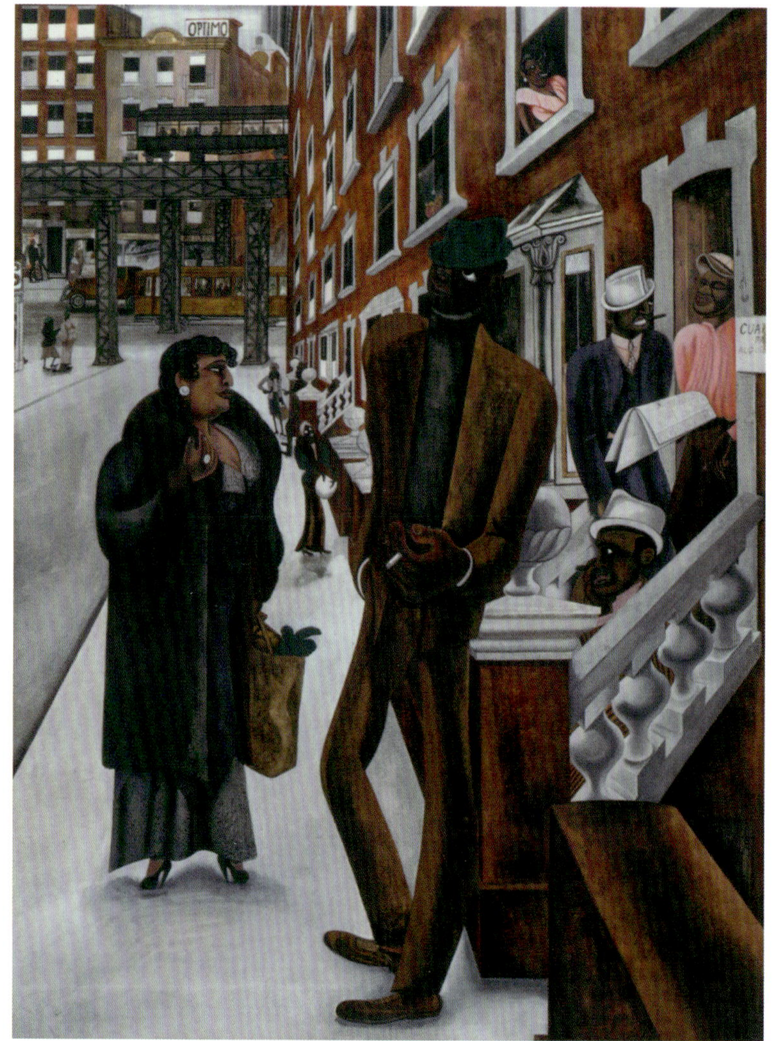

Burra had settled by his mid-twenties into a double life: the invalid painter at his parents' conventional home in Rye (sedately 'BOORGWAH', in his own spelling) but whose art was nourished abroad by rash breakouts to sailors' bars, drug haunts and burlesque theatres. His real subject was liberation from English upper-middle-class repression. As Burra wrote to Nash from Paris on 19 May 1931:

> My new occupation is going to the Boulevard Clichy to Minuit Chanson. The Clientele is enough to frighten you a bit what with listening with one ear and looking at the intrigues going on elsewhere. The people are glorious. Such tarts all crumbling, and all sexes and colours.

In *Minuit Chanson* (Midnight Song, 1931) [illustration p. 87] vamps and *hommes fatales* parade below the portico of the all-night record store, each one superb, most of all the blue-overcoated black man closest to us, surveying the scene with such an assured nonchalance. The flawless young dandy to the right, his huge-shouldered suit the same sandy pink as his exquisite head, seems plasticated, or out of a jelly-mould.

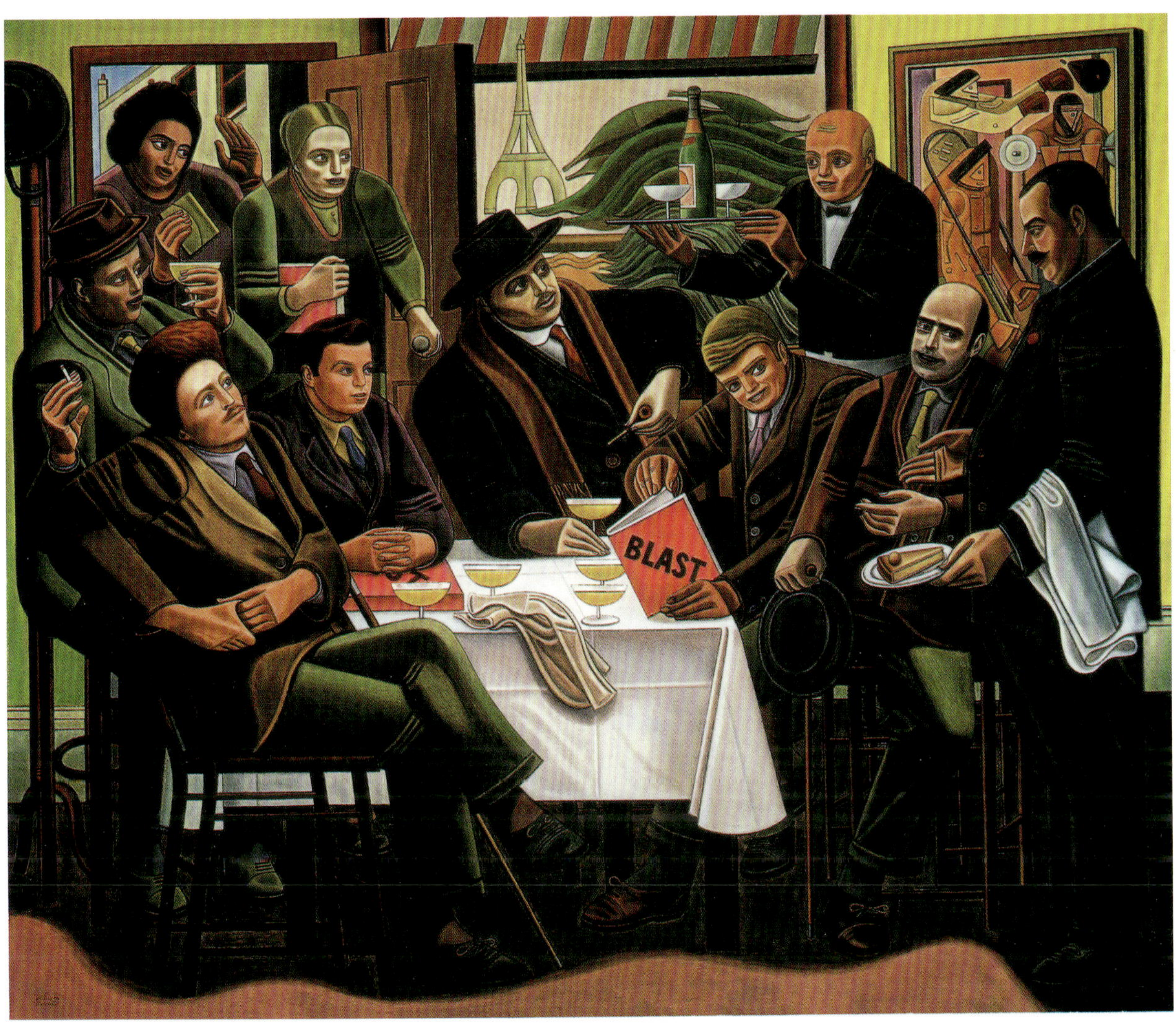

Although arthritis and anaemia restricted him mainly to watercolour, Burra's large sheets of the early 1930s attain a formal intensity beyond any other English painter of his time. His six months in New York were arguably the climax of his life's work. Burra arrived in Harlem in 1933, just before the end of prohibition, living for two months in the household of the black actress Edna Lloyd Thomas. Even after the 1929 economic slump that had shut down so much of the Harlem Renaissance, the dance halls were still supplying the 'Black Jazz' Burra adored. In *Harlem* [illustration opposite] the principal idlers are a Latino woman and an Afro-Caribbean dude twice her size, set against the steep perspective of a tenement street, the 'L' trainline as backdrop. We are a long way from Rye.

As both the political climate and his health worsened, Burra's foreign adventures ceased. Like Nash, he was diverted into a contrived Surrealism. By contrast, an unchanging style served Roberts for the next thirty years, culminating in his warm memorialization, *The Vorticists at the Restaurant de la Tour Eiffel: Spring, 1915*, painted as late as 1962 [illustration above]. Wyndham Lewis presides at a

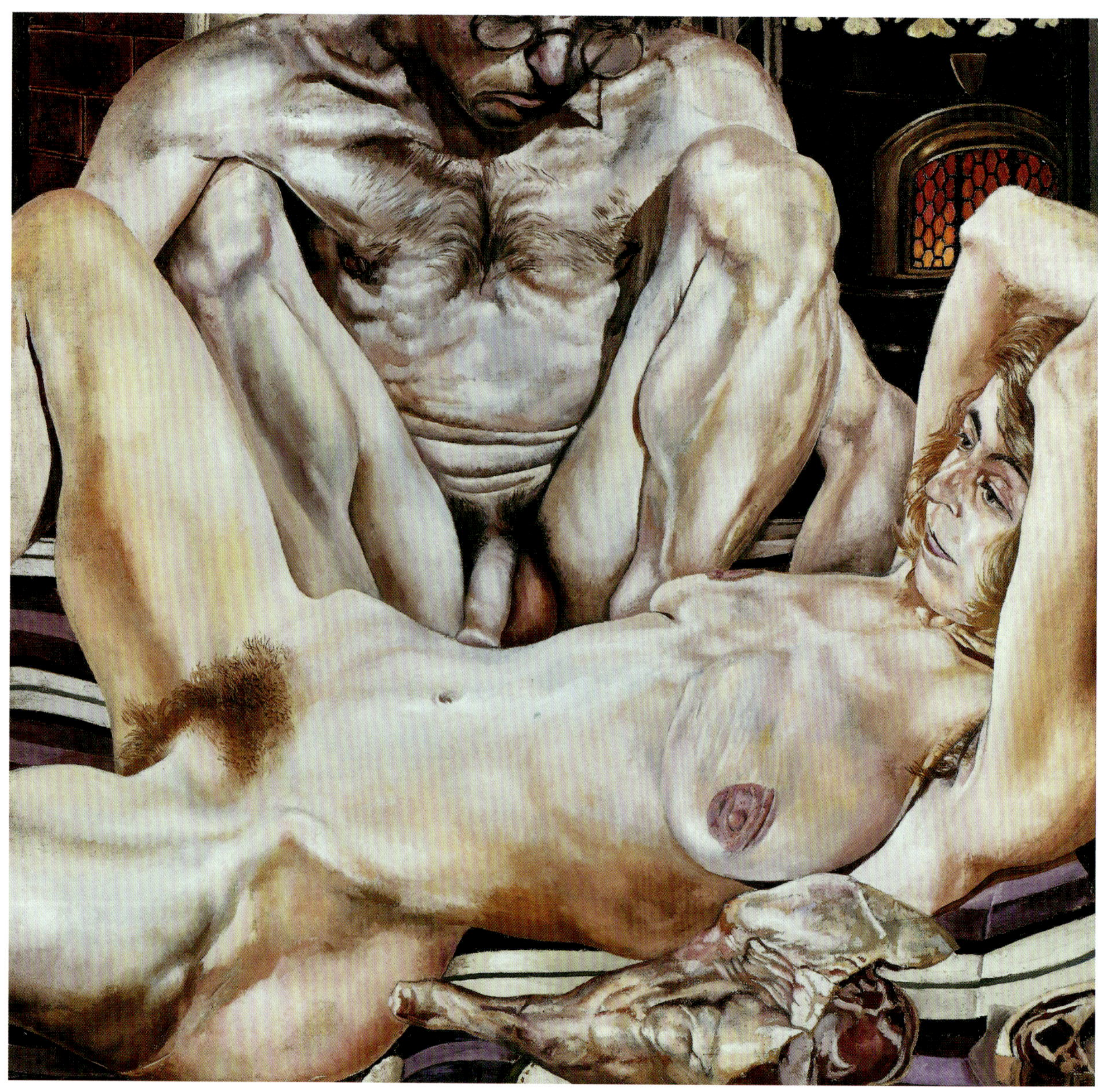

STANLEY SPENCER

The Leg of Mutton Nude (Double Portrait
of the Artist and His Second Wife)
1937

The two figures must have been painted
separately, as a kind of collage – the self 'set into'
the other. Patricia Preece had met her lifelong
partner Dorothy Hepworth at The Slade in 1918;
but in the early 1930s, facing destitution, she fixed
upon Spencer as a willing victim. He lavished gifts
upon her, divorcing Hilda, and eventually signing
away his house. He married Patricia two months
after completing *The Leg of Mutton Nude*; mission
accomplished, she returned to Dorothy.

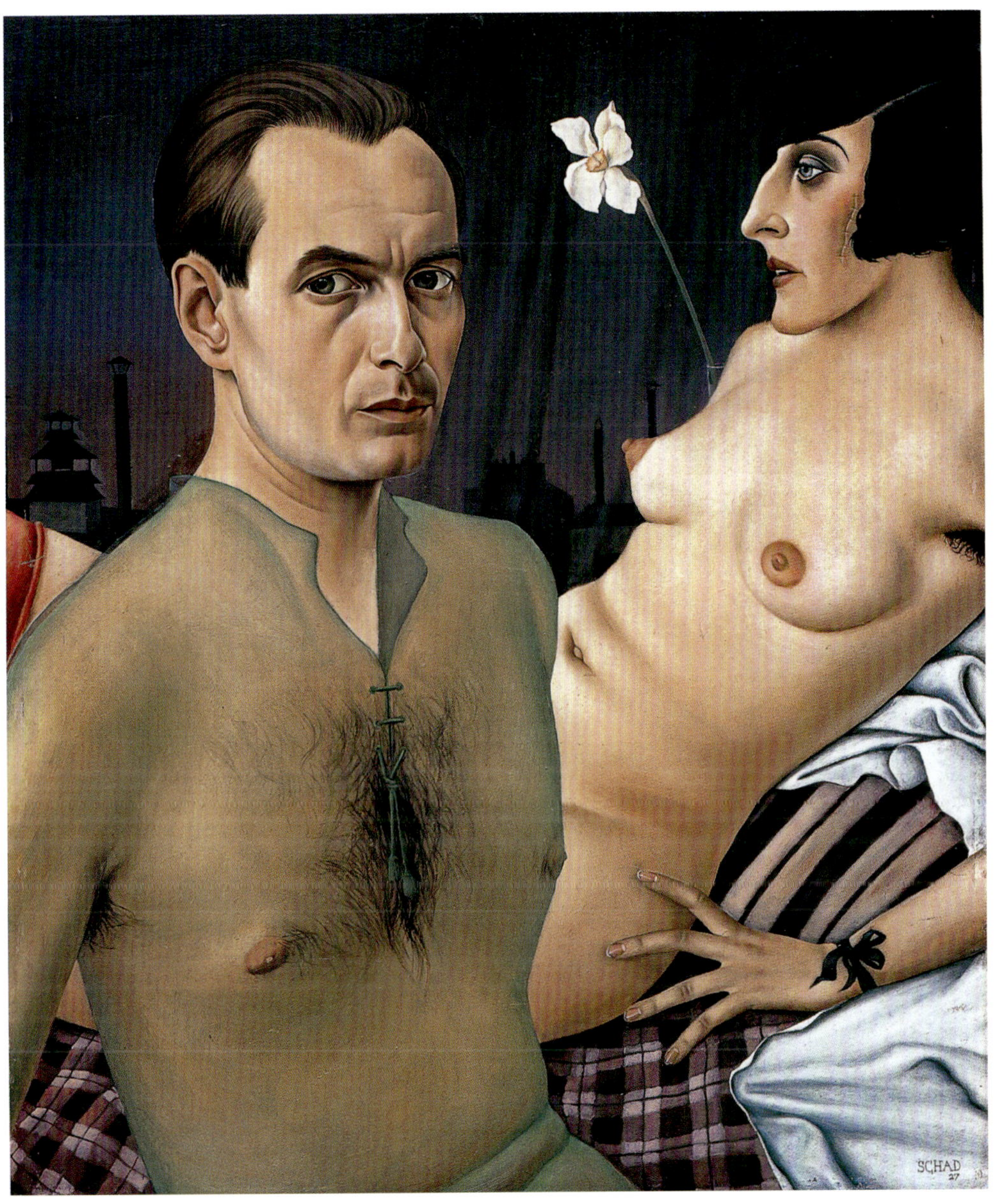

CHRISTIAN SCHAD

Self-Portrait with Model

1927

Schad was a former Dadaist; his compelling
portraits mimic 'bourgeois realism' (they were
admired by the Nazis) yet their cosmetic mask
cracks open to reveal an utterly corrupt society,
within which the artist implicates himself.

table that also includes the red-quiffed Ezra Pound and Roberts himself, all set against the repeated shocking-pink doorsteps of their newly published manifesto, *BLAST*.

Most unexpected of all was Spencer's later development. Even before Burghclere, in 1926, he'd written:

> I feel, really, that everything in one that is *not vision* is mainly vulgarity....
> It's awful after four years at The Slade to find oneself not in possession
> of an imaginative capacity to draw, but to find instead that one has
> contracted a disease.

From 1932 onwards, with the chapel completed, that conflict between visionary and 'vulgarity' pushed Spencer into crisis. He found himself producing 'a complacent stream of landscapes. Money need...doggedness.' Yet when he brought those 'dogged' landscape procedures to bear on his new love for Patricia Preece, an extraordinary psychological charge was created – a numbness that became expressive. It renders the flesh of those 'naked portraits' shockingly present, in its unidealized Thingness; a minutely detailed 'Realism' that runs utterly contrary to the spirit of *Zacharias* [see illustration p. 81]. He likened the slow movement of his tiny brush to 'an ant crawling over every inch of the skin'. In the most confessional [illustration p. 90] Spencer himself squats naked, a stove burning beside him, while alongside Patricia he has placed an uncooked leg of mutton. In a notebook of 1955, Spencer looked back:

> The big double nude is rather a remarkable thing. There is in it male,
> female and animal flesh...it was done with zest and any direct painting
> capacity I had.

The Leg of Mutton Nude was never exhibited in the artist's lifetime. When it entered the Tate Collection in 1974, it soon helped to reignite Spencer's reputation, surely influencing the later 'naked portraits' of Lucian Freud (see pp. 109–110). In 2000, in the opening hang at Tate Modern, London, it was exhibited alongside an icon of *Neue Sachlichkeit* painting, Christian Schad's *Self Portrait with Model* of 1927 [illustration p. 91] and at first glance, they seemed uncannily akin, even to the striped bed linen. Yet the icy-smooth flesh of Schad's model is impermeable; the narcissist and his scarred lover enact a cynical comedy. (We note the wit of the little segment of stockinged thigh at the left edge.) But the *Leg of Mutton Nude* is without irony. Out of a 'dogged' effort of perception, Spencer's committed verism attains the stature of a tragic vision, entirely outside his pre-war range.

EARLY BALTHUS: A PUPPET MASTER (1933–56)

Balthus (Balthazar Klossowski, 1908–2001) chose to present himself in his later
years as a classical figure-painter, last heir to the noblest Italian and French
traditions. But the reality was more complex; his art inherited German and Eastern
European components also, and his best work comes out of such tensions – an
'Expressionist' sensibility, yet overlaid by a Courbet-like 'realism'.

La Rue (The Road) [illustration p. 94], completed in 1933 when Balthus was
twenty-five, remains in some respects his masterpiece, much as *Bathers at Asnières*
for the twenty-three-year-old Seurat – warmer, more directly moving than any of
its successors. Balthus has gone down into the street only so as to create a silence.
De Chirico had written of the 'disturbing correspondence that exists between
perspective and metaphysics' and this counterpointing of figures against the tight
architectural grid of an urban stage-set tends to elevate the everyday scene to the
plane of the miraculous. It may also have to do with measure. Two simple relations:
the centre-line is defined vertically by the straight back of the figure in white, who
turns from it into the left half of the picture; while on the horizontal is placed –
balanced like a piece of fruit on a table-edge – the bulbous, infantile head of the little
man who walks towards us.

He alone of all the figures is open-eyed, and certainly the picture is his vision;
this child–man is the puppet-master, and all the rest move according to his invisible
wires. The adults turn their backs, their faces masked; he sees only children. As he
patrols the city, arm half-raised in a marionette-like gesture, the façade of order
breaks down into glimpses of sexual violence and desolating solitude.

The earliest version of *La Rue*, painted four years earlier, was a memory-image
of Balthus's bearded father out walking in Paris with his two little boys, painted
with the tender, impressionistic touch of Pierre Bonnard. But in 1933 the scene is
transposed from hazy remembrance to sharp-focused visionary enactment. For
the father and his little sons is substituted the adolescent pair in sexual struggle;
the dwarfish foreground child is also new. And yet for all their separateness
these scarcely overlapping, flat silhouettes remain absolutely convincing human
presences. Everything in this picture is *emphatic* – the pigment oily and rich, laid
over a hot crimson underpainting that seeps through at the edges of the cool greys
and browns.

That same year, Balthus made a long series of illustrations (quite roughly
drawn in pen and ink on large sheets) to the first part of Emily Brontë's 1847 novel
Wuthering Heights [illustrations p. 95]. They chronicle the thwarted childhood love
of Heathcliff (whose features are those of Balthus himself) and Cathy (Antoinette
de Watteville, child of a patrician Bern family, who Balthus first met when he was
nineteen and she fifteen). Each drawing is captioned, presenting a moment of
psychological crisis, a violent emotional outburst: '*You needn't have touched me…*';
'*No, no Isabella, you shan't run off…*'. The stumpy figures with their huge heads enact
their scenes in tiny, box-like rooms, in which the stark furniture is much too small
for them. It's as though we've lifted the front off a doll's house. Their graphic idiom

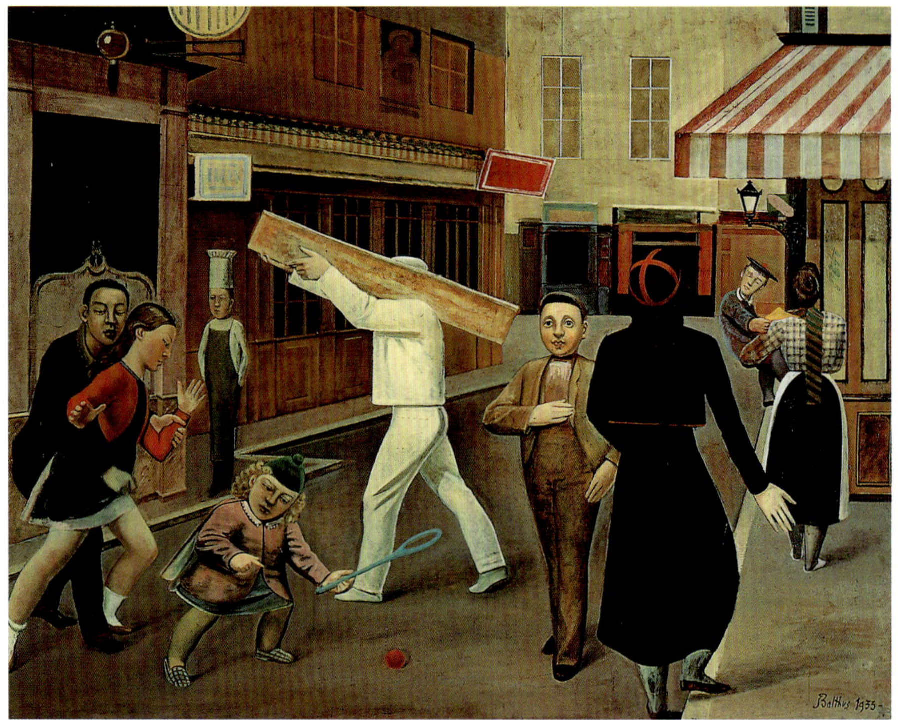

derives from John Tenniel's famous illustrations to *Alice.* The fire in Balthus's belly
has allowed him to create a convincing modern language out of Victorian cross-
hatching. At the end of that miraculous year Balthus embarked on *The Lesson*
[illustration p. 96]. He wrote to Antoinette on 1 December 1935:

> I am preparing a new canvas. A rather ferocious one. Do I dare speak of it to
> you? It is an erotic scene. I want to declaim in full light of day, with sincerity
> and emotion, all the palpitating tragedy of a drama of the flesh, proclaim
> with great yells the ineradicable laws of instinct. Thus to return to the
> passionate content of an art. Death to the hypocrites!...

The expression on the instructress's face, the harshness of her arm as it clenches
around the child's hair, speaks of a sexuality linked with cruelty. The child's
swooning, almost broken-backed pose has been variously related to the late-
medieval *Avignon Pietá*, to the dreamer of Fuseli's *The Nightmare* (1781), to the
arch-of-hysteria; this pose of sexual abandonment will be developed again and
again over the next twenty years. One of Balthus's lifelong friends was Georges
Bataille, eleven years his senior, in whose novella *The Story of the Eye* (1928)
adolescents are involved in manifold forms of intercourse – masturbatory,
urinary, lesbian and eventually sanguinary. For Bataille, 'the truth of eroticism
is tragic', and sexuality is viewed as a power utterly disruptive and subversive
towards society. Both Bataille and Balthus's elder brother Pierre had already
published admiringly on de Sade, as libertine and sexual revolutionary. *The
Lesson* (despite his denials in later life) was the young artist's own deeply felt
'proclamation' of the reality of sex, depicted in a language entirely 'realistic'.

BALTHUS

Drawings to Wuthering Heights:
'You needn't have touched me'
1933

The young Balthus was certainly familiar with Carlo Carrà's 1920s figuration (see illustration p. 28) but his illustrations to Emily Brontë are also nourished by children's books. Both *Alice in Wonderland* and *Wuthering Heights* were standard texts amongst Surrealists, though Balthus had read them in childhood. According to his brother Pierre Klossowski, he once began an essay on the imagery of children's books, giving a section each to Tenniel's Alice and *images d'Épinal*, as well as Dr Heinrich Hoffmann (the artist of *Struwwelpeter*).

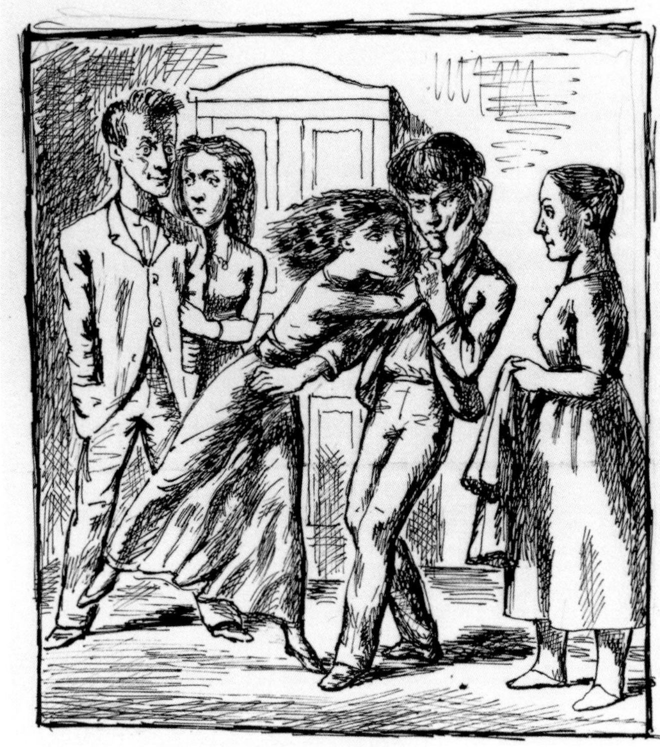

BALTHUS

Drawings to Wuthering Heights:
'Pull his hair when you go by'
1933

Balthus identified with Heathcliff, the sinister, rough-born and mysterious boy of Emily Brontë's narrative. As a half-Jewish, penniless young painter, he was unacceptable to Antoinette's grand family. But he would eventually marry his 'Cathy' in 1937.

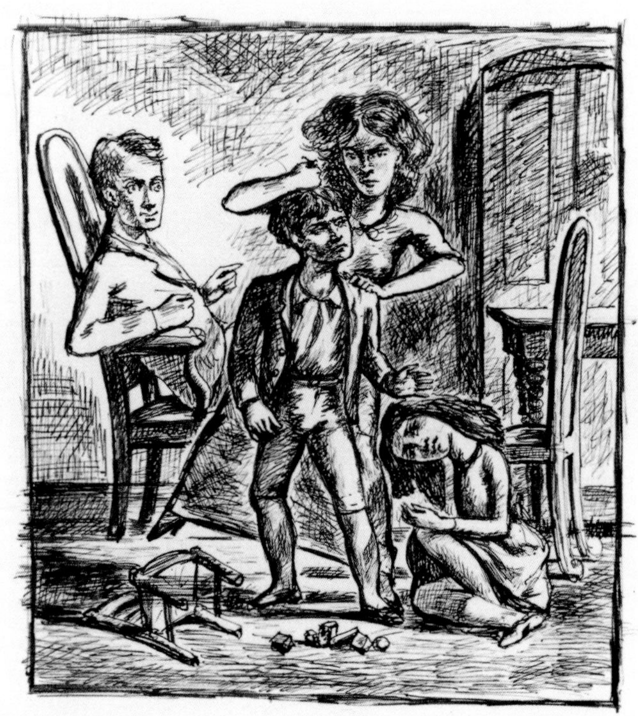

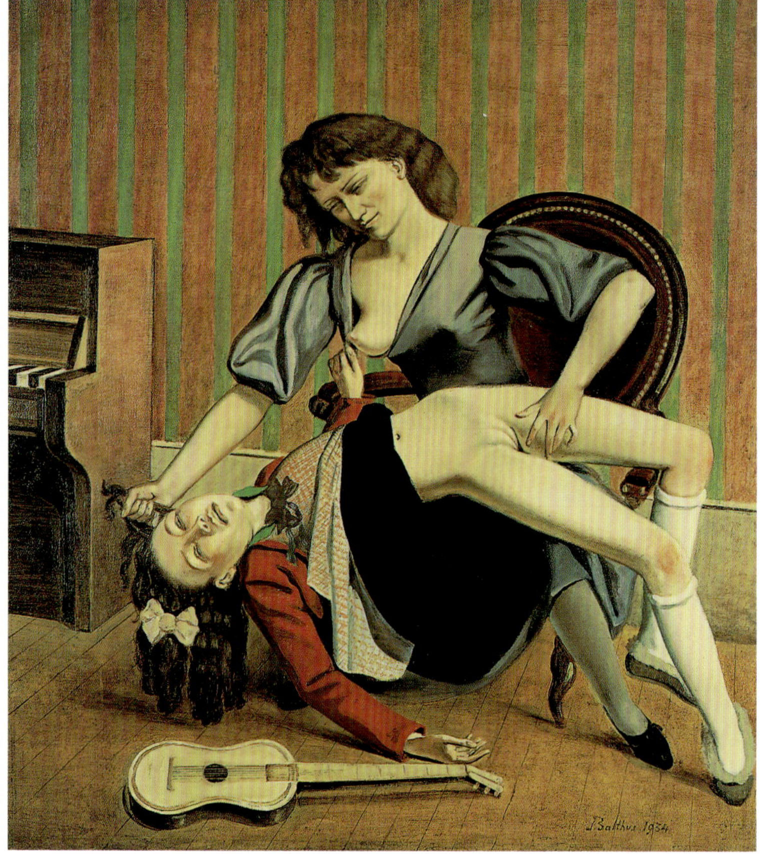

Like most of Balthus's best work, *La Rue* and the *Wuthering Heights* drawings reflect
the world of childhood and are permeated with nostalgia. It had been a childhood
so intensely lived that he was bound to be shadowed by it. The decisive figure was
the poet Rainer Maria Rilke, a Prague-German who first came to Paris as devotee
of the sculptor Rodin in 1902.

Balthus's father, Erich Klossowski (a Prussian art historian of Polish descent),
met Baladine Spiro in Breslau (where her father was Cantor in a synagogue). In
1903 the young German-speaking couple settled in Paris, where both painted,
sharing a large circle of artist friends, including Bonnard. But at the outbreak of
war in 1914, when Balthus was six, as German citizens they had to flee to Berlin.
They separated; from 1917 Baladine brought up her two boys alone in Switzerland;
and in Geneva in 1920, she became the 'Merline' of Rilke, his enchantress
throughout the creative spell that allowed him to complete *The Duino Elegies* and
the *Sonnets to Orpheus* (both published in 1923, often seen as the greatest of all
German twentieth-century poems). Impressed by a drawing sequence Balthus had
made aged eleven about the loss of a beloved cat, Rilke had them published and
contributed a preface.

When he abandoned Baladine she returned with the boys to Berlin.
Those years remain the most shadowy in Balthus's life, yet it seems evident that
something of *Sachlichkeit* did impinge on his formation. Thus by the time he

arrived as a sixteen-year-old in Paris, he'd been shaped at least as much by German culture as by French. It was Rilke who urged the boy to study Poussin in the Louvre and raised the funding to send him to Italy, where he made copies of Piero della Francesca's frescoes in Arezzo – from which *La Rue* derives its figure carrying the plank [illustration p. 94]. Out of such polyglot tensions Balthus's best work takes shape – a dark, moody Mitteleuropa *Sachlichkeit*, but overlaid with a veneer of French classicism and early Renaissance Italian purity.

Puppets were a persistent theme throughout Balthus's childhood. The Marionette theatre had remained significant in European culture. (For example, Alfred Jarry's *Ubu Roi*, of 1896, was first performed as a puppet play designed by Bonnard, later as 'Grand Guignol' – that is, by human actors imitating puppets.) The Klossowski family often performed home theatricals and *tableaux-vivants*. A puppet play by his father's close friend, the German art-writer Julius Meier-Graefe was published (with Erich's illustrations, much indebted to Bonnard) in the year of Balthus's birth. Rilke's own writing reflects a lifelong interest in dolls and puppets. 'They have no joints / And hang a bit obliquely / And woodenly in the system of wires', he wrote in 1907 in *The Puppet Theatre*. 'Their big faces / Are once and for all; / Not like ours; plainer, / Urgent and ideal, / Open as an awakening / From the depths of a dream...'.

To see *La Rue* as frozen *tableau-vivant*, the *Wuthering Heights* drawings as doll's house or puppet play – that may help define Balthus's relationship to the body, to narrative, as well as to 'realism'. When the radical theatre director Antonin Artaud began to collaborate with Balthus around the time of *The Lesson*, he found in the young painter an equivalent for his own aesthetic; here was an art that was 'cruel', yet which existed 'to make metaphysics'. He wrote in his 1932 *Manifesto of the Theatre of Cruelty*:

> The theatre cannot become itself again...until it provides the spectator with
> the truthful precipitates of dreams, in which his taste for crime, his erotic
> obsessions, his savagery, his fantasies, his utopian sense of life and of things,
> even his cannibalism, pour out on a level that is not counterfeit and illusory,
> but internal.

Balthus's work, wrote Artaud, 'carries the scent of plague, of storm and epidemics'. In 1934 he visited Balthus almost every evening, and it was Artaud who discovered the young painter after his suicide attempt, despairing that he had lost Antoinette.

Bonnard would remain an exemplar, showing how it was possible to be 'modern' without any stylistic ideology. (According to the critic David Sylvester, 'I remember in 1954 saying to Balthus that I couldn't make up my mind whether the greatest artist of this century was Matisse or Bonnard. He replied that if I didn't think it was Bonnard, we had nothing further to say to one another.') The dictum attributed to Balthus – commanding that artists should 'redo Surrealism' (as Cézanne had 'redone Poussin') 'from the life' – has complex overtones. It means we need to incorporate within any contemporary realism, those 'other' realities – of dream, of our unconscious life – that Surrealism took as its project, to liberate us

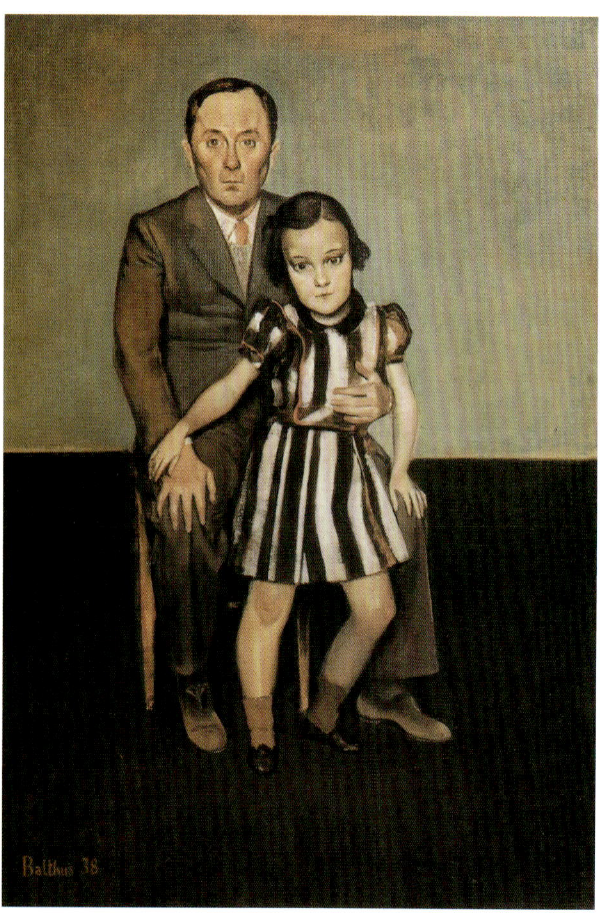

BALTHUS

*Joan Miró and His
Daughter Dolorès*

1937–38

The portrait was painted from
life over about forty sittings.
Throughout these months,
Miró was taking instruction in
painting from his eight-year-
old daughter. Balthus, who
happened to be born on 29
February, embraced a self-
identity as an ageless child.
In a late interview he recalled,
'What was important to me
was the *child atmosphere*, the
source of my inspiration.'

from bourgeois societal norms. But we should do this not from the top of our heads, not as a turning away from the everyday. The 'beyond-real' is to be found *within* bodily reality.

The company Balthus kept was largely Surrealist. When the *Wuthering Heights* drawings were first published in 1935, in the Surrealist magazine *Minotaur*, they looked at home alongside Man Ray's nudes, Brassaï's Paris, Hans Bellmer's dolls. From 1935 onwards his closest friend among artists was Alberto Giacometti; seven years older, he'd already created some of his greatest sculptures. The erotic violence of *Woman with Her Throat Cut* and the somnambulistic poetry of *The Palace at 4 A.M.* (both 1932) each have their equivalents in Balthus's painting. Most relevant is the plaster of 1934–35 sometimes known as *Person Holding the Void*, or *The Invisible Object* – a figure expressive of disbelief in any bodily reality. When Balthus affirms the human body it should be imagined with Giacometti's terrifying figure of negation lurking behind it. The writer Albert Camus recognized the paradox apropos of Balthus's *Portrait of André Derain* (1936): 'Such painting can best be defined, I think, by saying that its strangeness grows in proportion to its realism.' In the 1938 *Joan Miró and His Daughter Dolorès* [illustration above] fidelity to appearance – even to the contrast between suede and patent-leather shoes – does not impede intense psychological interrelation; and, as so often in Balthus, adult and child merge.

In the twenty years after *The Lesson*, Balthus returned in some forty pictures to the erotic experience of young girls. There is an element of comedy; we perceive them through narrowed eyes as the dolls and puppets of a peculiar imagination. A *Wuthering Heights* drawing, in which Cathy teaches Heathcliff to read, is transposed four years later into an almost 'straight' representation, the girl reading and the boy dreaming. (*The Blanchard Children*, 1937, is the picture purchased by Picasso in 1941 with the endorsement that Balthus and he were 'like two sides of the same coin'.) But this image in turn Balthus reworked into a more sexually charged scene, *Le Salon* (1941/43) – the reading girl obsessively 'getting into' her book on the floor, raising her rump, while behind her a phallic table presses itself between the legs of a second, dreaming child. Another sequence takes the Lycée half-holiday of Thursday afternoons, with two contrasted girls at the threshold of puberty, alone together in the silent room. The more daring presses herself back, sometimes naked, sometimes caressing a sportive cat quoted from Hogarth. Balthus's feline self-identification is most evident in his 1935 self-portrait,

BALTHUS

The Room

1952–54

Both *The Room* and
Le Passage [illustration
below] were conceived as
fully-realized *grandes machines*
in the exalted French tradition.
'If I have achieved something
up to the present,' wrote
Balthus in 1956, 'it is almost
uniquely, I think, in my large
paintings.'

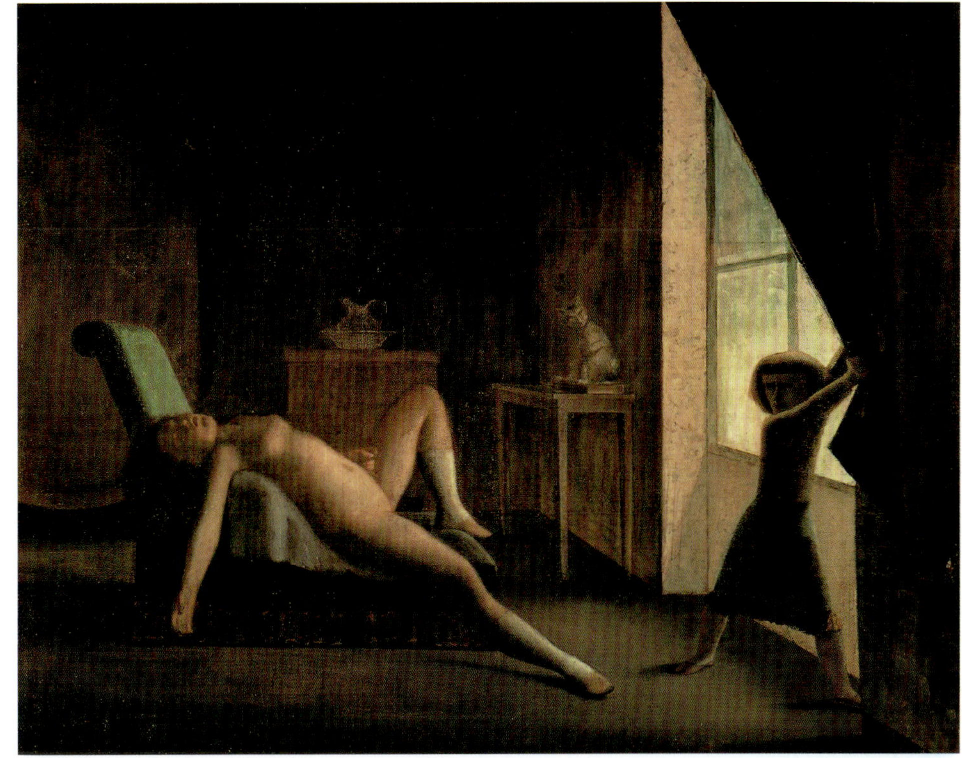

BALTHUS

*Le Passage du Commerce-
Saint-André* (Commerce-St-
Andrew Passage)

1952–54

The golden key and arrow
are not symbolic invention,
but together form a sign for a
locksmith; it was still visible in
the passage (close to Odéon
in Paris) well into the 1980s.
Balthus's studio, borrowed
from Derain, was close by.

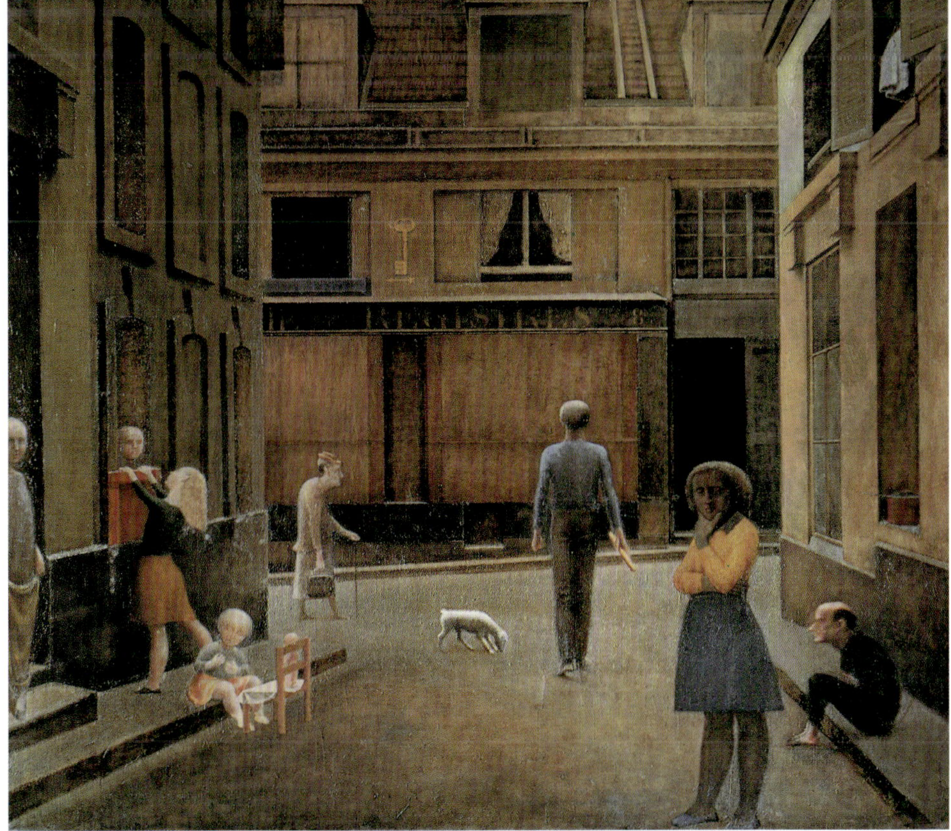

inscribed in English 'H M The King of The Cats'. Into the closed world of children awakening to sexuality, a cat has entry.

The most compelling of all those scenes is the huge canvas, eight by eleven feet, known as *The Room* [illustration p. 99], painted between 1952 and 1954. The shallow but enormously high space suggests a stage (and Balthus's actual theatre sets for Artaud and others seem to have been of this sparsely furnished kind, with menacing expanses of battered wall). The curtain rises on a strange tableau: a naked adolescent almost twice life-size is sprawled with disturbing abandonment, like a giant doll, one arm projecting stiffly. Against her rounded grace, the angular lines of her dwarfish companion contrast cuttingly; one seems a reproach to the other. Perhaps we should see these two figures as embodying two conflicting paths, two attitudes to life, between which Balthus finds himself divided: one languorously sensual in darkness, the other astringent, energetic, stark – the light-bringer. Melodrama? Grand Guignol? But the presence of the Mephistophelean cat who cocks his head to smile at us, establishes that we aren't in the adult world at all. *The Room* is the recreation of a child's experience in all its over-scaled, disproportionate intensity.

In the same years *The Room* was taking shape, Balthus completed alongside it the even larger street-scene *Le Passage du Commerce-Saint-André* [illustration p. 99]. On one level this is a reprise of *La Rue*, twenty years after, but its strangeness is far more oblique, owing as much to surface quality as to narrative. In *La Rue* the paint had been succulent and shiny, allowing him to create a razor-sharp clarity and illuminated starkness. With the Miró portrait he begins to drag the brush dryly across the grain, to give each surface its due weight and substance; until in *Le Passage* each figure seems to have been first incized as a silhouette into the thick, plaster-like casein, before being tinted with a pigment sometimes as transparent as watercolour. This process combines finality with insubstantiality. So for the urgent dream of *La Rue* is substituted an otherworldly evanescence – a stillness no longer frozen but muffled, muted under a pinkish, misty light.

The stage has grown but the players have shrunk. The self-figure walking away from us, his head touching the central horizontal, bears a *baguette* – that is, in French, a magician's wand. The puppet master now turns his back. Although the composition faithfully reconstructs an actual Paris location, the image suggests allegory; according to his brother, *Le Passage* has 'the importance of a kind of panorama' of Balthus's life. 'Depression haunts the picture in places; Balthus had to assign it some spot.'

Le Passage marks the great break in Balthus's work. In the subsequent almost fifty years there would be no more compositions of that scale or ambition. This break is as perplexing as in the work of Giacometti, or de Chirico and Derain before. After 1956, Balthus seems to create a new identity for himself, one that repudiates the whole thrust of his earlier achievement. He left Paris, sequestering himself in a dilapidated chateau with the teenage daughter of his friend Bataille and claiming the title of Count. (He had long since resigned his membership of the French Communist Party.) His new works appeared unshadowed, often insipid. Later, as director of the Académie de France at the Villa Medici in Rome (from 1961 to 1977), Balthus devoted himself to its redecoration: those distressed-plaster walls were echoed in the surfaces of his late canvases.

Having been left out of most accounts of twentieth-century art, Balthus became, from the 1980s onwards, a rallying point for revisionists and young 'resistant realists'; sometimes as a kind of Messiah, come to lead us back to the true path of classical figure-painting. Yet the whole flavour of Balthus's best paintings was deviant (as Pierre Klossowski well understood, taking up from where his brother left off in his own sequence of sexually transgressive images, first exhibited in Balthus's studio in 1956). However solidly embodied Balthus's early figures may appear, his remains a puppet world, envisioned from a child's viewpoint.

EDWARD HOPPER'S *NIGHTHAWKS* (1942)

Late in life, Balthus loftily claimed never to have heard of Edward Hopper (1882–1967). But in the 1980s, rediscovered together by a new generation, they were sometimes championed by the same young figurative painters. Nevertheless, their versions of realism point in very different directions. *Nighthawks* [illustration p. 102] is more impersonal than *La Rue*; Hopper's realism has something of the neutrality of the lens, eliminating not only the mark of the painter's hand but our sense of any process by which the image has come into being. In *Nighthawks* the space is clamped into a simple perspectival scheme, a kind of no-nonsense *normalization* of vision. (We might contrast the perceptual 'adventure' offered by a Bonnard of the same years [see illustration p. 130].) Yet *Nighthawks* is so intensely realized as to transcend its apparently banal representation, to create a strange, unforgettable icon, with its own new resonance.

Hopper had responded in his early twenties to the teaching of Robert Henri, recently returned from Europe, and urging his students towards the new American urban spectacle. 'The artist must be a spectator of life; a reverential, enthusiastic, emotional spectator.' That programme was immediately fulfilled by Hopper's fellow-student and exact contemporary, the prodigious George Bellows (1882–1925), who hurled himself into an exhilarating sequence of New York pictures between 1907 and 1911. To that already-quoted speculation of Léger, 'I sometimes wonder what would have happened to painting without Cézanne', Bellows provides one answer. In the revelatory retrospective of 2012–13, Bellows emerged as a magnificent, generous talent, fuelled by political conviction: a libertarian socialist, he exhibited at the People's Art Center; published illustrations in such journals as *The Masses* and *The Liberator*; taught at the Ferrer Center (named after the

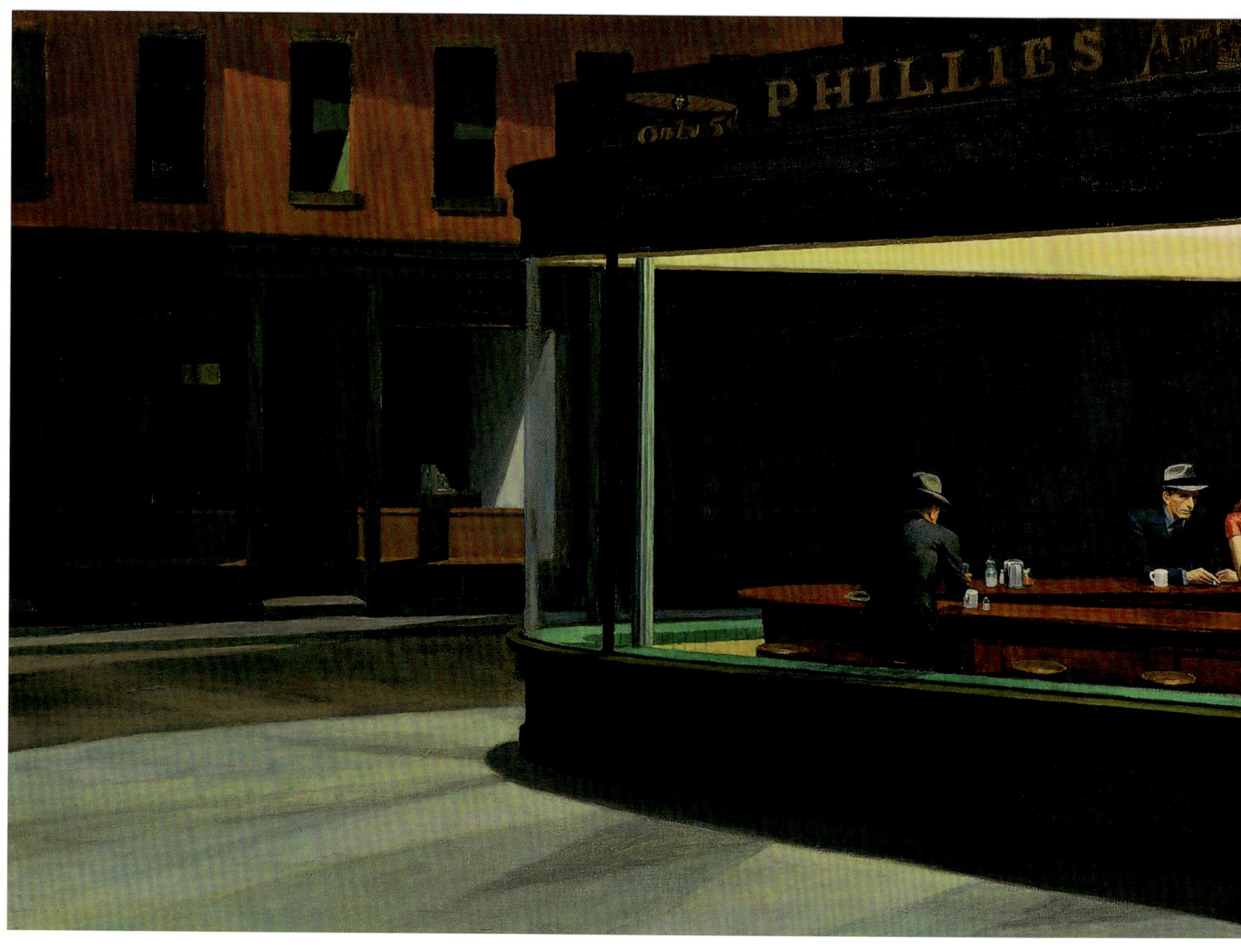

EDWARD HOPPER

Nighthawks

1942

At sixty, despite recognition, Hopper had earned barely US $1,500 the previous year. He was a slow painter: 'It takes a long time for an idea to strike. Then I have to think about it for a long time. I don't start painting until I have it all worked out in my mind.' Nor did he keep a regular studio routine: 'I wish I could paint more. I get sick of reading and going to the movies.'

Spanish anarchist executed in 1909); and he was a close friend of the activist Emma Goldman.

In these respects, as in so many others, the dour, hard-bitten Republican Edward Hopper was Bellows's opposite. In those same years, Hopper began work as a commercial illustrator, funding a series of lonely trips to Paris – Bellows never left the United States – and honing a sophisticated pictorial intelligence. Hopper too looked at Manet, but also at the reinvention of space accomplished by Degas and the *Nabis*. (His mature paintings sometimes bring to mind the framing-devices and hard, closed surfaces of Félix Vallotton around 1900.) When he returned from his last stay in Paris, in 1910, Hopper found it difficult to readjust: 'It seemed awfully crude here when I got back. It took me ten years to get over Europe.' In 1914 he made a conscious attempt at a masterpiece – the long-format (nearly three by six foot) *Soir Bleu* (Blue Evening), with its array of large, melancholic bohemians, centred on a sad clown; its artful design indebted to Degas. The following decade would become a painful retreat from that European figure-composition into a new, American estrangement, first achieved in his etchings.

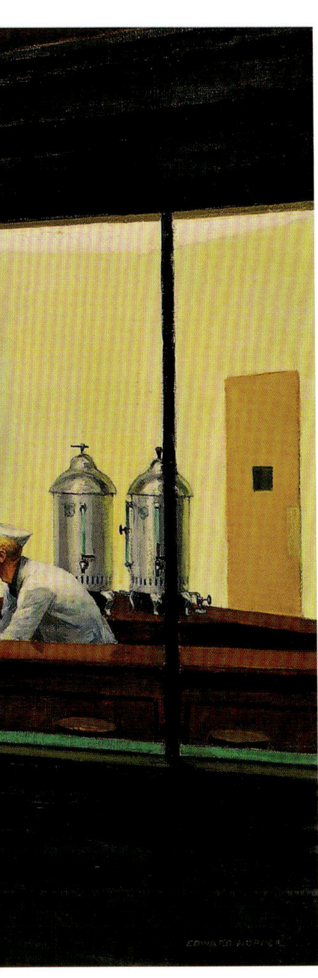

When Bellows died suddenly, in 1925, Hopper was 'distraught' at the funeral. Yet he was about to bring off the first of those long-considered oil paintings that would at last establish his own public identity – *Automat* (1927), *Night Windows* (1928) and *Early Sunday Morning* (1930); pictures that can also be seen as Hopper's sullen refutation of his friend's work. Beside them, Bellows's populist, affirmatory zest-for-life is made to appear crass. Hopper consistently dissociated himself from John Sloan and the Ashcan painters, from 'American Scene' art: 'It had a sociological trend which didn't interest me.' Recent writing on Hopper has emphasized his intellectual underpinning, his lifelong reading of Plato and the transcendentalist Ralph Waldo Emerson; that he carried in his wallet a quotation from Goethe, defining art as 'the reproduction of the world that surrounds me by means of the world that is in me…'. The conflict between mere naturalism and The Real was always in his mind. Whether or not he was aware of Carrà and Sironi (see Ch 1 pp. 26–33), that is the company in which I would place him.

That 'metaphysical' dimension is especially present in *Nighthawks*. The conté preparatory drawings are blandly efficient 'layouts'; what elevates the painting are the colour and the framing, and above all the contrast between lit, inhabited interior and the vast blue-green emptiness of the nocturnal street. At one crucial point, in the central figure – the figure seen from the back, nearest to us – that blue-green void strikes down into the interior, the hue of his shadowed suit rendered almost identical to the invasive night.

Nighthawks repays long scrutiny; it goes on *opening up* the more one looks. It could be seen, for example, as a wonderful pictorial equivalent to that Goethe quotation – the conjunction of inner and outer experience, the near figure as solitary protagonist (almost a Caspar David Friedrich *Rückenfigur*). The couple have their backs to the night, but the lone man gazes straight into that vast dark rectangle, which then takes over as the dominant motif. Its slant of shadow against light is extraordinarily 'abstract' – held between two verticals, the emerald and the almost-black.

Nighthawks also appeals as an icon of an era, and has often been paralleled with noir film-stills. Hopper loved cinema. But he was more ambivalent about the photograph, complaining (in dialogue with his younger urban-realist comrade, Raphael Soyer) 'Photography is so light. No weight to it.' Hopper and Soyer wrote together in the journal *Reality*, founded in explicit opposition to New York Abstraction. Hopper began to take a crudely anti-modern stance, declaring in 1953:

> Painting will have to deal more fully and less obliquely with life and nature's phenomena before it can again become great.

As it transpired, Abstract Expressionist painting would indeed be promoted *at the expense of* figuration (see Ch 5 pp. 193–98); soon, for young artists growing up in Europe and Britain during the 1960s, not just Hopper but all of twentieth-century American figurative painting would disappear from sight, *terra incognita*.

THE LIBERTARIAN LINE: ALICE NEEL AND THE MODERN PORTRAIT (1933–80)

Art is two things: a search for a road and
a search for freedom. It's very hard to get freedom…

ALICE NEEL, c. 1975

Alice Neel (1900–84) was eighteen years younger than Hopper and Bellows; her struggle for legitimation as a figurative painter within an overwhelmingly abstract painting-culture would be long and heroic.

During the Great Depression of the 1930s, President Roosevelt's New Deal (bitterly opposed by Edward Hopper) gave a role and a bare living to many young painters who might otherwise have given up. From 1933, under the Works Progress Administration (WPA) and related schemes, some 5,000 artists were paid to create more than 2,500 murals and at least 20,000 paintings. That new socially aware cultural bias eventually sparked the contrary reflex – in favour of the timeless, the universal – that would fuel New York Abstraction. (The painter Arshile Gorky called social realism 'poor art for poor people'.) But for Alice Neel, funding was intermittent for a decade, between the ages of thirty-three and forty-three, and to walk through a retrospective of her portraits is to experience a collectivity, a zeitgeist. She defined herself as an 'anarchic humanist'; we never lose the sense that in her painting she is challenging the authority of the prevailing status quo.

As a young woman, Neel participated in the Cuban *Vanguardia* movement, whose 1927 manifesto declared:

> The central issue of modern art is to return to emotions; situate oneself with
> pure intentions before the spectacle of the world and of life, and describe, with a
> simple and clear language, the emotion of everyday life.

To that prescription Neel remained faithful. She became heir to a broadly 'Expressionist' portraiture, linked to early Oskar Kokoschka, to Munch and Soutine – all artists she is known to have admired, whose sense of the solitary and singular individual is inflected with the tragic. But a further influence remained unacknowledged: her close affinity with the Weimar verists (see pp. 59–80) and above all with Otto Dix (one of whose portraits hung at MoMA as early as 1932). Alongside her directness – Frank Auerbach has praised 'her patent and shaming honesty' – in all her best portraits there is a dimension of grotesquerie, of comical and caricatural absurdity.

Her early portrait of *Joe Gould* (1933) [illustration opposite] is admittedly a special case. Gould was a vagrant in Greenwich Village, New York, something of a Holy Fool, and Neel was among many who befriended him with food, clothing or small sums of money. Harvard-educated, he claimed to be writing an 'oral history', a transcription of random conversational encounters, millions of words long. (This project may have held a special appeal for Alice Neel, who saw her own portrait-painting as a form of

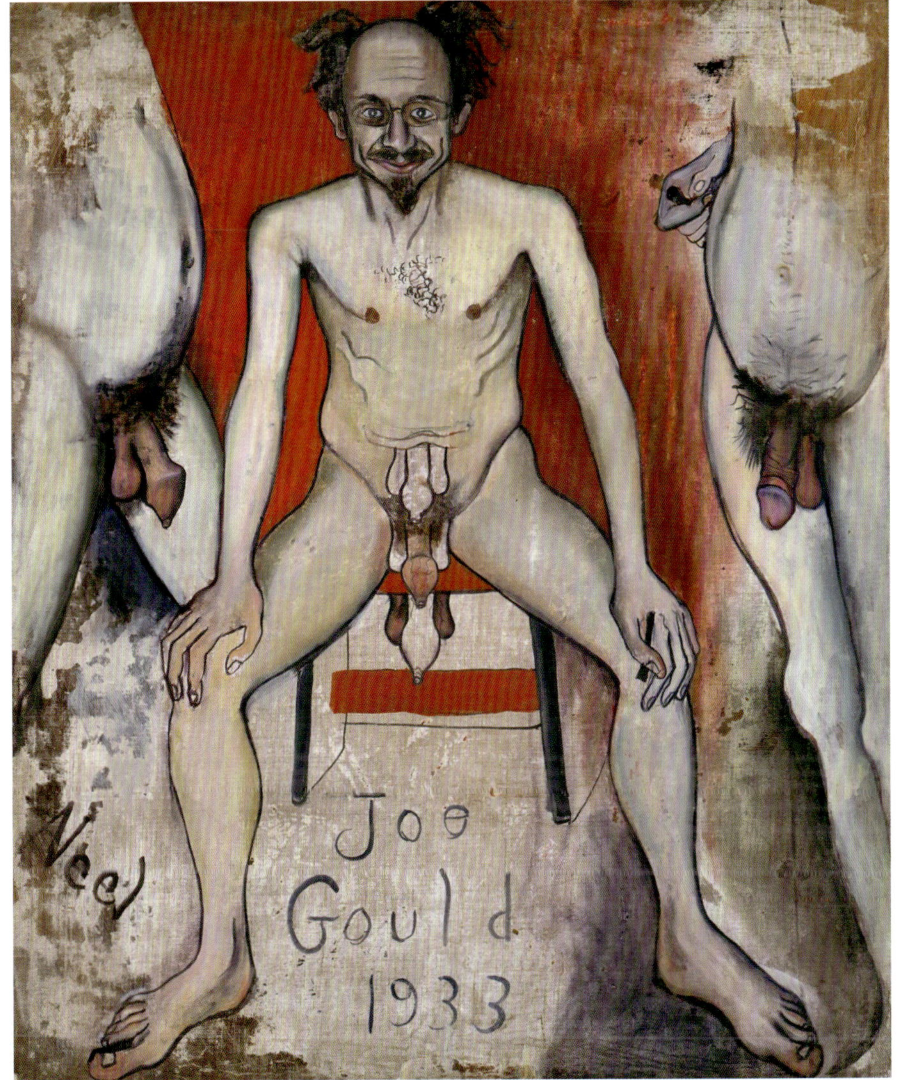

'history'.) He would later be the subject of two famous *New Yorker* pieces. At Gould's insistence Joseph Mitchell went in 1946 to search out 'Miss Neel'; 'the address turned out to be a tenement in a Negro and Puerto Rican neighbourhood in the Upper East side'. Mitchell had often witnessed Gould in drunken performance mode at bohemian parties. 'On his face would come a leering, gleeful, mawkishly abandoned expression, half Satanic and half silly. Miss Neel had caught that expression.' She had originally entitled the painting *Portrait of an Exhibitionist,* though the masculine appendage is here exposed only to be multiplied, a male udder. (Has Gould, who is clutching a piece of charcoal, inscribed his own name below, a willing participant in this mockery?)

Neel had become an art student only at twenty-one, after business courses and secretarial jobs. Immediately after graduation in 1925, she married a Cuban artist, giving birth in Havana, but losing the one-year-old to diphtheria back in New York. By the end of 1930 her husband had abandoned her, taking their second daughter. She suffered a breakdown. After a year in various hospitals, punctuated by suicide attempts,

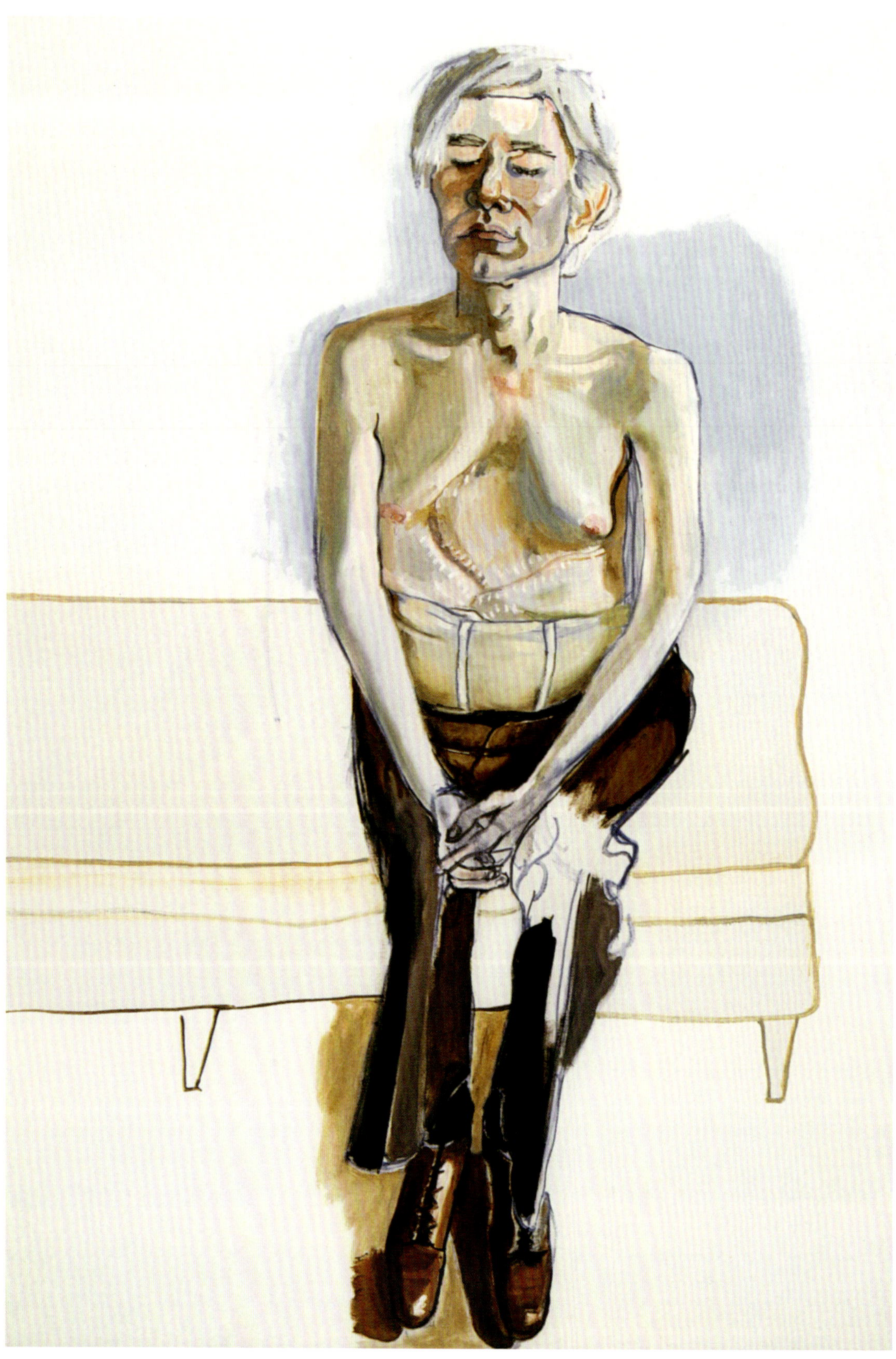

Although Warhol's own icons denied any psychological interiority, recent research has emphasized his own religiosity and inward torment. (His splendid early drawings have a comparable directness to Neel's wiry, ink line.) Warhol wears a corset, having recovered from the gun attack of 1968. The South African painter Marlene Dumas has pronounced this 'one of the most beautiful paintings of the twentieth century'.

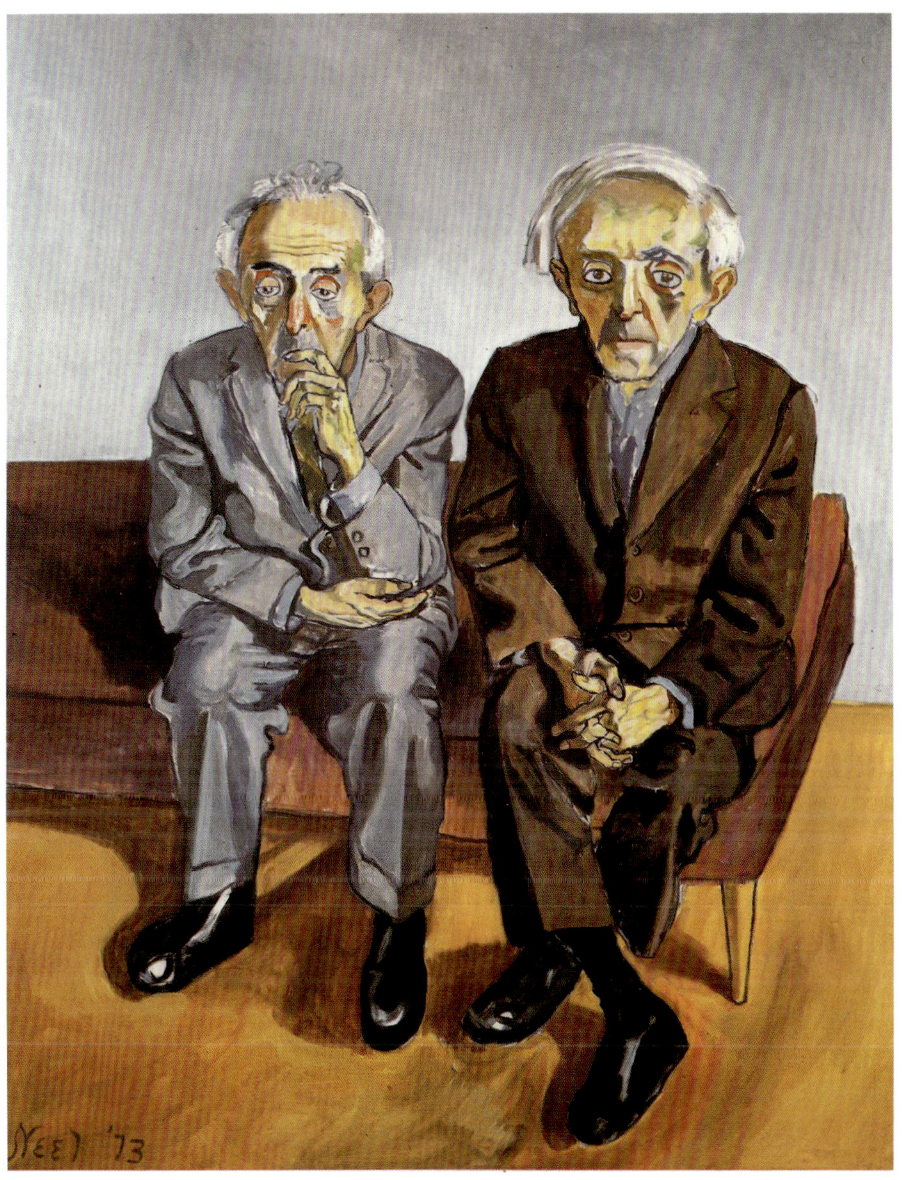

ALICE NEEL

The Soyer Brothers

1973

Raphael Soyer (1899–1987) was a Russian-Jewish immigrant who painted some of the most distinguished social realist images of the 1930s. Alice Neel had been associated with Moses Soyer in the American Artists' Congress as early as 1936. The twins were two of her dearest painter-friends, comrades in her quest to find meaning in the facts of modern life, rather than in subjectivity and abstraction.

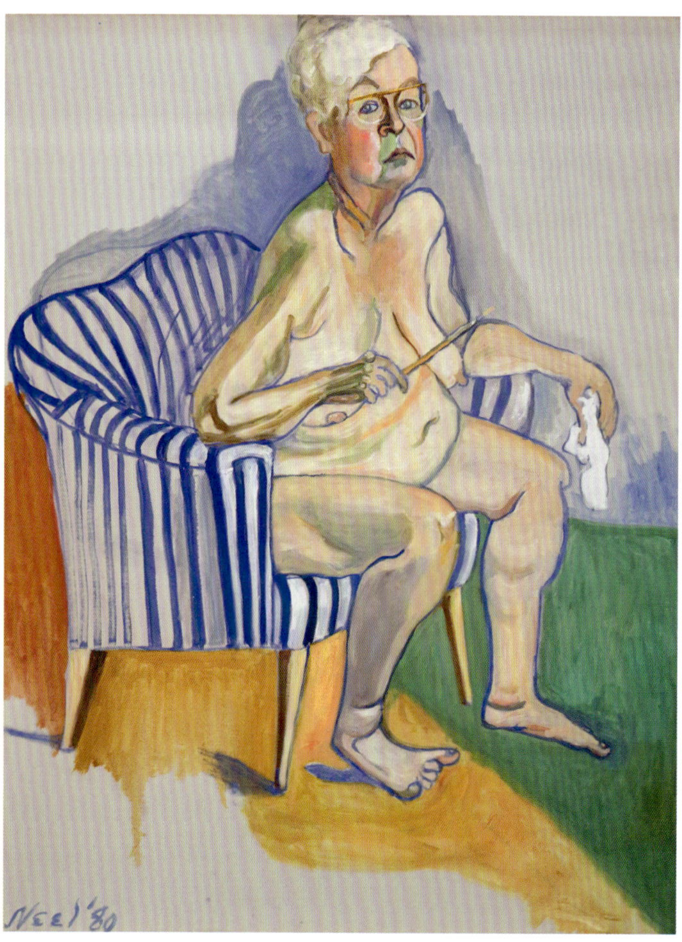

ALICE NEEL
Self-Portrait
1980

Commenced in 1975, but
abandoned for five years
in a crisis of confidence,
Neel's unsmiling self-scrutiny
resumed as she entered her
ninth decade.

she finally emerged onto the Greenwich Village scene in 1932, during the fourth winter of The Depression. The naked clowning of the *Joe Gould* portrait, painted the following summer, could have been a one-off – but for the next fifty years, Alice Neel continued to defy decorum. The critic Peter Schjeldahl has written of her 'poor etiquette and great art'; her coarse, tactless line becomes her instrument of truth-telling.

Like most of the artists in this book, Alice Neel was fully aware of the prevailing narrative of 'Modern Art', and she set out to construct her own contrary alternative. She understood Cubism to signify 'the human race torn to pieces' and her own role, if not to mend, at least to present the precariousness of our reconstruction. It was line that could knit together those shattered fragments of the dismantled body; the *Joe Gould* portrait provides one paradigm for a 'modern' portrait. She didn't peddle the illusions of academic portraiture (in which she'd been thoroughly instructed in Philadelphia); she de-skilled, and her 1930s pictures are often deliberately 'primitive'.

Other less extreme images, of Leftist activists or bohemian intellectuals, build a picture of the milieu of Greenwich Village, America's most art-friendly zone during the 1930s. But in 1938 she moved, with her Hispanic lover, several miles north-east to Spanish Harlem, where she would bring up two sons, by different fathers. Neel's work was seldom exhibited; she had no solo show from 1944 to 1950, or again from 1954 to 1963. Nevertheless, she did keep in touch with the New York scene. After The Club was founded (in 1949 in East Eighth Street) she would make the long journey downtown, where she witnessed the steady hardening of art-world attitudes against figuration. As she recalled in 1960:

> I decided to paint a human comedy.... Like Chichikov [Gogol's protagonist] I am a
> collector of souls. When I go to a show today of modern work, I feel that my world
> has been swept away. And yet I do not think it can be that the human creature will
> be forever *verboten*.

That '*verboten*' (forbidden) invokes fascist tyranny: abstract painting had become oppressively dominant. By the mid-1960s however, several new subcultures of figuration were sprouting, mostly under the protective umbrella of Pop. Among those who sat twice for Neel, Red Grooms and Mimi Gross, makers of the

'sculpto-pictorama' *Ruckus Manhattan* [see Ch 5 pp. 210–14, illustration p. 213],
as well as the gay city-poet Frank O'Hara and the art historian Meyer Shapiro,
were each representative of a changing intellectual and sexual climate. Alice Neel
had already come close to several gay or transgendered participants from Andy
Warhol's Factory; when Warhol himself sat for her in 1970 [illustration p. 106]
she persuaded him to bare both breast and wound. The feminist art writer Linda
Nochlin published *The Realist Criminal and the Abstract Law* in 1973, the year that
Neel portrayed her. (No preliminary drawings, six sittings.) Also that year, her old
friend and defender of realism Raphael Soyer is portrayed with his painter-twin
Moses, both looking baffled and lost [illustration p. 107]. These later portraits are
almost life-size in scale, high-keyed, verging on brash; and like the epoch they
depict, no longer 'innocent'. But somehow Neel herself had moved with the times.

The coarse immediacy of Neel's big, late pictures can be disconcerting; taken
singly, they can seem perfunctory (as can the late works of Edvard Munch [see
Ch 3 p. 161, illustration p. 160]), but their challenge is cumulative. Like Dix before
her, she finds a way to conjure a political and social milieu. Neel waited until the
age of seventy-five before embarking on a self-portrait, naked in specs, with brush
and rag, which would eventually become her most famous image [illustration
opposite]. But any widespread international recognition of Neel's achievement
would be delayed until the twenty-first century.

LUCIAN FREUD'S *INTERIOR AT PADDINGTON* (1951)

Although Lucian Freud (1922–2011) always spoke ill of twentieth-century
German art – making exception only for the drawings of George Grosz – his
Interior at Paddington [illustration p. 111] makes clear his affinity with Weimar
Sachlichkeit. It is now known that he visited in 1938 the large survey 'Twentieth
Century German Art', mounted in London as refutation of the Nazis' 'Degenerate
Art' campaign; among much else, it included Dix's portrait of his parents
[illustration p. 67], while Beckmann came over from Amsterdam to give a lecture
(see Ch 3 pp. 139 and 154). Shortly after, Lucian Freud emerged as a boy-wonder
into the English art world, where his own version of magic realism, as in his
tender and beautiful *Girl with Roses* of 1947–48, brought him recognition, even
if he was seen as 'Teutonic'. By 1952 David Sylvester could write of a widespread
'Modernist Realism', with Giacometti and Bacon as major protagonists; yet the
same critic would also pronounce Freud's imagery 'not radical enough in style
to be relevant to the future of painting'. His realism would always be without any
'critical' dimension. Set alongside Dix or Alice Neel, Freud entirely lacks their
sense of a contrarian witness, of a wider engagement with their society. Implicit
in Freud's art (and increasingly so as he grew older) was an unquestioning
confirmation of the status quo.

Yet *Interior at Paddington* commands recognition as an early masterpiece. Freud
was one of sixty artists commissioned by the Arts Council to make 'large paintings'

as part of the 1951 Festival of Britain. Throughout the 1940s he'd been almost a miniaturist, painting on a small scale with fine sable brushes. Those early pictures have a strange purity; in *Girl with Roses* the delineation, the radiant light, seems innocent, even if the girl's facial expression suggests fear. (Hence Herbert Read dubbing Freud 'The Ingres of Existentialism'.) But here the artist sets out to create a complete figure, life-size – Harry Diamond was a small man – standing within an inside–outside space that is almost a microcosm. Man is juxtaposed to Nature, which takes the form of a dry, spiky yucca, of equal height and presence. Its crown reaches out, but never to the edge of the picture, and never overlapping the figure – never breaking their mutual isolation. Through the grimy glass, we look down on a wintry street, a bleached, steel-etched monochrome, lifeless except for the little brown figure leaning against the wall.

Any close description of *Interior at Paddington* will sound drab and chilling: the plant-pot cracked, the cheap red carpet rucked up from the bare floorboards, the man pallid, with nicotine-stained fingers and creased mac. Yet the overall emotional charge of this image has always struck me as *comical*. The placement of that bespectacled male – a kind of Everyman, a kind of fool, a 'funny little man' – beside that monstrous potted palm is inherently ridiculous, grotesque. (And that is part of the picture's affinity with Dix.) Even though the figure was posed from life, the effect is of dislocation, of his having been put together slightly awry, head and hands too big, giving him the look of a child, or a puppet.

In the following year Freud would paint two close-up heads, *John Minton* and *Francis Bacon*, and in 1954, *Girl in a Green Dress*; all have a powerful psychological impact, capturing a sense of 'the human condition', and, emerging out of extremely intense observation, a *strangeness*.

From about 1960, and emphatically after 1985, in the paintings for which he would become most celebrated, Freud's art switches to a numb realism, an affectless representation-as-such; his neutral rendering of what is seen repressing psychological or literary overtones. His sometime dealer, Helen Lessore, has written: 'One cannot fail to recognize that Freud's early work had a beauty, something we call "poetry", and that then the muse left him.' Stylistically, these later paintings are not heir to the radical realism of Courbet, let alone to Dix or Balthus or Spencer; they hark back to what used to be called 'straight painting', the stodgy academic naturalism that Freud himself had never practised, even in his youth – the 'copying' against which all modernist painting has set itself, ever since the Impressionists.

'"Reality" is one of the few words which mean nothing without quotes', wrote Vladimir Nabokov in 1955. There was – perhaps especially prevalent in post-war England – a view of 'truth' as brutal and unfeeling; of naked 'reality' as aggressively dull and grey. Freud's portraits might be seen in that light, as monuments to disillusionment. Inherent in doggedly realistic painting may be a shutting-down of pictorial liberty – the kinds of mutability and free play that distinguish so much of the greatest twentieth-century art. Yet the persistent rediscovery of Thingness all through the twentieth century, often accompanied by intense pictorial invention, remains a vital resource for painters of the twenty-first.

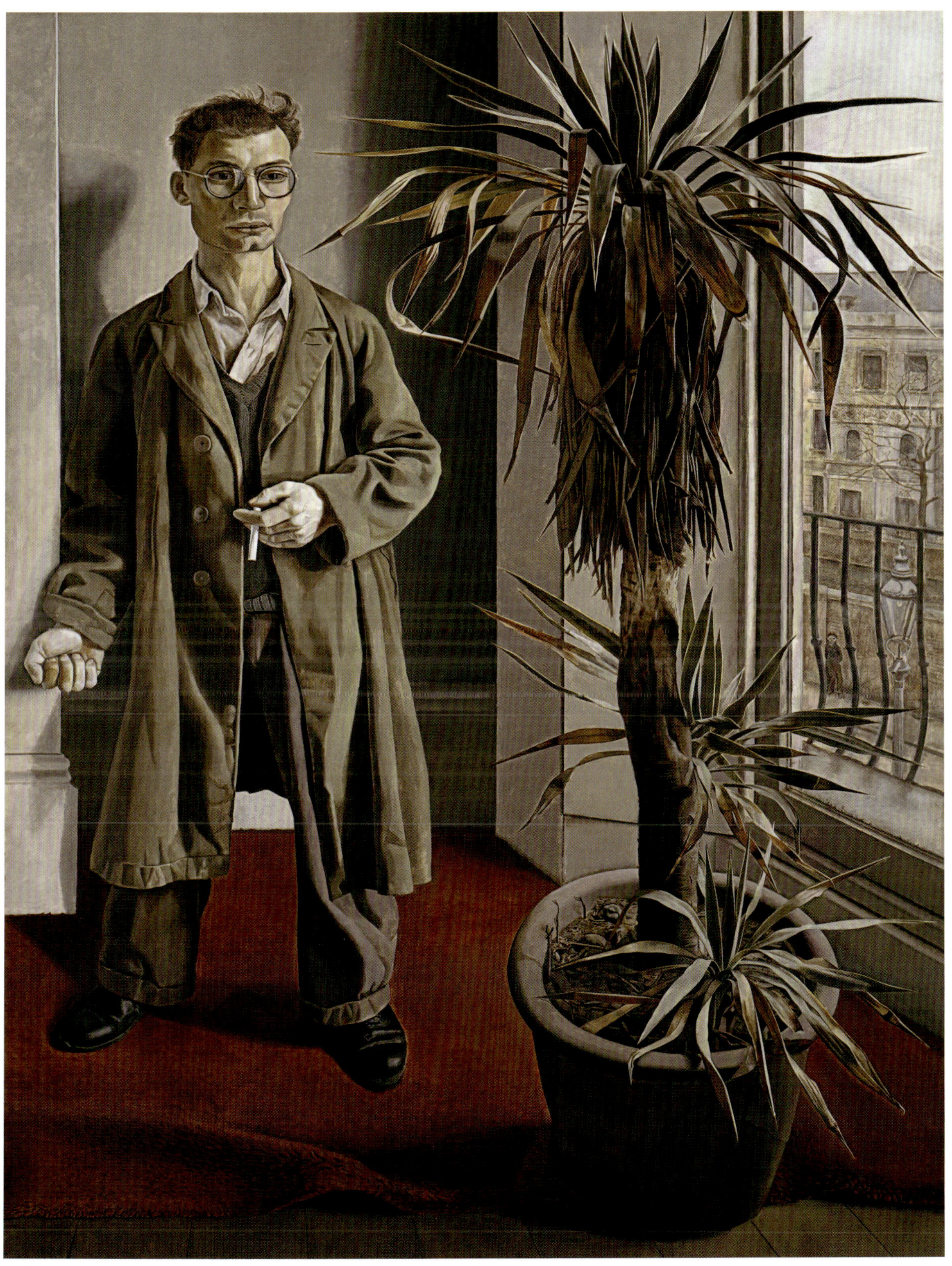

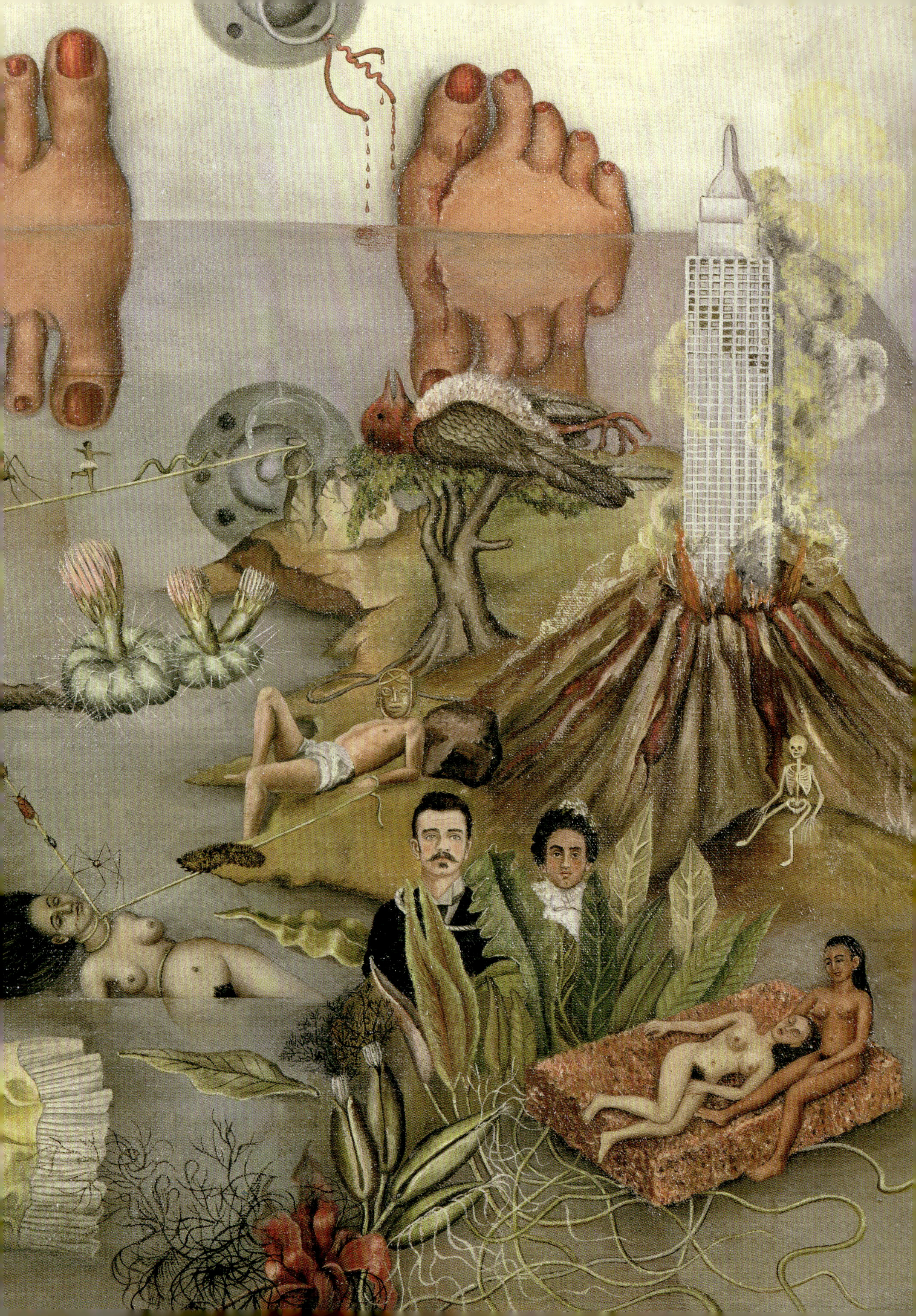

CHAPTER THREE

First-Person Painting

It becomes more and more difficult to say I,
and yet at the same time often imperative to do so.

CHRISTA WOLF, 1976

That is the catchword: his art is self-art...
The man always steps in front of his work

PAUL WESTHEIM (WRITING ON MAX BECKMANN), 1923

In the 1920s, several German art writers began to identify a category of *Selbst-Kunst* (self-art). The term never quite took on, partly because the very concept of painting *in the first person* seemed to contradict the modernist consensus, whereby the greatest art was the most formal, the most 'impersonal'. The immediate context was German (Kirchner, Modersohn-Becker, Beckmann), yet across Northern Europe artists since Van Gogh and Munch had begun to explore this essentially new role – the painter as protagonist of his or her own art, projecting the self as a dramatized persona.

As soon as we isolate that self-art vein, we realize how pervasive it has been throughout the twentieth century – even if, in Hans Belting's phrase, 'Modernism suppressed it'. In 1995 a huge survey exhibition was mounted to mark the centenary of the Venice Biennale, curated by the revisionist Jean Clair at the Palazzo Grassi. 'Identity and Alterity' assembled an astonishing international array of twentieth-century self-portraits, and the catalogue raised the provocative question: 'What if the twentieth century had been, more than any other, the century of the self-portrait, not of Abstraction?' In this chapter I want to explore the work of several of these 'first-person' artists, chosen because they were compelled to create not merely self-portraits, but a narrative of the Self.

FRIDA KAHLO
What the Water Gave Me
1938

(detail, see p. 136)

Intimism: Vuillard and Bonnard (1900-13)

In the 'Intimism' of Edouard Vuillard (1868–1940) and Pierre Bonnard (1867–1947) around 1900, something of that subjective, psychological view, was already latent.

Ten years earlier, as *Nabis*, they'd abandoned naturalism for Gauguin's gospel of inwardness. 'Painting,' Gauguin pronounced, 'must return to its original purpose: the examination of the interior life of human beings.' His 1888 *Vision After the Sermon* seems almost too schematic – that field of flat red that allows his Breton tribals to experience both the everyday cow and Jacob struggling with the angel, literally on the same plane. Yet this flatness would serve, from Munch's *Frieze of Life* (see Ch 2 p. 59) to Bacon's existential icons (Ch 1 pp. 54–55), to raise the material of our everyday lives to a symbolic resonance; flatness as a shortcut to the interior.

According to Vuillard's fellow *Nabi*, the painter/theorist Maurice Denis, naturalism was 'a false witness'. But *Nabi* flatness proved limited in its reach. Vuillard's painting took on full resonance only when, around 1895, he overlaid that underlying structural flatness with flurries of small, wild marks; the combination delivers a formal tension that allows him to trap extremely elusive, subjective emotions. Writing from Rome in 1898, thrilled by Raphael, Denis wrote, 'I know of no atmosphere so far removed from Impressionism.' He reproached Vuillard (along with Bonnard and Félix Vallotton) for moving away from the *Nabi* collective ideal towards individualism. But Vuillard's response was to declare his 'horror, cold fear, of ideas that I have not arrived at by myself.'

Mystically inclined as a boy (he even considered a monastic vocation), his art is consequent upon a loss of belief. Specific moments in specific rooms are the only certainties left to him. As he explained to Denis,

> There was in my life a moment when, either through personal weakness,
> or through a lack of solidity in my basic principles, everything was
> demolished...a sort of intimate whirlwind took over...the area in which I was
> quite certain of anything got smaller and smaller...

It is hard to know in our own lives what value to place on those small domestic epiphanies, which are Vuillard's chief subject. (In the same *Revue blanche* [White Review] circle, Stéphane Mallarmé and Marcel Proust created their literary visions from materials no less fragile.) Living at home, where Madame Vuillard ran a couturière business, Edouard was surrounded by pattern; the 1890s saw a vogue for *millefleurs* tapestry, flowered screens and wallpapers, and doors opening *in* the wallpaper. Pattern invades his figures and becomes a vehicle for feeling.

Vuillard's devastating *Married Life* [illustration opposite] of 1900 owes much to his work as stage-designer for the first French productions of Henrik Ibsen's dramas, with their themes of domestic incarceration. While gas lamps blaze outside in the blue urban night, there opens between this couple a terrible, shaming distance. The room silts up with suffocating brown patterned marks in which the figures are imbedded and entrapped.

Vuillard's reconstruction of a room to create a psychological truth would be developed further by Bonnard. Together the two painters pointed to the possibility of a new subjective language of representation, in many ways

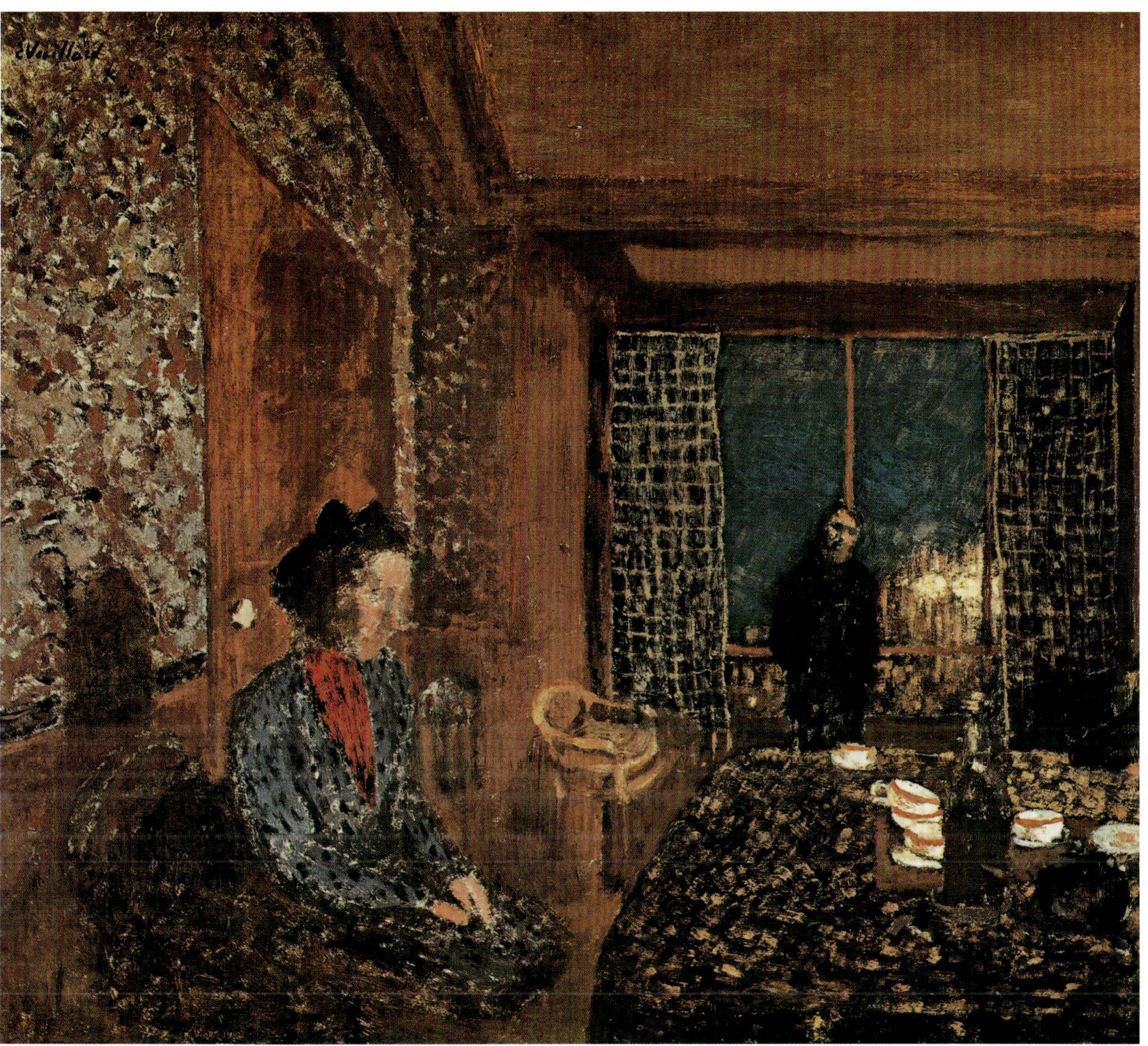

more flexible and closer to experience than the heavily stylized Cubism that superseded their Intimism. It is a mistake to see Vuillard and Bonnard as mere bourgeois individualists. Like many others of their circle (and notably the great editor of the *Revue blanche*, Felix Fenéon) they were committed to a relaxation of hierarchy, resolute supporters of Dreyfus during the political scandal that polarized French society, libertarians with a vision of a Golden Age future. The tension in Vuillard's best work, between flat design and improvisatory marks, may be equivalent to that other tension he discovered between the sensory patterned world of the everyday and his yearning for some more permanent structure of meaning. In his essay of 1863, Baudelaire had proposed a *Painter of Modern Life*, whose art would mirror not only the passing moment, but 'all the suggestions of eternity that it contains'. In both Vuillard and Bonnard, the fugitive vibrations and the 'suggestions of eternity' often came hand-in-hand.

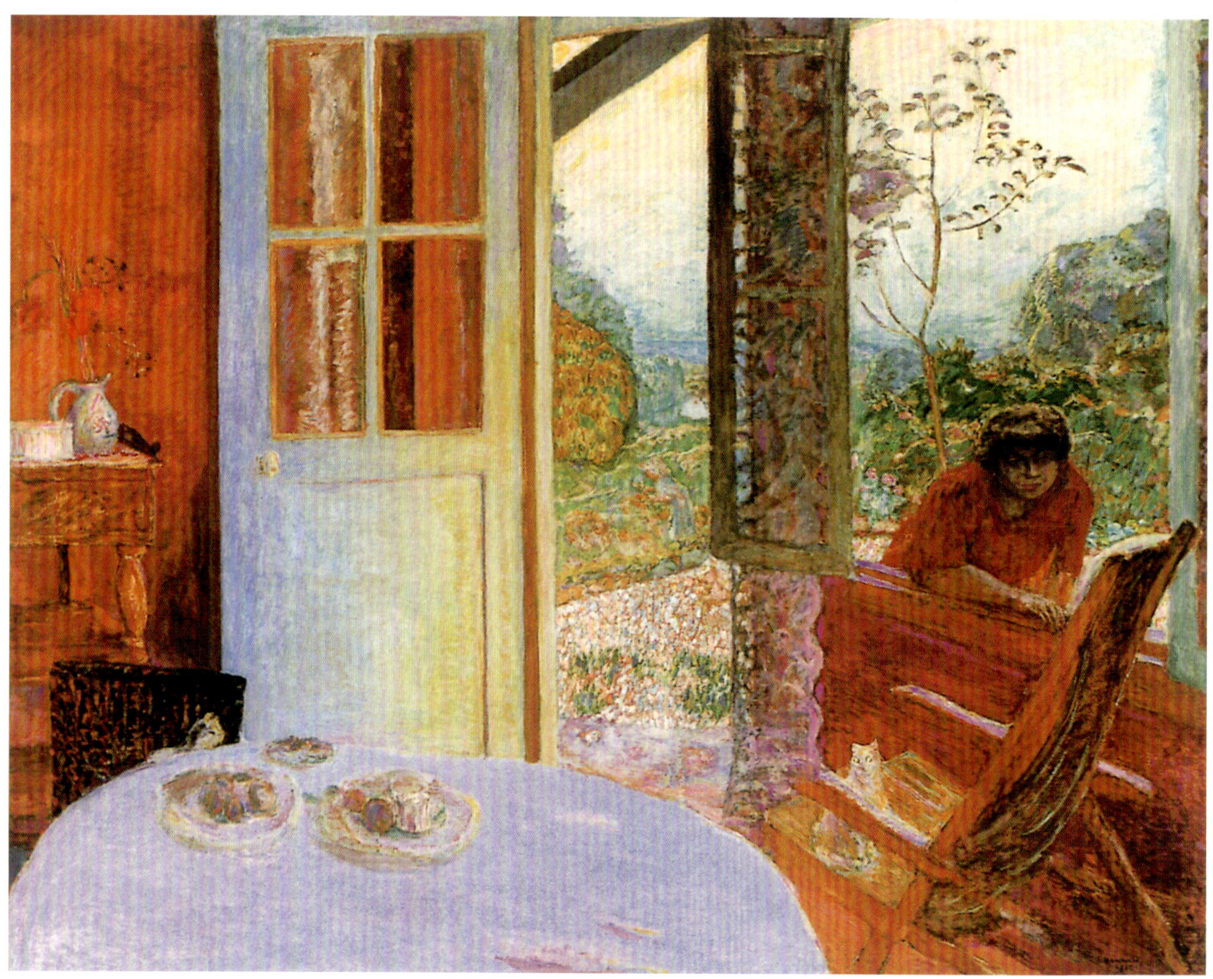

PIERRE BONNARD

Dining Room in the Country
1913

By 1913 Bonnard was no longer painting from the motif, but from drawings, allowing him to reinvent freely; not so much reality as remembered experience. One might suppose that crimson wall fanciful, but at Bonnard's Normandy house that wall really was painted red.

The early years of the twentieth century were a time of difficult transition for Bonnard. At their outset he had felt himself to be part of a group endeavour; the Intimists wanted

> to pick up the research of the Impressionists, and to take it further…. Art is not Nature. We were stricter in composition. There was a lot more to be got out of colour as a means of expression.

Bonnard had been interested in the philosophy of Henri Bergson, in his emphasis on the subjectivity of sensory experience: the self as rebuilding or reassembling the world into images. But meanwhile the notion of art as an evolutionary progression of movements took hold. After the ascendancy of Cubism in 1910–11 (see Ch 1 pp. 13–17), the Intimist quest appeared retrograde: 'We were left, so to speak, dangling in mid-air.' Yet by 1913, when Bonnard was forty, he was able to fulfil that project in a defining masterpiece, *Dining Room in the Country* [illustration above]. Bonnard employs here the approximate qualities of Impressionist mark-making to stress the personal, the individual. If the Impressionists had aspired to remove the self from perception, Bonnard would

put it back again, registering the place of the spectator – Bonnard's own place –
with a first-person emphasis new to painting.

The almost seven-foot scale is surprising – much larger than one might expect
from reproduction, and larger than such an intimate space might seem to call for.
The subject is not immediately evident, its inventory only slowly unpacked to our
sight. We are placed this side of a wide expanse of milky, mother-of-pearl table-
top, and at first we may think we are in an empty room, dominated by the bold
central geometry of door and frame; until we find ourselves in eye contact with
the shadowed figure off to the right, who looks in at us from outside the window.
(Eventually we make out also two little kittens, and – perhaps quite some while
later – a child picking flowers in the garden.) Once we have glimpsed her presence,
everything is charged with that relationship. The room becomes the vessel of an
extraordinary tenderness, its red walls an extension of that red, smiling figure.
We might see the table as a kind of wheel, turning the successive planes one after
the other, enacting the transformation: of the quotidian into the epiphany, of
solitude into love, and – as with all the other painters in this section – of 'reality'
into first-person experience.

PAULA MODERSOHN-BECKER: NOT 'THAT'S ME' BUT 'THIS IS' (1900-7)

Before her death at the age of thirty-one, Paula Modersohn-Becker (1876–1907)
made at least fifty self-portrait images, among them several of her most
significant paintings. It was her letters and journals that first brought her fame
in Germany, published posthumously in 1920; her art was seen as *Selbst-Kunst*,
and as proto-Expressionist. Yet her finest self-portraits, like her work as a whole,
sought to pass 'beyond' the self.

This paradox is central to Rainer Maria Rilke's *Requiem for a Woman
Friend* (1908) – his long poem reproachfully addressing her unquiet ghost,
still haunting him a year after her death. The poet and the painter had shared
a passion for Cézanne's still-life vision, which went beyond 'apples' into a realm
of objectivity. At the same time, Rilke supported her quest for an art that would
embody a specifically feminine view.

> Women too, you saw, were fruits and children moulded
> From inside, into the shapes of their existence.
> And finally you saw even yourself as a fruit, you stepped
> Out of your clothes and brought your naked body
> Before the mirror, you let yourself inside
> Down to your gaze; which stayed in front, immense,
> And didn't say 'That's me', but 'This is'.
> And at last your looking was so objective,
> So free of possessing, and of such true poverty
> That it no longer desired self...

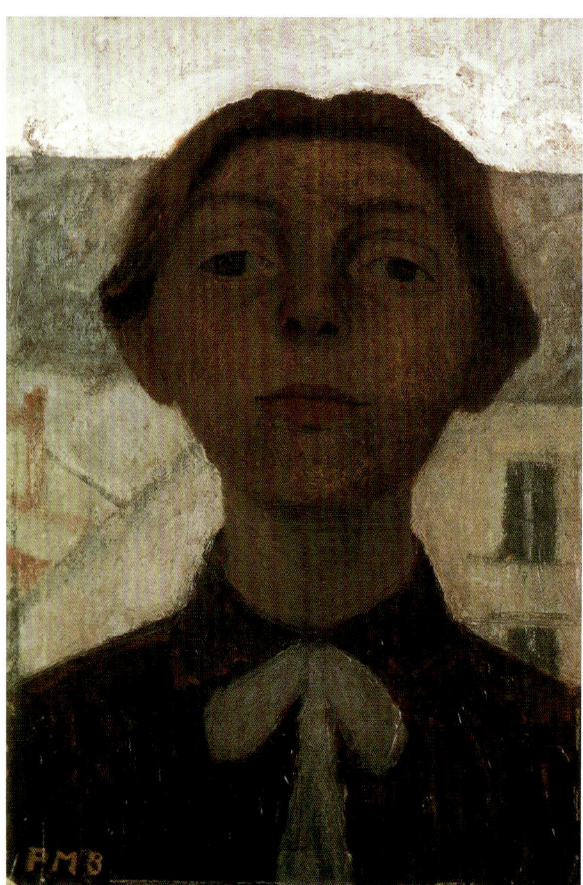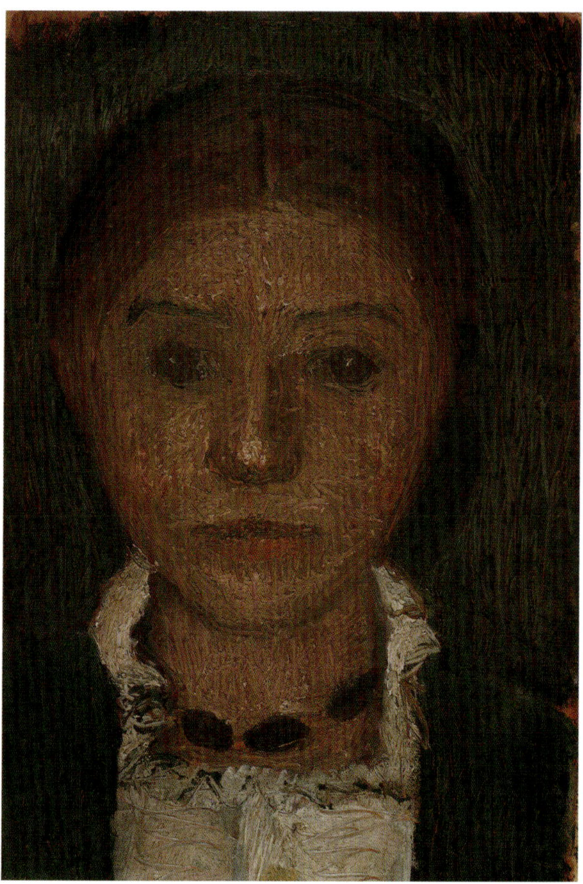

PAULA MODERSOHN-BECKER

Self-Portrait in Paris

1900

Her journal reflects her new freedom: 'I am becoming a woman…and life will be beautiful, wonderful. And I walk along the boulevards, encountering crowds of people, and a voice within me cries out…. Art speaks and wants two more serious, uninterrupted years of work' (13 April 1900).

Paula Becker first set foot in Paris on the first day of 1900. Her small *Self-Portrait in Paris* [illustration above] is painted close-up and *contre-jour*; stylistically remote from any contemporary avant-garde, memorable and original in its ardent self-scrutiny. She came across several Cézanne still-lifes at Vollard's gallery; as she later recalled, this discovery 'affected me like a thunderstorm, like a great event'. By the time Rilke encountered her, later that same year, she'd returned to Worpswede, a north German 'art colony' that combined New Age counter-culture with back-to-the-soil wholesomeness. Although already committed to an older painter, Otto Modersohn, she drew close to the young poet.

In Paula Modersohn-Becker's second long stay in Paris she was excited by the recently rediscovered Fayum mummy portraits at the Louvre – vividly naturalistic heads, from the first and second centuries AD, painted in encaustic, which sometimes requires graving into the waxy impasto with a sharp tool. In her 1903 *Self-Portrait with Necklace* [illustration above] she seems to have emulated that effect in oil with the end of her paintbrush. She wrote in her Paris journal (20 February 1903):

> I must learn to express the gentle vibration of things, their granular surfaces [*das Krause in sich*]. The strange quality of expectation that hovers over mute objects.

**PAULA MODERSOHN-
BECKER**

Self-Portrait with Necklace
1903

In Berlin in 1901, she'd seen
a pioneering exhibition of
Daumier's still scarcely known
paintings. Their radically
unfinished handling helped
liberate her own approach
to painting. Eventually, in
emulation of the wax medium
of the Fayum mummy portraits,
she would sometimes switch
between oil and *wurmsche
tempera farbe* (a specialist
tempera medium), as can be
seen in the matte density
of *Mother and Child*
[illustration p. 122].

**PAULA MODERSOHN-
BECKER**

Standing Nude Self-Portrait
1906

From the surviving nude
photographs of herself (which
one recent writer speculates
may have been taken by Rilke)
the artist was broadly built, with
a rounded belly. It seems likely
that this seldom-reproduced
and exceptionally large picture
is the one referred to in Rilke's
Requiem. After June 1906 the
two friends never met again.

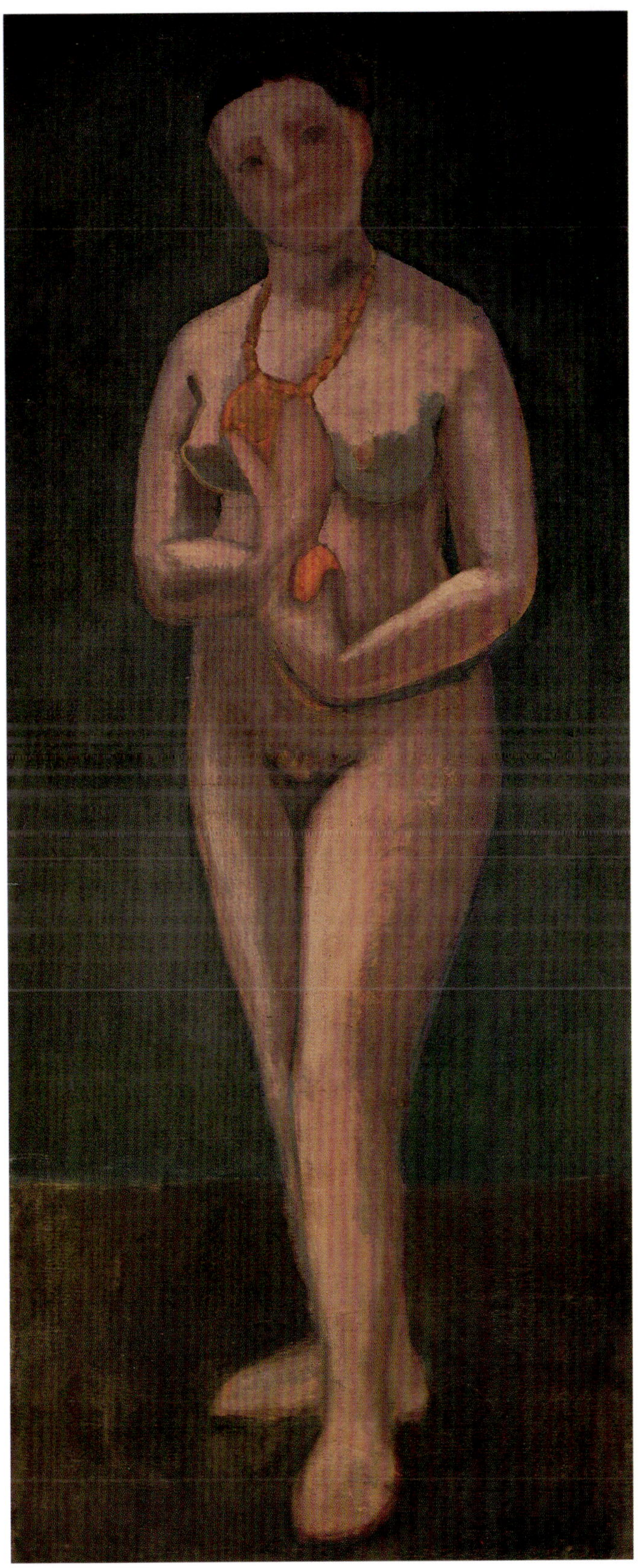

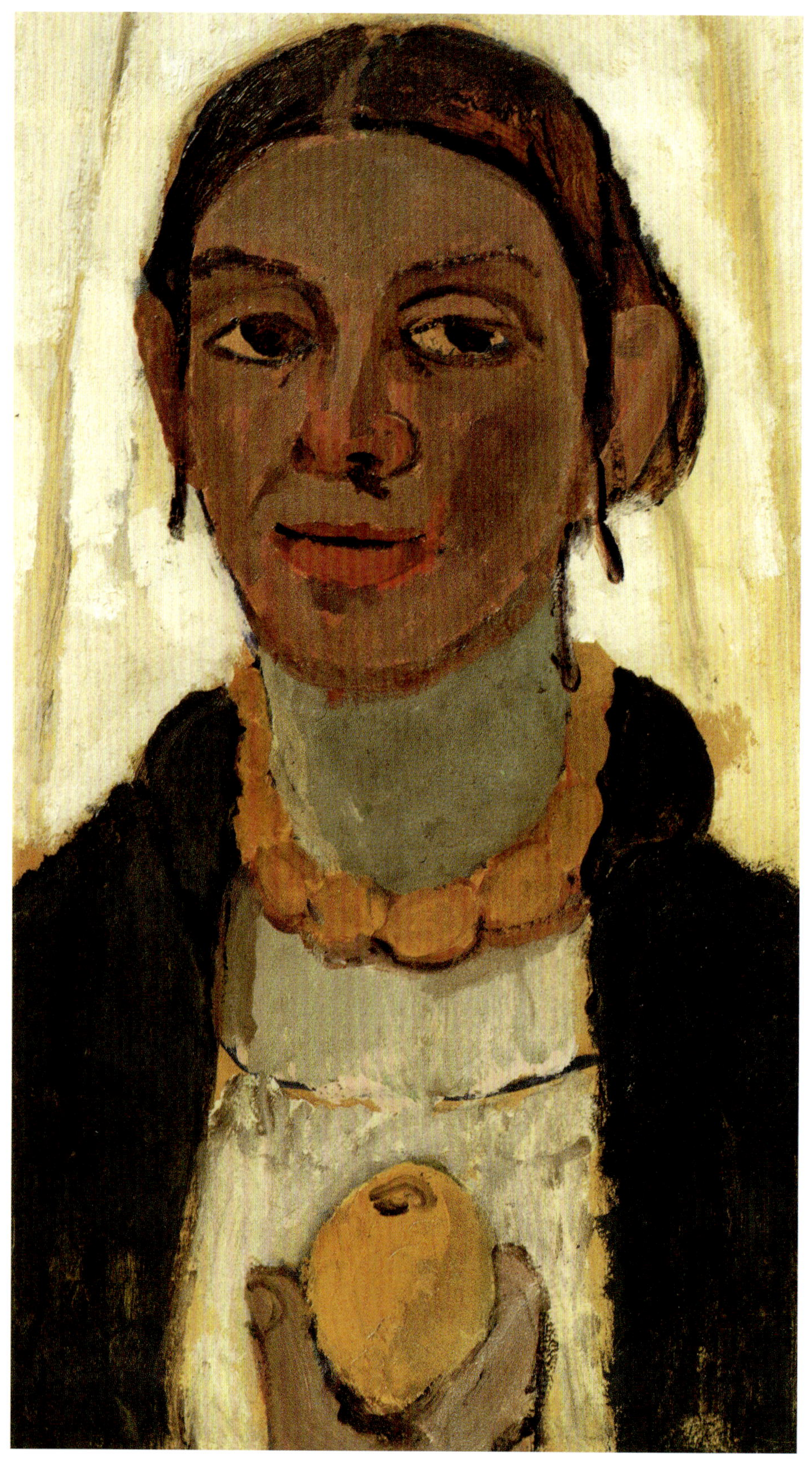

**PAULA MODERSOHN-
BECKER**

Self-Portrait with Lemon
1906

This is one of a sequence of
self-portraits that explicitly
parallels her quest for identity
outside and beyond marriage.
We now know that she both
painted and slept with the
radical sociologist Werner
Sombart (who in the year of
this portrait published *Why
Is There No Socialism in the
United States?*). She wrote
in a letter in May, 'Now that
I'm free, I'm going to make
something of myself.'

Rilke recognized her growing authority, purchasing the powerful *Infant with Mother's Hand* (one of only three pictures sold in her lifetime) and, later, introducing her to Rodin. For Rilke then, as for many writers subsequently, Modersohn-Becker became a kind of emblem of the woman-artist, and beyond that, of some more equal future relation between the sexes. He wrote in his journal (16 July 1903): 'The great renewal of the world will perhaps consist in this, that man and woman, free of all false feelings and reluctances, will seek each other not as opposites, but as brother and sister, and will come together as human beings.' And, Rilke believes, women will prove 'more human' than men: 'carried to term in pain and humiliation, this humanity of women will...become evident, and those men who cannot feel this coming today will end up being surprised and vanquished.'

In 1906 she made the momentous decision to abandon Modersohn. In a key letter of 8 February, Clara Rilke reports a conversation: 'Paula says that for all those five years her husband was not able to perform sexual intercourse.... She believes herself able to bear children – and would still like to.... Her only real desire is: not to be married.' On 17 February, the painter herself wrote to Rilke:

> And now I do not know how to sign my name. I am not Modersohn, neither
> am I Paula Becker any more.
>
> I am
>
> Myself,
>
> And I hope to become myself more and more.

And a week later, in her journal, on the way to Paris: 'Now I have left Otto Modersohn and am standing between my old life and my new life. And what will I be like in my new life? Now it is all about to happen.' It was Rilke, ever supportive of her independence, who met her at the Gare du Nord.

In many of the twenty or more self-portraits she painted over the following months, she is holding a fruit, especially striking in the *Standing Nude Self-Portrait* [illustrations pp. 119, 120]. Although the non-consummation of her marriage often goes unmentioned, it is obviously germane to this whole sequence. The Paris self-portraits are fuelled by her quest for a new identity, not least a freely sexual identity. There are often overtones of Gauguin's Tahitians – the primal woman, stripped of bourgeois convention.

Her two most celebrated paintings both date from this same brief period. *Mother and Child* [illustration p. 122] comes out of a long sequence of beautiful charcoal drawings, and at least one other painting, in which the relation of the unknown model to her baby is subtly varied. In this, the final and largest version, the head is almost lost in darkness, the body's massive bulk rising whale-like above the tiny infant. The heavily impastoed pigment takes on a wonderful fleshy density; any Worpswede stodginess has been transcended in a majestic physicality. This archetypal 'Mother' embodies a modern rediscovery of the archaic or primordial woman – I think also of Carrà's *The House of Love* [illustration p. 28] – closer to the Willendorf Venus (*c.* 28000–25000 BC) than to the early 20th-century bourgeois wife.

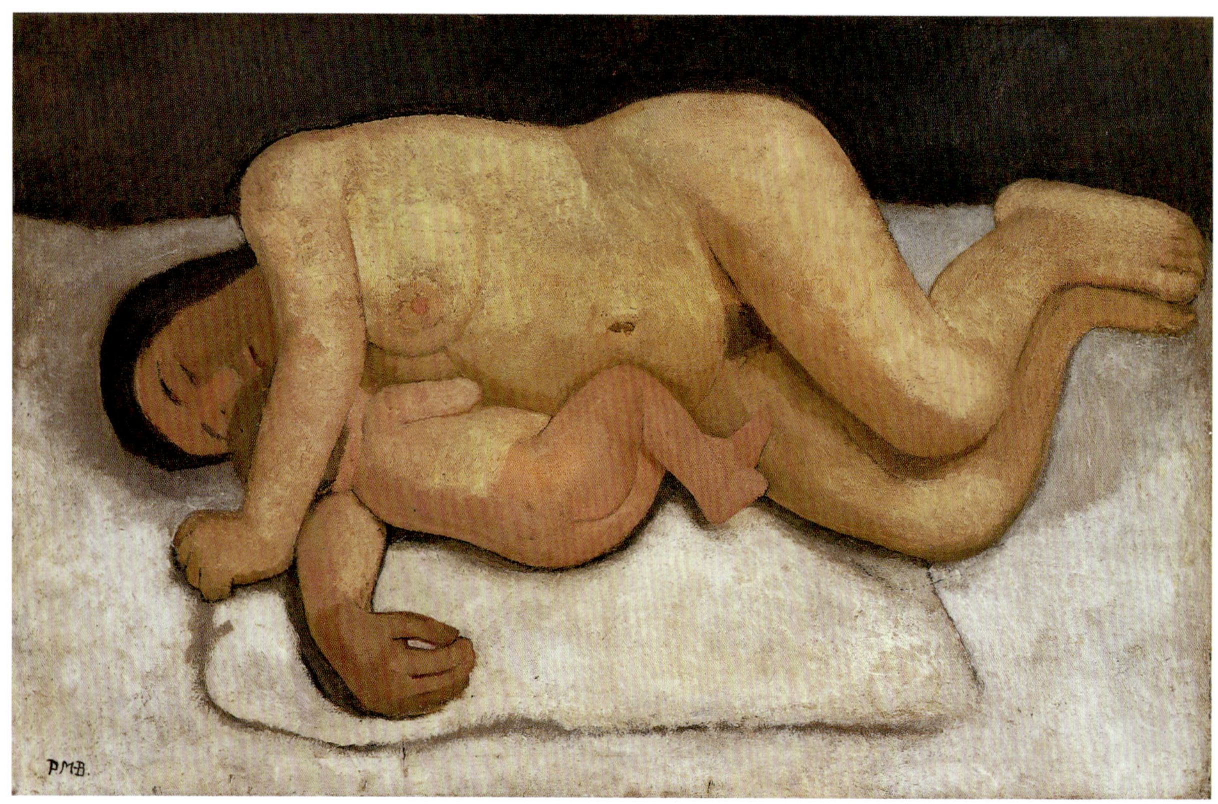

PAULA MODERSOHN-BECKER

Mother and Child

1906

The 'archaic' nude can be viewed in the context of Montparnasse and a general cult of the primitive. It is likely Modersohn-Becker was taken by a mutual friend to visit Henri Rousseau, her neighbour on Avenue du Maine, and she may also have met Picasso, five years her junior and soon to embark on *Les Demoiselles d'Avignon* [see Ch 1 pp. 13–17; illustrations pp. 14, 22].

PAULA MODERSOHN-BECKER

Self-Portrait on My Sixth Wedding Anniversary

1906

Her most explicit manifesto of liberation, this painting is perhaps the best known of Modersohn-Becker's works. Two weeks earlier, on 10 May, she wrote from Paris to her mother: 'Now I am beginning a new life. Don't interfere, just let me be. It is so beautiful. This last week I have been living in ecstasy. I believe I have achieved something good.'

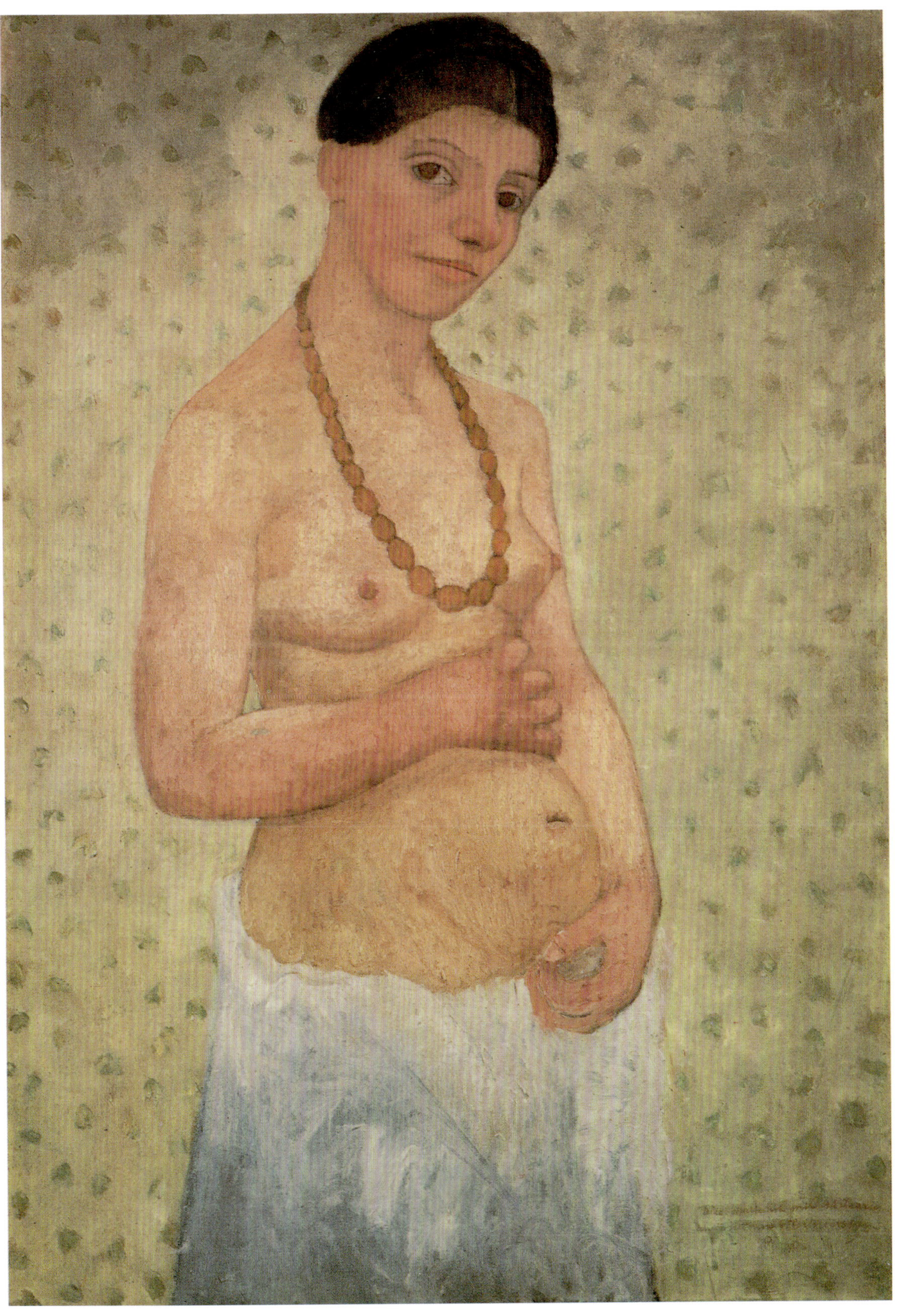

Her best-known self-portrait [illustration p. 123] is explicitly autobiographical and set in a specific moment, inscribed: 'I painted this aged 30 / on my sixth Wedding Day / PB.' Thus, on 25 May 1906, 'PB' turns to the spectator with an almost knowing smile, breasts bared, her hand oddly cupped to the curve of her belly. That empty hand – sometimes seen as charged with sexual, even masturbatory significance – was originally, I suspect, intended to clasp a 'fruit'. Yet the belly is so pronounced that pregnancy is surely implicit – not with a child but with that unborn new self, which must be 'carried to term in pain and humiliation'; her hand is cradling it tenderly.

That September, still in Paris, she wrote pitilessly to Modersohn, demanding a divorce. But a week later, she backed down, eventually returning to Worpswede. In November 1907, two weeks after giving birth to his daughter, she suffered a fatal embolism.

Exhibitions of her roughly five hundred paintings began, both before and after the First World War. But from 1937, Paula Modersohn-Becker was condemned as a 'degenerate' artist. After 1945, as New York's Museum of Modern Art set about defining the twentieth-century canon, her work remained absent from the collection. Only in recent monographs has she come into focus, not only as 'The First Modern Modern Woman Artist', but as a participant in modernity's quest for radical self-realization. And it is in that role that she has sometimes been viewed as precursor of Kirchner and other 'German Expressionists'.

KIRCHNER'S 'HIEROGLYPHIC' STREET SCENES (1913-14)

The nervy calligraphy of Kirchner's best work gives off a charge unlike that of any other twentieth-century painter; he stands or falls by the vibrancy of his brushstroke, the electricity of his drawn mark. There had long been a tradition of the swift line, even in the French Academy – of drawing as a medium responsive to a world that is not fixed. But such notations were not greatly valued; the 'sketch' (whose Latin derivation is 'a poetic improvisation') became synonymous with the preparatory, the superficial, the insubstantial. From about 1907, however, Ernst Ludwig Kirchner (1880–1938) made 'the sign' the basis of his painting. The art historian Pierre Schneider has defined the sign as 'a form that has been made buoyant through simplification...condensed by the swiftness of the draughtsman's hand'. The sign calls attention to the act of drawing, shifting the emphasis away from the object seen, towards the presence of the artist. Much later, as the fictitious French critic, 'L. de Marsalle', Kirchner would write an essay in praise of his own drawing:

> The images are not in themselves representations of definite objects; their significance lies in their placing, their size, their juxtaposition with others on the page. They are *hieroglyphs*, in the sense of reducing natural forms to simplified flat shapes.

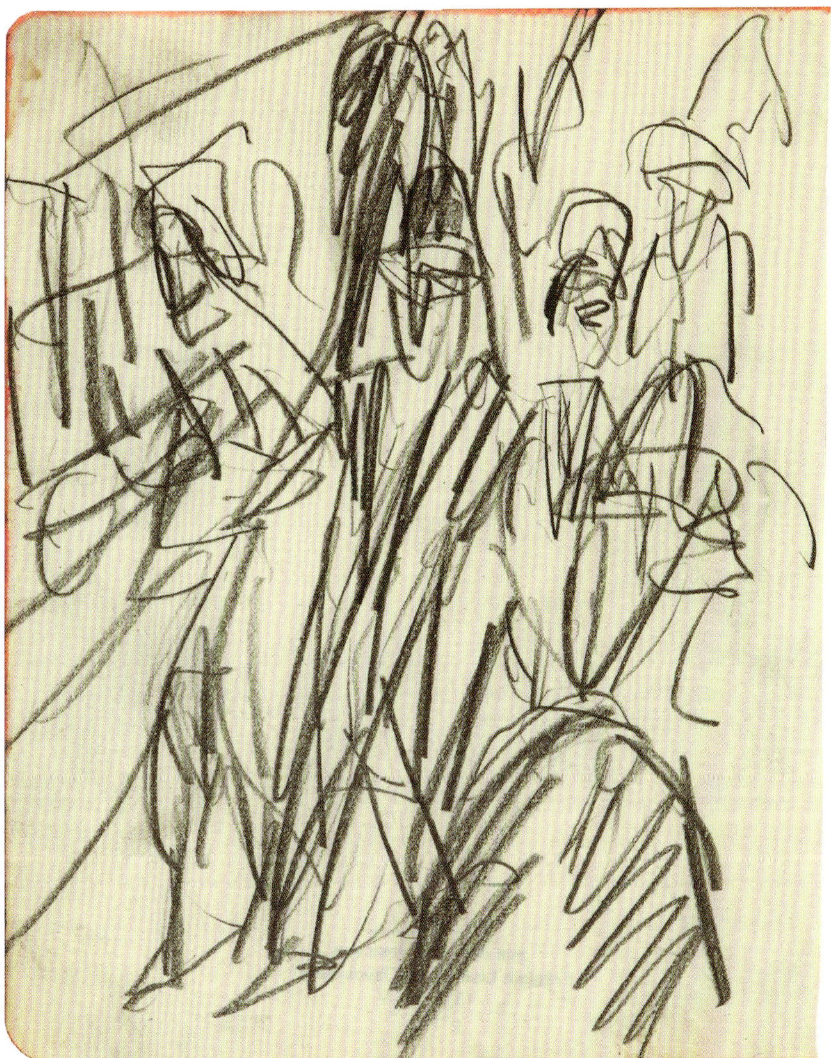

Kirchner had spent four gruelling years qualifying as an architect in Dresden before cutting loose as a painter, alongside a group of fellow students that included Erich Heckel and Karl Schmidt-Rottluff. From 1905, they lived and worked together as a commune under the Nietzchean sign of a bridge to the future, *Die Brücke*. They experienced hardship: as Kirchner would recall, 'the artists of the *Brücke* had nothing but struggle, and the poor people fed me and patched my clothes.' They felt linked to a wider, pan-European fraternity that included Van Gogh, fifty of whose works were shown in Dresden in 1905. Gauguin's search for the primitive became part of the *Brücke* myth, while Munch (see p. 161) and Nolde (Ch 2 pp. 60–61) provided exemplars nearer to hand. At some quite early stage, Kirchner must also have encountered the work of Matisse; for the next few years, his high-voltage colour could be called a Fauvist dialect, though bounded by a much racier outline.

That line implies movement; it has some of the headlong wit of free play, exuberant and celebratory. But around 1911 (coinciding with his move to Berlin, which triggered the dispersal of *Die Brücke*), Kirchner's line altered. Losing the cursive contours of Munch and Matisse, it acquired a spikier edge, with potential for spite, for acid negativity – but also for vertiginous enjoyment.

He begins to draw very rapidly in the thick of the crowd in central Berlin [illustration p. 125], and although he once described his art as 'the life story of a paranoid', the emotion conveyed is as much zest as fear. Drawing here is Kirchner's means of asserting his own presence within the alienating metropolis, not as spectator or moralist, but as participant. His drawings are, in his own words, 'born in the ecstasy of first sight'; his sensations 'set down unmediated'. His imagery moves excitedly across the city, from pencil to ink to pastel, from etching to lithograph to woodcut.

To achieve a painting of equivalent graphic immediacy proved more of a struggle: 'How often have I failed to pull off and consciously complete on canvas that which in the sketch I threw off without effort, in a trance.' In his 1914 masterpiece, *Potsdamer Platz* [illustration opposite], Kirchner's line does create a viable painterly language. Two women stand almost life-size on their grey island – very close, and, at the same time, quite unreachable. On the periphery, tiny male figures set out to cross the enormous gulf; the women tower above us, barbaric deities, angels of death.

This kaleidoscopic vision of the street is not Kirchner's invention; he was aware of the splintered cities of the Futurists, and there may also have been cross-fertilization from his fellow Berliner Ludwig Meidner, whose apocalyptic cityscapes were painted during these same years just before the First World War. Among Kirchner's closest friends was Alfred Döblin, a Jewish neurologist with a prophetic sense of the doomed city, eventually fulfilled in his 1929 novel *Berlin Alexanderplatz*, with its multiple viewpoints and cinematic montage-effects. Yet unlike all of these, Kirchner's conception of the city is not panoramic, and perhaps because his imagery is so closely based on the immediacy of drawing at street level, it retains the haptic feel of first-person experience.

In the 1920s, a new generation in Germany would condemn the pre-war Expressionists: instead of the needed societal critique, their forebears had supplied an art of the Bohemian individual, the effect of which was 'narcotic'. Under Nazism, and even in the reinvented, cleansed Germany post-1945, that view of Kirchner and his contemporaries as *dekadenten* (decadents) persisted. Yet Kirchner's bounding line speaks now with a kind of lucid purity; one might call it his dance, or his song – not a scream or a shout but a new urban self-realization.

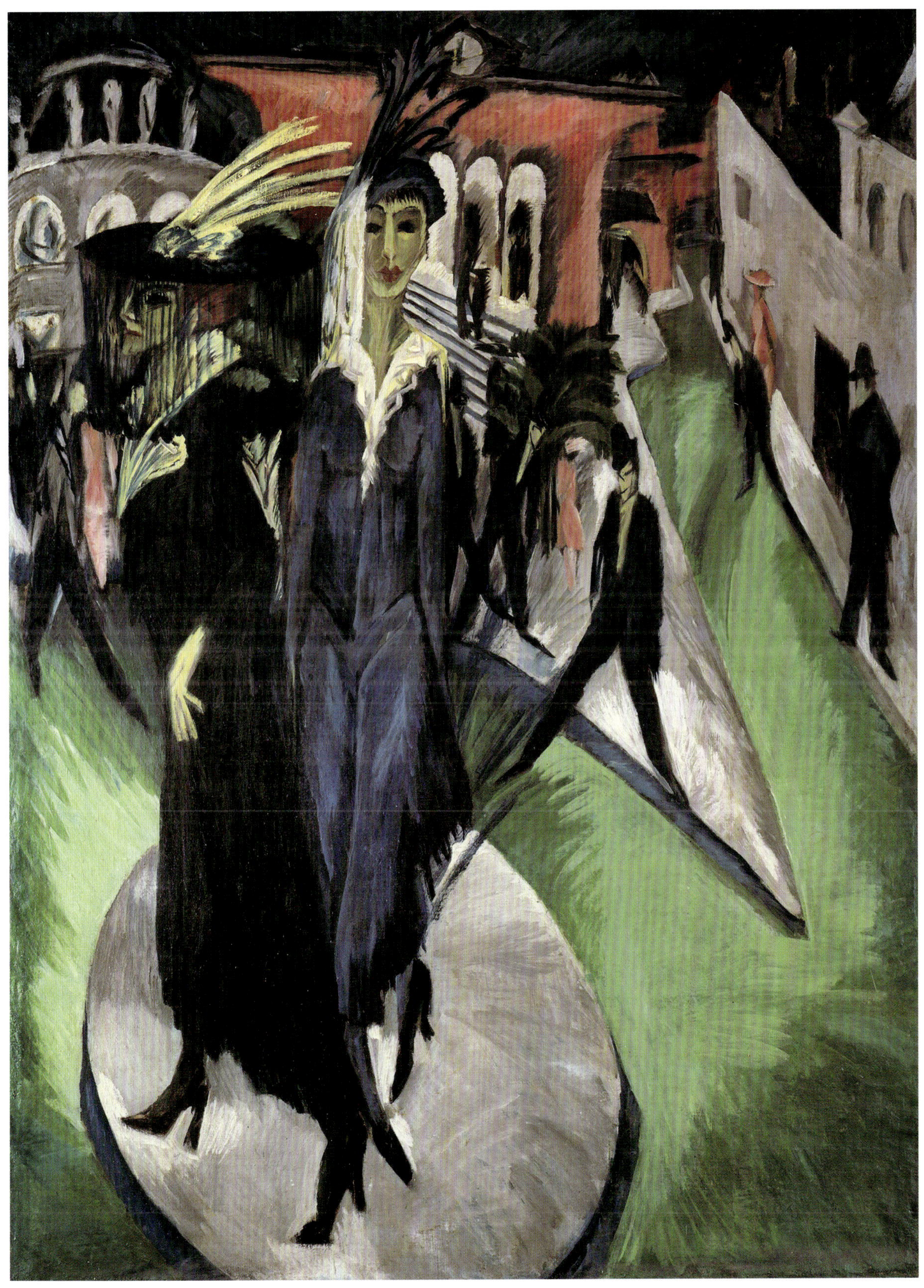

PIERRE BONNARD: A NEW SPACE FOR THE SELF (1924–46)

Painting, or the transcription of the
adventures of the optic nerve

PIERRE BONNARD, 1 February 1934

Like Kirchner, Bonnard developed his own radical procedures of very rapid drawing – accumulating those small sheets on which nearly all his greatest paintings depended. In his later works, Bonnard makes explicit, more than any artist before, the space that extends between the self and the world. He becomes acutely attentive to the mechanics of seeing; those 'adventures' increasingly set in question the conventions through which earlier artists had conveyed our experience of space. Phenomena that had long been observed in the literature of perception (such as the bending lines at the junction of wall and ceiling, or the darkening and striation that occurs on the periphery of the visual field) begin to appear in painting after painting.

Pencil in hand, Bonnard set himself to unlearning the kind of seeing associated with the fixed stare of the art-school life room. After 1916, he'd ceased to use his Kodak camera, which has been described as 'a little Brunelleschi box'; that is, the image restricted to the same forty degrees as one-point linear perspective. He'd become more aware of the disparity between lens and seeing:

> The eye of the painter gives to objects a human value and reproduces
> things as the human eye sees them. And this vision is mutable, and this
> vision is mobile.

To monumentalize the glimpse, to make altarpieces out of the ephemeral; in his later work, Bonnard transfers the terms of an 1890s symbolist quest (the storing-up of aesthetic moments) to the harsher world of twentieth-century modernism – renewing it, and in a sense redeeming it. (That seems to me also true of the writings of, say, Proust and Yeats, Robert Musil and John Cowper Powys: they all explore the epiphany through the medium of the self.)

When Bonnard in so many of his bathroom pictures signals his own presence within the image, he marks out a special territory of feeling. I suppose we are all familiar with seeing a part of ourselves intrude into the visual field: the tip of one's nose, a spectacle-rim, a knee, a hand. In his *Large Blue Nude* (1924) [illustration opposite] Bonnard's pale leg edges in, and a 'nude' is transformed into a relationship; not Artist and Model, but Pierre and Marthe. We now know that throughout much of her life 'Marthe' (Maria Boursin) was afflicted with a mania for cleansing herself. Bonnard had come close to leaving her. But having committed at last to marriage, he moved with her to the south of France, where they became increasingly isolated. As he wrote to his friend Georges Besson in 1930:

PIERRE BONNARD

Large Blue Nude
1924

The left and lower edges are bordered with a pencil-ruled strip: a mirror-frame, a door or simply a compositional device that intensifies the presence of the artist's own leg and hand. After the age of forty, Bonnard never painted directly from life, but only from drawings and memory. 'I like to work always on a piece of unstretched canvas larger than the final image. This gives me room for alteration.'

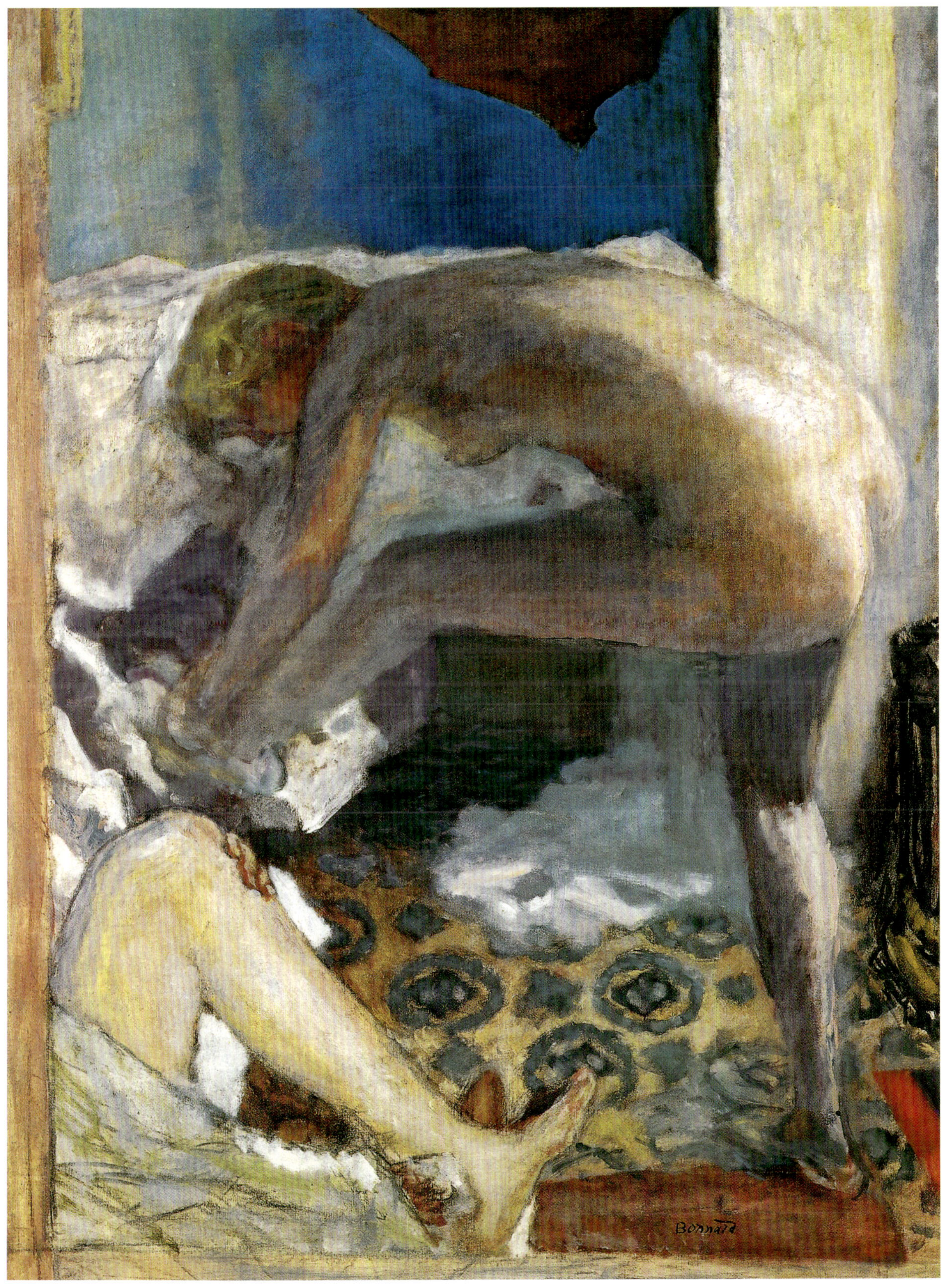

For quite some time now I have been living a very secluded life as Marthe has become completely antisocial and I am obliged to drop all contact with other people. I have hopes though that this state of affairs will change for the better but it is rather painful.

The presence of the self charges everything with subjectivity, with emotional ambiguity and psychological complexity. Bonnard sits, holding his knee, gazing in contemplation – perhaps not so much at Marthe as the dazzling patch of light on her back, rendered in thick impasto. The shadowy blue and purple surrounding this radiant form evokes an underwater world, and Marthe, reaching into darkness, seems more remote than ever.

Bonnard associated the inception of each picture with a sudden involuntary heightening of emotion. 'Consciousness…', he writes, 'the shock of feeling and of memory.' The myopic spectator's gaze drifts through a floating world, until arrested by that sudden seeing/feeling – and that transition, from blur to focus, is an essential component of Bonnard's language. His art, centred on the exceptional moment – on the moment that detaches itself from the flow of everyday living – discovered new constructions of wide-angled space, and astonishing intensities of colour,

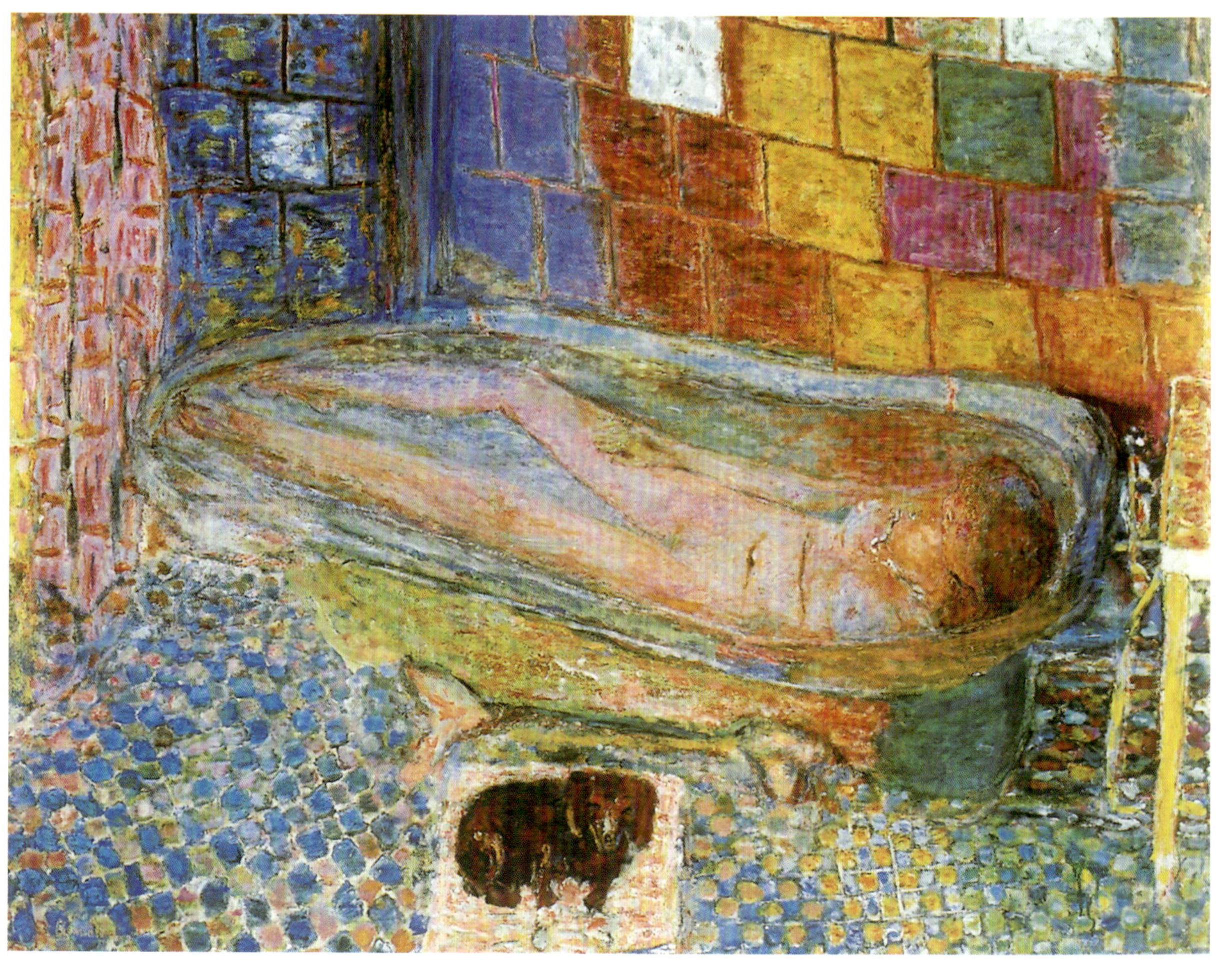

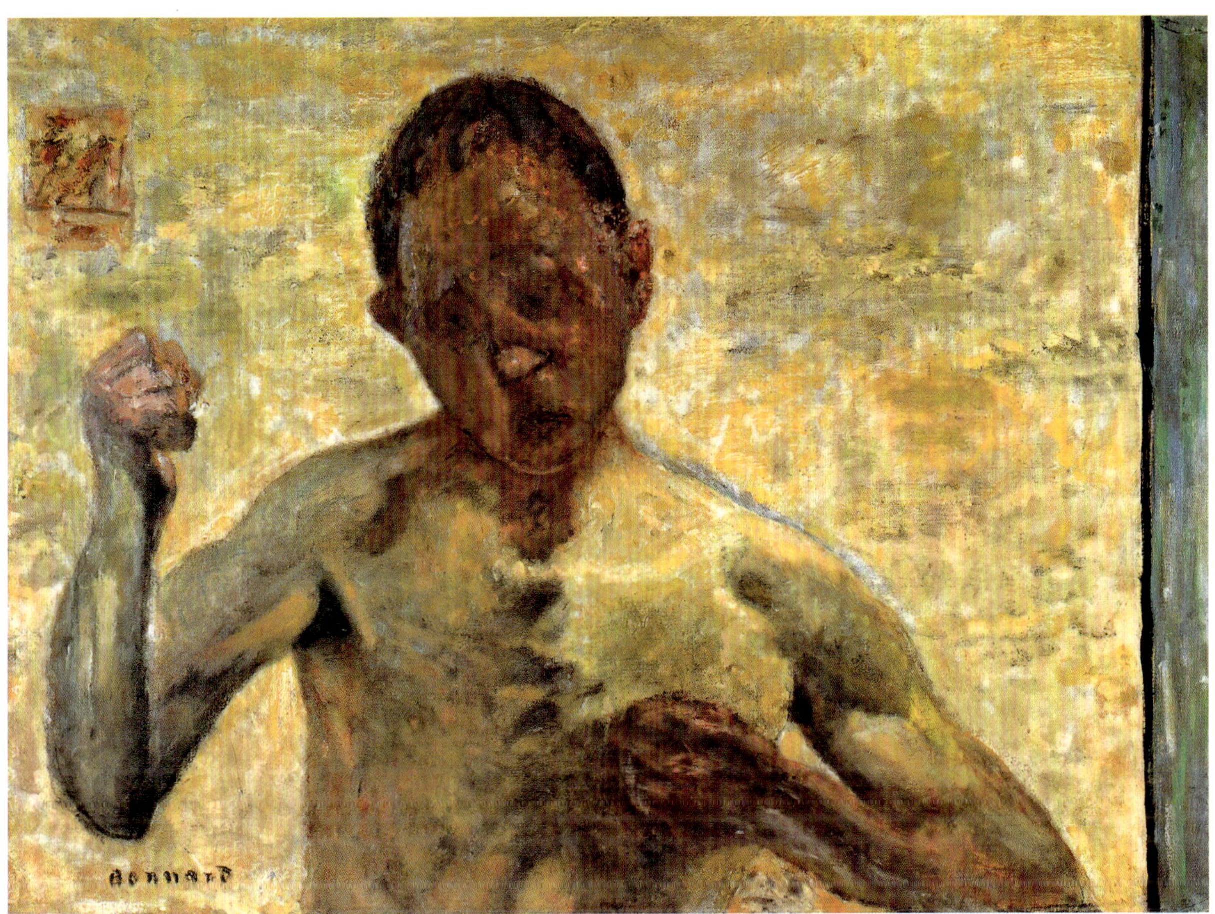

PIERRE BONNARD

The Boxer

1931

A kind of tragicomic clowning is transformed – by the exquisite violet line along the shoulder, by the magically shimmering yellow-and-blue field in which the figure is embedded – into an image of unforeseen beauty.

pictorial equivalents to his startled epiphanies. In the previously uncharted territory of peripheral vision, it was as though the central area of fact were surrounded by much less predictable, almost fabulous margins; where subjectivities – imagination, reverie, memory – could be asserted.

The third and by far the most extreme of Bonnard's large *baignoires* [illustration opposite] was begun two years into the Second World War, in 1941, when Marthe was already in her seventies, and completed in 1946 four years after her death. The stricken woman took her hours-long baths in full sunlight, in the middle of the day. Dazzlingly reflected in tiles and floor, the Riviera sun is shown flooding in from the two windows – those inexplicable shifts of light and hue that seem to stand here for the passing of time, extended in reverie. A pale-tiled, very ordinary bathroom has over several years become utterly transformed, until it wraps the bather in a kind of crazy quilt. Most amazing of all are those passages where the bath narrows, then seemingly exhales and expands, buckling, merging with the vibrating floor; the paint here is crusty, layer upon layer, and the drawn edges of bath and figure just barely defined, by a brush – or a fingertip – dipped in crimson, dragged loosely across the surface. The bath appears a crystalline sarcophagus, in whose light the dead woman becomes transfigured.

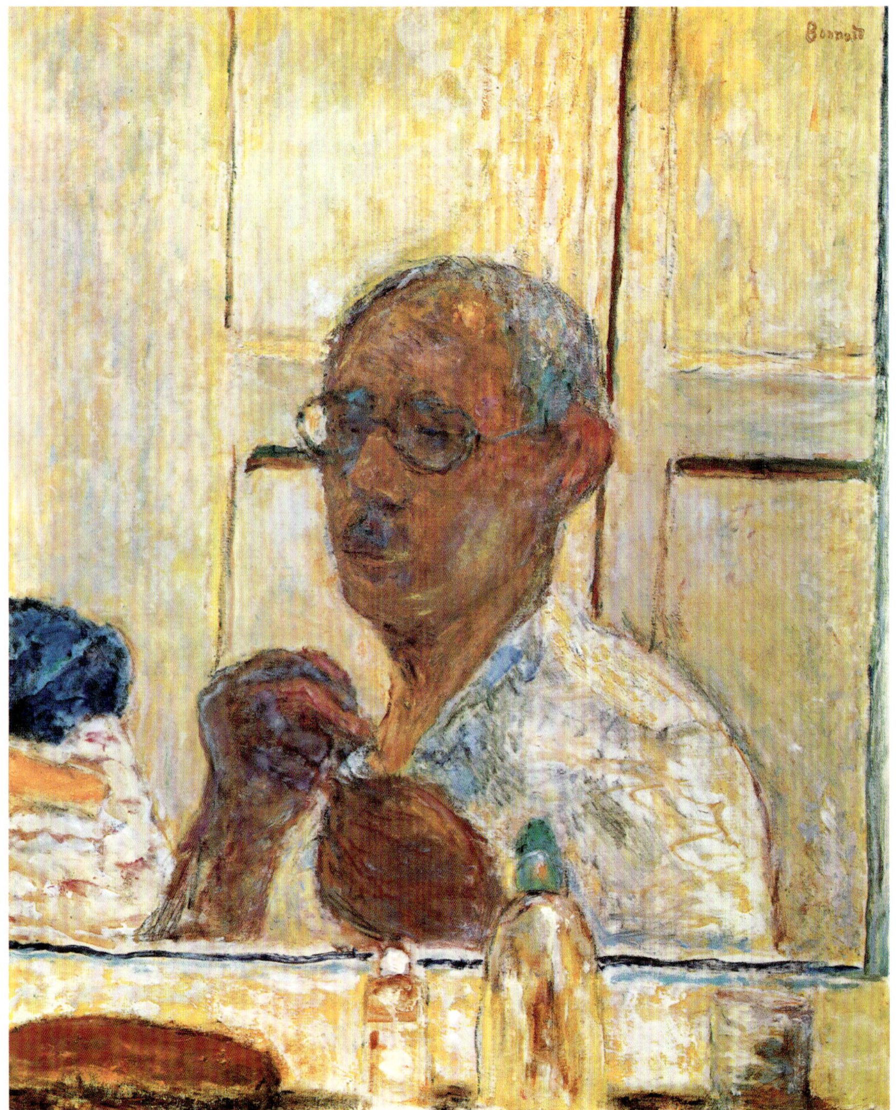

Bonnard's late self-portraits (most of them glimpsed in the bathroom mirror under artificial light) are among the most poignant in all painting – linked formally by their use of *contre-jour*, rendering the self always in shadow. The most disquieting and confessional is *The Boxer* of 1931 [illustration p. 131], squaring up to the mirror with puny fists. From the battered red pulp of the head – a lump of raw meat set atop the naked torso – there emanates a terrible pathos, eyes lowered in impotent defeat.

In a self-portrait completed nearly a decade later [illustration above] the bathroom shelf in the foreground presents a dazzling treasure trove: ruby hairbrush, golden bottle, emerald stopper. The wall behind is a fiery Indian yellow, streaked with orange and pale green. Bonnard's white shoulders retreat into the gold, but the hands are crimson and mauve, silhouetted against the light – and rising from them, the astonishing hot darkness of the head. As our eyes adapt, we make out all the colours that are stored in shadow: the vermillion ear alongside the apple-green

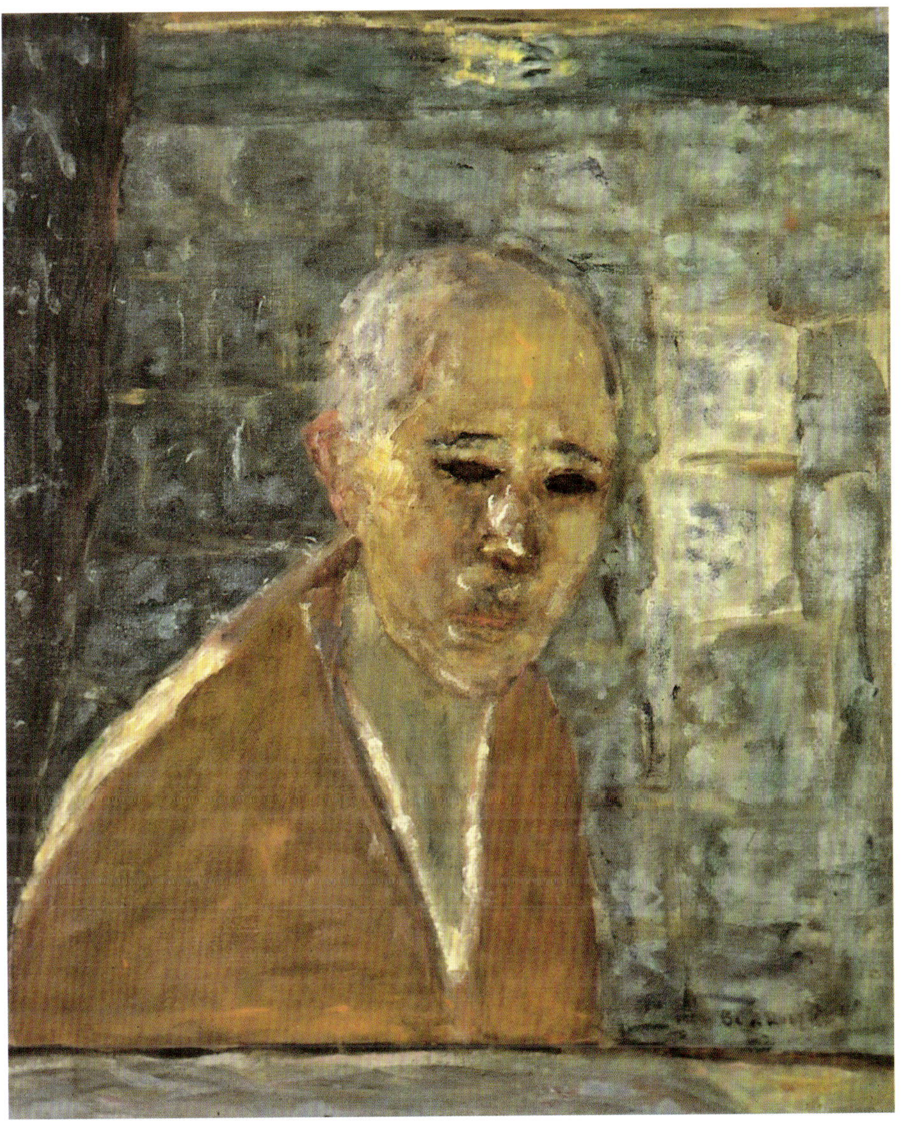

jowl; the bristle of blue eyebrow and moustache; and on the forehead, burning, an impastoed highlight of brightest cadmium yellow. Photographs of Bonnard in his final years make him look strangely Japanese: sometimes a sage; sometimes, as here, the shabby, grief-stricken penitent of Akira Kurosawa's 1952 film *Ikiru*.

His last self-portrait dates from 1945, some eighteen months before his death [illustration above]. The face has become a Noh mask; the eyes, empty greenish-black slits, the darkest notes in the picture. Everywhere, the brush has been supplemented by the artist's fingerprinting, yellow and white, blobs and smears of an unmatched tenderness. The bathroom's tiles are now painted so fluidly we could be in an aquarium. A visionary *dissolving* – a watery, boneless melting of all division – pervades Bonnard's last paintings; as though the fabled Age of Gold really has come round again; and with it a new, more fluid and vulnerable self has come into being.

SOUTINE AND INSTABILITY (1919-22)

I like my brush to slide...

CHAIM SOUTINE

Soutine's *Le Pâtissier* (The Baker's Boy, The Little Pastry Cook, *c.* 1919) [illustration opposite] was the canvas that in 1922 first caught the eye of Dr Barnes, whose subsequent purchase of at least fifty more would change the young painter's life.

The academic training of painters had always tended towards the immobile, the fixed forms of classical statuary. One strand of modernist liberation was a new emphasis on flux, from Van Gogh and Soutine to de Kooning and Baselitz (see Ch 5 pp. 193–97, 214–16). Chaim Soutine (1893–1943) had undergone a conventional academic training in Vilnius, before enrolling at the École des Beaux Arts soon after he arrived in Paris in 1913. He joined the cluster of Yiddish-speaking Litvak painters at *La Ruche* (see Ch 1 pp. 17 and 41), and he probably saw Chagall's wild early canvas, *The Studio*, of 1910, its heaving rhythms oddly anticipatory of his own art. Like Chagall, Soutine was excited by the stretched figures of the newly rediscovered El Greco; and by the instability in Cézanne's paintings, played down by later art historians. D. H. Lawrence wrote of Cézanne in 1929, 'He set the unmoving material world into motion. Walls twitch and slide, chairs bend or rear up a little...'. The earliest Soutine portraits date from 1915, and they show him looking towards Bonnard's quiet, yet off-kilter and subjective, apprehension of the world.

That year the raw, uncouth twenty-two-year-old became protégé and boon-companion to the much older Amedeo Modigliani (1884–1920); in whose own portraits elements of Cubist language combine with El Greco's verticality in brilliantly effective likenesses, suspended between icon and caricature. It was Modigliani's dealer Léopold Zbrowski, a former fellow-student of Soutine at the Beaux Arts, who funded the three years Soutine spent in Céret. The seventy or so surviving landscapes from that episode are often seen as the core of Soutine's work. Far more explicitly than Cézanne, or even Van Gogh, Soutine here 'set the unmoving material world into motion': steepening the region's gentle gradients into pyramidal pile-ups; animating trees and houses, almost as cartoon characters. He painted always directly from life, setting up his easel in the landscape, but employing as many as forty separate brushes, completing the image in a single session. Each became partly about his own motion, his own vitality and ardour.

When painting indoors, he would sometimes, like Bonnard, tack a piece of unstretched canvas straight onto the studio wall. The young *pâtissier* would have been seated to his right, back to that wall, as Soutine plunged to and fro, occasionally peering very close – hence the astonishing invention of that enormous wrenched ear. One sitter recalled the artist in constant motion,

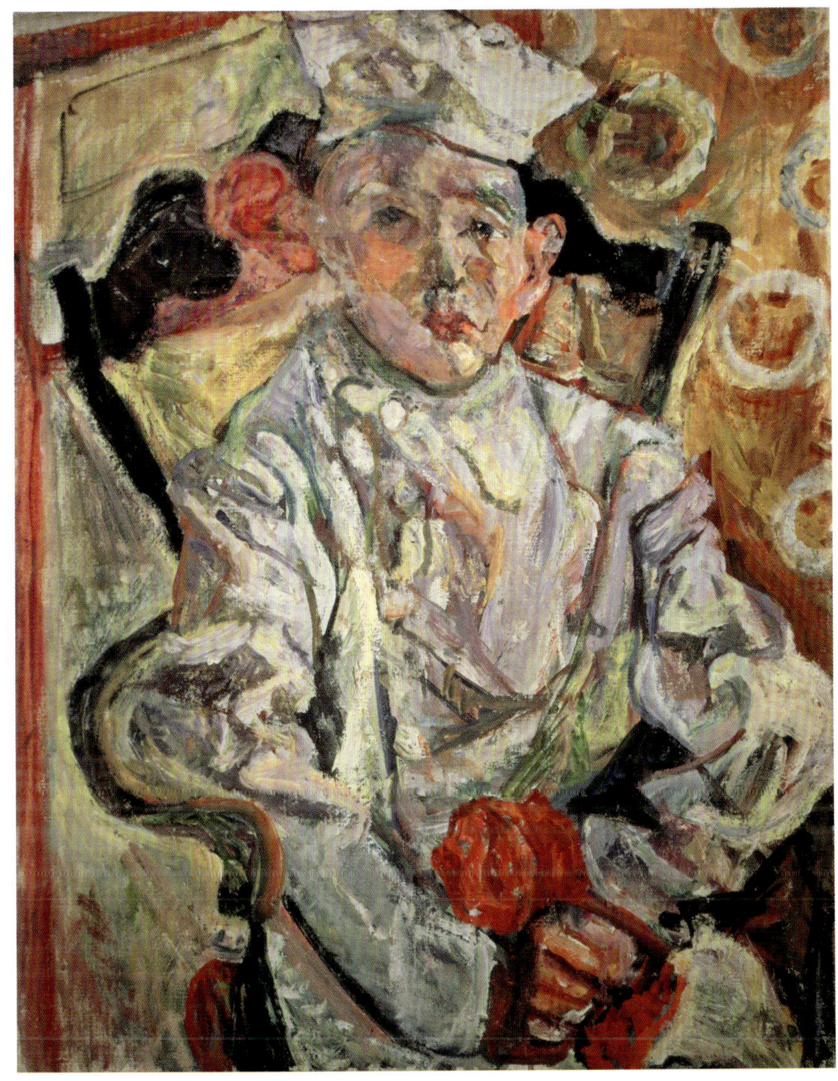

sweating, becoming red in the face. 'He loves his torment,' wrote Drieu la Rochelle of Soutine in 1930. 'But it is a torment'. We read of his passion for wrestling matches; *Le Pâtissier* is no-holds-barred. Without preliminary drawing, he made enormous changes wet-into-wet and that white coat and cap ended up broken into by yellows, purples, greens. The pathos of *Le Pâtissier* comes from the boy's face looking out helplessly from the maelstrom of push-and-pull, a human personality that has slipped its optical moorings, adrift among so many jostling, conflicted perceptions. The circles to the right, the boa-constrictor chair-arm, the zigzag leaping rhythm of chair-back – all reinforce instability.

Soutine's process restricted his scale. Thirty years later, his admirer Willem de Kooning took up the challenge of sustaining that intensity across a much larger surface (see Ch 5 p. 194). Clement Greenberg found himself 'disappointed' by Soutine's pictures: 'They do not stay in place the way paintings should. They do not "sit" decoratively.' There is evidence that the artist himself came to a similar conclusion, whenever possible buying back his Céret landscapes in order to destroy them. By 1930 he was declaring his contempt for Cubism, Van Gogh, Cézanne – all of them 'incapable of giving any joy'.

In Le *Pâtissier* that slithering near-dissolution of the figure does not preclude a magnificently monumental presence. Soutine's agitation and 'morphing' is more viscerally convincing than in equivalent figures by Francis Bacon – less formalized, and less forced (see Ch 1 pp. 54–55). Soutine is making an authentic response, however convulsive, to a specific experience. We have the sense that 'reality' is taking shape before our eyes, and *Le Pâtissier* commands our recognition as a truth about the instability of human identity.

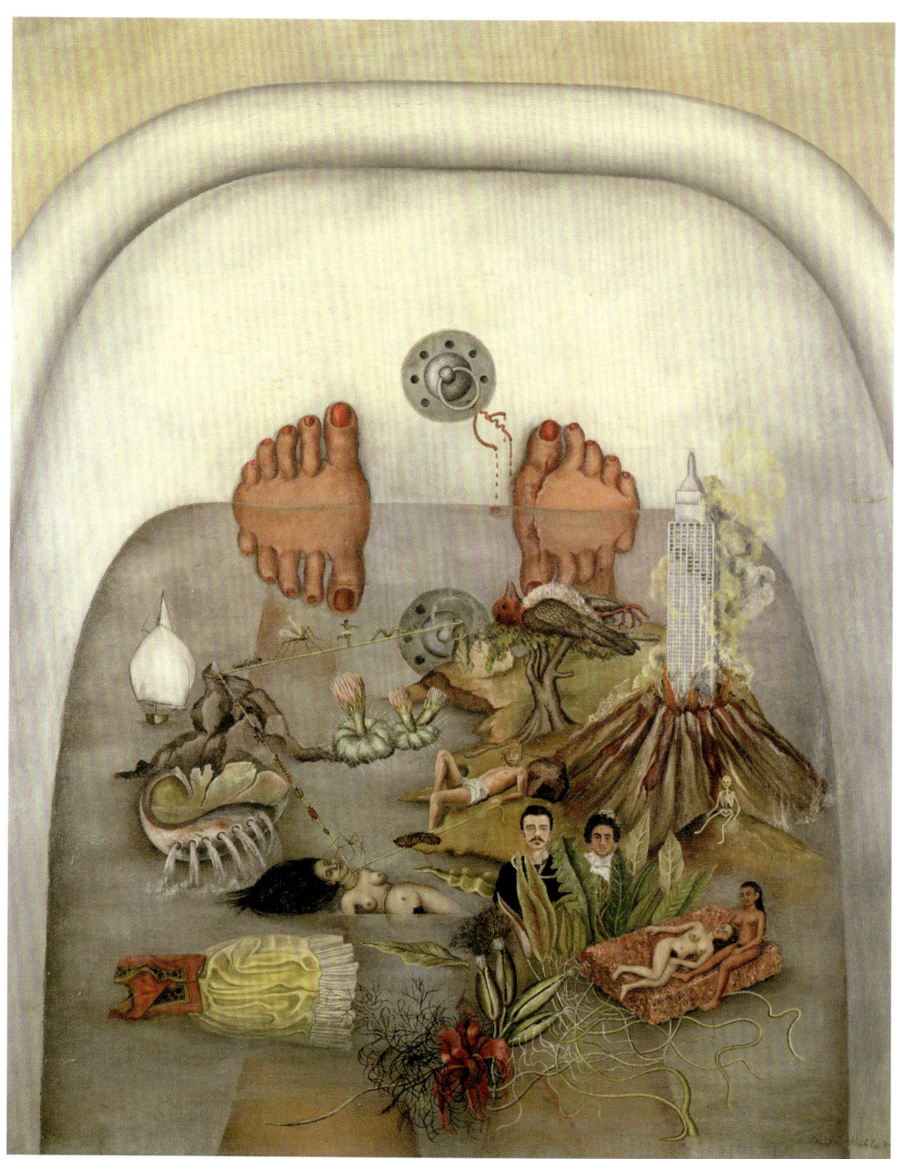

FRIDA KAHLO: *WHAT THE WATER GAVE ME* (1934-38)

*Since my subjects have always been my sensations, my states of mind, and
the profound reactions that life has prompted in me, I have often objectified
all this in figures of myself; which is the most real, most sincere thing I could
do to express what I felt, within and outside myself.*

FRIDA KAHLO, 1939

In her masterpiece [illustration above], Frida Kahlo (1907–54) dissolves her own
body into a complex microcosm – or rather, an archipelago: floating islands of
reverie and reflection, filling the space that extends between her feet at the bath's

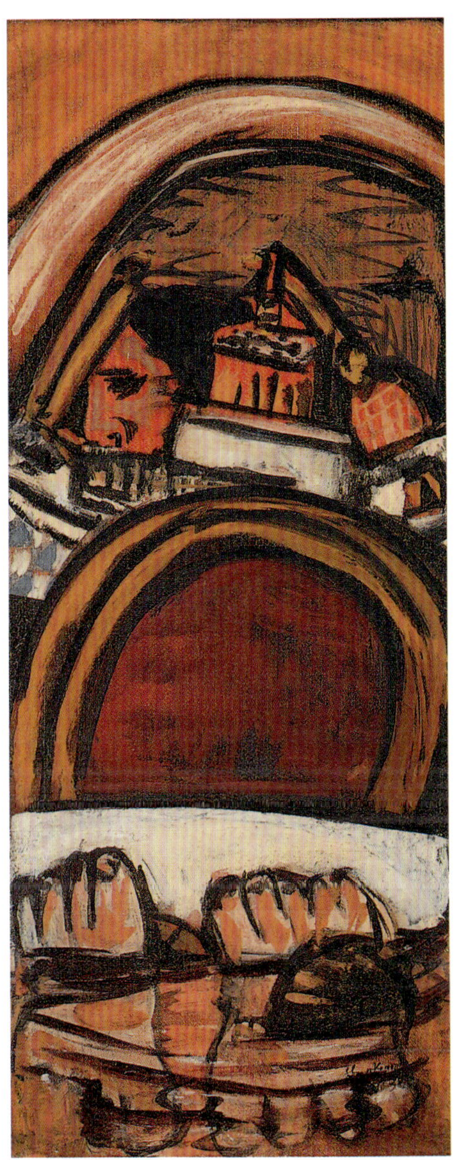

rim, and her unseen self. We are made to enter her world. What this imagery most resembles is the residual flotsam after the floodwaters recede. Her right foot has snagged on the bath-plug's wire, which now drips blood. Yet despite the skeleton, the dead bird in the tree, the drowned, strangled or sleeping nude, and even the skyscraper that rises from the volcano's smoking crater, the overall sense of this miniature world is one of calm rather than catastrophe. We are close to the infant playing with her bath-toys. The tangled fronds that wave in the foreground suggest pubic hair, overlapping dreamily with the floating dress and the divan upon which two naked women – one white, the other brown – are making love. *What the Water Gave Me* was the canvas on Kahlo's easel that so struck André Breton in 1938, visiting her husband, Diego Rivera (see Ch 1 pp. 43–45), and his guest, the Soviet ex-leader Leon Trotsky. It became the centrepiece of her solo exhibition in New York, and of a show organized by Marcel Duchamp in Paris; and it was in front of this image that Kahlo asked her New York dealer, Julien Levy, 'Where is the I?'

What the Water Gave Me was first conceived in the crisis of 1934 when Kahlo learned, after five years of marriage, that Rivera was sexually involved with her sister, eventually triggering a sequence of separation, divorce and remarriage. Kahlo's extramarital love affairs, with both men and women, culminated in her passion for the Hungarian-American photographer Nickolas Muray, who paid four hundred dollars for the picture in 1939. Muray's famous colour portraits of the artist would become central to the 'Kahlo-Cult'.

I want here to juxtapose *What the Water Gave Me* with Max Beckmann's *Feet in the Bath* [illustration left] where the reverie is reversed; feet and reflection at the base, so that one is made to move upward, beyond the bath's rim, to a wider circle – a human profile imbedded within a kind of city panorama (which could also be a perfume-atomizer). Begun in 1931, but completed only in 1950, Beckmann's little picture starts from solipsism but looks beyond to the larger world; Kahlo finds the world more explicitly within herself, however broken that self may be. 'I am disintegration', she would write in 1944.

She had begun to paint in her late teens, after a near-fatal bus accident. (A metal bar pierced her hip, exiting through her uterus.) Her right foot had been damaged by childhood polio; toes were amputated in 1934, and, eventually, the entire foot. Her finest early paintings were very simple metaphoric self-images – *My Birth* (1932), *My Nurse and I* and *The Dress of Memory* (both 1937) – on small pieces of metal, emulating the anonymous local retablos she collected. But when she transfers that magic realist precision to canvas, in the far more diffuse imagery of *What the Water Gave Me*, the effect is close to hallucination. Kahlo turned to both drugs and alcohol after the crisis of 1934, recalling in a letter of 1938, 'I drank to drown my sorrows, but the little devils learnt to swim.'

In 1938 Breton, Trotsky and Rivera were co-signatories to a manifesto that sought to bring together Surrealism and revolution.

> We believe that the supreme task of art in our epoch is to take part actively and consciously in the preparation of the revolution. But the artist cannot serve the struggle for freedom unless he subjectively assimilates its social content, unless he feels in his very nerves its meaning and drama and freely seeks to give his own inner world incarnation in his art.

Despite that insistent 'he', it was Frida Kahlo, not Rivera, who was 'giving incarnation' to a radically new, complex and shifting configuration of identity. Looking back on her pictures, Kahlo mused, 'They have a message of pain in them…. But they're not revolutionary, so why do I keep on believing they're combative?' The feminist slogan 'The personal is political' has rightly been invoked for Kahlo. In her total of 140 paintings, at least sixty are self-images. Her repeated head-and-shoulders self-portraits of the 1940s could sometimes become mechanical; the reality of her art was internal. Rivera pronounced her 'the only painter in the history of art to tear open her chest and heart to reveal the truth of her biological feelings', but it was her wit and lucidity that rendered *What the Water Gave Me* truly revelatory.

STANLEY SPENCER: THE SACRED SELF AND THE *CHURCH OF ME* (1937–59)

solemnizing and celebrating…by taking solid chunks of my own life and putting it on canvas. I like my own life so much that I would like to cover every empty space on a wall with it.

STANLEY SPENCER, 1922

Stanley Spencer thus defined his paintings; the experiences he went on to depict at Burghclere the Sandham Memorial Chapel (see Ch 2 pp. 85–86) were autobiographical, yet nowhere on those crowded walls did he represent himself. Only in the mid-1930s, in the 'naked portraits' of himself with Patricia (see Ch 2 p. 92) did his art turn decisively towards the first person. But a second mural project was already taking shape: his imaginary *Church House*, which he sometimes referred to as 'The Church of Me'. In this ever-expanding 'Forest of Rooms', his personal autobiography could be set within a religious context and painting's sacred function could be reclaimed within a domestic setting.

In the winter of 1937, with his marriages to Hilda Carline and Patricia Preece both having collapsed, Spencer found himself alone, and gave himself up to a prolonged meditation and fantasy about relations between 'husbands and wives'. His *Beatitudes of Love* were conceived as part of the *Church House*: the spectator would encounter each couple in 'cubicles about bathroom size'. Each is a praise-image for the existence of love. In *Toasting* [illustration p. 140] he relives a lost era of intimacy and fire-lit cosiness – a memory of those occasions when Hilda and Stanley would strip and continue their everyday lives in naked companionship. Hilda towers above the little self-figure (a kind of shrivelled child). In striking contrast to the naturalistic Thingness of his *Leg of Mutton Nude* [illustration p. 90] painted just a few months before, Spencer here reconfigures the body expressively, as in Hilda's weirdly extended neck. We are brought much closer to those Gothic figures he'd seen in Germany in 1922 (see Ch 2 p. 87); but they also seem akin to 'low art' genres, such as children's book illustrations, or even end-of-pier postcards.

The couple in *Consciousness* [illustration p. 141] are wilfully, monstrously repellent. She is bespectacled, her mouth all gristle and teeth; he strains his scraggy neck towards her, desperate in his open-mouthed need. (In the preparatory drawing, their tongues stick out and meet.) When Lucas Cranach in the 1520s or James Gillray at the turn of the nineteenth century depicts an 'Ill-Matched Couple', we share their laughter; but these two are made for one another, and any potential mockery dries in our throats. And so we are made to feel the force of Spencer's vision: that human love is most truly mediated not through beauty, but through the grotesque. Ugliness, awkwardness, gaucheness – in the *Beatitudes*, these become almost a value. In an accompanying text he declares:

> It would be better and truer to say 'Spencer likes degenerate and deformed-
> looking people', than to impute me with sniggering and laughing derisively....
> These people, every one of them, are the beloved of my imaginings.

'Degenerate' may be a significant word here. In 1937–38 Spencer was aware of the 'Degenerate Art' exhibition in Nazi Germany, through his brother-in-law Richard Carline's work for the Artists' International Association; it mounted the exhibition 'Twentieth Century German Art' in London as a riposte (see Ch 2 p. 109). In parallel with the *Beatitudes*, Spencer conceived a much larger apocalyptic cycle, intended for the nave of his *Church House*; the denizens of Cookham led by Franciscan disciples to a public love-making, centred on the village war memorial. In this vein, Spencer is neither Late Romantic nor neo-primitive, but can be located in a far more disruptive tradition of English 'dissenters' – antinomians, Blakean prophets, purveyors of home-baked mythologies.

Spencer's redemptive vision was, at core, sexual. In Munich he'd purchased a book on Indian sculpture, including the temples of Khajuraho, encrusted with love-making groups; as Spencer intuitively understood, the total effect is not licentious, but rather, a celebration of the multifariousness of love. Now he reimagined Cookham, in his own phrase, 'assembled in sexuality', swept up in a universal love that extends to plants and animals. *Sunflower and Dog Worship* [illustration p. 142] depicts a husband who rises in ecstatic flower-fusion, and 'holds his wife's bag so she can do it better' – clasping a leaf to her breast as she plunges her face into the flower's yellow crown. Elsewhere in the garden, reaching

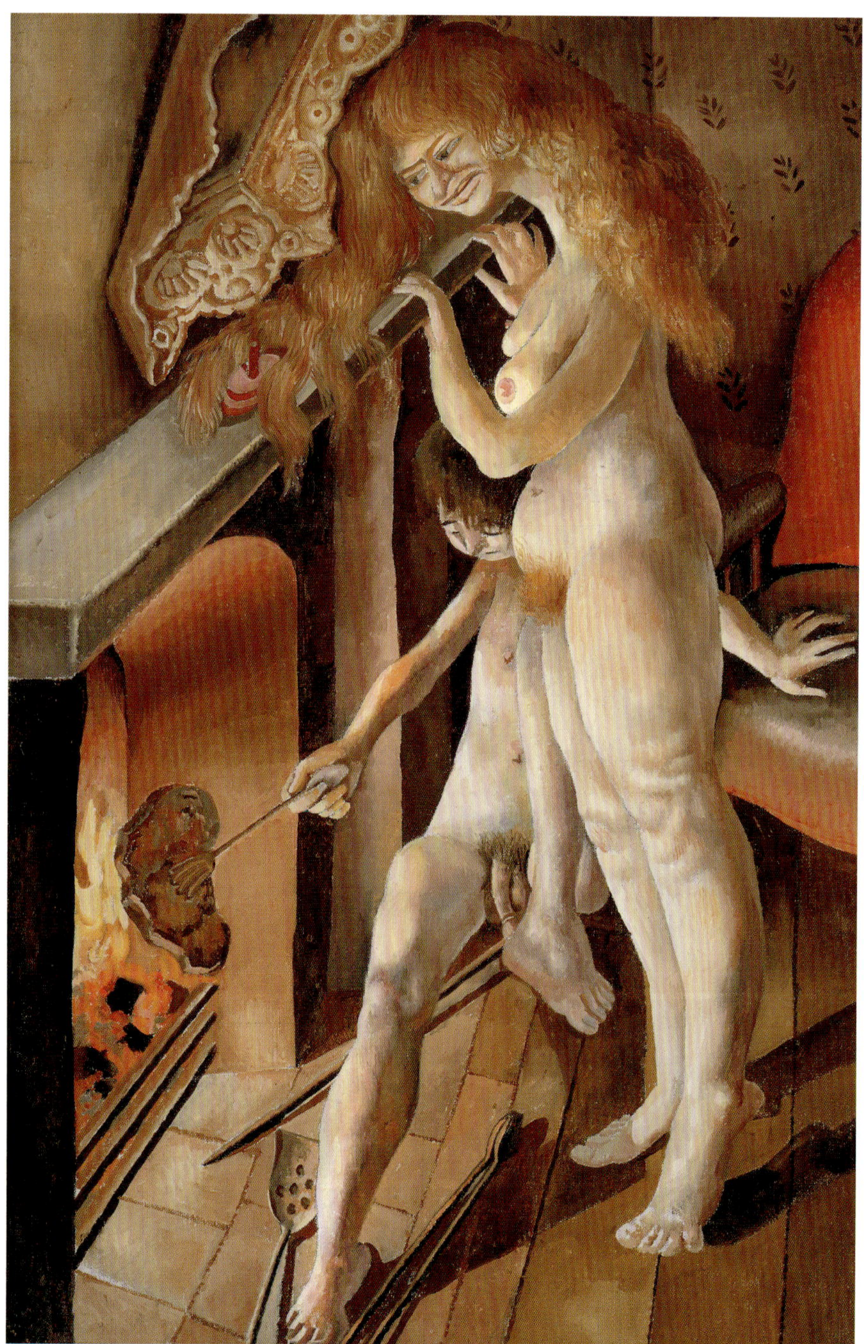

STANLEY SPENCER

The Beatitudes of Love:
Toasting
1937–38

Hilda towers above the little
self-figure, who becomes
a kind of shrivelled child;
the fire illuminates his genitals
and her flame of red pubic hair.
'Being naked,' wrote Spencer,
'helps them in the realization
that the species called civilized
conventional beings is different
from the species husband
and wife.'

STANLEY SPENCER

The Beatitudes of Love:
Consciousness
c. 1938

Spencer wrote of his
Beatitudes: 'These people are
all me, really…. Only I make it
other people as much as I can.'

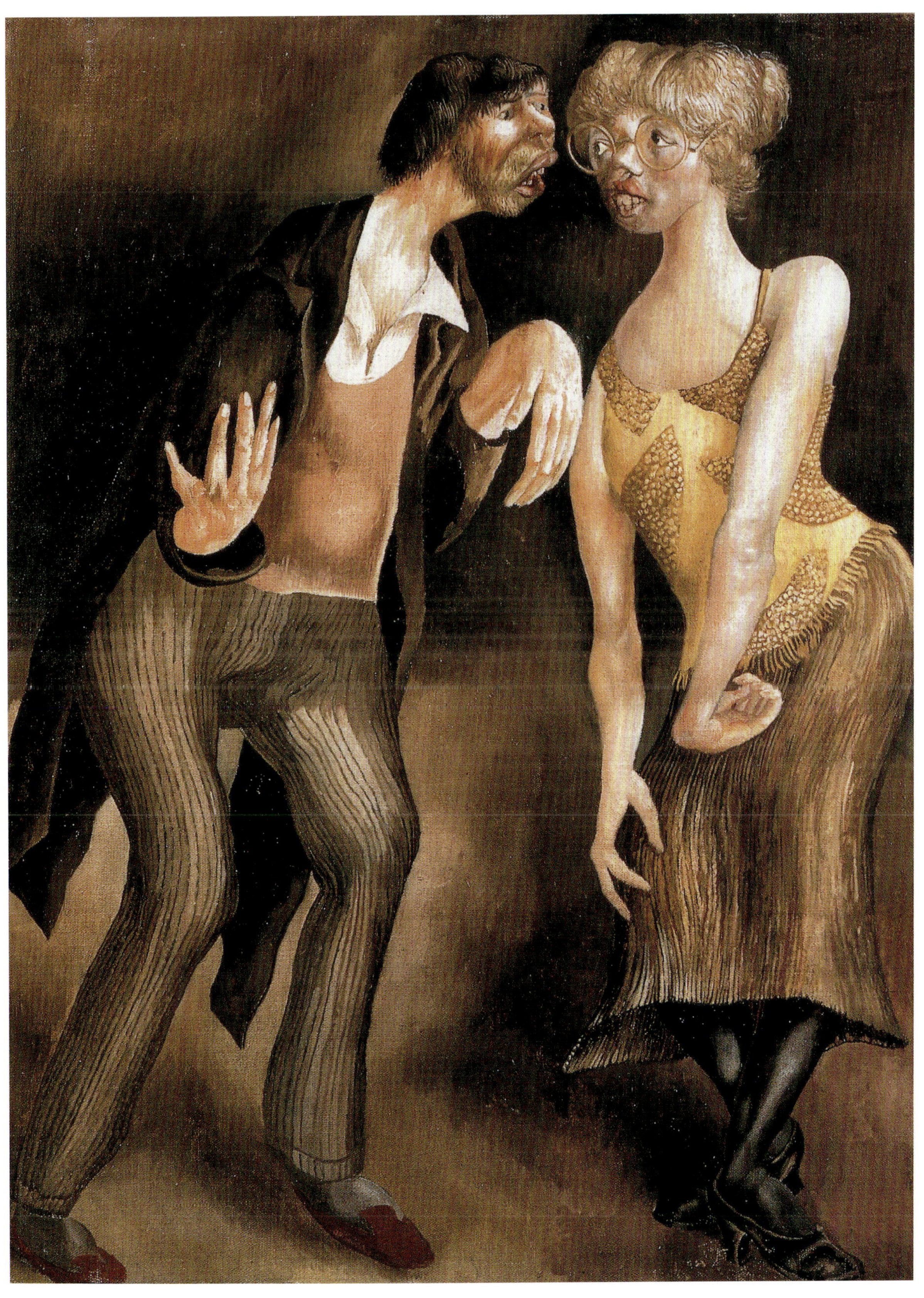

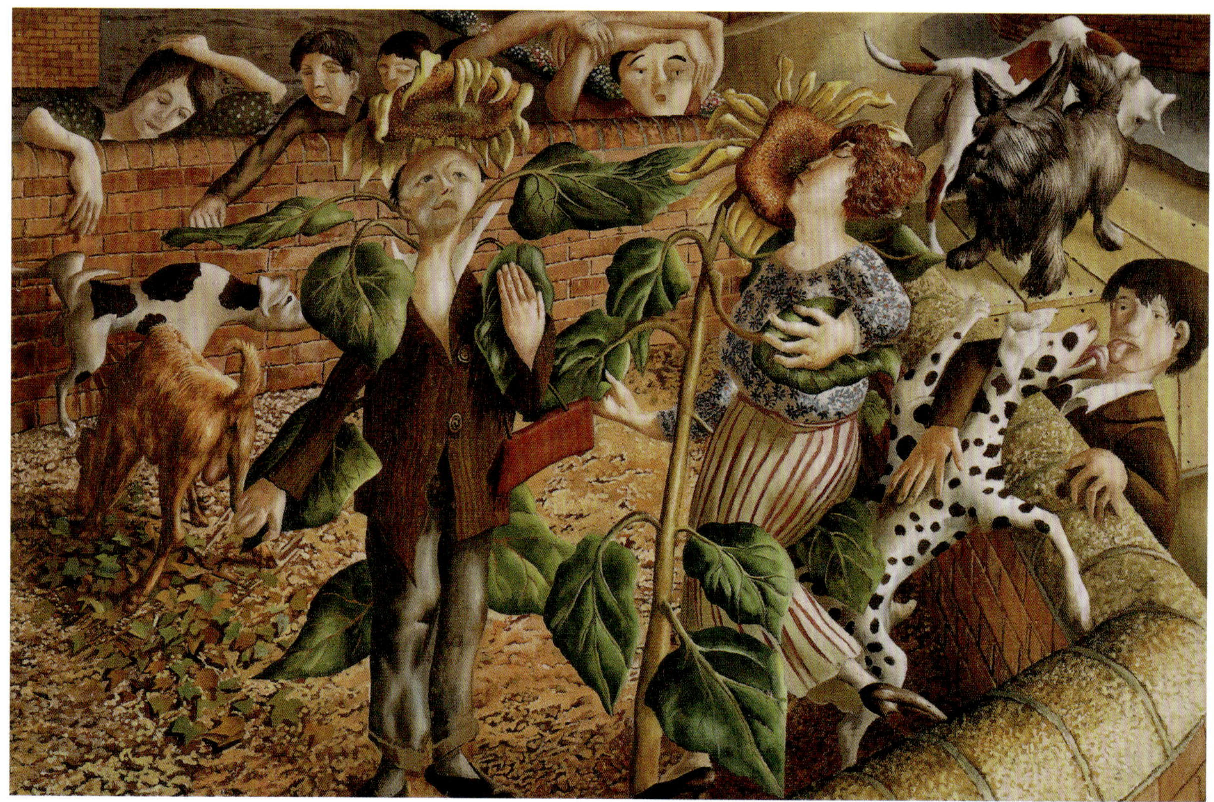

STANLEY SPENCER

Sunflower and Dog Worship
1937

An extreme episode from
Spencer's *Last Day* cycle, the
transformation of a village
garden party into a universal
love-in. As he recalled: 'During
the war, when I contemplated
the horror of my life and the
lives of those around me, I felt
that the only way to end the
ghastly experience would be
if everyone suddenly decided
to indulge in every degree and
form of sexual love, carnal love,
bestiality, anything you like to
call it.'

across the brick walls, the pissing dog is adored, and an excited Dalmatian leaps up erect to lick the outstretched human tongue. In the *Church House*, the liberating power of sex goes far beyond Cookham. *Love Among the Nations* moves along its nine-foot length between the Near East, Africa and China; in Spencer's words, 'There is a girl adoring a negro's toes and an English woman in ecstasy as she feels a Turk's cheek.'

All this could be dismissed as mere puerile folly. Spencer often speaks to us in the language of arrested development, his childish self-absorbtion essential to his silly-profundity. 'I love myself', he wrote to Hilda 'in much the same way as a baby loves a tin soldier.' But the carnivalesque imagery of the *Last Day* cycle brings to mind Mikhail Bakhtin's vindication of the comic–grotesque as a counter-culture 'disclosing the potentiality of an entirely different world…. It always represents in one form or another, the return of Saturn's Golden Age upon Earth – the living possibility of its return' (see Ch 1 pp. 33–41). In 1938 Spencer's exuberant figuration – impure, ignoble – challenged the styles enforced by dictators, both the pseudo-classicism of the Third Reich, and the debased academic realism of Soviet Russia. (Spencer's *Church of Me* could be seen as kin to another continually evolving monument of anti-authoritarian solipsism – Kurt Schwitters's lost Hanover *Merzbau*, 1923–37.) By the end of the 1930s, the *Church House* had become an amorphous structure, in which many imagined compartments could accommodate Spencer's multiple identities and stylistic contradictions; and, in bringing all together, could rebuild the shattered self.

The *Church House* may be best understood alongside those other post-1918 mural initiatives – in France and Italy, Mexico, India and the USA – all of them looking to early Italian fresco painting as model for a reformed relation between the artist and society. Richard Carline visited the United States in 1928, keeping his brother-in-law up to date on Thomas Hart Benton and, later, on the WPA projects (see Ch 2 p. 104). Spencer had read about Diego Rivera, who shared so much of his own aesthetic of crowding, in the magazine *The Studio*, as early as 1927. With the outbreak of the Second World War he would make his most Rivera-esque imagery, as an official war artist attached to the Clyde shipbuilding yards in Scotland.

The first drawing for the masterpiece of all Spencer's post- 1945 paintings, *Love Letters* [illustration below], appears in an actual letter to Hilda of 1930. In 1942 she suffered a mental breakdown; Spencer often visited her at the asylum, and the exchange and reading of one another's letters became their central ritual, a consolation for the impossibility of physical love-making. When in 1950 he at last set brush to canvas, *Love Letters* had complex overtones. He knew Hilda was dying of cancer, and the painting became emblem of all they'd experienced together – a return to childhood, with Stanley and Hilda together at play, dwarfed within the 'cosiness' of a huge upholstered armchair. By that time, his writing held as much

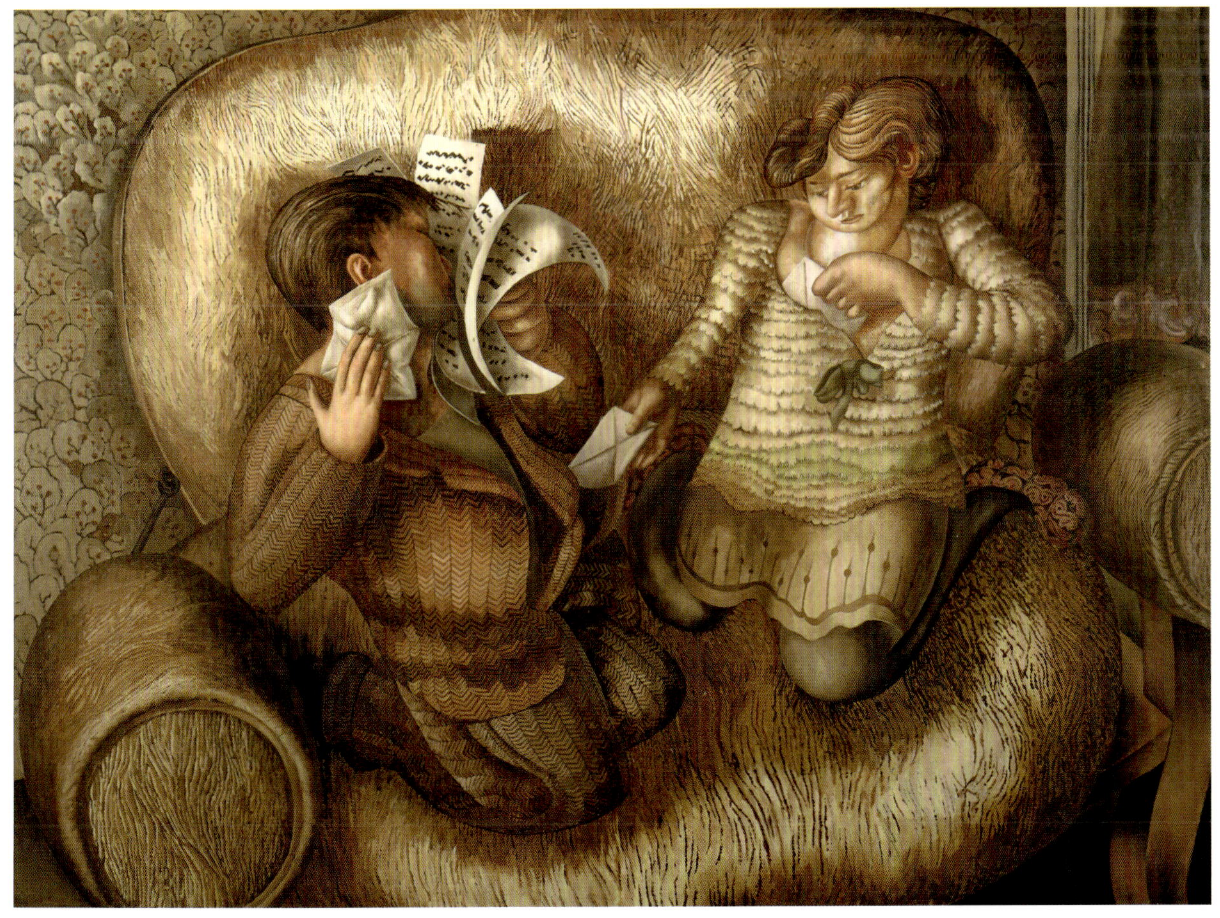

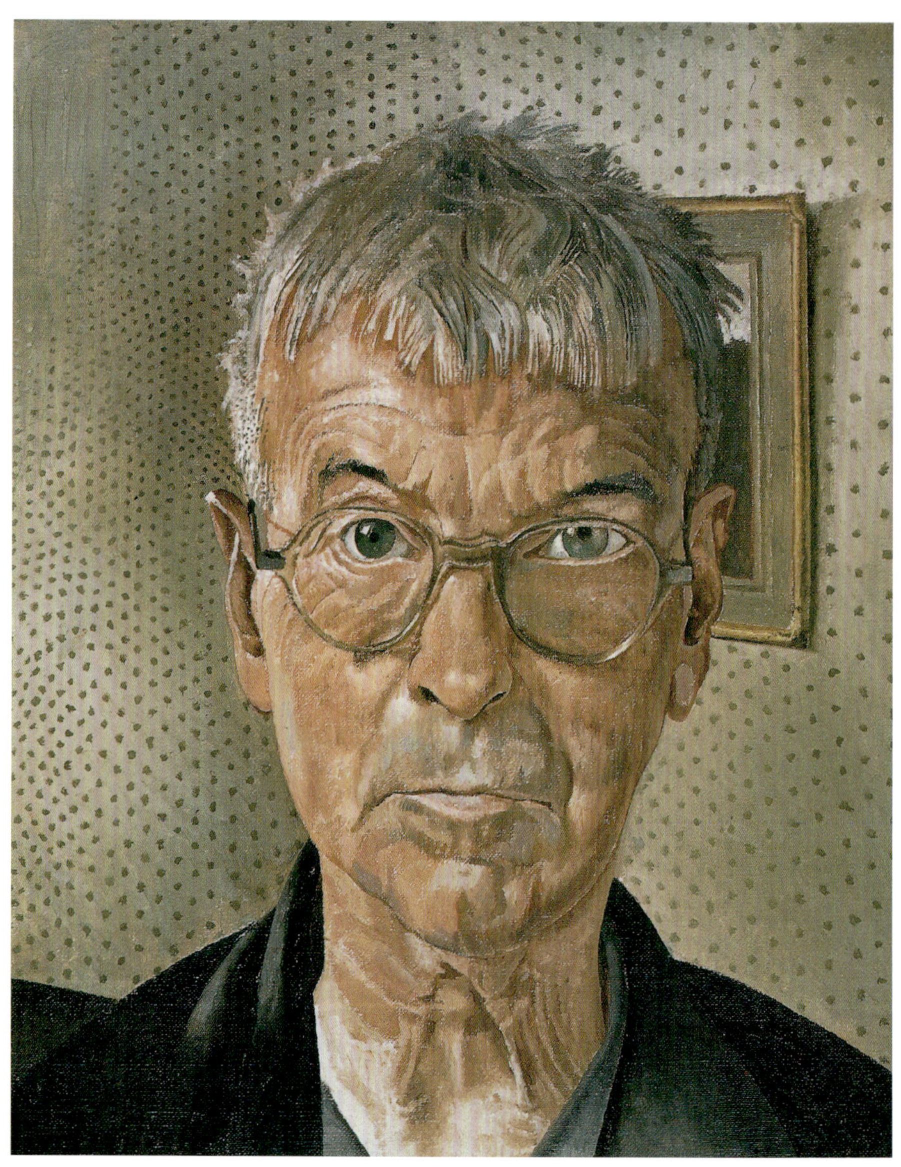

significance for him as his painting: 'I would almost prefer that other people should paint them in order to leave me to write about them.' The obsessive, dry linearity of *Love Letters* signifies Spencer's prioritization of narrative over form. (The painter/critic Merlin James has likened Spencer to William Blake as 'a literary artist who writes his paintings'.)

His final *Self-Portrait* [illustration above] was completed over five days in 1959, 'holding a mirror between his knees'. However desiccated, *Sachlichkeit*, and disillusioned his mode of representation, the gaze is of compelling intensity. (No other painter had so powerfully shown how a spectacle lens enlarges the eye or how behind lenses of different strengths, the two eyes pull apart.) In the decades following his death, Spencer became something of an unmentionable, seen as a mere isolated eccentric. Only in the twenty-first century has he received international recognition – for his astonishing emotional range, and as the sole English artist of his generation to engage with those issues of Self and Identity shared by so many of the painters in this book.

CHARLOTTE SALOMON'S *LIFE? OR THEATRE?* (1940-42)

*The war raged on and I sat by the sea and saw deep into the
heart of humankind. I was my mother and my grandmother,
yes I was all the characters in my play. I learned to walk
all the paths and I became myself.*

CHARLOTTE SALOMON, 1942

I want to focus on Salomon as a painter, even if she remains difficult to place among her contemporaries. Most of us encounter *Life? Or Theatre?* first in book form. It presents as a fully realized project – far more complete than Spencer's *Church of Me*, for example – yet question marks hang over the entire enterprise. What kind of book is this? I am inclined to say – a children's book, the main subject of which is the experience of a young girl, and for which this academically trained artist de-skilled herself, adopting the idioms of the child and the adolescent. (There is often a disjuncture between the sophisticated poise of her text and the primitiveness of the image.) *Life? Or Theatre?* might be classed as a graphic novel, though that fails to convey its scale and substance. When exhibited *en masse* (as at London's Royal Academy in 1998–99, when about four hundred were hung) these small sheets assert a powerful physicality.

Almost all we now have by Charlotte Salomon (1917–43) is this product of about twenty months working in the limbo of the French Riviera under Italian occupation – 'scorching sun, purple sea, and luxuriant blossoms' – in the midst of war-torn Europe. Between the ages of twenty-three and twenty-five, humming as she painted, she covered some 1,675 sheets in watercolour and gouache; of which 769 constitute the brilliant quasi-autobiographical and quasi-comic narrative she entitled *LEBEN? ODER THEATER? EIN SINGSPIEL* (Life? Or Theatre? A Song-Play) [illustrations pp. 146–49].

Charlotte Salomon would have been familiar with the 'novels without words' of Frans Masereel (1889–1972). His 1919 masterpiece, *Passionate Journey*, was brought out with a new introduction by Thomas Mann in 1926 as *Mein Stundenbuch* (My Book of Hours), its 167 woodcut images preceded by an epigraph from Walt Whitman, 'When I give, I give myself.' But *Life? Or Theatre?* is above all a unique *fusion* of image with text. The closest analogy is with the cinematic storyboard. Her writing often refers to cinema (*Kino*); she'd grown up, until the age of sixteen, with silent film – that is, narrative imagery interspersed with still captions, accompanied by music. Charlotte Salomon is not a linear storyteller;

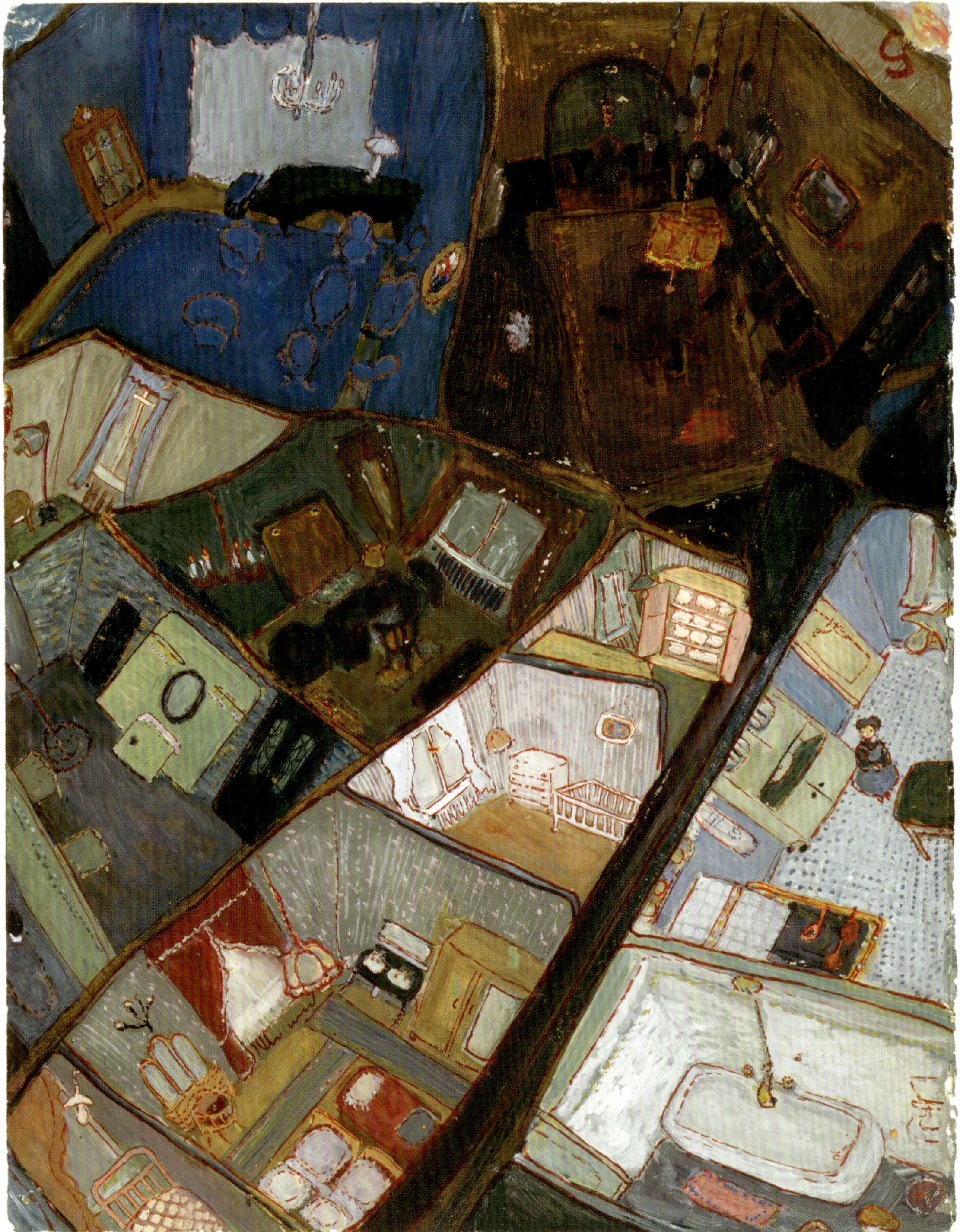

CHARLOTTE SALOMON

Pages from *Life? Or Theatre?*

1940–42

Number 19. 'The apartment is really, one might almost say, beautiful…. A long passage leads to the rear of the apartment, at the end of which are the linen-room with its well-stocked linen closets, the nursery for the anticipated additions to the family, the bedroom, the kitchen, where Augusta is already sitting, waiting for her mistress's orders, the pleasant bathroom…. To the tune: "we twine for thee…"'

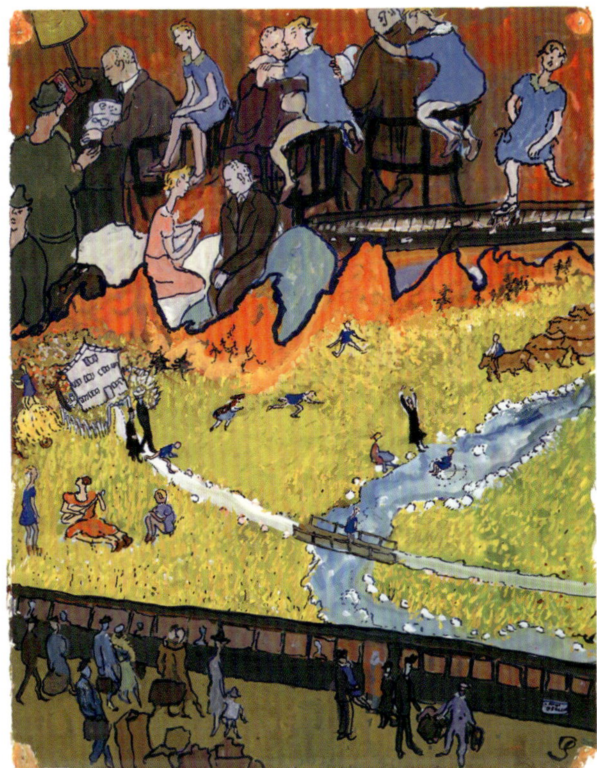

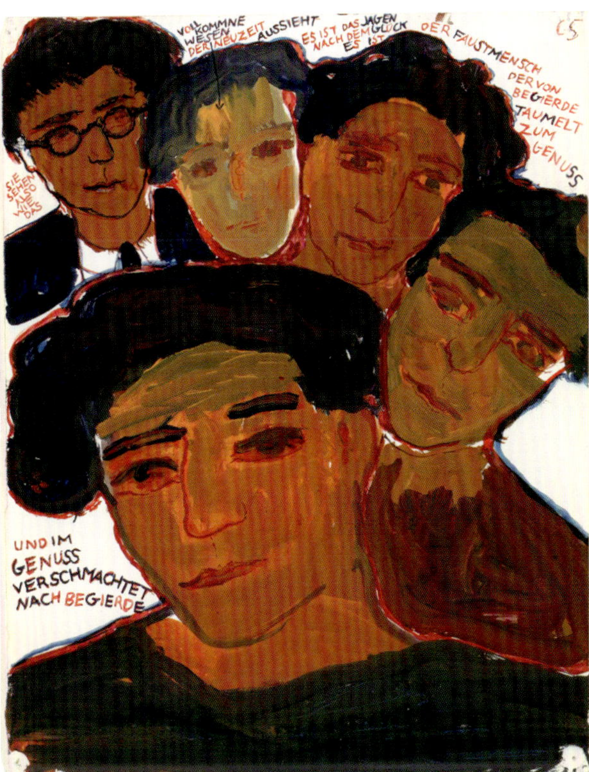

Number 46. 'One day on a meadow…'. The same brown train that forms the lower border is inserted again above the mountains – and behind Charlotte's foot. The fifteen images of the protagonist culminate in her changing her dress from blue to red as she clinches the deal with her father; who to the left is hiring the governess.

Number 249. One of many episodes from the gush of 'Daberlohn's' monologues, based on the actual utterances of the musicologist Alfred Wolfsohn. 'So you see what the perfect creature of the modern era looks like. It is the pursuit of happiness, it is the Faustian man who, driven by desire, staggers towards sensual pleasures and in those pleasures languishes for desire…'.

she is constantly time-travelling, employing jump cuts, flashbacks and close-ups – 'sculpting in time', as Tarkovsky would later define cinema. And in the twenty-first century, we can conveniently access *Life? Or Theatre?* on the computer screen, complete with text and her selected musical accompaniments.

The images that initially excited me are complex, detailed, multi-compartmented; among the two hundred or so that make up her *Prelude*, for example, the cutaway view of the first home of her parents, with an ironic overlaid text that begins 'The apartment is really, one might almost say, beautiful…' [illustration opposite]. On this intricate sheet, she recreates the domain of her childhood – twelve rooms with their carpeted or tiled floors, their variegated light fittings, their elaborate dressing tables, all the paraphernalia of the affluent Berlin bourgeoise – but almost empty, with just one servant seated in the kitchen, next to the up-to-the-minute white bathroom. We float across the cursive spaces opening below us, mapped fluidly, with no wall at right-angles. This is the labyrinth in which her mother suffered and, when Salomon was eight, committed suicide – *Selbstmord*.

In another composite image [illustration above], we see at the lower edge the train that took the young motherless girl and her grandparents to the Dolomites – where 'One day on a meadow she comes across a maiden playing a lute as she watches a child.… Charlotte decides she must have that governess for herself.' And thus above the mountains we see in continuous narrative 'Charlotte', having returned to Berlin by another train, repeatedly pestering her widower father to employ the governess. It was this lute-player who first encouraged Salomon

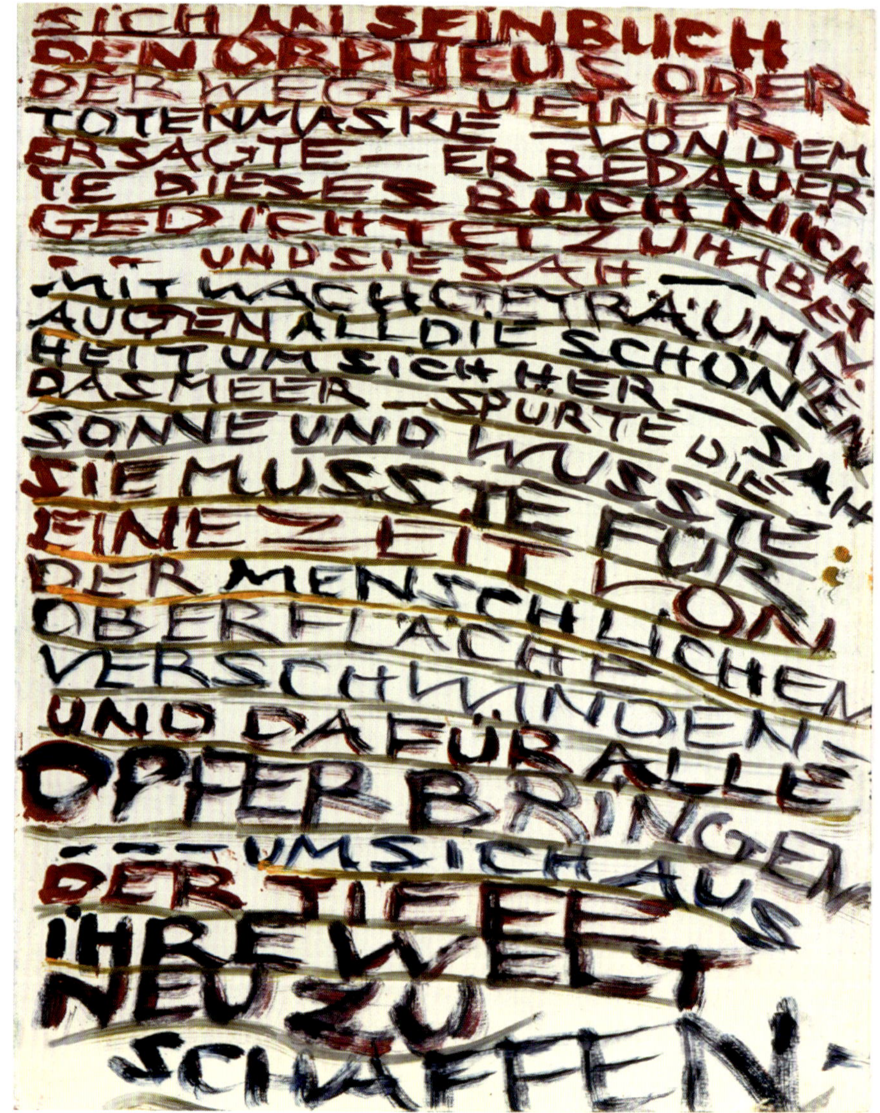

to draw. Leaving school at sixteen, she studied Fashion Design and Illustration at the Berlin *Kunstgewerbe* (commercial art) Academy. A final sequence shows her drawing from plant and life-model, from 1935 to 1938.

With her *Prelude* completed, she stopped for reflection. She hinged transparent paper to many of the sheets: overlaying dialogue and commentary, sometimes a diagram, and an indication of the accompanying music she was humming. Those early, exuberant, map-like tableaux reflected her training as an illustrator. But as she embarked on the main section of the story her graphic language switched to a far more direct idiom, often incorporating text within the image itself.

'Amadeus Daberlohn, prophet of song, enters to the tune of "Toreador" from *Carmen*.… And now our play begins.' For the next several hundred images Daberlohn is the central character, coaching Charlotte's beloved stepmother, the singer 'Paulinka Bimbam', and eventually becoming the object of her own schoolgirl crush.

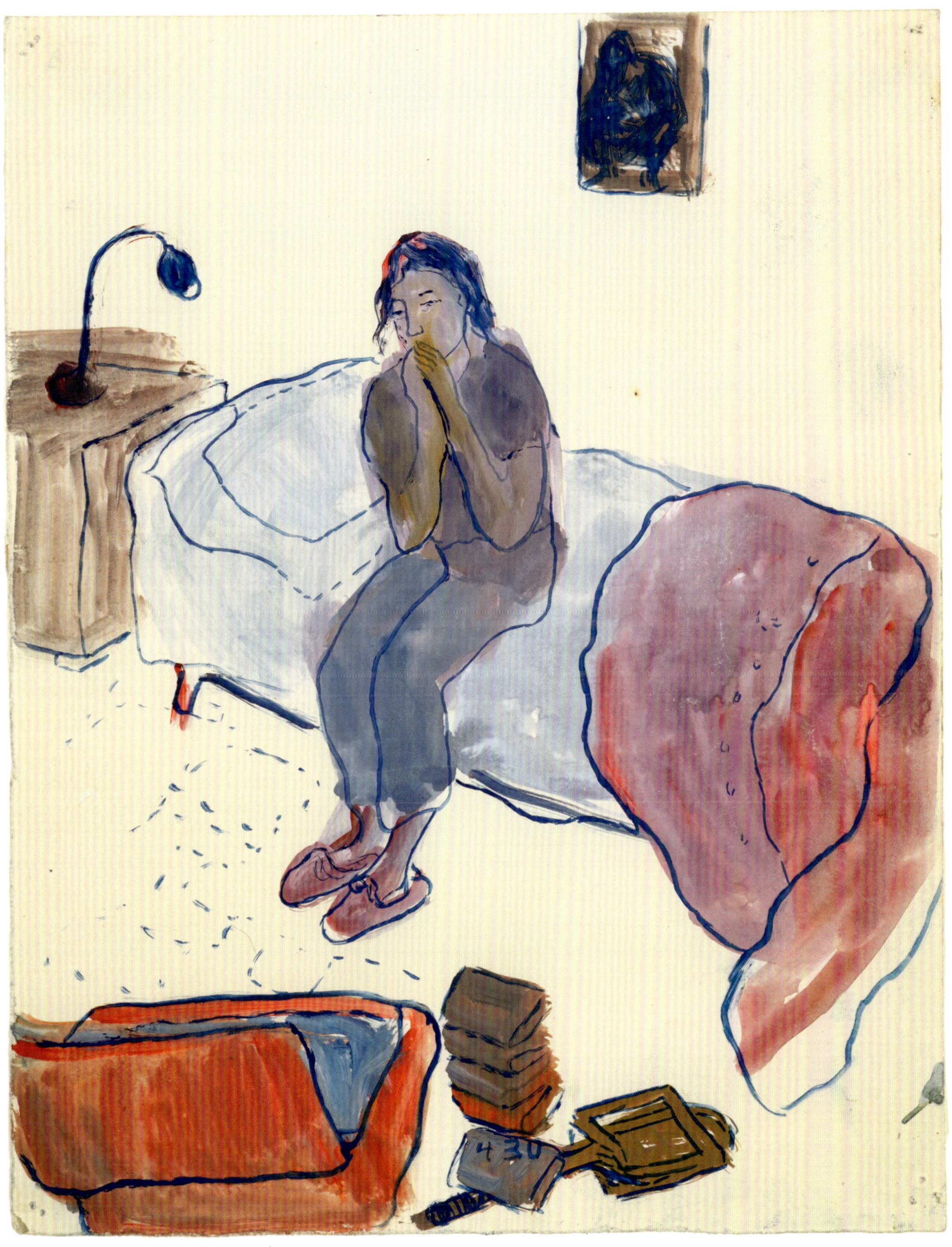

Daberlohn is seen in all his ambivalence: charlatan and windbag, creep and crank, fool and scoundrel – but also an impassioned man-of-art, and thereby a freedom-bringer. Salomon renders his monologues in a chancy procedure, starting each sheet with rows of orange-red smears, which are then overlaid with bluish outlines forming multiple heads and busts – that is, multiple Daberlohns, with or without his specs, pouring out his confessional gospel [illustration p. 147]. He has been shaped by a wartime experience: left for dead under a heap of corpses, he has recreated his identity as Orpheus returned from the Underworld, with song as his medium. His words gush out and swirl around the multiple heads – sometimes five Daberlohns to a sheet, sometimes sixty-two. Charlotte mocks him, but she is also fired up by his utterances.

If that four-hundred-image flashback stands at the centre of Charlotte's narrative, that is because – in the terrible crisis that sparked off the whole project of *Life? Or Theatre?* – Daberlohn had taken on new meaning. Salomon's crush on Wolfsohn had ended disastrously in 1938, destroying her relationship with her stepmother, and ensuring, as the persecution of Jews deepened in Berlin, that she would be sent away to her grandparents in France. In 1940 her grandmother carried out her long-threatened *Selbstmord* and the young woman became aware that in her maternal family, four women and two men had committed suicide. As she recalled, 'My life commenced when I found out I was the only survivor and when deep within me I felt the same inclination, the urge towards despair and dying.'

A few weeks later Germany invaded France; she and her grandfather were interned as enemy aliens. (The real Charlotte Salomon was incarcerated in the hellish, rat-infested concentration camp of Gurs, but in *Life? Or Theatre?*, the horror of those three weeks remains virtually unmentioned.) We rejoin 'Charlotte' only after her release, as companion to her grandfather (who has attempted to share her bed). And now, 'alone with her experiences and her paintbrush', she 'found herself facing the question: whether to take her own life, or to undertake something eccentric and mad'. And it is at this point Charlotte recalls how Daberlohn commissioned her to illustrate his Orphic gospel; and also, his final words at the railway station, 'May you never forget that I believe in you.' Her 'eccentric' undertaking will be a *song-play*, and she is a female Orpheus, resurrected after her own descent into hell. With Daberlohn as half-comic muse, she can commence her work of self-fulfilment. As Salomon wrote to her parents in May 1940, 'I will create a story so as not to lose my mind.'

Near the end of the Daberlohn story the 'illustrational', lyrical tableaux briefly return; as the narrator explains (number 667):

> Here the visual concept changes once more. It is Charlotte who once again
> begins to sing: the song of farewell to her native land.

That interpolation clarifies Salomon's conceptual sophistication – her conscious deployment of multiple visual languages within the same work. Even if we can't fit *Life? Or Theatre?* into any of the customary 'Movements of Modern Art', we should recognize that Salomon was fully aware of contemporary painting, both in the Berlin galleries, and in the library at home. The Salomons' social circle included not only musicians, but the painter Max Liebermann and the architect Erich Mendelsohn. Her art school's library remained unpurged; and in 1938, along with her fellow students, she would have seen the several hundred modernist works, which toured in the 'Degenerate Art' exhibition.

From the outset, Salomon restricted herself to only three pigments – a red, a blue, a yellow; initially entitling her undertaking *The Three Colour Song-Play* (invoking *The Threepenny Opera* of Brecht and Weill). In her epilogue, the imagery becomes almost infantile – so primal as to challenge the very notion of *Kultur* itself. In many sheets the writing dominates, sometimes elbowing out the image altogether [illustration p. 148]. The overall effect is of an extraordinary 'modernity'; jettisoning any trace of academic accomplishment, Salomon now attains a rawness of pictorial language beyond mere style.

In making her enormous picture series, Salomon followed Daberlohn's prescription, repeated four times in the cycle: 'you must first go into yourself – into your childhood – to be able to get out of yourself.' 'Charlotte' was a necessity; like Proust embarking, as 'Marcel', on 'The Book of Himself', Salomon set out to encapsulate an entire life, but transcending the first person through use of the third.

> I had to go deeper into solitude, then maybe I could find – what I had to find!
>
> It is my *self*: a name for myself. And so I began *Life and Theatre*.

She delivered those parcels of fragile watercolours into her doctor's safekeeping with the words *'C'est toute ma vie.'* (It's my whole life.) We now know the facts: pregnant in 1943, she married, thereby alerting the authorities to her presence as an alien; the couple were sent to Drancy, and onward to Auschwitz; where, arriving by transport number sixty, Salomon was immediately, as a pregnant Jew, directed to the gas chamber. Inevitably, any account of her work will be inflected with tragedy.

Yet our experience on opening that vast *Book of Life* is of affirmation, buoyancy, invention. We are made to revisit our earliest pleasure in picture books – Griselda Pollock calls *Life? Or Theatre?* a 'modernist fairytale' – and the wit and charm of Charlotte Salomon's imagery join with her wisdom and self-knowledge to create one of the most rewarding works of narrative art of the twentieth century.

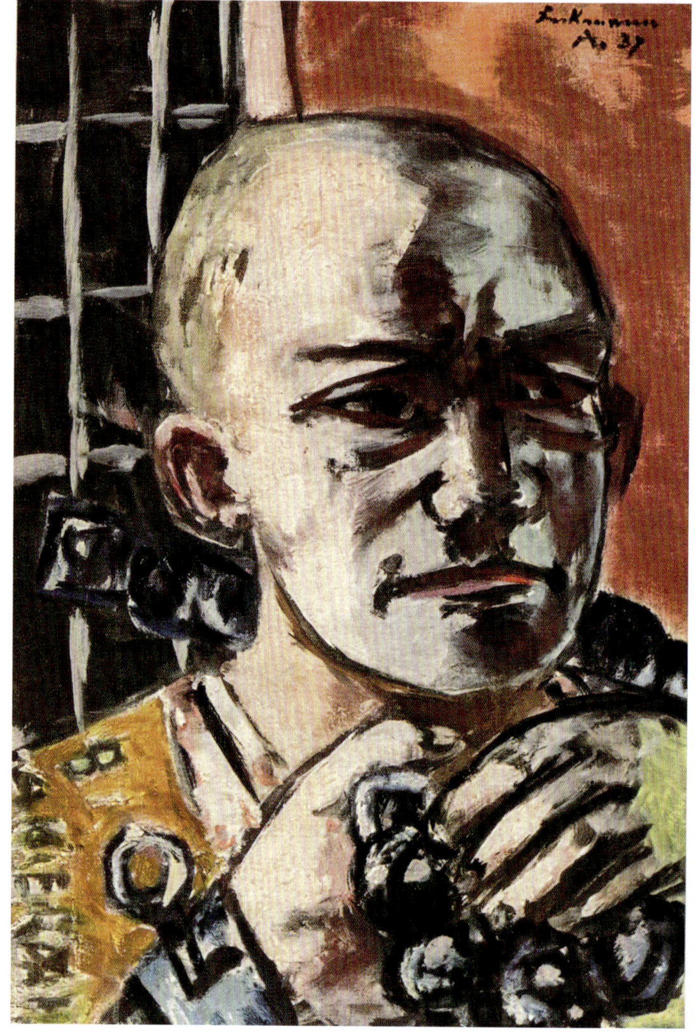

MAX BECKMANN: EPICS OF SELF-ART IN AMSTERDAM (1937–46)

*The role you're playing at the moment is the most difficult
and the most magnificent that life could have offered you –
don't forget this, Max Beckmann – precisely as it is.*

MAX BECKMANN, 1940

A first-person pictorial space becomes as significant in Max Beckmann's later work
as in Bonnard's. His mode of composition constantly asserts the positioning of the
self, especially in his smaller and less complex images, where we look out – from
a bathing cabin, a balcony, a ledge, a window; and in each, a dark, near-to-hand
framing element stands in for the self. From the 1930s onwards, the emphasis
shifts from *Sachlichkeit* 'Thingness' (see Ch 2) towards pictorial construction –
that is, to the relation between self and world. As the critic Carl Einstein already

understood in 1931, the result is a kind of self-inflicted rift, a tension and disharmony: 'Beckmann does not attempt to avoid the conflict, but sets out rather to deepen that conflict into an almost tragic confrontation.'

In Beckmann's pictures, space is made to convey a much wider range of meanings than we're accustomed to in twentieth-century painting. When modernism eschewed 'illusion', it separated itself from some of the most rewarding experiences offered by earlier Western painting – the cosmic journeys of Brueghel and Lorenzetti; the airborne diagonal thrusts of Tintoretto and El Greco. After 1910, pictorial space was too often shut down, rather than liberated, typically amounting to little more than a shallow shelf, parallel to the picture plane. In Beckmann's imagery (as in Bonnard's) those doors of perception were reopened, not as illusion, but as subjective and transcendent experience. Beckmann wrote in 1938:

> To transform height, width and depth into two dimensions was for me an
> experience full of magic, in which I glimpsed for a moment that fourth
> dimension my whole being was seeking.

Beckmann's 'first person', unlike Bonnard's, is tangled with historical events, which affect every aspect of his imagery. *Departure* (1932–35) and subsequent

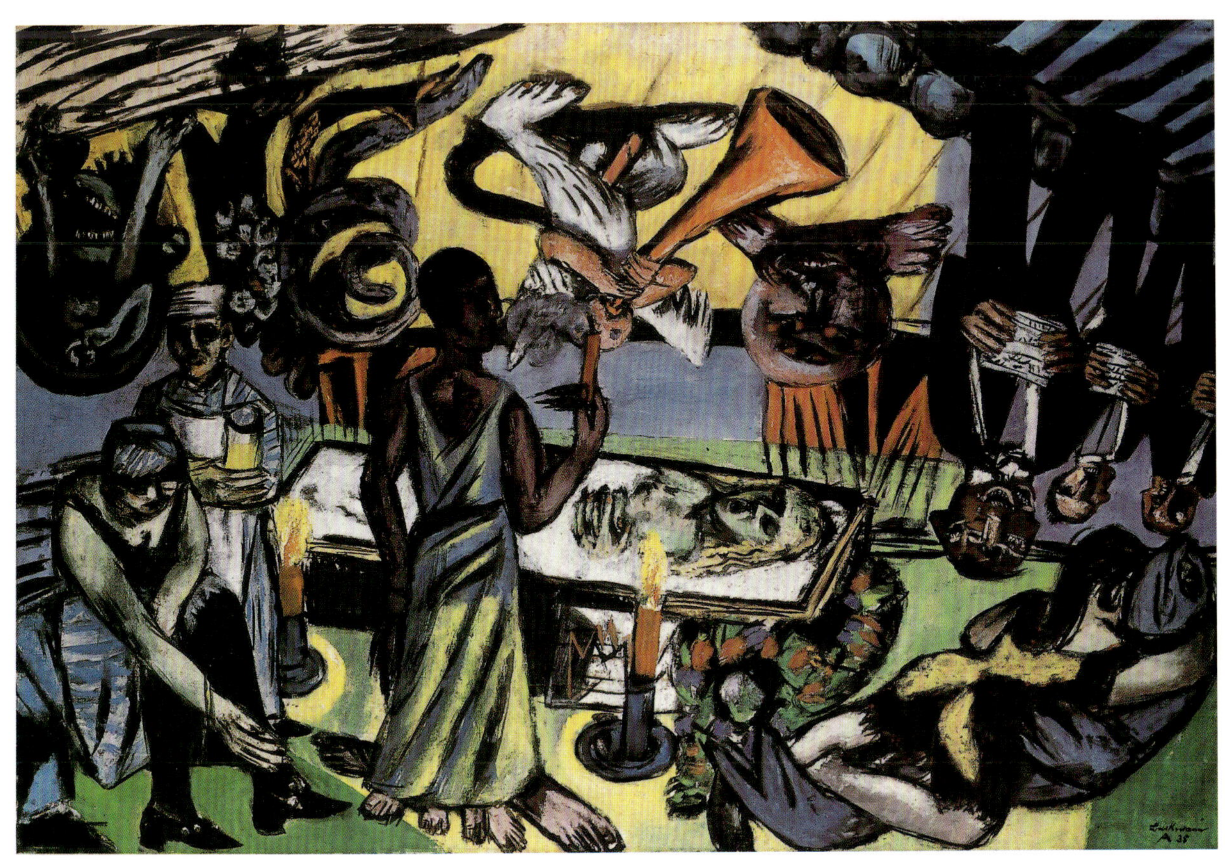

triptychs [illustrations pp. 78–79, opposite and 156–57, see Ch 2 pp. 77–80] could be described as history paintings, but with a first-person emphasis that filters public experience through the internal structures of dream and archetype.

By 1936, Beckmann's situation in Germany had become precarious; it was difficult for him to sell or exhibit, and his works had been confiscated from German museums. On 18 July 1937, Hitler himself inaugurated the House of German Art in Munich. He condemned all modernist painters as sick, suggesting it might be necessary to have these defectives sterilized, 'to prevent hereditary propagation of these gruesome optical disturbances'. Two days later Beckmann boarded a train for Amsterdam (just missing the opening of the 'Degenerate Art' exhibition, in which his paintings were prominently displayed). *The Liberated* [illustration p. 152], is exceptional among his eighty or more self-portraits, in being tied to a specific moment: having put the prison-house behind him, the shaven-headed convict removes his shackles. It marks Beckmann's entry into an exilic existence, which he often experienced as a kind of afterlife.

The pair of large nocturnes *Birth* and *Death* [illustration p. 153] were begun while his new life was split between Amsterdam and Paris. *Birth* is staged in the caravan of a travelling circus. In *Death*, completed several months later, the stage boards are inverted, and the black-suited chorus is suspended upside-down above a green corpse. William Kentridge (see Ch 5 pp. 231–34) has observed, we are thereby invited 'to take part in the construction of the painting'; this upside-down space 'evokes the world as a contested arena…the ambiguities, uncertainties and arcane ways in which we shape our sense of ourselves…'. The world of the hospital-nurse is made to intersect with that of archetypal monsters, of the multi-footed African goddess, and the girl making love to a fish.

Beckmann visited London for two weeks in July and August of 1938, where he delivered a lecture to accompany the exhibition 'Twentieth Century German Art' (see p. 139 and Ch 2 p. 109). Visiting the Tate Gallery, he had felt an affinity with 'the rainbow-hued cosmic fantasies' of William Blake's drawings to Dante. In the dream-soliloquy of his lecture, Beckmann encounters Blake, who counsels him: 'Do not let yourself be intimidated by the horror of the world.'

> I awoke and found myself in Holland, in the midst of a boundless world-turmoil. But my belief in the final release and absolution of all things, whether they please or torment, was newly strengthened.

The identification with Blake, creating his own encrypted mythology in the midst of the Napoleonic wars, was real; Beckmann too wanted 'to create a new mythology from present day life; that's my meaning.' But in his second triptych, *Temptation* (1936–37), the props and costumes of his figures are from amateur theatricals, fancy-dress charades, tacky provincial circuses. And in *Acrobats* [illustration opposite] he again exposes myth to the light of carnival. Completed in August 1939, its central panel presents the gods backstage, off-duty, during an interval. To the right, Mars, with blood-dabbled hands, is chatting up the ice-cream girl; while stage-left, in the vertiginous space above the safety net, a trapeze artist

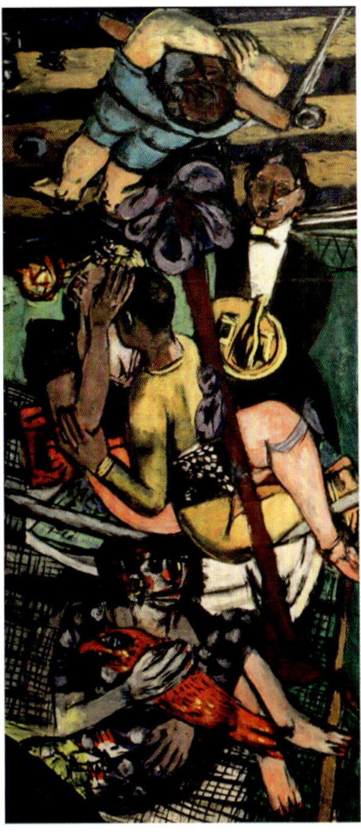
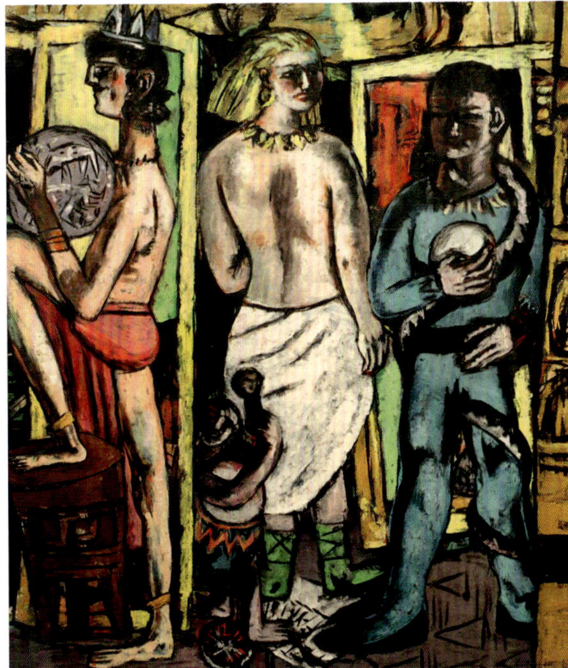
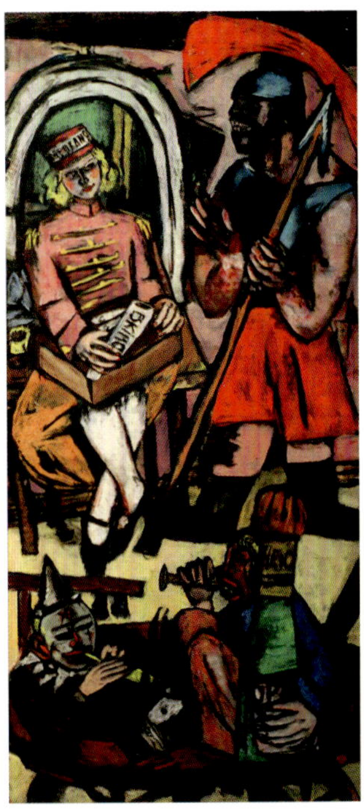

MAX BECKMANN

Acrobats

1937–39

Begun in Paris, then continued
in Amsterdam, *Acrobats* was
completed just before the
invasion of Poland – and the
return of Mars to centre-
stage. From 1940, Amsterdam
was under Nazi occupation,
with Beckmann, a self-exiled
German, lying low throughout
the war (see also detail, p. 2).

soars past the pair risking coitus on the tightrope. Far below, a flunkey brings congratulatory champagne.

That central, life-size Venus turns her gaze upon us; she possesses a massive physicality, not easily conveyed in reproduction [illustration above, detail p. 2]. Her flesh is thickly painted, with surprising flashes and flurries of bright colour – carmine, purplish-grey, viridian, orange – enlivening the pink. Across the whole triptych the paint surface is as discontinuous as a Bonnard, thin scumbles juxtaposed to sudden strokes of impasto. It seems Beckmann began these triptychs without any preliminary planning. Making radical changes over the course of a year or so (Beckmann sometimes used commercial paint-stripper), he often stumbled into unexpected imagery. In the triptychs, complexity is internalized; it is the individual who carries the multiplicity *within*.

When the young painter Eric Fischl first encountered *Departure* [illustration pp. 78–79] at the Museum of Modern Art in New York, he found its complexity 'daunting': 'My fear was that I could never penetrate its content without first reading what he and others had to say about it.' Yet detailed exegesis probably isn't the best route into Beckmann's triptychs. The most helpful texts were written by his young patron Stefan Lackner. *Max Beckmann's Mystical World-Pageant*, published in 1938, locates *Departure* within the *Welttheater* (world theatre) tradition of Goethe's *Faust Part II* (1832), a text for which Beckmann would later make illustrations. Lackner sees the triptychs as both 'post-Christian altarpieces' and 'three-act dramas': the shallow stage in the two wings of *Departure* (which at one time bore the title *Scenes from The Tempest*) is obviously theatrical, and later triptychs include *Acrobats*, *Carnival* and *Actors*. Yet the content remains provisional, improvisatory and, in its jostling carnival absurdity, ultimately humorous. As Lackner puts it, 'Several meanings cross one

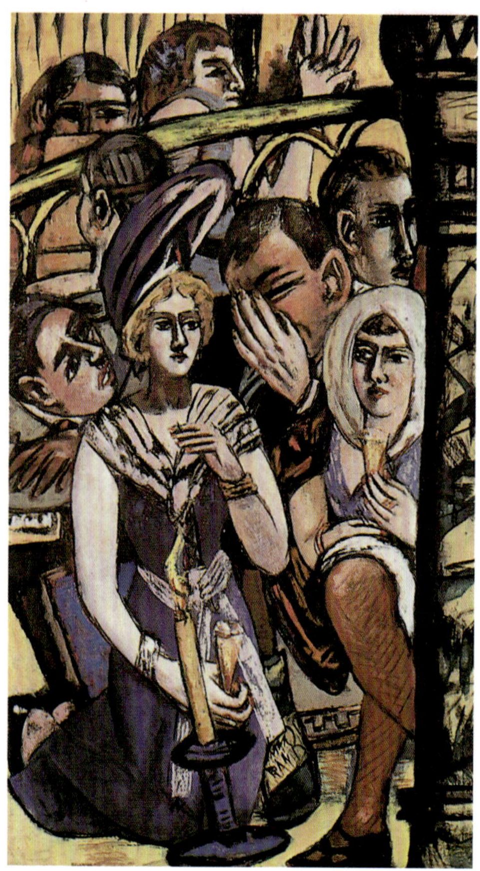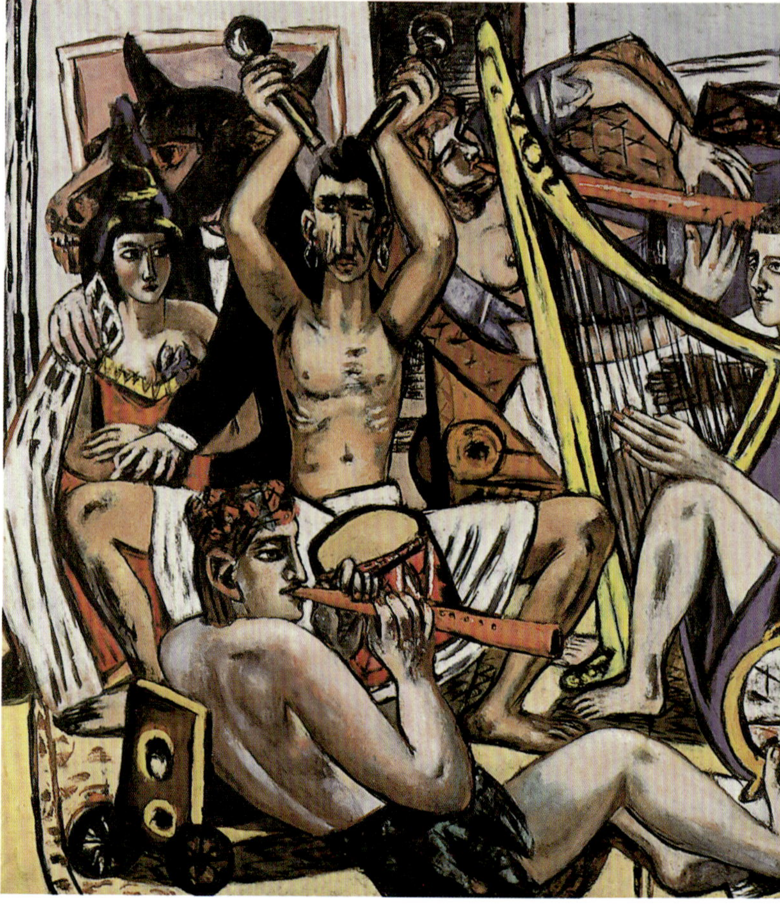

another, aboriginal heathen drives and Christian salvation wishes, preconscious memories, subliminal anxieties and aimless bliss.'

Beckmann, now in his fifties, was still physically imposing. 'His solid round head looked like a boulder. His massive body moved slowly, deliberately, swaying from side to side, like a captain on the deck of his ship.' But Lackner recalled a reception in Paris where 'Beckman suddenly walked out on the lawn, pulled his derby a little more firmly down on his forehead, and did several cartwheels, whirling sideways on stiff arms and legs without losing his hat.' The triptychs cease to be alarming in their congestion when we become alert to the 'cartwheels' across their surfaces – the sudden, wild bursts of exuberance out of which each of these apparently impermeable structures is cobbled together. What he is really doing is *filling the void*; and his greatest triptychs are painted on a black ground, so that we have a sense of glimpsing the Void through the interstices. What might appear most grandiose in Beckmann turns out to be most fragmentary, broken, vulnerable; as he explained to Lackner: 'Basically my thing originates in an almost demented mirth, but then it aims at not leaving anything out.'

Beckmann read the fifteen-hundred pages of *The Secret Doctrine*, Madame Blavatsky's 1888 Theosophical compendium, six times between 1934 and 1950.

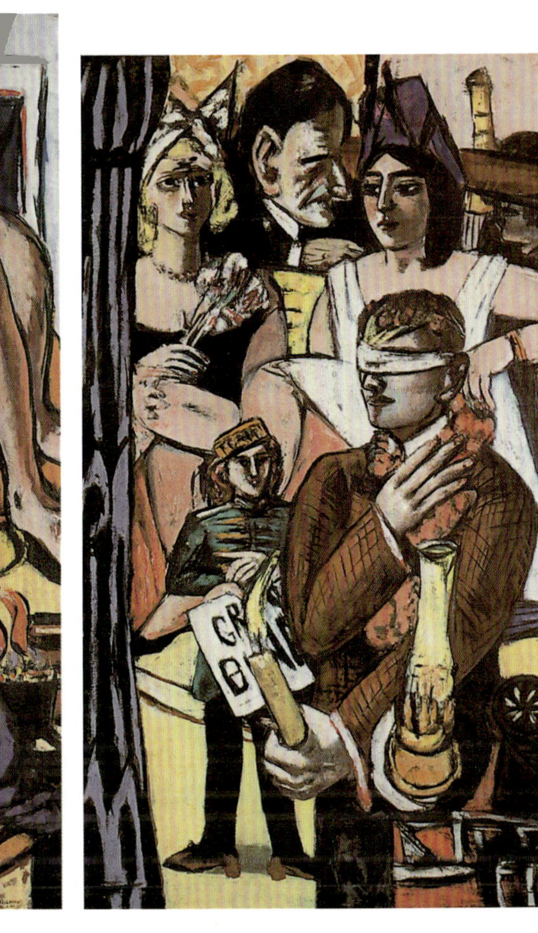

Her invocation of multiple worlds and cosmic zones had already fuelled painters (including Kandinsky, Malevich and Mondrian) to create abstract works; but for Beckmann, those compartments needed to be stuffed with figures. Together with books on Atlantis and crystal-ball-gazing (as well as the philosophic speculations of Schopenhauer and psycho-alchemical writings of Jung), Beckmann's esoteric reading supplied an unstable mythic resource, where giants might morph into angels, hermaphrodites into four-armed or three-eyed divinities.... It is the crowding that is essential, to the point of absurdity, and out of which *anything* might take shape. Beckmann gropes his way through the labyrinths of dream and myth, like one of his own blindfolded sleepwalkers, led by the figures of his own creation.

He painted his largest triptych, *Blindman's Buff* [illustration left] during Amsterdam's 'Hunger Winter' of 1944–45; there was no electric light, and the occupied, blockaded city starved and froze. Beckmann had already suffered his first heart attack, and was living a very confined existence. With all access to the coast long since prohibited, he found himself painting consolatory images of beaches or even the French Riviera, from memory and drawings. In parallel, the epic-scale triptych, his seventh, constantly transformed itself, Beckmann variously referring to it as *The Concert*, *Grand Café*, *The Great Bar*, *Cabaret*, *Ox-Feast*, *The Gods* and *Dionysus*. It is a reminiscence set in the glamorous nightlife of the lost Weimar era. A previous triptych, *Carnival* (1942–43), had shown Beckmann and his wife being expelled from the Eden Hotel. Now the party-goers crowd in, and a drummer and a foreground reveller have 'gone primitive', Nietzschean devotees of Dionysus (see Ch 2 p. 60); the alarm clock is ticking away. The young figures with candles to left and right were identified by Beckmann as Pamina and Tamino, the separated lovers from Mozart's *The Magic Flute* – except that here they never will meet, because there is so much socialite clutter piled-up between.

While most German artists have appeared briefly in small, vivid character parts, only to drop away as the scene changes, Beckmann has moved like the protagonist of some Expressionist quest-play – a Baal, or a Peer Gynt – through all the disaster-filled five acts of his country's history. When Kirchner commits suicide in 1938, Beckmann writes, 'we have to hold out, we have all gone through terrible times' and in January 1944, 'Munch has died.... He held out for a pretty long time.' I see Beckmann's 1944 *Self-Portrait in Black* [illustration p. 158] as a 'holding-out' – the self carved brutally out of the black ground, like an act of defiance against the Void. In 1945, he wrote to Stephan Lackner:

The world is rather *kaput*, but the spectres climb out of their caves and pretend to become again normal and customary human beings who ask each other's pardon instead of eating one another or sucking one another's blood. The entertaining folly of war evaporates, distinguished boredom sits down again on the dignified old overstuffed chairs...

Beckmann's most complex configuration, *The Cabins* (1947–48) [illustration opposite], became a kind of rite-of-passage between his wartime experience and his new life. After years of entrapment in occupied Holland, to cross the Atlantic twice

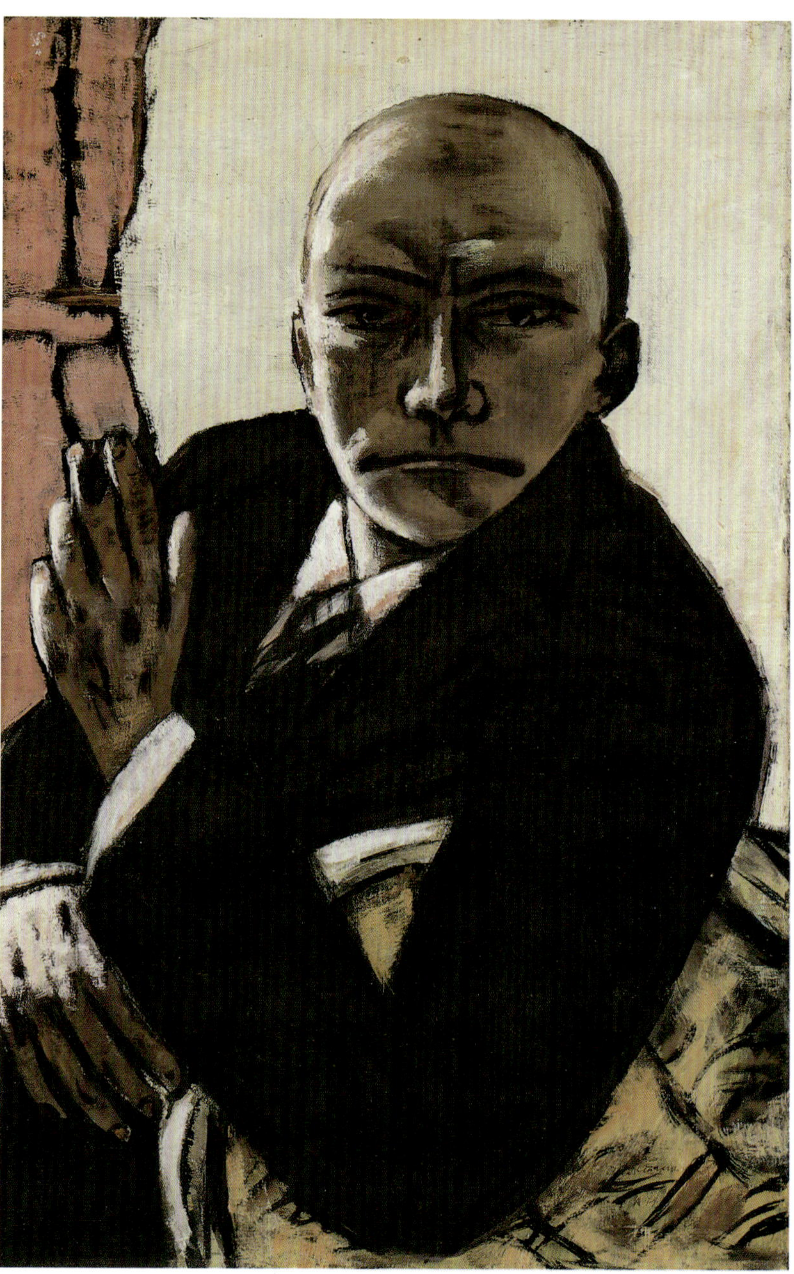

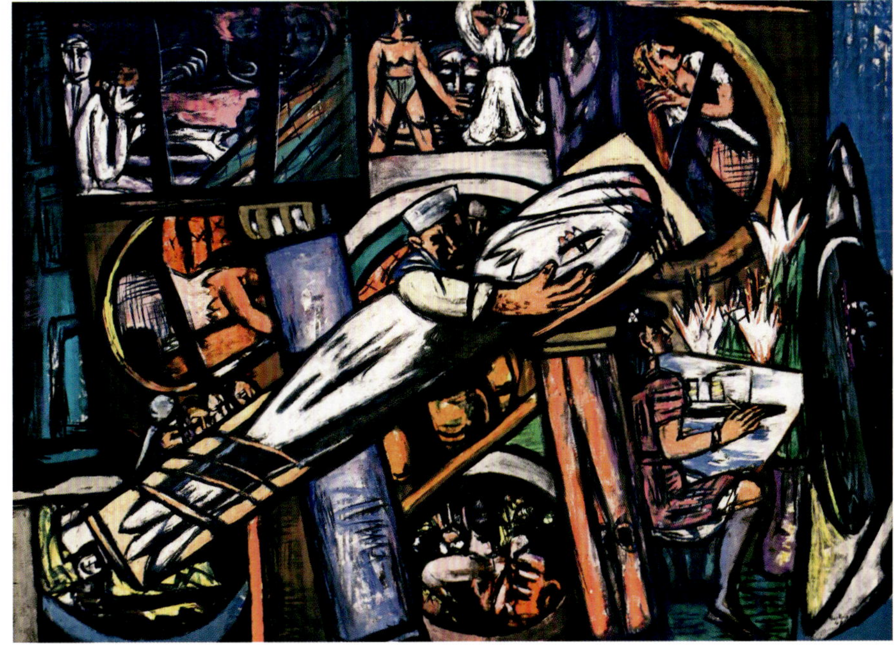

in an ocean liner was an overwhelming experience. Beckmann here creates a skewed, polyphonic space, perhaps best read from the band of green sea at the right, where a two-funnelled boat steams along a vertical horizon, vignetted through a porthole. From her cabin, a young woman-artist gazes out, and makes an image; and all the rest of this weird composition could be interpreted as her apprehension of the many-decked boat piled up behind her. The compartmented, conglomerate cascade of *The Cabins* seems to imply an entire cosmology; perhaps William James's proposal (and Madame Blavatsky's) that the world is not a universe, but a multiverse.

In *The Cabins*, as in *Acrobats*, pictorial space – not a design, but the space thrown up by the processes of painting – becomes the vehicle by which Beckmann searches for his place in the world. Leon Golub (see Ch 5 pp. 237–38) wrote in 2003 of

> the impacted, dislocated stresses of the triptychs... [Beckmann] lumps
> incongruities together...he doesn't seem so deeply invested in symbolism
> *per se*, because he was so involved in the fragmented context in which he was
> living, the disorder...

What is registered is a structure equivalent to the complexity, and disorder, of our own lives. The movement made explicit in *Departure* [illustration pp. 78–79], of entrapment transcended, could be extended to Beckmann's work as a whole, which becomes an epic of self-liberation.

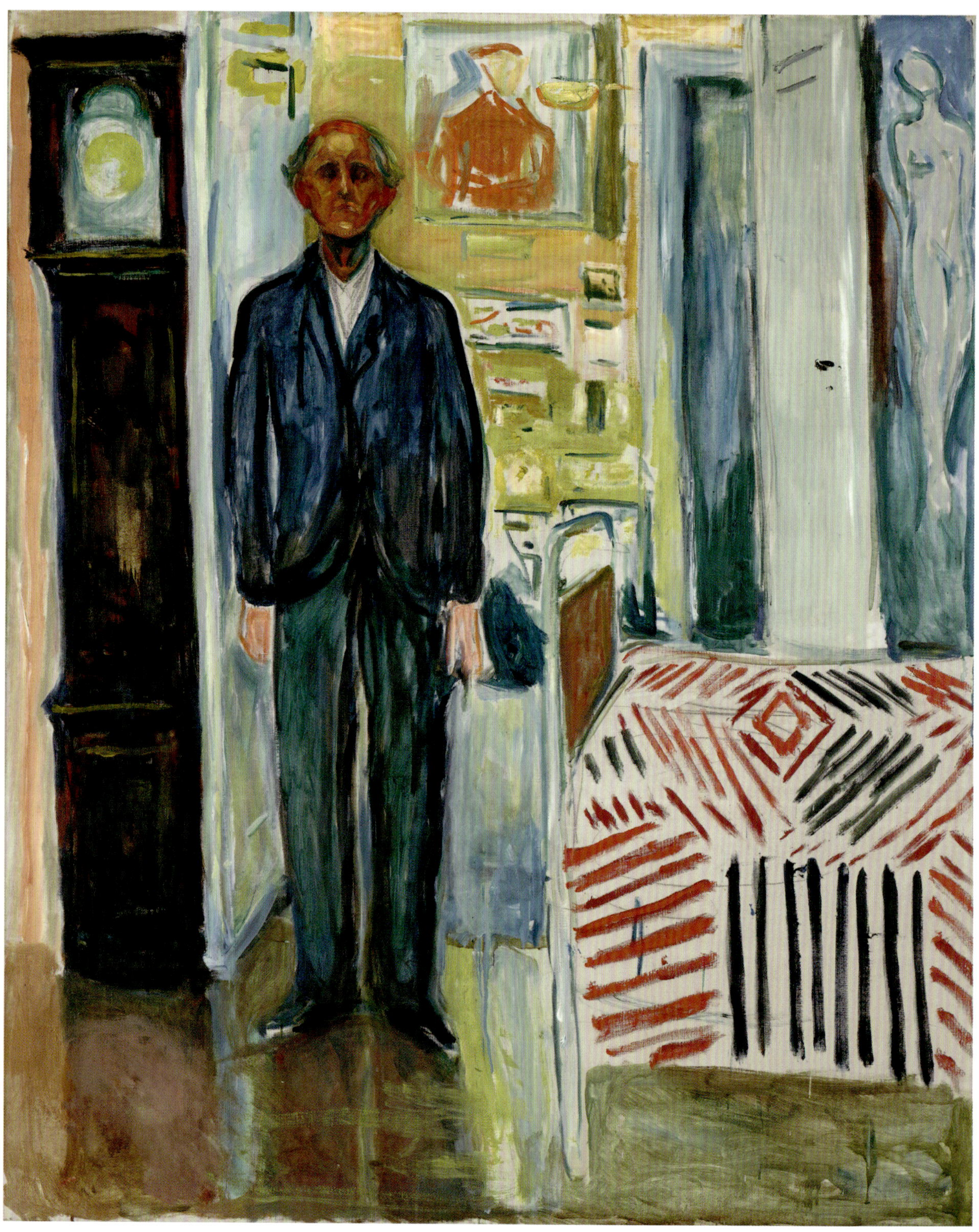

EDVARD MUNCH: BETWEEN CLOCK AND BED (1940-43)

The second half of my life has been a battle
just to keep myself upright.... Anxiety about life
has followed me ever since my mind became aware.
My art has been a personal confession.

EDVARD MUNCH, c. 1940

EDVARD MUNCH

Self-Portrait: Between Clock and Bed

1940–43

Munch's confessional cycle, *The Frieze of Life*, began to tour across Germany in the 1890s under various titles: *From the Modern Life of the Soul*, or *A Man's Life*. Paintings such as *Puberty*, *The Scream*, *Ashes* can still surprise when encountered in their original versions; R. B. Kitaj called them 'the last real fire-and-brimstone in European painting'. In 1908, Munch's 'time of alcohol' ended in breakdown; his subsequent paintings can often seem thin or even unfinished.

By the time Edvard Munch (1863–1944) painted his last self-portrait [illustration opposite] he had long since renounced the histrionic intensity of his early work. This late refusal to self-mythologize, his implicit admission of weakness and insignificance, is part of what makes this disconcerting picture so moving. The figure has some of the bare starkness of the dethroned King Lear, reduced to 'the thing itself' – that is, to an old man, close to death. In *Between Clock and Bed*, it is as though he no longer has the spirit to bring the painting to any pitch of solid realization. Drips and raw half-hearted scumbles hang in mid-air. Munch faces us frontally, but diminished, made to echo the rigid 'upright' of the grandfather-clock that has no dial, just as his own mouth almost disappears into the face, as mute existence. Living in increasing isolation within his estate on the outskirts of Oslo/Kristiania, and refusing all contact with the German occupiers and their Norwegian collaborators, Munch finds a new pictorial language for disillusionment and non-transcendence – for the obliteration of identity.

In the course of the twentieth century, any fixed, continuous character of the individual was set in question; the confident 'self' of the nineteenth-century bourgeois unmasked as illusory. Concepts of structuralism and deconstruction filtered into artists' everyday lives, threatening to negate and invalidate the authorial dimension inherent in so much figurative painting. Yet when, in 1976, the East German writer Christa Wolf made the declaration with which this chapter begins – 'It becomes more and more difficult to say "I", and yet at the same time often imperative to do so' – she was pointing to some irreducible core of identity and authenticity, upon which the continuity of painting, and the novel, depends. A 'post-authorial' view of modern culture had abolished the very notion of the Self; painting seemed impossible to assimilate within 'Theory'. But painters were able to reflect that new *uncertainty* of identity, and out of their self-questioning and self-construction, a wonderful new figuration had come into being.

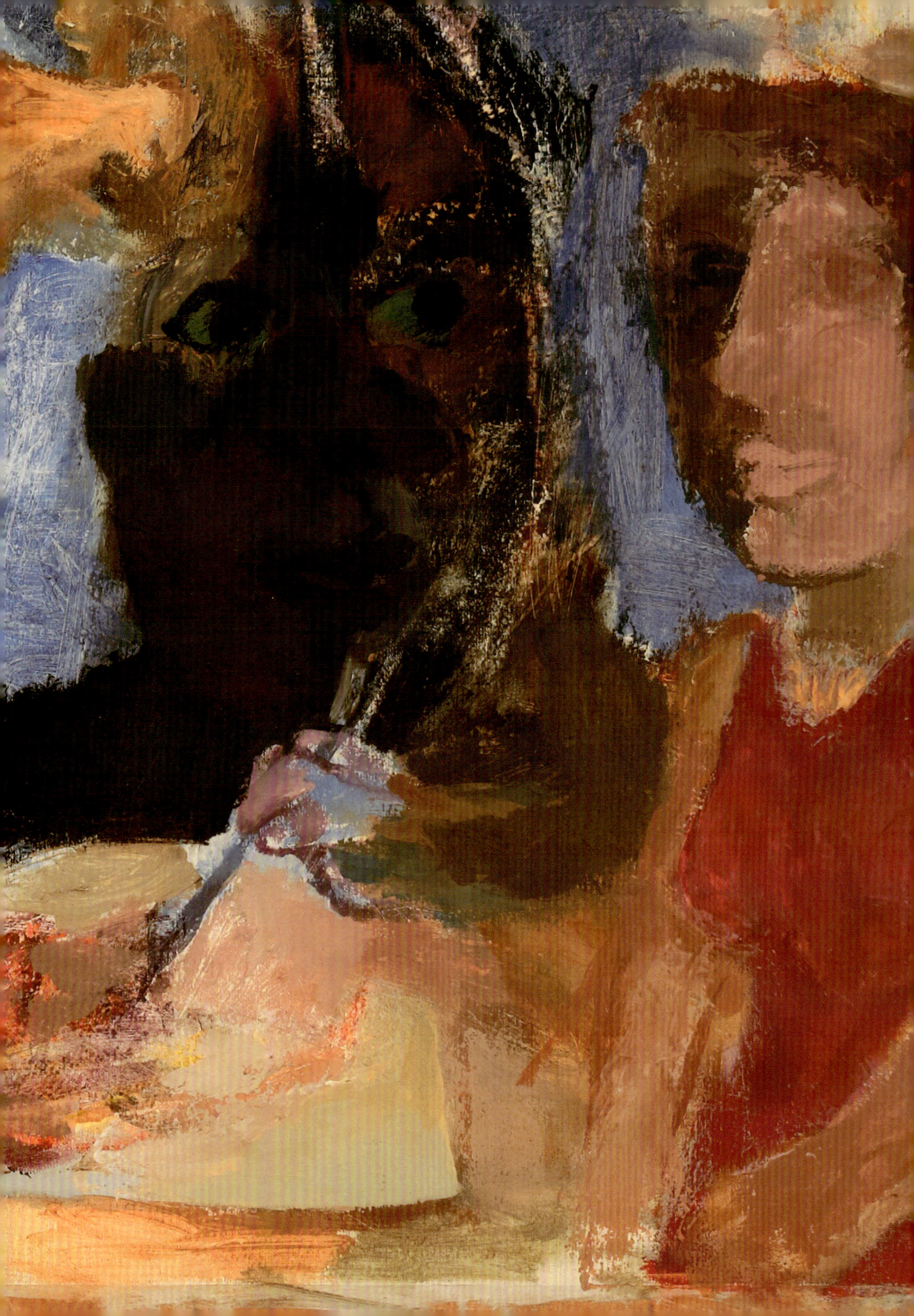

CHAPTER FOUR

Beyond the Formalist Canon: Visionaries, Dreamers, Outsiders

Some of the twentieth century's most vivid imagery has been the work of visionaries or outsiders – *exceptionals* – who cannot easily be inserted into any account of painting's 'progress', yet who together stake out new territory for artists. Each embodies a challenge to exclusionary orthodoxies, whether academic or formalist; each affirms a role for the solitary image-maker, creating ambitious projects and narratives independent of the art-world mainstream.

Modernism, defined by the Mexican writer Octavio Paz as 'the revolt of suppressed realities', often took a psychological turn. The honouring of Dream and The Unconscious – a recognition that we may be most fully ourselves when not in our waking mind – transformed twentieth-century painting. 'Of the dream,' wrote Jung in 1911, 'it may truly be said, the stone that the builders rejected has become the head of the corner.' The impact of Surrealism, assisted by the growth of art publishing and colour reproduction, helped lift out of obscurity several forgotten 'fantastic' artists, singularities such as Hercules Seghers or Richard Dadd.

In that spirit, the American painter Leon Golub (see Ch 5 pp. 237–38) often insisted that 'true Modernism began not in Paris, but in Ostend in the 1880s' – the decade in which James Ensor (1860–1949) completed all his most significant works. *Tribulations of Saint Anthony* of 1887 [illustration pp. 164–65] hangs majestically at the Museum of Modern Art in New York, where each new generation of painters, from de Kooning and Guston (see Ch 5 pp. 193–98) to Paula Rego (Ch 1 pp. 56–57) and Dana Schutz, has drawn inspiration from Ensor's reconciliation of modernist painting with a complex, literary imagery.

Many artists before Ensor had depicted the legend of Saint Anthony – the earliest Desert Father, who separates himself from mankind and seeks solitude, only to be tormented by the world he carries within him. As in Hieronymus Bosch's great Lisbon triptych of 1515, Anthony is depicted by Ensor hunched over his holy book, peering uneasily behind him as the void fills with self-generated monsters. Ensor, working alone through long, silent days in his fifth-floor attic high above the family's carnival shop, conjures a more visceral language for his own tribulations; a disquieting imagery neither nocturnal nor fiery, but high-keyed, focused around the central swamp or waterfall of white. He transfers the beautiful nacreous palette

KEN KIFF

From *The Sequence* Number 97. *Writing*

1977–79

(detail, see p. 189)

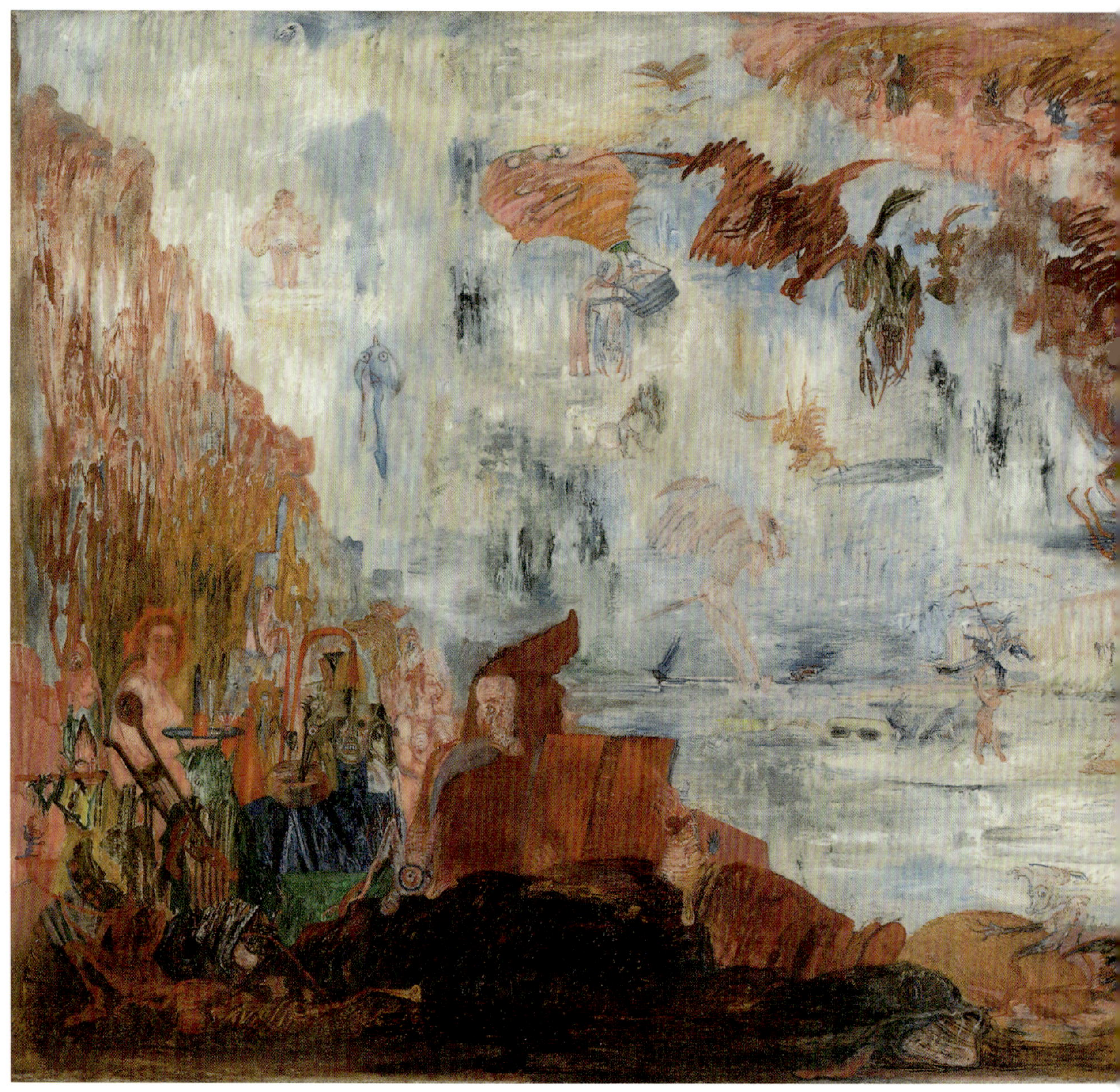

of his seascapes and still lifes to his inner wilderness – broken pinks beside rose-reds, though always set against that ridged and seamed, impastoed whiteness. Lead-white becomes a substance independent of any descriptive function, into which Ensor zigzags the end of his brush, as a kind of seismic doodling; and out of this matrix there emerge wonderful miasmas of hallucinatory imagery. The longer we look, the more we discover: insects and polyps morphing into demons; the animal-headed creature bearing a lyre, merging with the red-haired woman at the café table; a hot-air balloon with a face, and in its basket, a flayed figure. Enemas, projectile vomit, a ship-of-fools, bottoms that become faces, witches on broomsticks – the familiar imagery of the Flemish Carnival is here recast to suggest the unbounded and anarchic freedom of the individual imagination.

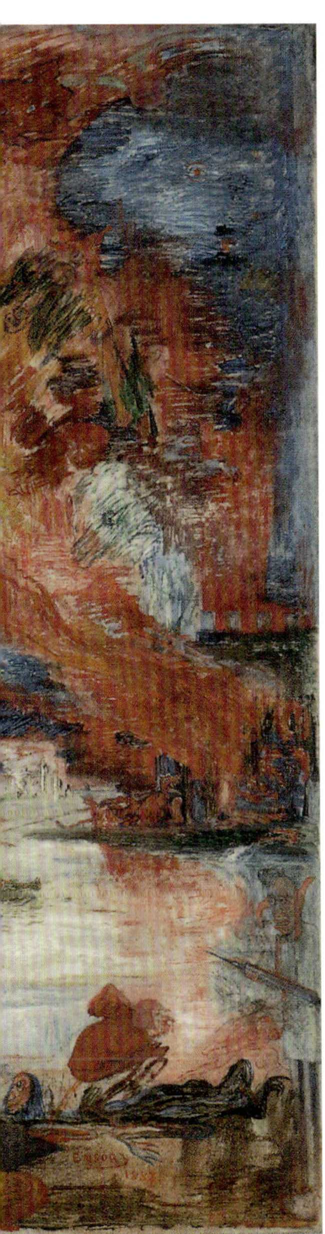

It was also in 1887 that an enormous canvas by the twenty-five-year-old Georges Seurat, *A Sunday Afternoon on the Island of La Grande-Jatte* (1884–86), took the Belgian art world by storm, converting many to divisionist procedures. Ensor railed against this 'art of cold calculation...dry and repellent'. He especially resented the claim of divisionism to be the *true* painting idiom, equivalent to the libertarian/anarchist tenets Ensor himself espoused. The following year he embarked upon his own over fourteen-foot refutation, *The Entry of Christ into Brussels in 1889*, a disorderly carnival realized with an utterly unpredictable wildness of mark.

Ensor's paintings and etchings of the 1880s became widely known only in the twentieth century. In 1906 the young Paul Klee (1879–1940) became fascinated by the autonomy of Ensor's line, sending him two etchings of his own: and in 1911, Emil Nolde (see Ch 2 pp. 60–61) visited Ensor in Ostend. By mid-century his art had become an essential component within the modernist canon, while remaining outside any 'movement'.

Almost a century after Ensor's *Tribulations*, Ken Kiff (1935–2001) in London made his own assertion of the inward imagination. In *Talking with a Psychoanalyst: Night Sky* (1973–79) [illustration pp. 166–67] the mild-faced patient is Kiff himself. As he and the shadowy analyst become polarized, the room fills behind him with grotesque presences, pouring in through the half-open door – huge-nosed, multi-testicled, bestial or bowler-hatted. On the floor, perhaps suggesting the potential violence of this transaction, are a saw, a hammer and a pitchfork.

When, in his mid-twenties, Kiff had first begun to paint fantasy pictures, he'd experienced a sense of helplessness: the images that appeared were often extremely frightening. He had needed help. He began seeing a psychotherapist, whose orientation was broadly Jungian. (It wasn't merely an intellectual adventure; as Kiff later insisted, 'I wasn't right in the head.') Those sessions put him on easier terms with his imagination and taught him to avoid closure on any one interpretation. He wrote of receiving 'moral support' from his analyst; but also, especially relevant to this image, that the analyst 'provided a polarity'. And in thinking about the prevalence of the self in art over the past century, he saw it as an assertion of the individual – against negativity, against the collective and the corporate, but also, more generally, against the not-self. 'It's like a discovery.... It's an unknown.... It isn't self-aggrandisement.... An image of oneself in the painting never merely represents one's self.' For Kiff, each painting was the outcome of a complex exchange, between an underlying 'abstract' stratum of colour and potentiality, and the 'figurative' image that eventually emerged from it. 'The hill was yellow now. But if it stayed yellow, it might not stay a hill; and if it stayed a hill, it might not stay yellow.'

That process of image-forming is evident in all the 'modernist symbolists' of this section. Ensor, Kubin, Tagore, Yeats, Kiff – each in their different way participates in that shift of language which separates their figuration from any copying of reality. As Kiff wrote in 1979:

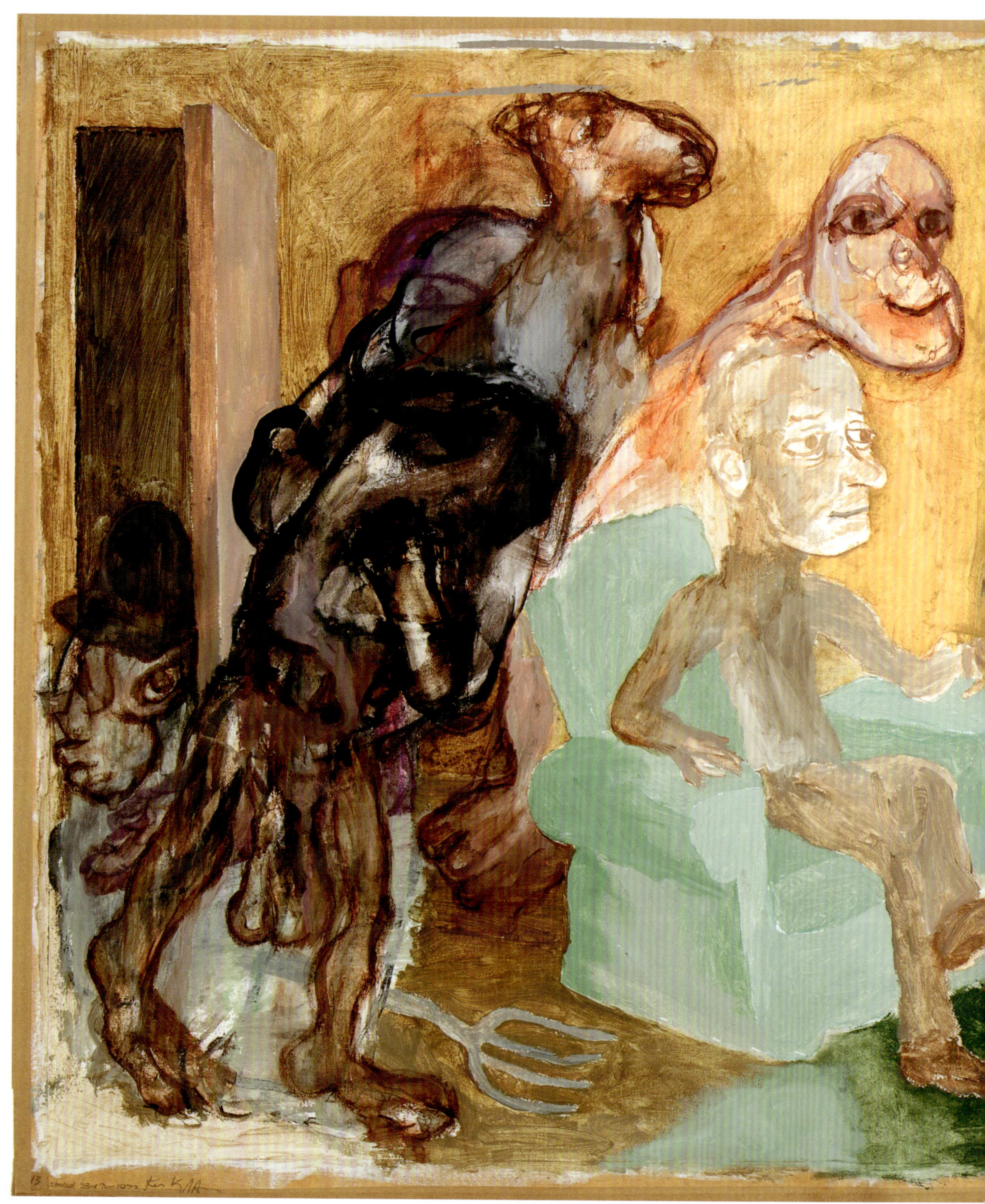

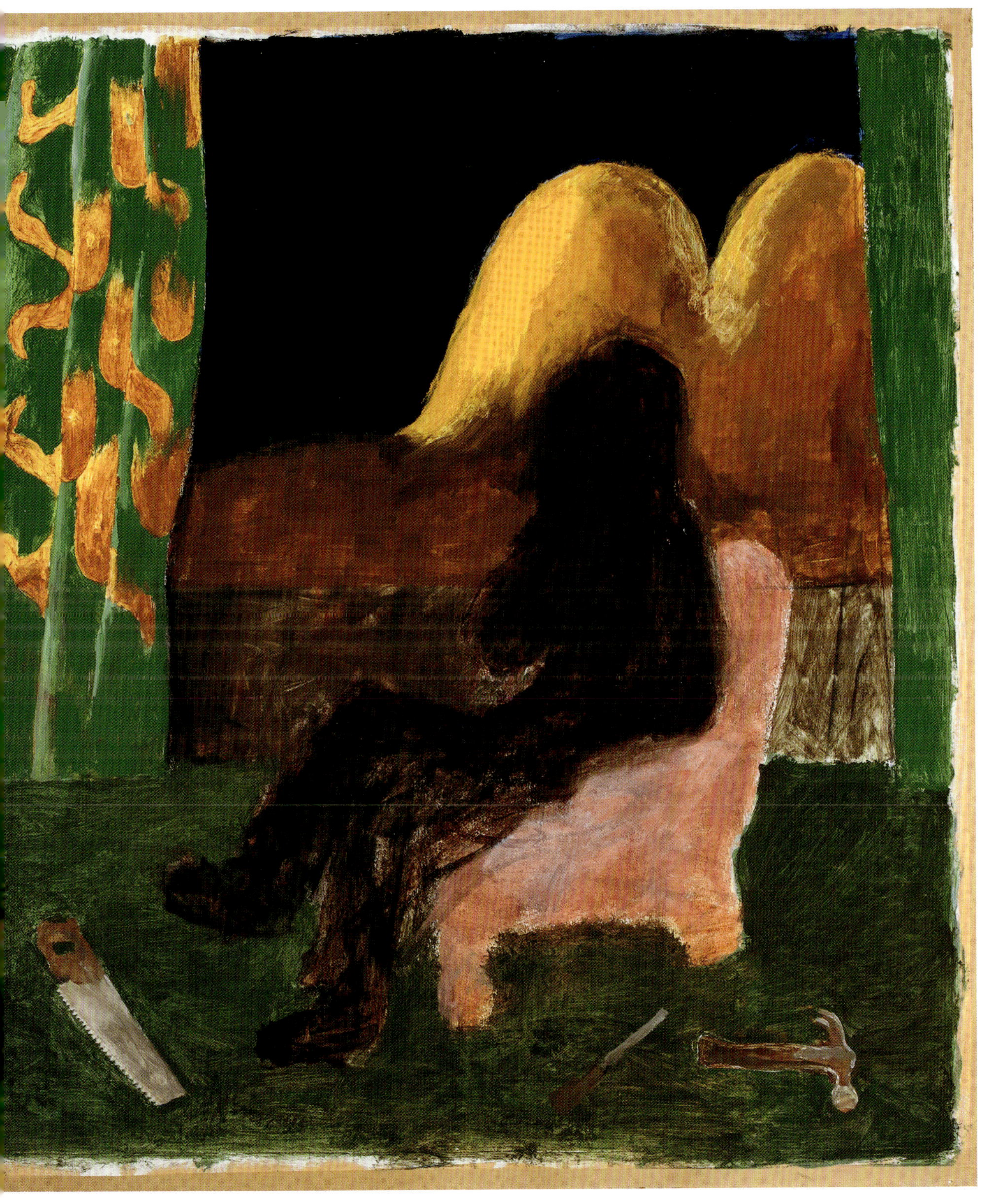

The symbol-construction that a dream is, presses towards the future...
So with the symbol-construction that a painting is: using the present and
the past, it presses towards the future.

The world has to be remade, its forms – figures, objects, spaces – dragged out of an inward Void, constructed anew in an unpredictable exploration.

ALFRED KUBIN'S *OTHER SIDE* (1900-30)

*I hit upon the idea of capturing dreams in picture form
as they are still reflected in one's memory immediately
after waking. For years, night dreams as well as so-called
daydreams or waking dreams were a rich mine....
I made a really methodical study of dreams. I read
old as well as quite recent theories about them....
Finally I became completely at home in this
phantasmal dream-world....*

ALFRED KUBIN, 1917

When Alfred Kubin (1877–1959) recalled his turn-of-the-century beginnings as a dream-artist, he emphasized not his solitude but his discovery in his late twenties of a graphic 'family' to whom he could relate intimately. He wrote of his childhood isolation after his mother's death; rejection by his father; failure, mental breakdown, attempted suicide; but also of how, from this personal crisis, art rescued him. His first inspiration came from seeing Max Klinger's sophisticated etching cycle *The Glove*, of 1881; that evening, Kubin was 'suddenly overcome by a whole avalanche of black-and-white imagery'. Soon he had constructed a lineage that went back to Goya's last great aquatints, the *Disparates* or 'Incongruities' (1819–24) – nocturnal worlds that create an absurdist imagery; fear and black humour in tandem. Kubin looked also to William Blake; to Ensor and to Félicien Rops; above all, to Odilon Redon's *noirs*, those lithograph cycles dedicated '*À Goya*' (1885) and '*À Edgar Poë*' (1882).

Kubin visited the aged master in 1906. Redon had been a dissident in his own generation; as he recalled, 'I decided not to embark on the Impressionist Boat, because its ceiling was too low.' Kubin's imagery around 1900 is openly about sexual need and obsession – not (as in Rops's) with any pornographic purpose, but more akin to the transgressive truth-telling of Sigmund Freud's contemporaneous *Interpretation of Dreams* (1899). A naked man is whipped, and produces an enormously long continuous sausage of excrement. A severed head is on the ground, looking up appalled at a headless man in his underpants, standing with his back to us; his posture makes clear he is masturbating. Elsewhere, genitalia and colossal breasts abound, alongside more philosophic fantasies: a head on a stalk flowers out of a marsh, its lichen moustache identifying it as Nietzsche.

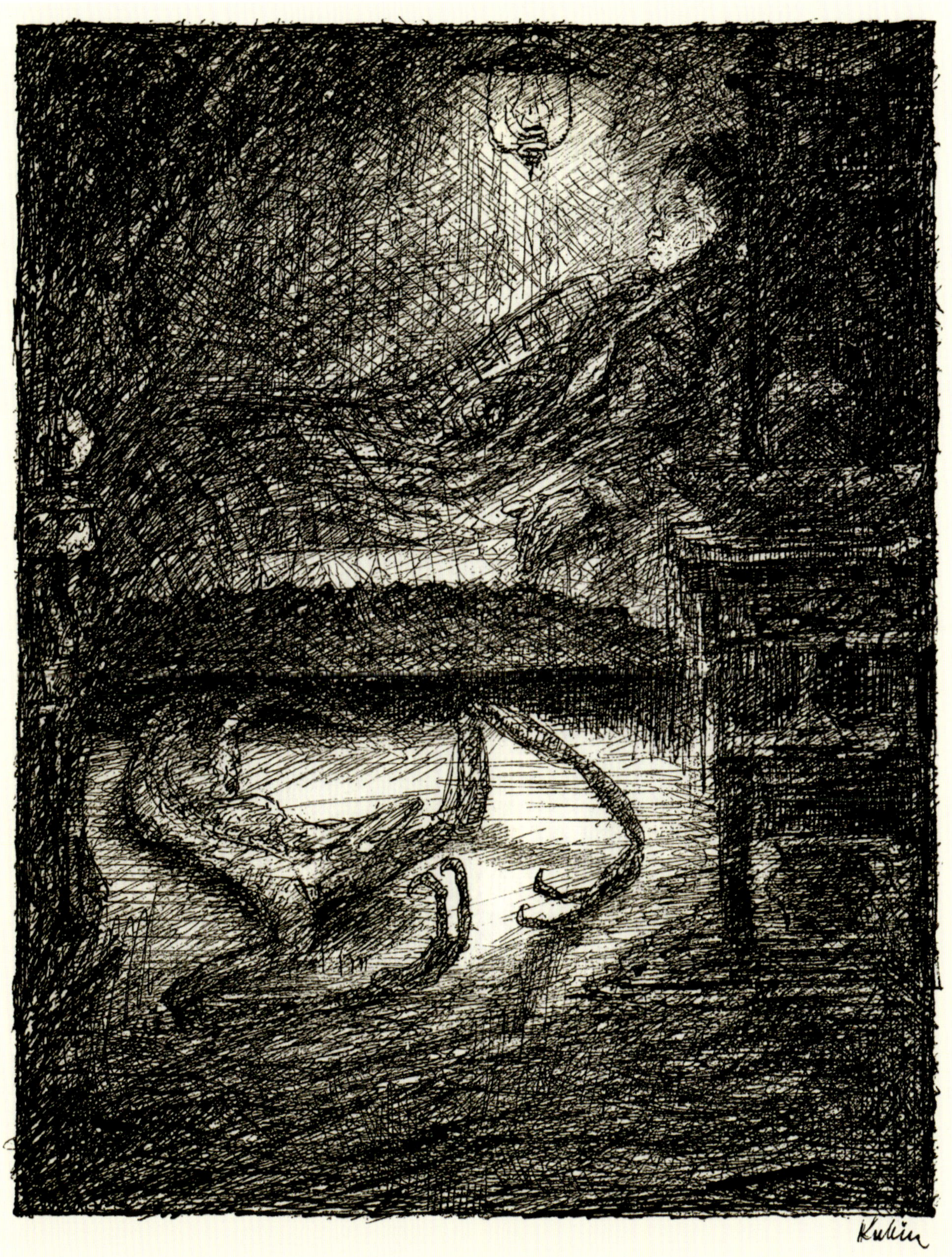

Kubin

These several hundred nocturnal images are elaborately realized in ink, blown through a filter. Such serio-comic spookery needs to be rendered plausible by means of naturalistic tone: following Redon's formulation, 'placing the logic of the visible at the service of the invisible'.

In 1909 Kubin published his dream-novel *The Other Side*, with his own illustrations – the work for which he is now best known. It reads uneasily, both darkly symbolic and ironic; for example, at one point in the dream-kingdom the narrator comes across 'a genuine Grünewald', but its subject is *The Seven Deadly Sins Eating the Lamb of God*. In 1903, Kubin had drawn the cover for Thomas Mann's novella *Tristan*; he would become the greatest of all German illustrators, serving especially Edgar Allan Poe, but also Dostoevsky, E. T. A. Hoffmann, Gogol (see Ch 1 pp. 33–40) and Strindberg. In Prague he came to know the then still-obscure Franz Kafka – a fellow dream-transcriber, and, like Kubin, a German-speaker born in Bohemia. 'I should have liked very much to have provided illustrations for Franz Kafka's novellas, which touch me so intimately', he wrote in 1931. *The Scorpion* (*c.* 1922) [illustration p. 169] recalls the horrific transformation into an insect enacted in *Metamorphosis* of 1915 (among the few stories Kafka published in his lifetime). As in his drawings for *The Other Side*, Kubin was now building tone with a kind of filigree scribble made with a thin nib. He conjures authentic night-fears out of countless repeated little marks, with something of a *graphomane* obsessionality; he felt affinity with the art of the insane and acknowledged in a late statement, 'I am a visionary, or even someone who suffers hallucinations.'

It was Kubin's somnambulistic line that brought him into the orbit of the Expressionist group *Der Blaue Reiter* (Blue Rider), whose leader Kandinsky (1866– 1944) wrote of Kubin pulling us 'into the terrifying atmosphere of the implacable void'; according to fellow-member Klee, 'his art grasps the world as poison, as collapse'. The fragile lines of Klee's 1911 drawings to Voltaire's satire *Candide* bring him close to Kubin; they share a comic-phantasmagoric vein (which exhibitions of Klee's work often suppress in favour of its structural component). Kubin's conception of art as 'inseparably bound up with the unconscious' was an influential corrective, and he has been described as 'a father figure to the world of fantasy.' One sees echoes in the work of many later twentieth-century artists – in the flow-of-thought drawing sequences of Günter Brus; in the hatched lines of Mervyn Peake's *Gormenghast*; in the comical-terrifying animations of Jan Švankmajer and his disciples the Brothers Quay.

Both Klee and Kubin visited the Prinzhorn Collection in Heidelberg, in 1920. Kubin's response was explicit:

> We were standing before miracles of the artistic spirit, dawning from the
> depths, free of any intellectual overlay; the creation and contemplation of
> which must bring happiness.

This was prior to the publication of Hanz Prinzhorn's *Artistry of the Mentally Ill* in 1922. 'In our time', wrote Klee, 'worlds have opened up which not everyone can see into...perhaps it's really true that only children, madmen, and savages [*Wilder*] see into them. An in-between world...'. To see madness as a kind of liberty was part of modernism.

IMAGE AGAINST THE WORD:
RABINDRANATH TAGORE AS A PAINTER (1928-40)

Beginning in his late sixties and continuing until the year before his death, Rabindranath Tagore (1861–1941) created at least two and a half thousand paintings. Since 2011, almost all have at last been reproduced, in four huge volumes. All are untitled, and this flow of small images on paper remains hard to bring into focus. They are his oddest, most anarchic achievement; everything in them counters the prevailing notion of Tagore as Olympian Sage and Educator (see Ch 1 pp. 45–47). He wanted, he said in 1928,

> to recapture the play of forms, not in any emotional, sentimental or intellectual manner, but purely for the sake of assembling individual forms together.... It is immaterial whether these creations are good or bad; what is important is that some form has *emerged* out of all those lines and colours.

Nevertheless, his art did change: from a stylized, not altogether convincing modernity before 1930, towards the looser, more atmospheric and accepting images of his final decade.

His painting had its origin in an assault on the written word. It was in 1925 that 'erasures' first erupted onto the poet's manuscripts – doodles that gradually, like a fungus, overwhelmed the lines of Bengali script, rendering them illegible. Those doodles refused to be ignored: 'They cried out, like sinners, for salvation, begging to be rescued into a merciful finality of rhythm.' Tagore was at that point perhaps the world's most celebrated public poet; in 1913 he'd been awarded the Nobel Prize, and, two years later, a knighthood. But by 1928, with the Indian Independence campaign gathering strength, every word he wrote was weighed for its political significance. In his darkest moment, when words had failed him, painting opened up as the most disinterested activity left to him.

His working pattern seems to have been constant: each image completed in one sitting, often four or five in a day; his main tools an ordinary fountain pen and Pelikan inks. 'I am so taken with this new game that all my various responsibilities, extraneous to myself, peep in from outside my door, only to withdraw the next minute with much shaking of the head.' As he wrote in 1930, 'I nourish a desperate hope in my heart...to play truant to all obligations that are compulsory. The artist in me ever urges me to be naughty and natural.'

At the beginning, Tagore's typical forms were concentrically banded enclosures, designs filled in with coloured inks: animals, plants, birds, serpents. Their visual sources might include totem poles, Batiks, the Vorticist drawings of

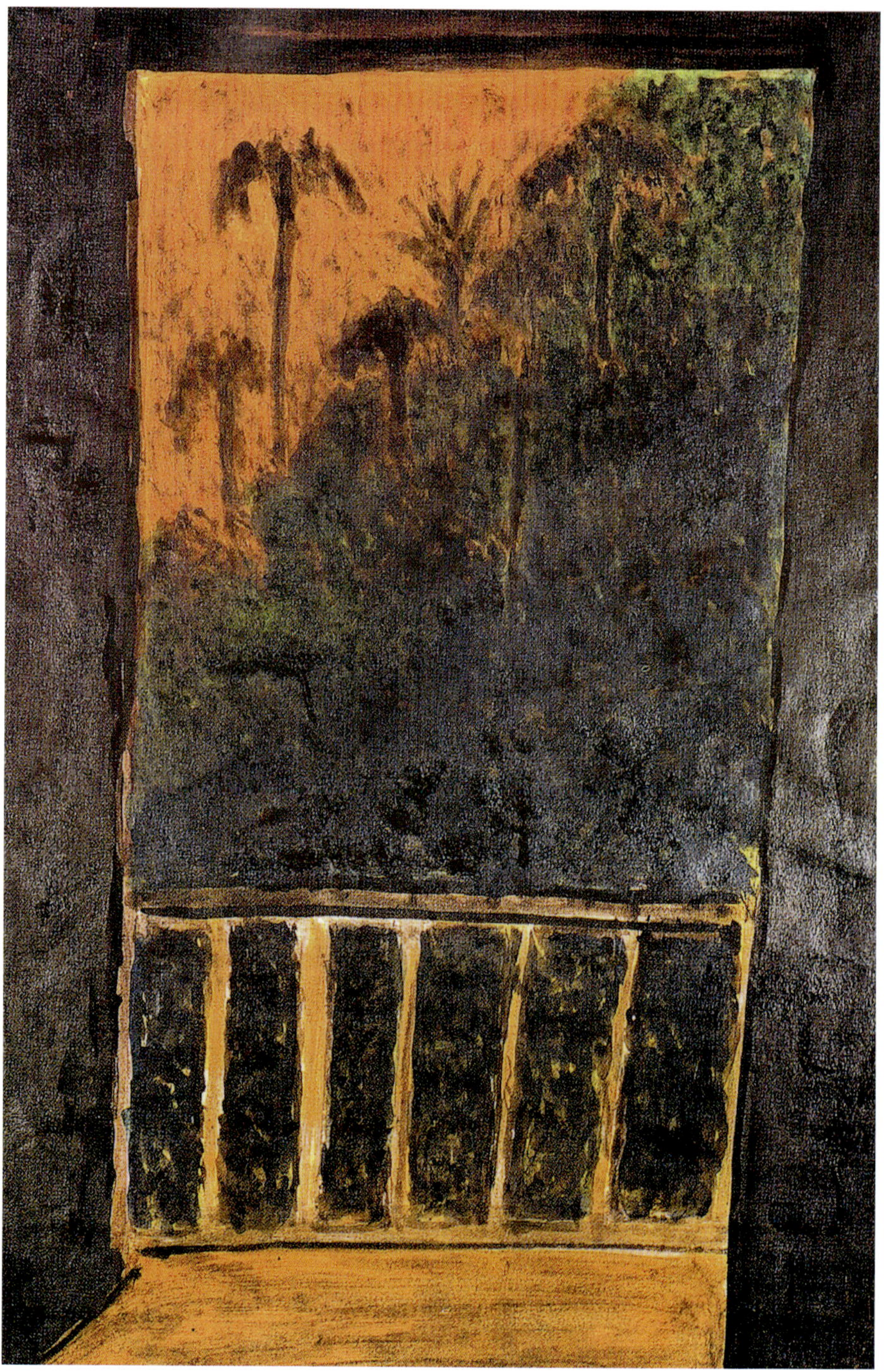

Wyndham Lewis (exhibited in Calcutta in 1922) and the woodcuts that illustrate Kandinsky's *Concerning the Spiritual in Art* of 1912.

But after his first exhibition in 1930, Tagore's handling became more fluid. Tone and touch developed the image more unpredictably; if it threatened to set rigid, he spoiled it. As he explained in 1939, 'I spill ink or scratch haphazard lines. After it is thoroughly spoilt, I start salvaging it until it assumes some other aspect.' Light is the new dimension in his imagery – building the surface by veils of transparent colour. He wrote of his art as 'a memory of light, treasured by shadows'. Trees and bushes are silhouetted against the dusk, or the grey starlight, conjuring a furry, atmospheric warmth and tenderness. In the image chosen here [illustration opposite] a hillside is viewed from a balcony, with palms waving up a steep green slope, and above, a wonderful yellow-gold sky – each mark visible in the saturated, spreading colour. We often see old people, like children, looking with a hungry wonder at the natural world, and Tagore's late apprehension of trees and flowers is of this kind. As he told a friend, two years before his death, 'That is why there is so much joy in the very act of seeing.'

In 1912, Tagore had lived in London; a friend of W. B. Yeats, in the aftermath of the 'Celtic Twilight'. But in the 1920s his contacts were more with Germany; Jungian ideas about the therapeutic value of automatic drawing, and the teachings of Klee and Kandinsky, fed into his aesthetic – he visited the Bauhaus in 1921. That winter, he invited the Viennese art historian Stella Kramrisch to Santiniketan, attending many of her forty-three lectures. As Kramrisch recalled, 'He accepted...the linear exclamations of Munch, and the monsters of Kubin', along with her own input of Rudolf Steiner's theories and Theosophical 'thought-forms'. When, a decade later, Tagore's own imagery emerges, his visual language is inflected with a strong German accent, and his pen drawings (such as *Fox in the Night*) often echo Kubin's filigree tonal scribble.

Nearly all are dark in tone; the unpeopled landscapes nocturnal, the heads looming in shadow. A bird flies, a flower bursts, in a field of colour, not as a scene but as an emblem. This is a genre of graphic art that depends on a creative flow; as with Redon or Kubin, discrimination must be suppressed. Yet while we may agree that perhaps one in three succeeds, we may find we differ as to which. The pictures are best seen in bulk, and in long sequences; the occasional misjudged or mawkish note is often swiftly counterbalanced by a more robust restatement.

As we look through his later images, everything works to deepen Tagore's *silence*. Refusing interpretation either as narrative or as ethical statement, his paintings are allowed to carry only those meanings words cannot express. He evades that web of allusion and aspiration that thickens most great painting, to become one of those fortunate 'outsiders' who so regularly put trained artists to shame. Many twentieth-century painters have conceived of themselves as – in Josef Herman's words – 'the last inheritors of a pre-verbal culture'; of art as a silent negation of the verbal construction of the world. Tagore, so eloquent in verse and prose fiction, in song and in his essays, became in the 1930s the *elective mute* of twentieth-century art.

JACK YEATS: TOWARDS 'THE HALF-DREAMING STATE' (1932-55)

No one, not even his wife, was allowed to see Jack Yeats (1871–1957) at work in his later years. He painted behind closed shutters, always by electric light – one of several procedures he developed, as though deliberately to sabotage technical control. He often squeezed a blob of pigment from the tube directly onto the canvas, and then cut into it with a palette-knife, perhaps smearing it with his fingers also. The result is a kind of tattered impasto, a broken blur that serves as metaphor for what he called 'The Half-Dreaming State' – for imaginings almost intangible, and memories almost irretrievable. It is a surface very different from that other memory-blur used by Bonnard for the re-creation of the stilled and perfected moment (see Ch 3 pp. 128–33). The raw, chaotic instability of Yeats's surfaces rules out any designed, formal integration; but it makes of each picture a matrix, allowing him to fumble figures and imagery out of the Void.

Born in London, Yeats had started out in 1894 as a jobbing black-and-white draughtsman for a periodical called *Lika Joko*, and he continued to work as a humdrum illustrator. In his late thirties, however, when he was living in

JACK YEATS

The Clown Among the People
1932

The weird white face is hemmed in by a mostly female 'People', and set against the arch of a horse's neck and a showgirl, half-glimpsed in the darkness behind.

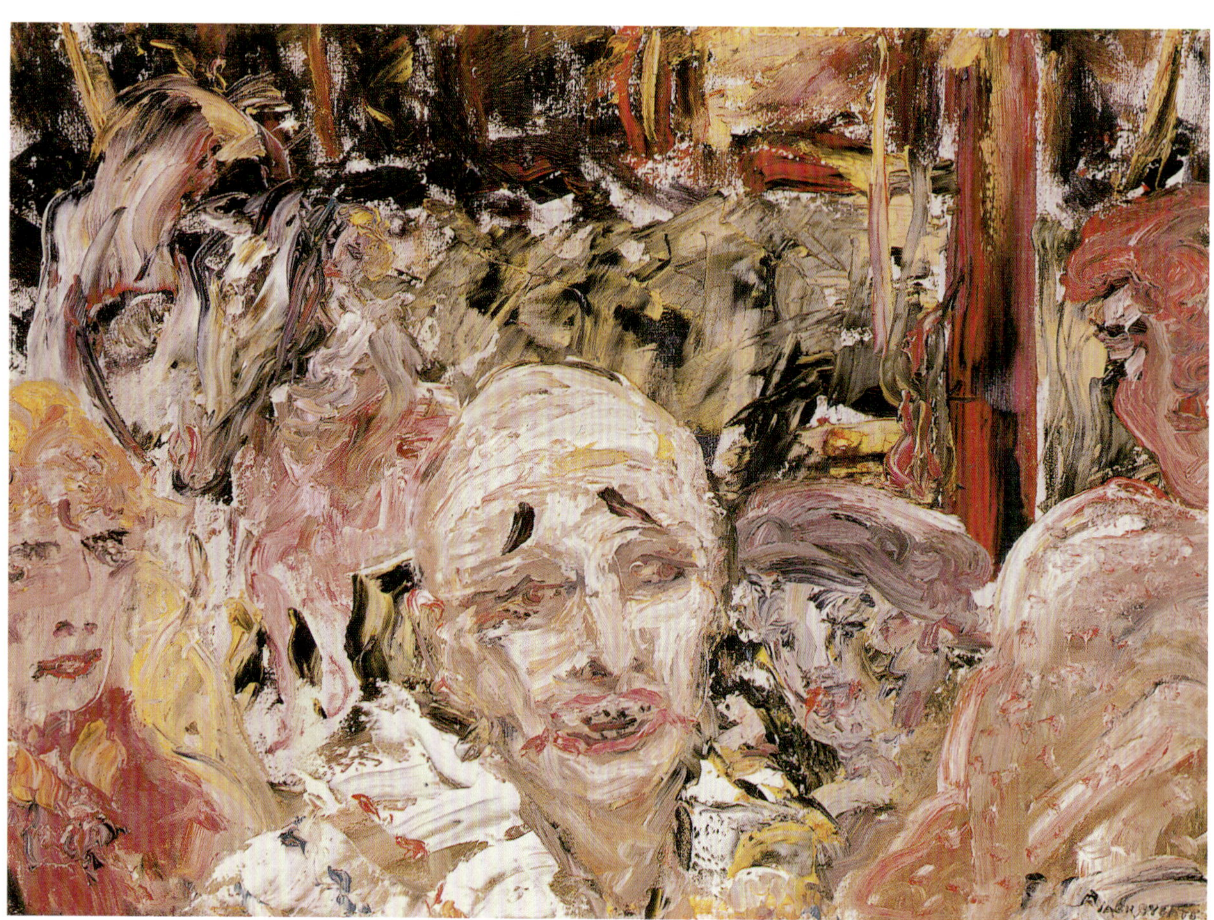

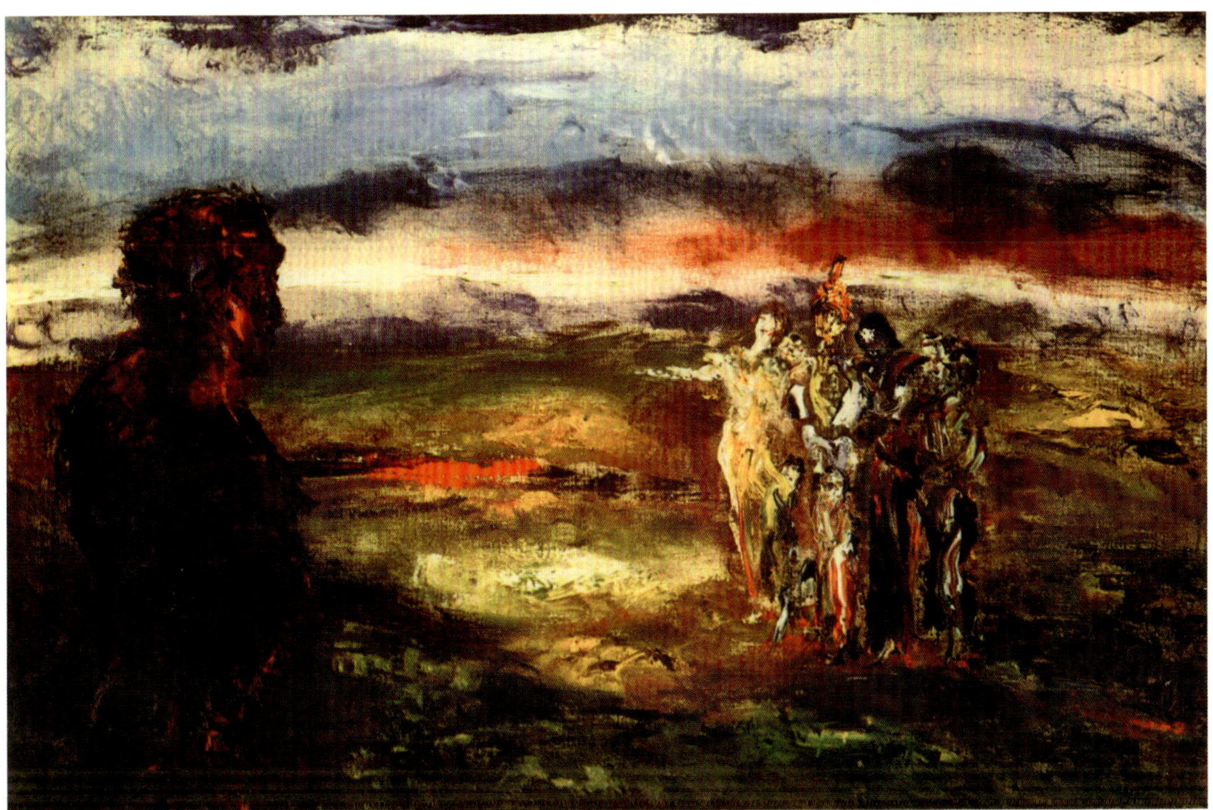

Ireland in the first years of the new century, he'd begun to paint in oil; and after a mid-life breakdown (coinciding with the defeat of the Republican cause he'd espoused), he entered a wonderful decade, in which he became Ireland's truest 'painter of modern life'. Jack Yeats did for Dublin what John Sloan and George Bellows did for New York, and Walter Sickert for London. These were the compositions characterized by Sickert, in 1924, as 'Life above everything. The movement of figures true and felt, and the landscape, water, sky, houses ruffling like flags in support of them.'

In 1922 Jack Yeats had travelled to Europe, visiting Paris, and perhaps (as some believe) first met Oskar Kokoschka in Dresden, glimpsing also the paintings of Lovis Corinth. Whatever he saw on that journey may have been midwife to his third and final manner. The painter Frank Auerbach has likened Yeats's development to that of Philip Guston (see Ch 5 pp. 197–98 and 216–19) in the 'radical changes of style without loss of conviction' that both artists underwent. Yeats's late paintings seem to abandon every element of his earlier achievement – no line, none but the vaguest indications of place: all dissolved in air and light. Yet, in practice, his raw material was in the hundreds of tiny ring-backed sketchbooks he'd filled before 1910, fugitive pencil notations from his wanderings along western Ireland's roads; chance encounters, and sudden effects of sunlight, recorded long ago. 'Being an ocean island', he wrote in 1929, 'the clouds are thin, and the light filters through softly, and with perpetual change, in a way you can never forget.'

That mobility finds its equivalent in the vehemence of his handling, which both obscures and transcends any ostensible subject. *The Clown Among the People* (1932) [illustration p. 174] may come from a circus seen in the 1890s. All the components of the original sighting are endowed with a new significance by the wild surface; universalized into an image of solitude and distress.

This sense of the artist looking back at his own self-created pageantry – a world of circus and fairground, seen always as dream, with an impassioned wistfulness – converges unmistakeably with the tone of his brother's late poems. I am thinking especially of 'The Circus Animals' Desertion' (1933); but so many of W. B. Yeats's tags and phrases – 'In exalted reverie', 'My fanatic heart', 'Grant me an old man's frenzy' – cluster about this brother also. Jack Yeats increasingly saw painting as 'greater than writing. Painting is direct vision and direct communication.' From 1929 onwards, James Joyce (having purchased two pictures) was sending him draft passages from *Anna Luvia Plurabelle*, the future *Finnegans Wake*, to which the painter felt a real connection. Joyce found in his paintings 'great silences'. When he pronounced 'Jack Yeats and I have the same method', he partly meant recollection in distant memory, but also, I suspect, dissolution in language.

Blocked by recurrent depression between 1933 and 1935, Yeats emerged in his late sixties into a final fierceness, completing another six hundred paintings before his death in 1957. *The Expected* (1948) [illustration p. 175] comes from that most fertile period. (The catalogue raisonné lists seventy-nine pictures in that year alone.) Smouldering and fiery, this is Yeats at his most visionary. Through the dark foreground figure, we are made to witness the approach of some legendary hero in armour and plumed helmet – an Arthur or a Saturn returned as saviour, coming to meet us across the boggy, tree-less plain. That bareness and dissolution made Yeats a modernist, an exemplar and mentor to Samuel Beckett. Invoking an affinity between the aged painter's imagery and the weightless procession of *The Pilgrimage to Cythera,* the playwright marvelled: 'He grows Watteauer and Watteauer.' For Beckett, the late painting of Jack Yeats 'brings light to the issueless predicament of existence'.

HENRY DARGER AND *THE REALMS OF THE UNREAL* (1937–73)

Henry Darger (1892–1973) began writing *The Realms of the Unreal* in 1911, at the age of nineteen, having recently escaped from an asylum: it was the 50th anniversary of the American Civil War, and he now conceived a parallel conflict, in which child slaves – pre-pubertal girls – rebel against adult male oppressors. By 1934 the narrative ran to fifteen thousand closely typed pages, millions of words bound in fifteen volumes. Only long after this huge labour had been completed, perhaps shortly before the Second World War, did Darger commence the new project that would occupy him for much of his remaining life – the creation of pictorial narratives to accompany his text. He had already made ambitiously scaled collages (Civil War battle scenes with myriad tiny figures glued in); that panoramic imagination was eventually carried over into the strange format of his enormous watercolours (each typically around two by nine feet, and often double-sided). The hundred or so long, scroll-like images in which Darger's vision is at full stretch establish him as one of the significant artists of the twentieth century.

Darger's very extended format is appropriate for the depiction of an immense inner world, cosmic in scope. The same composition can encompass multiple experiences; not just transitions from inside to outside, from near to far, but also conflicted states of being. The flower-filled idyll to the left of *[Storm] Brewing* [illustration pp. 178–79] is registered alongside the brown tornado clouds billowing up from the distant right edge, above that terrifying flat-black wedge piercing the pale grasslands; an image divided, yet harmonized by his astonishing colouristic and compositional gifts.

Darger has been recognized as the greatest of 'outsider artists' – innately talented but untrained, without knowledge of cultural tradition or role. As defined by the author of by far the best monograph on Darger, John MacGregor, 'Outsider Art requires that the artist create a vast, encyclopaedically rich and detailed alternative world – not as art – but as a place to live in over the course of a lifetime.' This entails 'a considerable rejection of reality'. Perhaps solipsism shading into autism; another definition might be *autism made communicative.*

In his imagery of the Vivian Sisters, the seven young princesses who lead the child slaves to liberty, Darger invented a new visual mythology that still resonates among contemporary poets and artists. Each watercolour began with Darger laying out big sheets of paper on a long table, and making a pencil drawing – in which every element was the result of tracing. The room Darger rented in North Chicago for some forty years was ankle-deep in detritus (balls of twine, old shoes and spectacle cases) that he'd 'rescued' and brought home. But among all this was also the raw material of his art: discarded newspapers, fashion illustrations, and comics (such as the *Little Annie Roonie* strip); 'Kiddies' Colouring Books' with titles like *Let's Do Dots*; several volumes of Frank Baum's *Oz* series. (The Vivian Sisters might be described as a multiple Dorothy.) Somehow Darger was able to weld these elements together – along with silly stickers, comic Tweety Pies – into his wonderfully coherent tableaux.

From 1946 onwards he employed a new procedure. Having traced his chosen figure from its source – typically no more than an inch high – he would take the little sheet to the local drugstore, enlarging it photographically, sometimes to fourteen inches. Then he would retrace – at this stage the figures were often, as he explained, 'nuded', – and sometimes added to his girls a little penis. By 1959 Darger had built up a repertory of at least 250 figures, which could be deployed at various scales, whether reversed, or more likely, shamelessly repeated. Thus in *[Storm] Brewing* the pile-up of seated girls in polka-dot

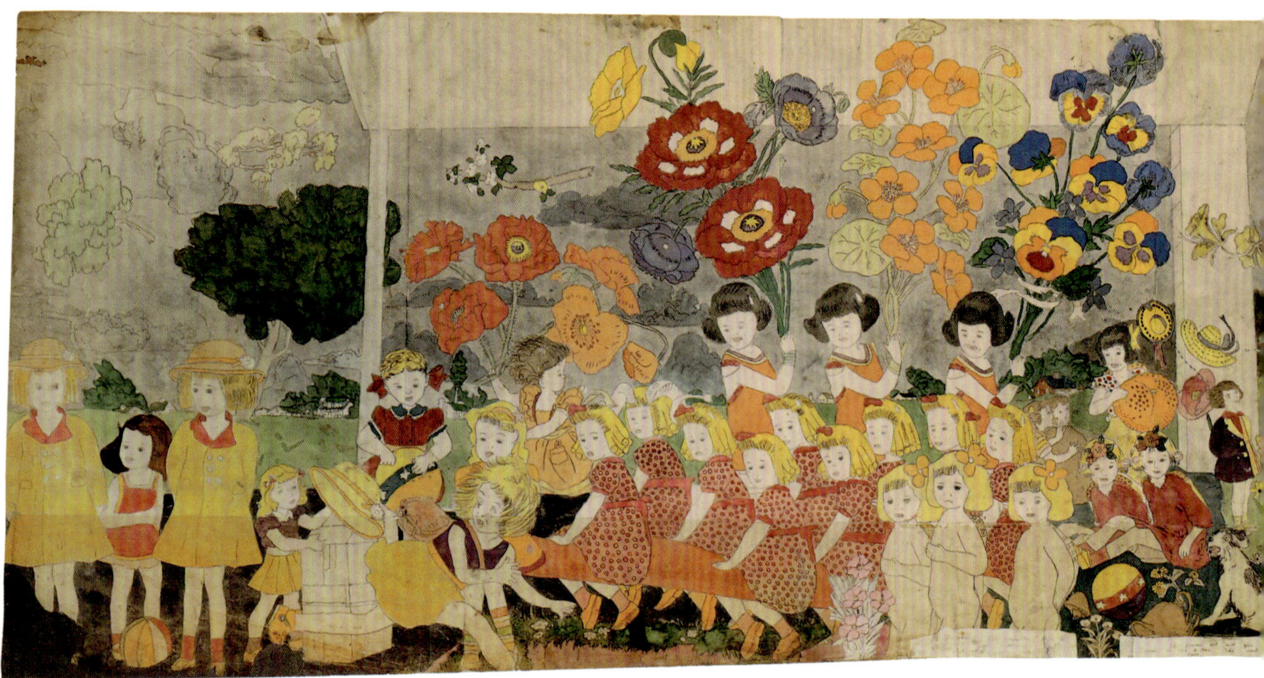

party dresses is assembled from a single identical tracing; and four of the girls fleeing from the storm clouds at right are also repetitions.

As interpreted by MacGregor, Darger 'adopted' the girl-images he found abandoned in the street, and his bedsitting room became a kind of orphanage. At one point in *The Realms* the Vivian Girls stumble upon the works of Darger. 'He must have been a very odd man…. He had to use them [the figures in the paintings] as company as he was childless.' Darger described himself as a 'Man of Child Worship'. In his most famous works little girls are swarming in all directions. While the Vivian Sisters wear pretty frocks, the slaves are often naked, kitted out with the penises that have caused so much discussion. My sense is that the transformation into the *Unreal* demanded this extra dimension; the girls were rendered thereby not so much androgynous as a new genus – celestial, seraphic, running and romping within their Edenic landscape.

His collage process was a kind of 'dream-work', and Darger's *Realm* is his dream-kingdom, endowed with a strange familiarity by its being assembled from American popular culture. The gorgeous early Technicolor of the 1939 *Wizard of Oz* – Emerald City above Yellow Brick Road – fed into his aesthetic, as did that young heroine, battling through the tornado, emancipator of misfits and munchkins. Yet the evil confronting the Vivian Girls goes far beyond any mere 'wicked old witch'.

Darger's gifts were most fulfilled in horror and atrocity. *The Massacre at Norma Catherine* (*c.* 1950) [illustration pp. 180–81] has been described as 'The Isenheim Altarpiece of Outsider Art' – a great panorama of cruelty, which, like Grünewald's,

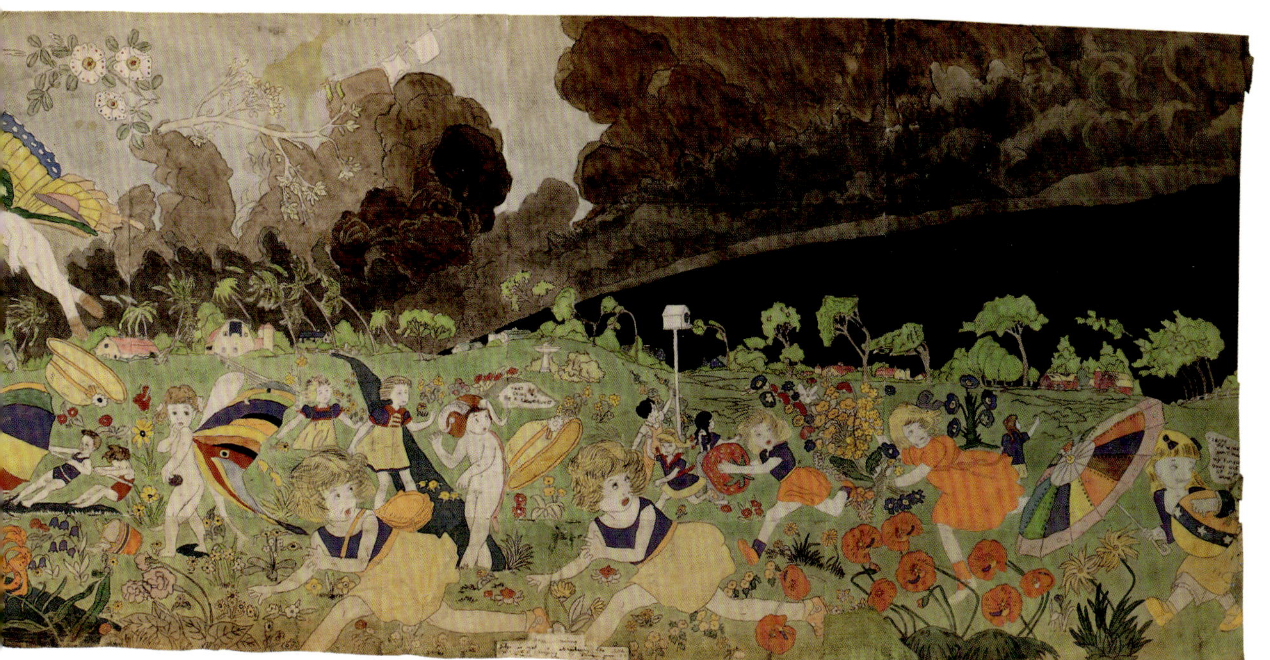

makes all other imagery appear insipid. The triptych depicts the culmination of repeated massacres by the anti-Christian 'Glandelinians'. The Vivian Girls 'have a thrilling time fleeing through a field of gutted bodies of children'. An extract from a typical text reads:

> Many children looked as if they had gone through the meat chopper. Even little girls, from the ages of nine, eight or even younger, were tied down stark naked, and a spade of red hot live coals would be laid on their bellies…. Hearts of children were hung by strings to the walls of houses.

In his central panel, flanked by two highly inventive orgies of slashing and disembowelling, Darger constructs a kind of Sadeian sculpture park: massive plinths on which the child corpses are decoratively arranged. Tracing now from a body-atlas, he delineates the internal organs, red against the snow. (MacGregor writes of 'a refrigerated museum of anatomy.')

The triptych was exhibited at London's Hayward Gallery as part of an *Outsiders* survey in 1979, alongside thirteen other Darger watercolours. Coming just at the moment when the formalist canon was crumbling, this previously unknown artist had a lasting impact on a new generation of painters, among whom Paula Rego and Grayson Perry are the best known. Rego made her pilgrimage to Darger's home in Chicago, and has spoken of the Vivian Girls as a constant exemplar for her own narratives (see Ch 1 pp. 56–57). Perry, in *Portrait of the Artist as a Young Girl*, names Darger as 'the artist I identify with most'. Yet *The Massacre at Norma Catherine* was

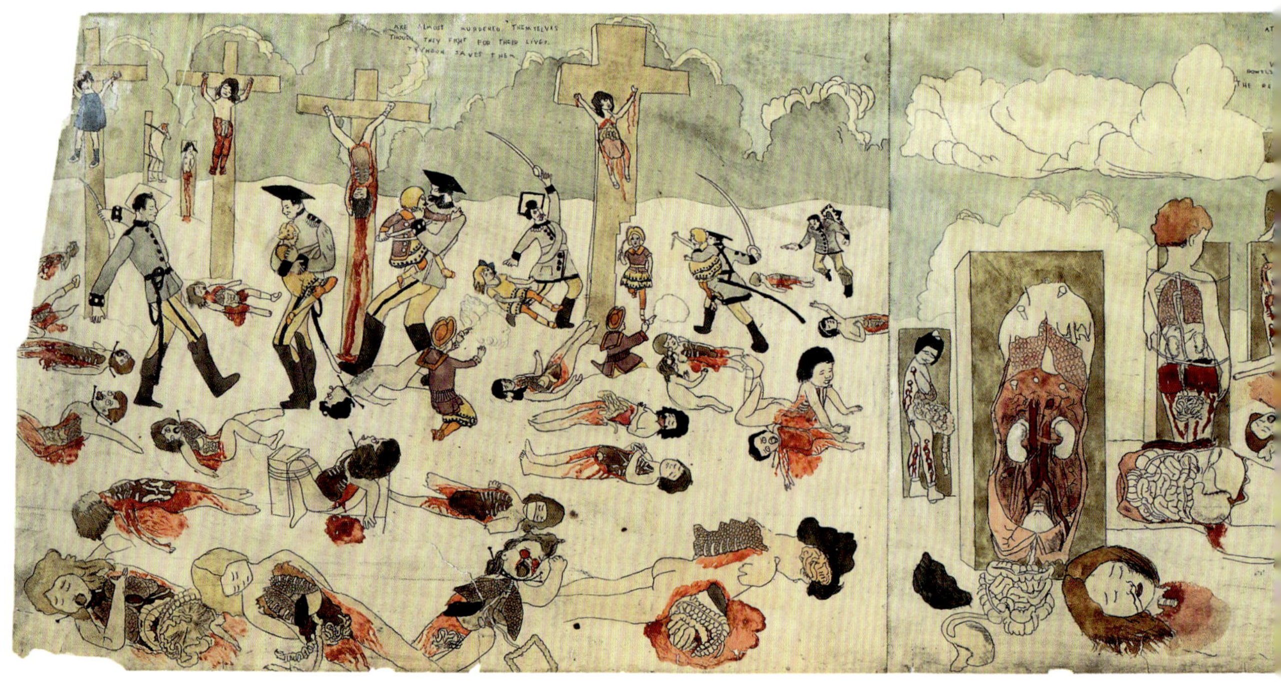

HENRY DARGER

From *The Realms of the Unreal: The Massacre at Norma Catherine*

1930–1972

AT LEFT: *THEY ARE ALMOST MURDERED THEMSELVES THOUGH THEY FIGHT FOR THEIR LIVES. TYPHOON SAVES THEM.* AT CENTRE: *AT NORMA CATHERINE VIA JENNIE RICHEE. VIVIAN GIRLS WITNESS CHILDREN'S BOWELS AND OTHER ENTRAILS TORN OUT BY INFURIATED GLANDELINIANS. THE RESULT AFTER THE MASSACRE. ONLY A FEW OF THE MURDERED CHILDREN ARE SHOWN HERE.* AT RIGHT: *VIVIAN GIRL PRINCESSES ARE FORCED TO WITNESS FRIGHTFUL MASSACRE OF CHILDREN – VIVIAN GIRLS NOT SHOWN IN THIS COMPOSITION…*

neither exhibited nor reproduced for the next twenty-one years; and would surely remain unexhibitable were it not for Darger's positioning outside society, allowing him the licence of the mad.

Darger made his art for no one other than himself, while working as a janitor in various Chicago institutions. His prolific output was discovered only shortly before his death. When the Chicago Bauhaus photographer Nathan Lerner inherited Darger as a tenant, he was utterly unreachable. ('How're you doing, Henry?' might elicit 'Storm approaching, north-north-west, thirty degrees.') When we insert this outsider into twentieth-century art, the possibilities of painting are expanded. With Darger on board, American art looks different; one might, for example, find his appropriation of popular culture more interesting than Roy Lichtenstein's. Or one might be struck by the affinities between his *Massacre* and the roughly contemporaneous triptych by Francis Bacon [see Ch 1 pp. 54–55, illustration p. 54]. Darger does, after all, fulfil Daumier's famous injunction that an artist 'must be of his time'.

JACOB LAWRENCE: *THE MIGRATION OF THE NEGRO* (1940–41)

Although essentially untaught, Jacob Lawrence (1917–2000) never conceived of himself as an outsider. From the poster-like idiom of his initial paintings made as a boy-wonder at the Utopia Children's House embedded within the Harlem of the WPA years (see Ch 2 p. 104), he developed a crisp, modernist vernacular. That 'schoolroom' or 'carpenter' – or, in his own phrase, 'dynamic' – Cubism

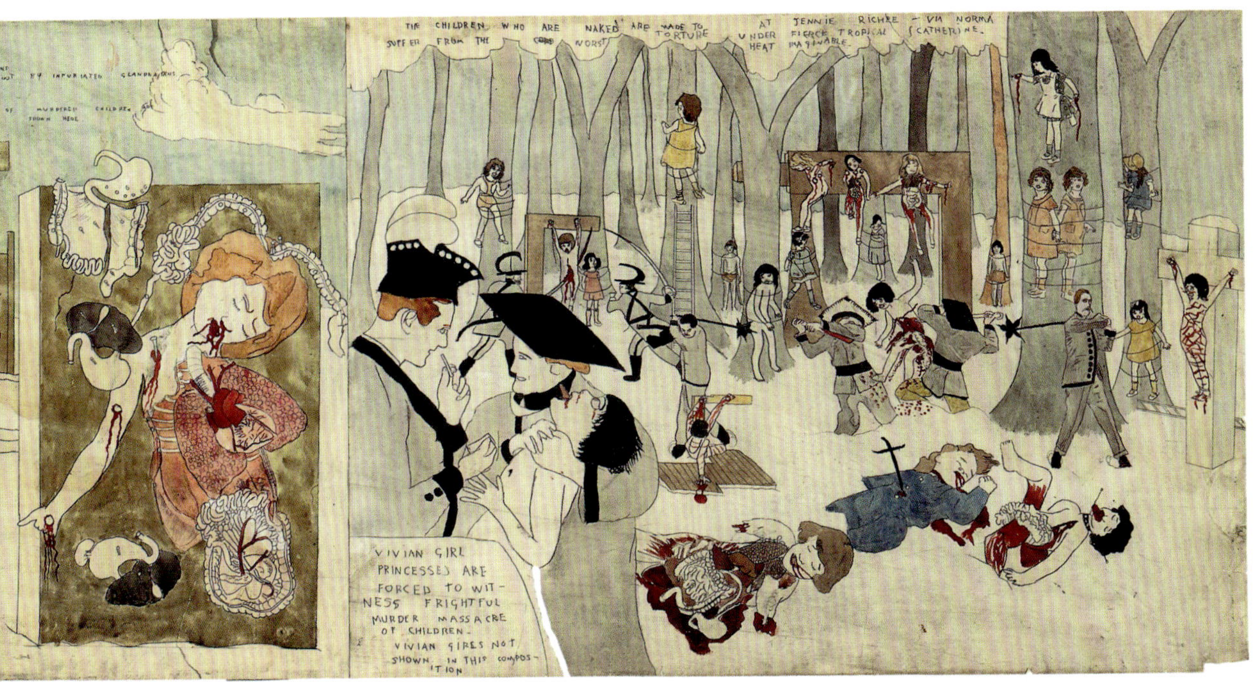

delivered an intensely formal language, allowing him to depict the 'suppressed realities' surrounding him: what Lawrence himself called 'the black experience, which is our heritage'; and to become, in his wife's terminology, a *griot* – a community storyteller.

He completed his first great narrative project, *The Life of Toussaint L'Ouverture* (1938), before the age of twenty-one. It was a new subgenre within history painting, intimate in scale, to be shown as a wall of multiple, captioned images. Two more *Lives* followed – of Frederick Douglass (author of a great slave autobiography), and of Harriet Tubman (guide to runaway slaves) – further heroes of black emancipation.

The *Migration of the Negro* (1940–41) [illustrations p. 183] is his most ambitious series – sixty small panels (each 12 x 18 inches), presented in both vertical and horizontal formats. Like Charlotte Salomon in those same years (see Ch 3 pp. 145–51), Lawrence took cinematic montage as a paradigm. (He'd become close friends with Eisenstein's American associate Jay Leyda, who was at the time setting up the Museum of Modern Art's Film Library in New York.) Leyda also introduced the twenty-three-year-old to the Mexican muralist José Clemente Orozco (see Ch 1 p. 42), whose compressed, anti-naturalistic figures confirmed to Lawrence the direction and style of his own art. Lawrence's theme was the 'Great Migration' that took millions of Southern blacks north, both during and after the First World War. All his series began with research. Yet, as he explained of *Toussaint*, 'I didn't do it as a historical thing, but because these things tie up the Negro today.' Making a grant application before embarking on

the *Migration* series – which he envisaged exhibited in schools, and as a book –
he declared:

> I feel that my project would lay before the Negroes themselves a little of what
> part they have played in the History of the United States.

His earnest, pared-down captions are an essential part of the panels; his words,
like Salomon's, interacting with the visual in unexpected ways. He laid out all the
panels on the floor of a studio hired specially. He wanted the images to be not
just stylistically compatible, but united in a single motion of thought, alternating
between South and North. Both the lynch rope and the family discussion –
emblems rather than scenes – are components within this cumulative narrative,
ending 'and the migrants kept coming.'

Stylistically, his imagery still seems extraordinarily fresh, by contrast with
the attempts by the Harlem Renaissance generation to create a 'New Negro' idiom.
Unlike them, Lawrence did not have to overcome any academic conditioning.
Not a naïf but rather a *puer aeternus*, he felt on easy terms with the early Italians
in The Metropolitan Museum (finding inspiration in the tight linearity of Carlo
Crivelli), while being nurtured equally by the bold patterning of fabrics in the
tenement rooms of his neighbourhood. His own family had migrated north from
Virginia shortly before his birth; he was raised in Pennsylvania, coming to New
York only at thirteen. He wrote:

> I was part of the migration.... The series came out of that – people talking
> about people coming up from the South.

Lawrence unfolds each stage of the migration experience with intimate proximity;
avoiding false optimism, acknowledging the bleakness of the North and the
disappointment, yet communicating 'people on the move' as some kind of
emancipation. His voice is that of a chorus. Asked whether he'd considered what
the black community might think of his painting, he replied, 'I am the black
community.'

The series gained immediate recognition: exhibited at a downtown
commercial gallery, widely reproduced, eventually purchased jointly by The
Phillips Collection in Washington, DC, and the Museum of Modern Art in New
York (who had toured it across the United States during the war). Yet although
Lawrence continued to produce magisterial work, in 1949 he suffered a severe
depressive breakdown and was hospitalized for eleven months. In the following
decades he often had to defend his highly formalized art against the prevailing
pressure to go abstract:

> The *human* subject is the most important thing. My work is abstract in the
> sense of being designed and composed, but it is not abstract in the sense of
> having no human content.

After the triumph of New York Abstraction (see Ch 5 pp. 193–98) the work not
only of Jacob Lawrence but of his older, white mentors from the social realist

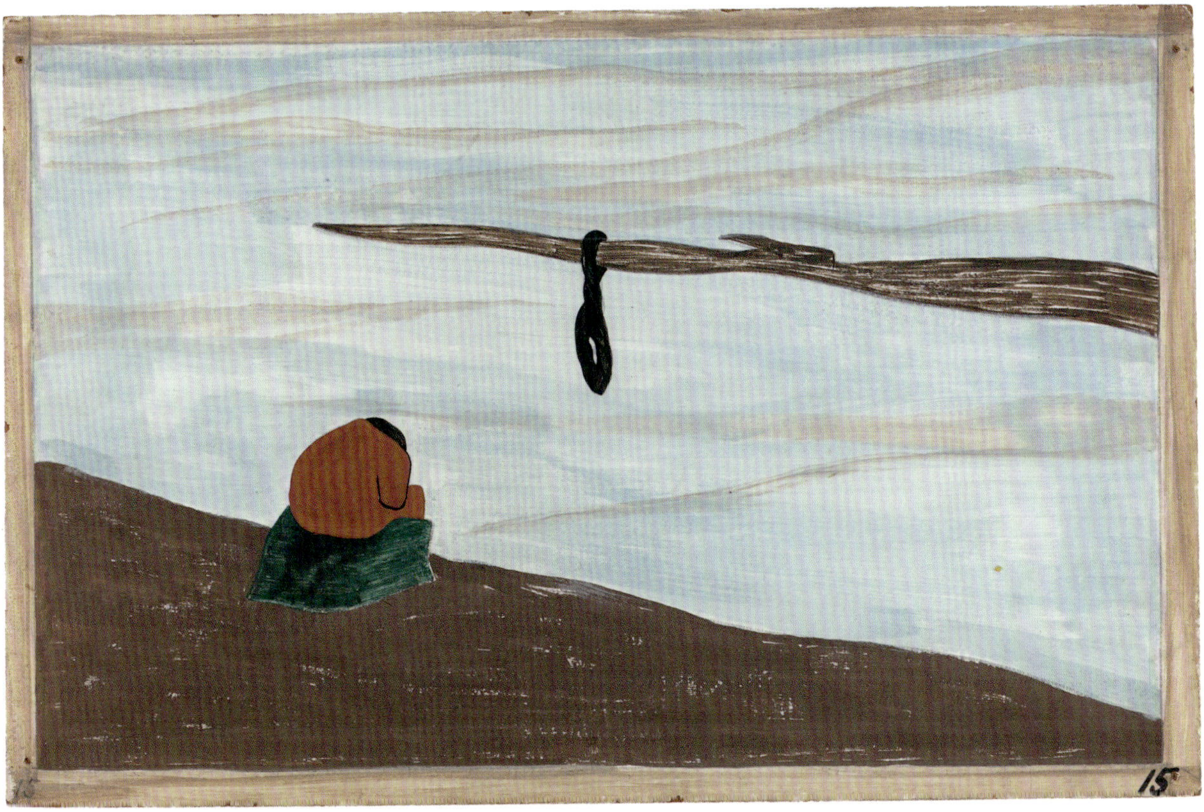

15

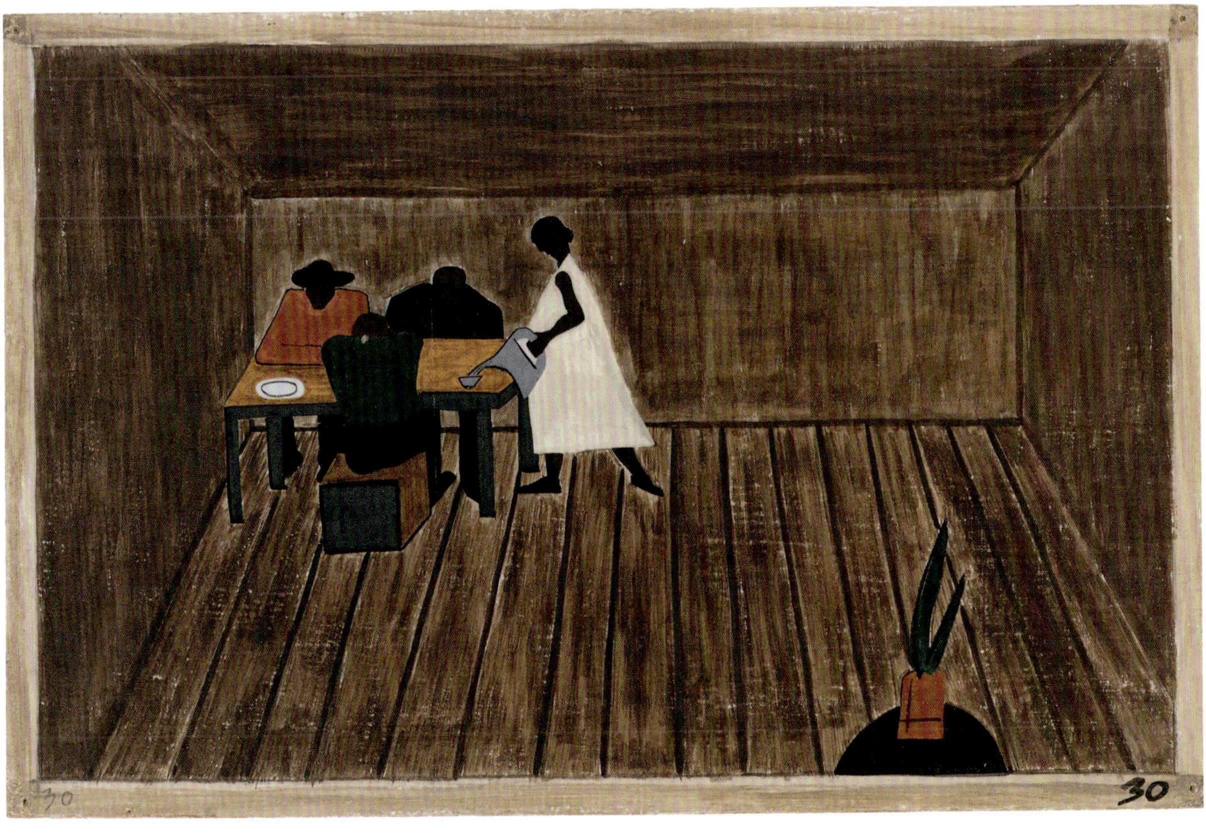

30

generation – such as Philip Evergood and Ben Shahn – were 'disappeared' from most art histories. The recent reassessment of Lawrence has helped to consolidate a new perspective on American art: a retrieval of memory which reignites another emancipation.

KEN KIFF AND *THE SEQUENCE* (1971-90)

*If you go through a nothingness period and come out
the other side, what you come out with could be some
kind of imagery. One might speak of 'flexible realism':
painting interacting with the life inside one and outside.
More of reality can be rediscovered, reclaimed, brought into
a new wholeness. Some understanding of the manifestations
of the unconscious, and of the 'feminine' in ourselves –
do these point towards a revolution in art beyond what
seems to be happening in the West?*

KEN KIFF, 1979

In 1971 Ken Kiff adopted a new strategy: each week he would hope to begin at least one or two images, in acrylic on paper, usually on a modest scale. *Sequence number one* [illustration p. 186] was entitled *Something Unknown Has to Be Eaten or Drunk*. Below two yellow hills a little man is seated, hand on chin, staring at the huge bowl and spoon set before him. Close by, at the lower right corner, a long-nosed, comic creature rises up from the floorboards; and above, to the left of the curtain, two smiling masks look down. Throughout the 1960s he'd painted mostly in tempera on a thick gesso ground, allowing him to change each image constantly, 'literally hundreds of times, radically'; 'to an almost crazy extent'. Few were completed. Kiff resolved *Person Cutting an Image* [illustration p. 187] after six years, just before he started *The Sequence*. It is a middle-of-the-night image, not so much about The Artist as The Dream-Work. That symbolic act – tenderly, resolutely scissoring into a smiling self-image – becomes an assertion of being, pressing into the black Void.

From the beginning, *The Sequence* released a new lightness, an intimacy and refinement of touch, that is central to Kiff's achievement. Working on as many as a hundred images – free to leave each and return a year, or three years, later – removed any pressure to force a picture through to some monumental conclusion. Swallowing 'something unknown' might suggest both an initiation and a submission; we might make associations with *Alice in Wonderland* – but also with shamanistic mystery cults. Many of the two hundred or so subsequent images chronicle a journey through some archetypal *terra incognita*, through Cave, Mountain, Boat, Castle. In several, a Little Man is protagonist, reappearing at different stages of his pilgrimage. (Kiff was reviving that structure of 'continuous narrative' found in early Sienese predella panels of the fifteenth century, among his favourite paintings.) Sometimes his figures are in modern or Victorian dress; more often, naked men battle with worms, excrete, or carry off girls, invoking our primal ancestry. On the shores of Hell, a tree bears human heads as fruit; in *Sequence* number eighty-eight, a *Spitting Man* spews heads out of his mouth.

Yet these primitive, often violent, adventures are punctuated by more reflective images, as already seen in *Talking with a Psychoanalyst: Night Sky* [see p. 165, illustration pp. 166–67] – an exceptionally large image within *The Sequence.* Kiff tried out various overall titles – *Journey Towards Realism, Acceptance, Movements of the Spirit* and even *Psychoanalysis Remembered* – before settling on 'The Sequence'. He cautiously likened the whole series to 'a long episodic dream', in which each image 'may be a fresh attempt to make a symbolic structure, commenting on the situation in oneself which the dream is about.' As a whole, *The Sequence* does resemble a dream-analysis, in which archetypal situations recur and are reformulated. At one point he envisaged publication, with commentary by 'a social anthropologist, a psychotherapist, an art historian.'

The conviction that painting has to do with processes of healing and integration came to Kiff very much at first hand. His wartime childhood was shadowed by his father's death in an air raid; he suffered nervous attacks, misdiagnosed as epileptic fits. After art school he taught 'educationally sub-normal' children part-time. In looking at *Sequence* number thirty-five, entitled *Walking (The Dead Father)* [illustration p. 188], it may be helpful to register first the faint Little Man, striding along the left periphery. If this is The Walker, then all those other, larger and more forceful elements in the picture might be seen as his imaginings: through this change in orientation, we can enter his mind. Above the torso of the naked figure, instead of a head, is a platform on which two smiling figures converse. Yet this is not an apparition of horror. The sense is of all being rendered benign, brought into harmony within a golden light.

In *Sequence* number ninety-seven, *Writing* [illustration p. 189, detail p. 162], the artist gazes swivel-eyed at his Muse; Kiff's doubling of profile with full-face (redeploying Cubism) creates an ambiguous reciprocity between them. The left hand is 'writing' an image, and from the split head spills a wild cargo of creatures. In the unlikely medium of acrylic, Kiff has created a wonderfully alive surface, with breaks and blank areas, and ultramarine sandpapered into translucency, alongside the density of that greenish-black head. Our sense is of each image being crystallized gently *from the touch*, out of a matrix of possibility.

Kiff once defined fantasy as 'a way of thinking about reality'. Conceiving each painting as composed of 'floating chunks of stuff', Kiff achieves a wonderful flexibility, as in *Sequence* number ninety-one, *Earth Face* [illustration p. 191] where one leg becomes crimson, the other resting upon a green animal. Yet an ordinary English house stands behind him, and, in the lower

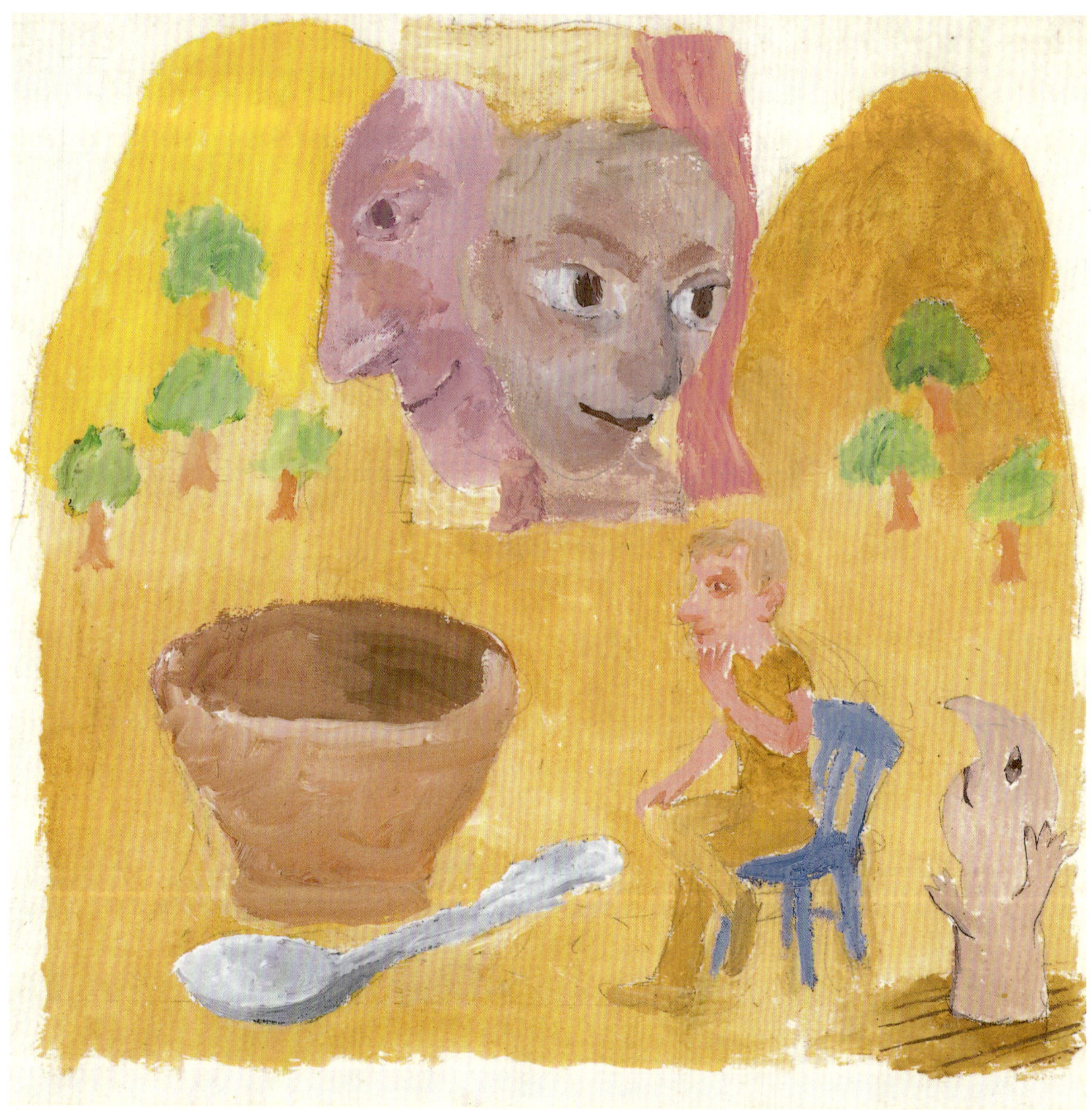

KEN KIFF

From *The Sequence*
Number 1. *Something Unknown
Has to Be Eaten or Drunk*
1971

That 'something unknown' might have been – as in
Herman Hesse's *Steppenwolf*, Lewis Carroll's *Alice*,
or Carlos Castaneda's *The Teachings of Don Juan* –
a hallucinogenic substance; but here the bowl and
spoon signify some more everyday mind-alteration,
perhaps psychoanalysis itself.

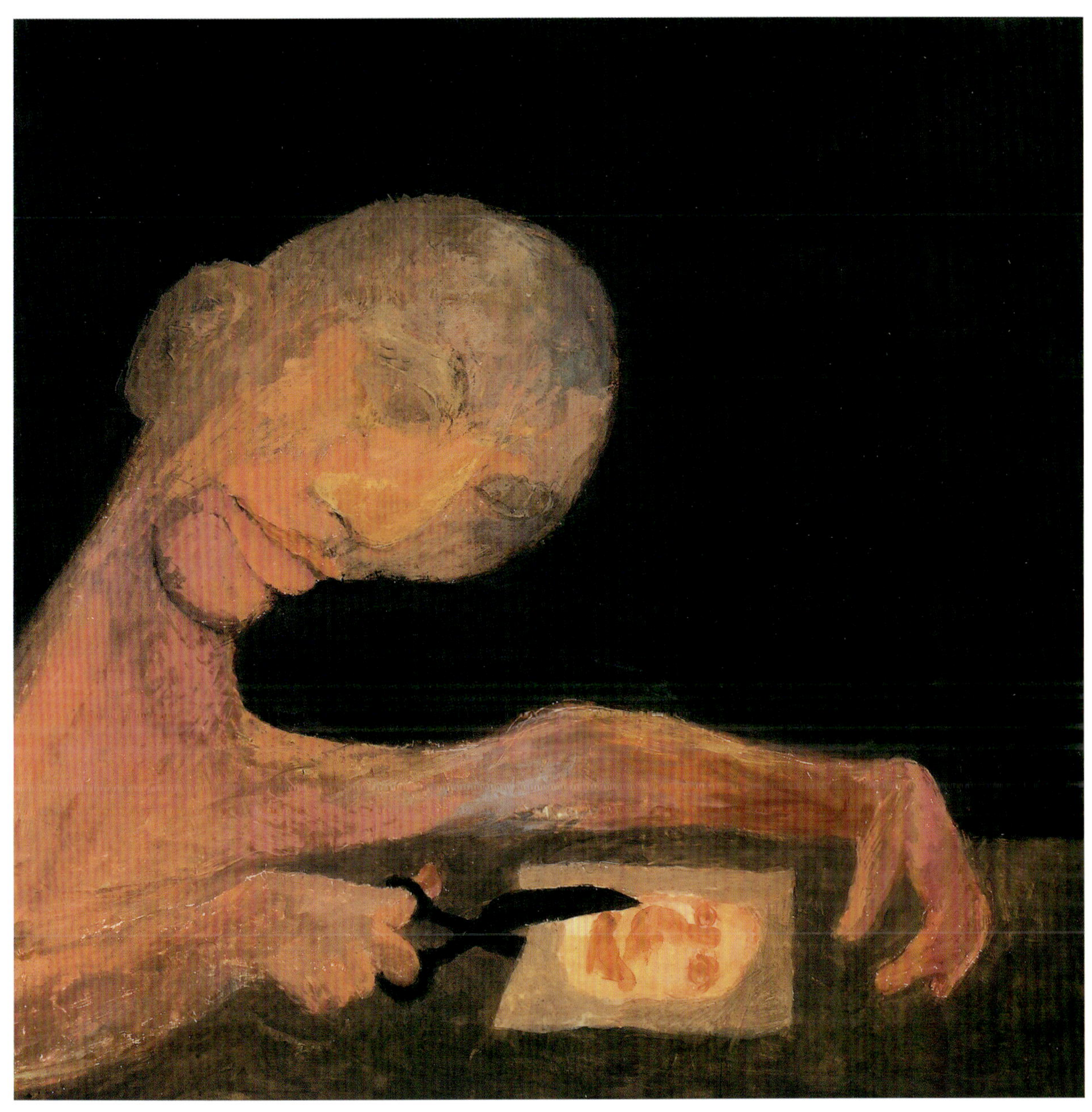

KEN KIFF

Person Cutting an Image

1965–71

The internalised 'person' or protagonist emerges
as a kind of unborn child, with an embryo head.

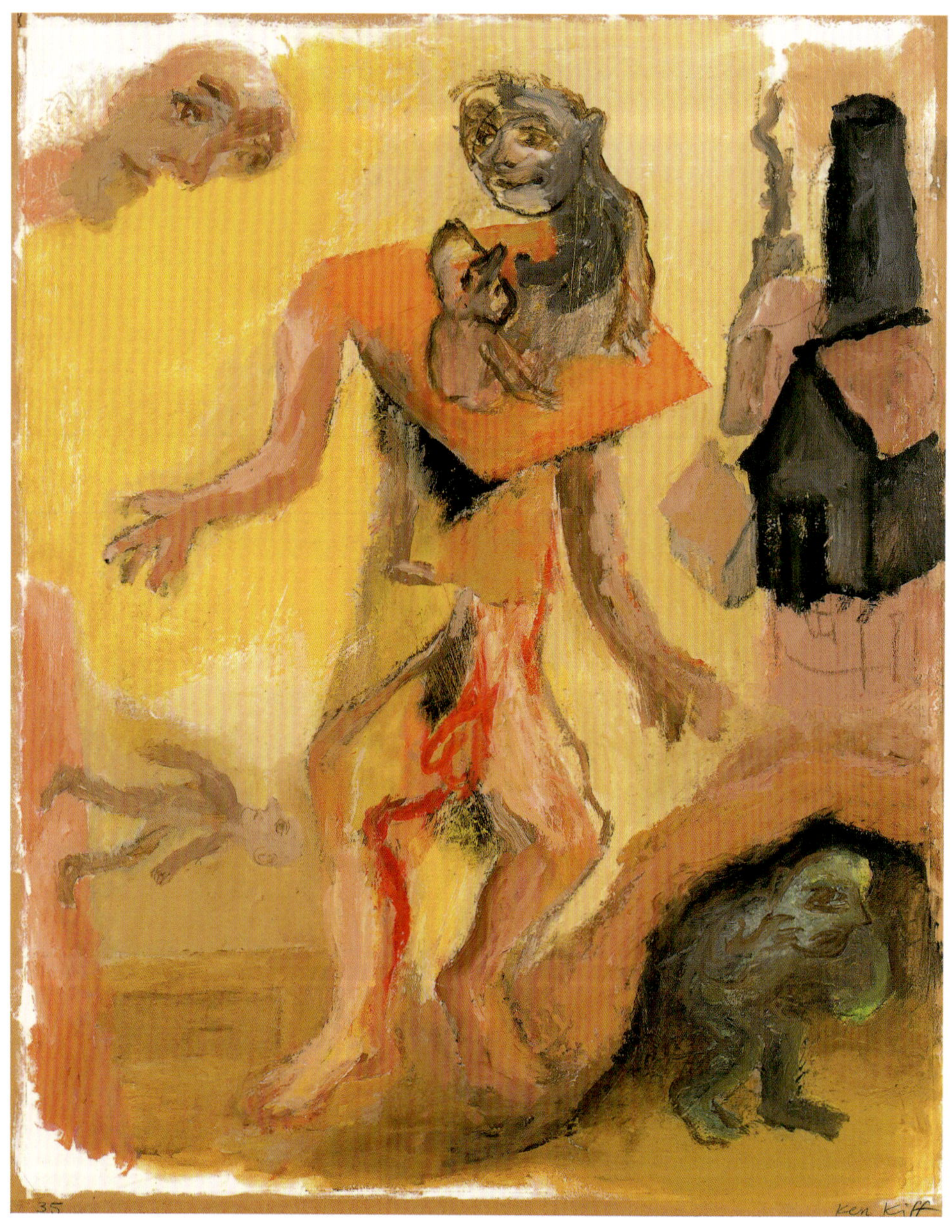

KEN KIFF

From *The Sequence*
Number 35. *Walking (The Dead Father)*
1972

As a water-based medium, acrylic tends to
be more buoyant than oil, more frisky and
fancy-free.

KEN KIFF

From *The Sequence*
Number 97. *Writing*
1977–79

When asked whether *The Sequence* was
autobiographical, Kiff replied, 'No. Except as
painting inevitably is…. There's no avoiding that
aspect of painting.' Like his favourite Paul Klee
(and like Tagore) Kiff watches himself at play
(see also detail, p. 162).

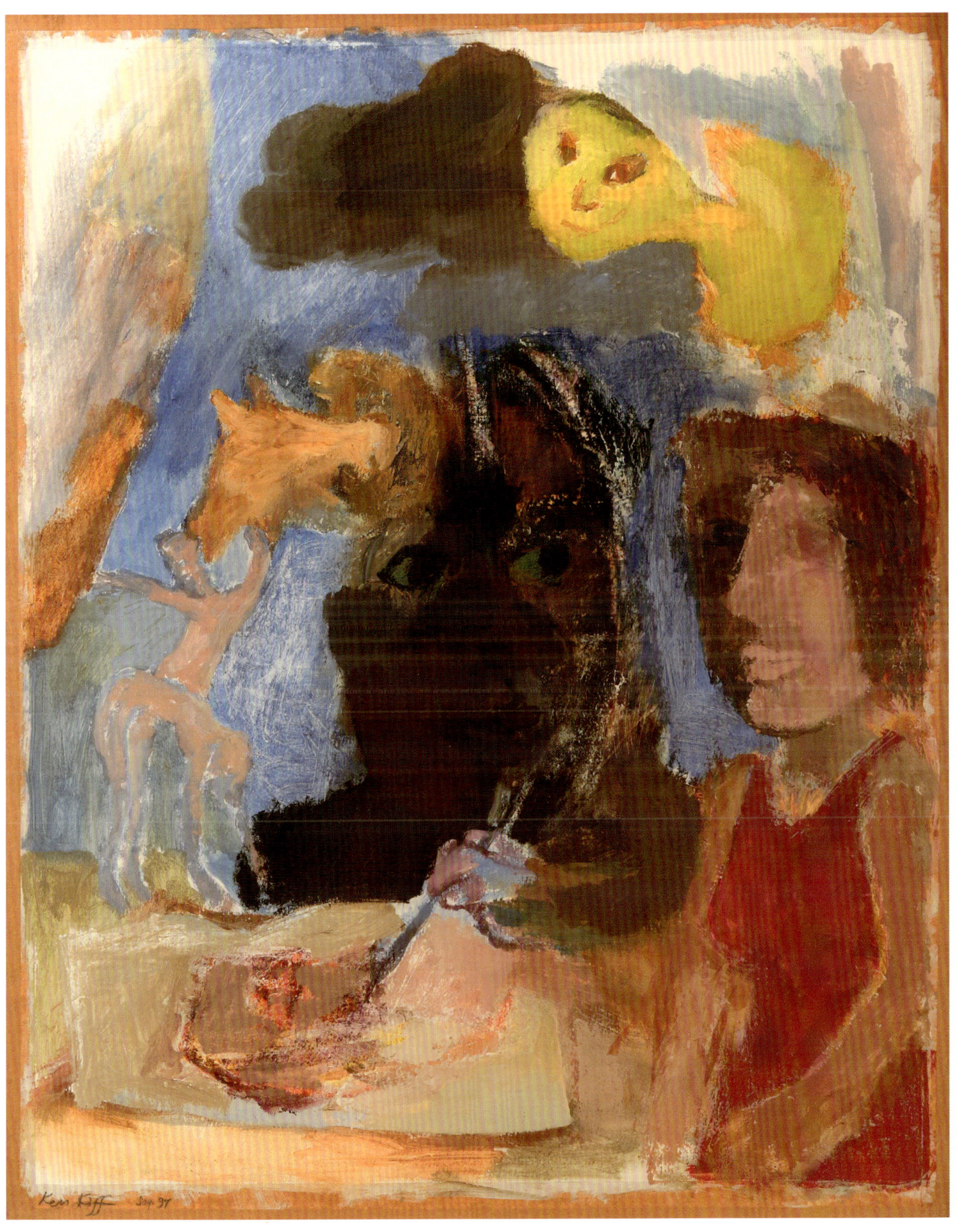

foreground, a table with cup and saucer. The critic Andrew Lambirth has summarized Kiff's theme as 'The Everyday invaded by the Unknown'.

As late as 1980, the British abstract painter John Hoyland (1934–2011) saw Kiff as a kind of cautionary tale: 'But if you turn your back on all that understanding of what's gone on in modern art, you're going to end up doing some idiosyncratic little kind of painting that doesn't belong to anything, like an escape…like Ken Kiff or somebody, painting your own nightmares.' Kiff, however, situated his work within the whole gamut of twentieth-century painting and Pollock was as important to him as Klee and Chagall, Picasso and Miró; he wrote or lectured on all five. He was sometimes critical of contemporary abstract artists, as failing 'to make a sufficiently rich connection with the world', and the choices he made, towards nuance, towards 'the feminine', eventually pitted his art against the large-scale bravura of American painting (see Ch 5). Already forty-four at the time of his first London solo exhibition in 1979, Kiff became associated with the 'refigured painting' of the 1980s, when younger artists reclaimed liberties of description and narration, after an era of prohibition. 'Even now, at this period of painting,' wrote Kiff in 1979, 'a new eloquence is possible. I think it will take on a much wider range of possibilities than seems available to the Western art world.'

In 2005, four years after Kiff's death, the French poet Yves Bonnefoy wrote, in an article entitled 'What is Poetry?':

> Our use of words can be alienation, an exile, if it lets itself be overrun by
> conceptual thinking, and it is poetry's role to work on words, so as to free
> them from just such entrapments.

I believe painting in the twenty-first century has a parallel role, within an art world overly 'conceptual' in emphasis. My sense, in writing this chapter – and indeed this book as a whole – is of marginalized individuals assembling together to become a collective force. Looking at Kiff or Tagore or Darger, we are challenged in any limiting notion of art as mere strategy or communication. Like true poetry, true painting goes deeper than concepts.

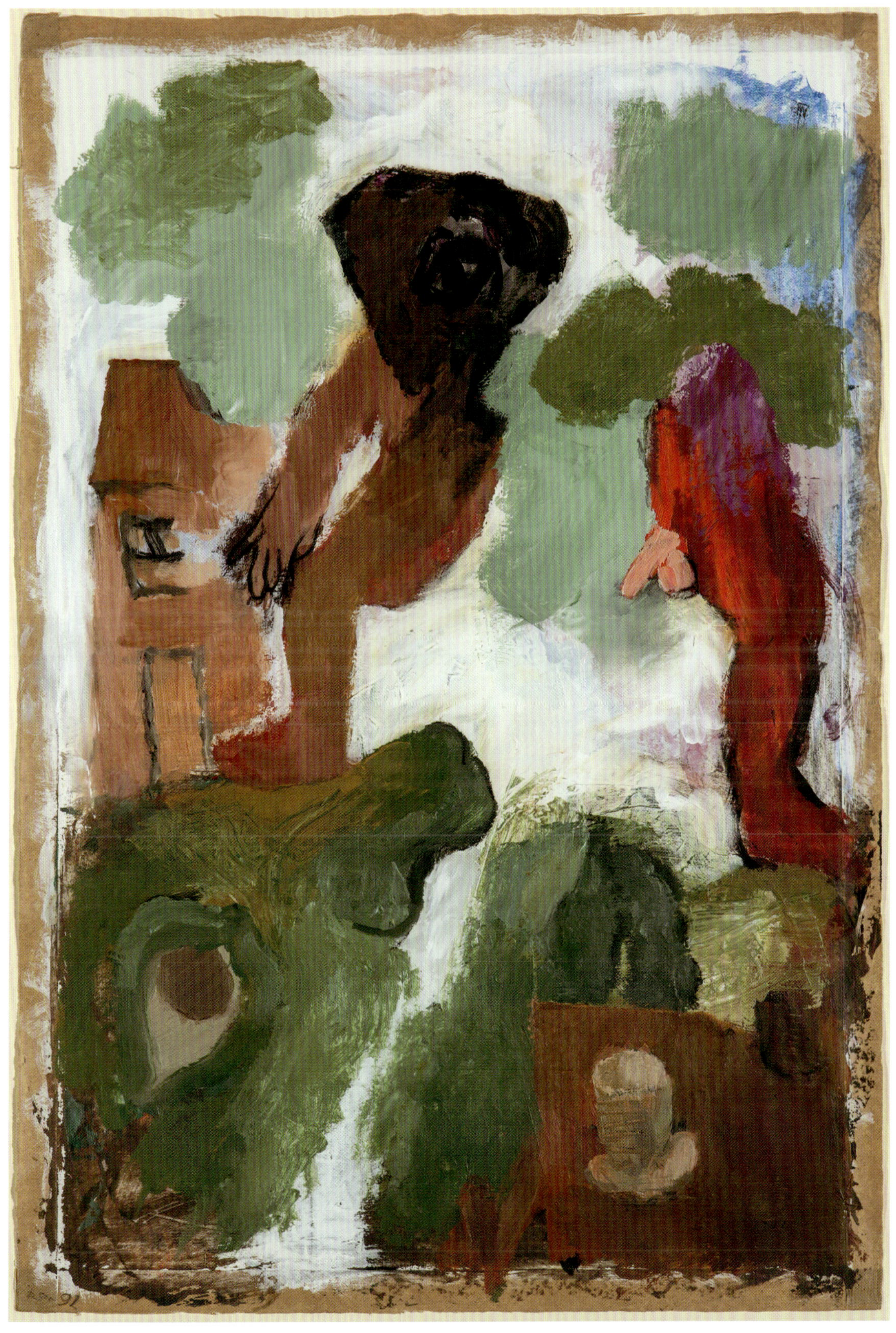

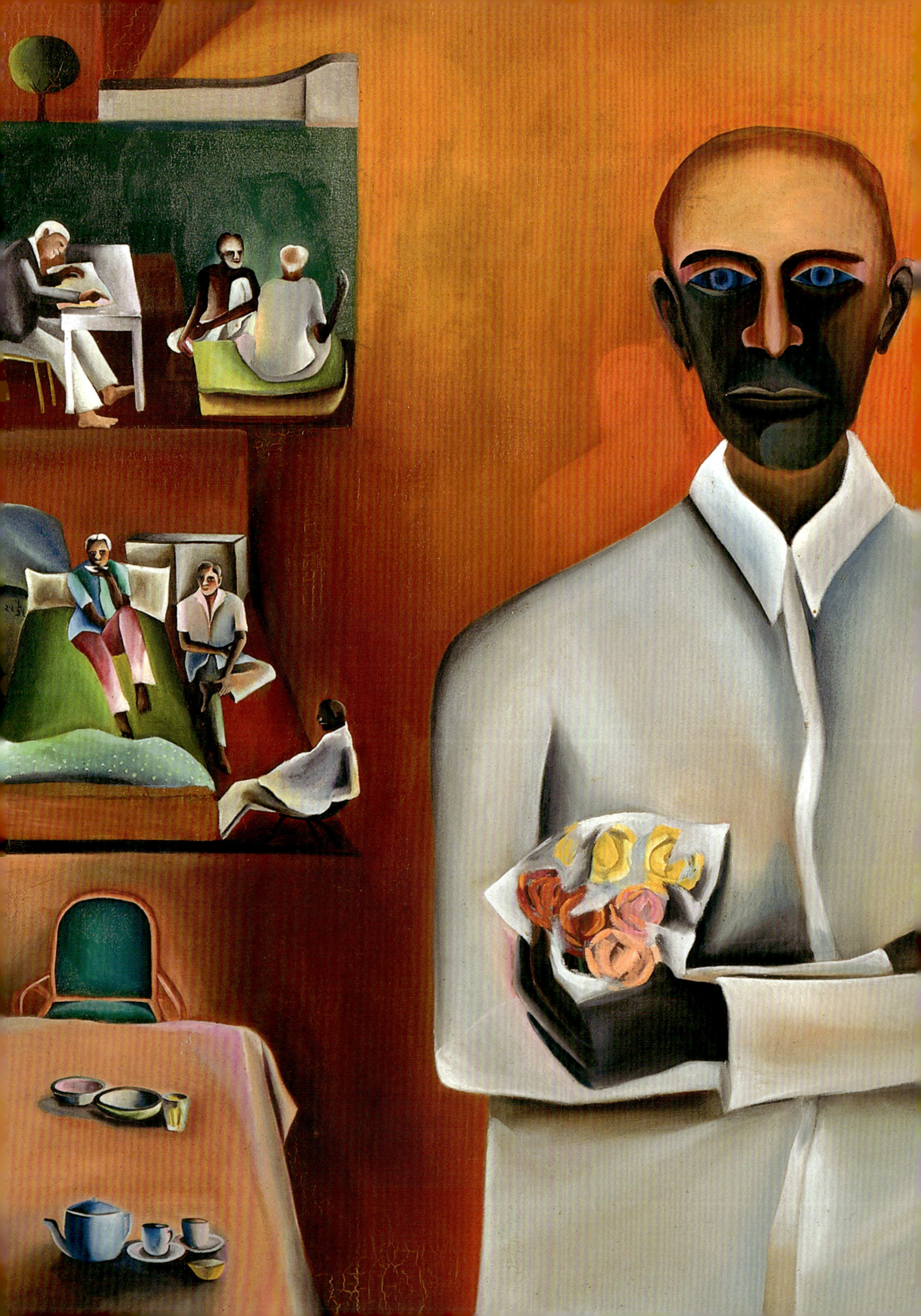

CHAPTER FIVE

After Abstract Expressionism: Towards a New History Painting

*In Genesis, it is said that in the beginning was the void and
God acted upon it. For an artist that is clear enough. It is so
mysterious that it takes away all doubt...you can float in it,
fly in it, suspend in it, and today it seems, to tremble in it is
maybe best or anyhow very fashionable...*

WILLEM DE KOONING, 1949

*American Abstract Art is a lie, a sham, a cover up for a
poverty of spirit. A mask to mask the fear of revealing oneself.*

PHILIP GUSTON, 1970

The greatest abstract painting emerged not from a stylistic, but a metaphysical, imperative. Each of those astonishing artists from Mondrian and Malevich to Rothko and Agnes Martin had to find a new pictorial language for the unsayable, for an absolute that was often identified as 'The Void'. Although de Kooning was writing in 1949 when abstract painting was still uncommercial, he hinted at the Void as already a 'fashionable' positioning. Over the next thirty years, New York Abstraction would be transformed into what has been called 'a mandatory world-style'.

Willem de Kooning (1904–97) arrived in New York in 1926, after a full commercial and academic training in Rotterdam. The distinctive character of all his painting, whether figure-centred or trembling-in-the-Void 'abstract', would be its openness, its refusal to resolve conflicts – its acceptance of uncertainty. Speaking at a 1951 Museum of Modern Art symposium on 'What Abstract Art Means to Me', he mocked abstraction's doctrinaire founders:

> But all of a sudden, in that famous turn of the century, a few people thought
> they could take the bull by the horns.... They began to form all kinds of
> groups, each with the idea of freeing art, and each demanding that you
> should obey them. Most of these theories have finally dwindled away into

BHUPEN KHAKHAR

*Man with Bouquet of
Plastic Flowers*

1976

(detail, see p. 222)

politics or strange forms of spiritualism…. I have learned a lot from all of them and they have confused me plenty too…. I am completely weary of their ideas now.

He had recently completed the very large canvas *Excavation*, compressing layer upon layer of imagery into a single structure, not so much abstract as indecipherable. Like many before and since – Cézanne and Picasso, Guston and Giacometti among them – de Kooning was haunted by Balzac's description, in his story *The Unknown Masterpiece*, of a painting by the fictional Frenhofer: 'confused daubings of colours contained by a multitude of strange lines, forming a high wall of paint.' De Kooning was working on a new image (closer in subject-matter to that of Frenhofer's quest), a life-size *Woman* [illustration opposite]. A grand archetype and icon resulted, variously seen as Kali-like goddess and smiling sex object, but essentially another superimposition of infinite possibilities, shifting before our eyes. Picasso had declared each of his paintings 'a sum of destructions', and when *Guernica* (1937) was hung at the Museum of Modern Art in New York, it was flanked by photographs of the drastic changes he'd made to it across several weeks. In *Woman* de Kooning extended that process of disassembling and reassembling to eighteen months.

When the increasingly doctrinaire critic Clement Greenberg told de Kooning 'It is impossible today to paint a face', the artist replied, 'That's right, and it's impossible not to.' So the 'impossible' figure, wrenched out of the matrix of the pictorial field (an idea already latent in many twentieth-century painters, from Picasso to Beckmann), was fulfilled in de Kooning's *Woman I*. At the beginning of its long gestation he had seen the 1950 Soutine retrospective at the Museum of Modern Art (see Ch 3 p. 135). Although painted from life, Soutine's figure-images remained exemplary for de Kooning, even as he became subsumed within Abstract Expressionism (AbEx), alongside Arshile Gorky, Jackson Pollock, Philip Guston and Franz Kline; with Mark Rothko, Clyfford Still and Barnett Newman as another grouping; all familiar to one another, and all emerging into the spotlight together over the course of a decade.

The structures of European culture – of 'Western civilization' – had been devastated by the two world wars. Even if Paris remained physically intact, even if significant paintings were still emerging from Picasso and Matisse, Léger and Balthus, there was no longer the sense of a cohesive European modernist painting. In the 1940s the New York painters had inherited existentialism; as de Kooning recalled, 'It was in the air. Without knowing too much about it, we were in touch with the mood.' That mood was essentially tragic. Politically of the anti-Stalinist Left (utopian socialists, shading into anarchists), the Abstract Expressionist painters were at odds with McCarthyite America, their isolation reinforced by an absence of either patronage or market for their paintings. When Harold Rosenberg and Clement Greenberg began to write on these artists, they were championing a small subculture within a vast, blandly philistine nation.

All this suddenly changed in the later 1950s. Much has been written about the adoption of abstraction by the Central Intelligence Agency (CIA) as a weapon

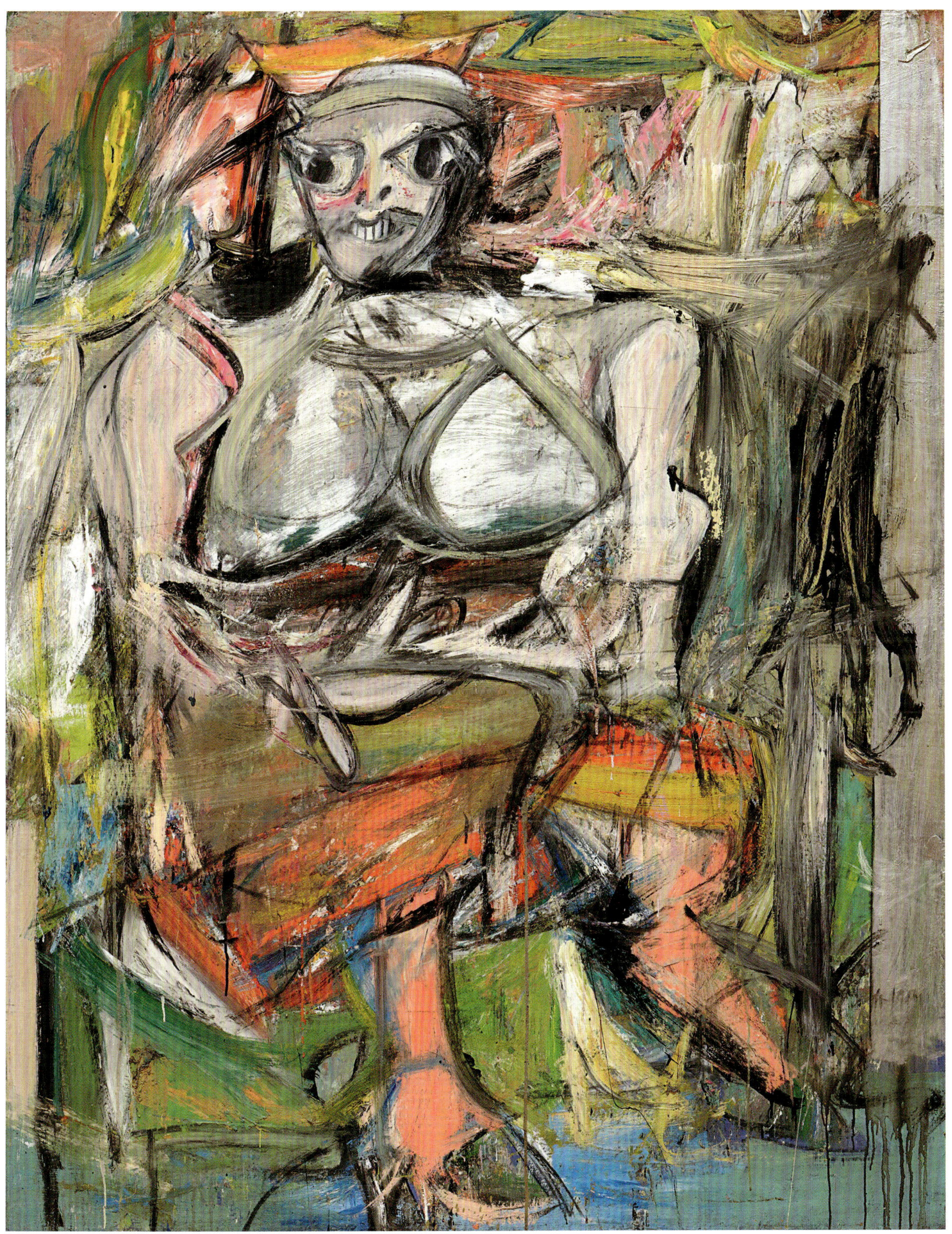

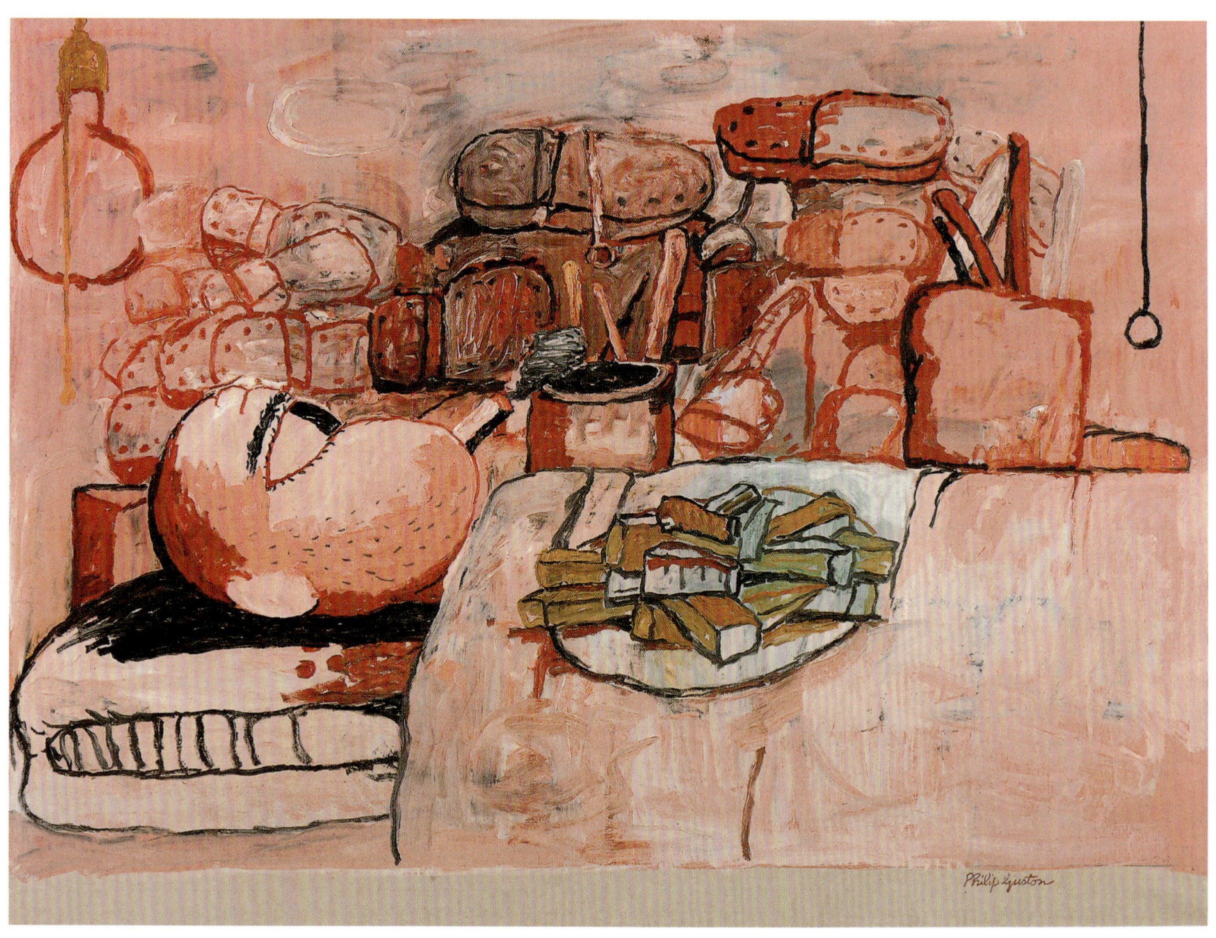

PHILIP GUSTON
Painting, Smoking, Eating
1973

of the Cold War, as part of its covert cultural propaganda operations, notably the Congress for Cultural Freedom (CCF). Surprisingly large funds were channelled via the Rockefeller, Ford and other foundations into grants and publications, museum and touring exhibitions (not always to great effect; for example, only fourteen thousand visitors saw MoMA's 'The New American Painting' at the Tate Gallery in London in 1959). But a more significant factor, too often neglected by historians, was the large-scale acquisition of abstract paintings direct from international dealers, through both individual and corporate dummy-purchasers – according to some sources, running to several thousand works. That manipulation distorted art markets all over the world.

Inflated most famously by Greenberg (a former Trotskyite who now sat on the executive committee of the CCF), American abstract painting was raised up as the evolutionary culmination of all previous painting. With AbEx enthroned as an imperial orthodoxy, twentieth-century non-abstract art was marginalized, rendered invisible; in Robert Storr's formulation, 'Greenberg deprived subsequent generations of their true intellectual heritage.'

Abstraction had become a kind of iconoclastic crusade. By 1959, according to critic John Canaday, 'an unknown artist trying to exhibit in New York couldn't find a gallery unless he was painting in a mode derived from New York Abstraction'. Yet many of the leading painters were uneasy with this stylistic straitjacketing; as de Kooning told the dance critic Edwin Denby, 'I'm not that crazy about my style – I'd just as soon paint some other way.'

Philip Guston (1913–80), sometime disciple of the Mexican muralists, admirer of Beckmann and de Chirico, found himself trapped in a false position, his beautiful informal brush marks taken to be the quintessence of art for art's sake. Already in 1960 he was articulating his discomfort:

> There is something ridiculous and miserly in the myth we inherit
> from abstract art – that painting is autonomous, pure and for itself....
> But painting is 'impure'. We are image-makers and image-ridden.

In those same years, a younger generation rose in open rebellion against AbEx, initially under the umbrella of Pop. Guston condemned the 'soulless commercialism' of early Pop Art; and, de Kooning, when he met Warhol, burst out, 'you're a killer of art, you're a killer of beauty, you're even a killer of laughter. I can't bear your work.'

The strange, painful transition made by Guston in the years 1965 to 1967 will be explored in detail later (see pp. 216–19). After many years of abstraction, he re-emerged in his hooded Klansmen, his heaps, his smoking-and-drinking selves, as the great seriocomic carnivalesque painter of the second half of the twentieth century. The comic-strip visionary Robert Crumb (b. 1943) felt the affinity:

> It was as though we'd both tapped into this great grungy unconscious
> – all the unconscious imagery of lower middle class America.

Just as the tragicomic art of Goya and Gillray was a corrective to the hegemony of neoclassical taste at the end of the eighteenth century, so the grotesque hilarity of such paintings as *Painting, Smoking, Eating* in the 1970s [illustration opposite] broke in upon cool American formalism (whether of the Greenbergian or the Warholian variety). The scandal of Guston's later canvases was that they came not from some young marginal, but from one of the AbEx masters. In 1953, when de Kooning first exhibited his *Woman* series, there had been a shock-response – though *Woman I* was swiftly purchased by the Museum of Modern Art. But in 1970, on the night Guston at last exhibited his new imagery at the Marlborough Gallery in New York, the outrage was far greater; de Kooning was among the few to approach him, saying, 'You know, Philip, what your real subject is? It is freedom.'

The fortress of formalist abstraction had been so reinforced and armoured over the previous two decades that any effective challenge had to come from *inside*. For Guston, the immediate consequences were catastrophic: the Marlborough Gallery dropped him, and he found himself excommunicated as a traitor and heretic. 'They said I was finished.... Some painters of the abstract movement – my colleagues, friends, contemporaries – refused to talk to me.' For several more years Guston had difficulty exhibiting or selling. With hindsight it is obvious that

Painting, Smoking, Eating could only have been created by an artist steeped in the scale and handling of American abstraction. The other new varieties of figuration that emerged after 1960 often had AbEx buried somewhere in their foundations. The ambition, the seriousness, the sense of the tragic, all carried over into 'history painters' as various as R. B. Kitaj and Leon Golub, Ida Applebroog and Kiefer. Yet almost all the artists in this chapter were motivated by a need to challenge the exclusionary and restrictive ideology constructed around Abstract Expressionism. Guston's quest to tear off the 'mask' of abstraction became a paradigm for a new generation from the 1980s onwards.

R. B. KITAJ: AVATAR OF EZRA (1960–76)

Across thirty years, one project would remain constant in Kitaj's work: the creation of a new kind of history painting. Reappearing in different stylistic guises, we can recognize the same picture – squarish in format, altarpiece in scale, crammed with incident, readable on many levels. All imply the same argument: that modern painting (even now, once again, after all) might embody a complex subject matter, might include all the world, anything and everything.

The Red Banquet (1960) [illustration opposite] and *Reflections on Violence* (1962) [illustration p. 200] present two contrasting possibilities within that project. In 1960, aged twenty-eight, R. B. Kitaj (1932–2007) was an American postgraduate at the Royal College of Art in London, emerging as a new star alongside his younger fellow-student David Hockney (see pp. 206–7) under the flag-of-convenience supplied by Pop. A decade earlier, in New York in 1950, he had found his first experience of art school unrewarding: 'I wanted to learn to paint like Memlinc, and they only wanted to teach me that Bauhaus shit.' At Oxford, he had been excited by Edgar Wind's lectures, and he was into Warburg Institute arcana. *The Red Banquet* was his first real history painting, in which the past is conceived as a phantasmagoria, the weightless wraiths of Karl Marx, Aleksandr Herzen et al., somehow all inhabiting a Corbusian villa. Despite his handwritten text, incorporated at lower left, the painting presents as a single unified space.

But *Reflections on Violence*, completed two years later, is an image-assembly of a different kind, owing something to Rauschenberg's silk-screened canvases of the same years, but far more bookish and wayward. It is a 'crazy chart' (a phrase that occurred to Kitaj while reading the great Warburgian historian Frances Yates on the 'diagrammatic' art of Ramon Lull). The painting becomes a haunted house with many rooms, again peopled by wafting eidolons, an advent calendar with doors that open onto sinister little nocturnal transactions. Thus what Kitaj called 'the outlandish imagery of such Warburg nonsense-visions' throws up a wondrous puzzle-picture.

The strongest influence of all on Kitaj's early painting was his identification with the poet Ezra Pound (1885–1972). In later years he would be rueful about this: 'sometimes I think I would be further on in my maturity as a painter if I had been

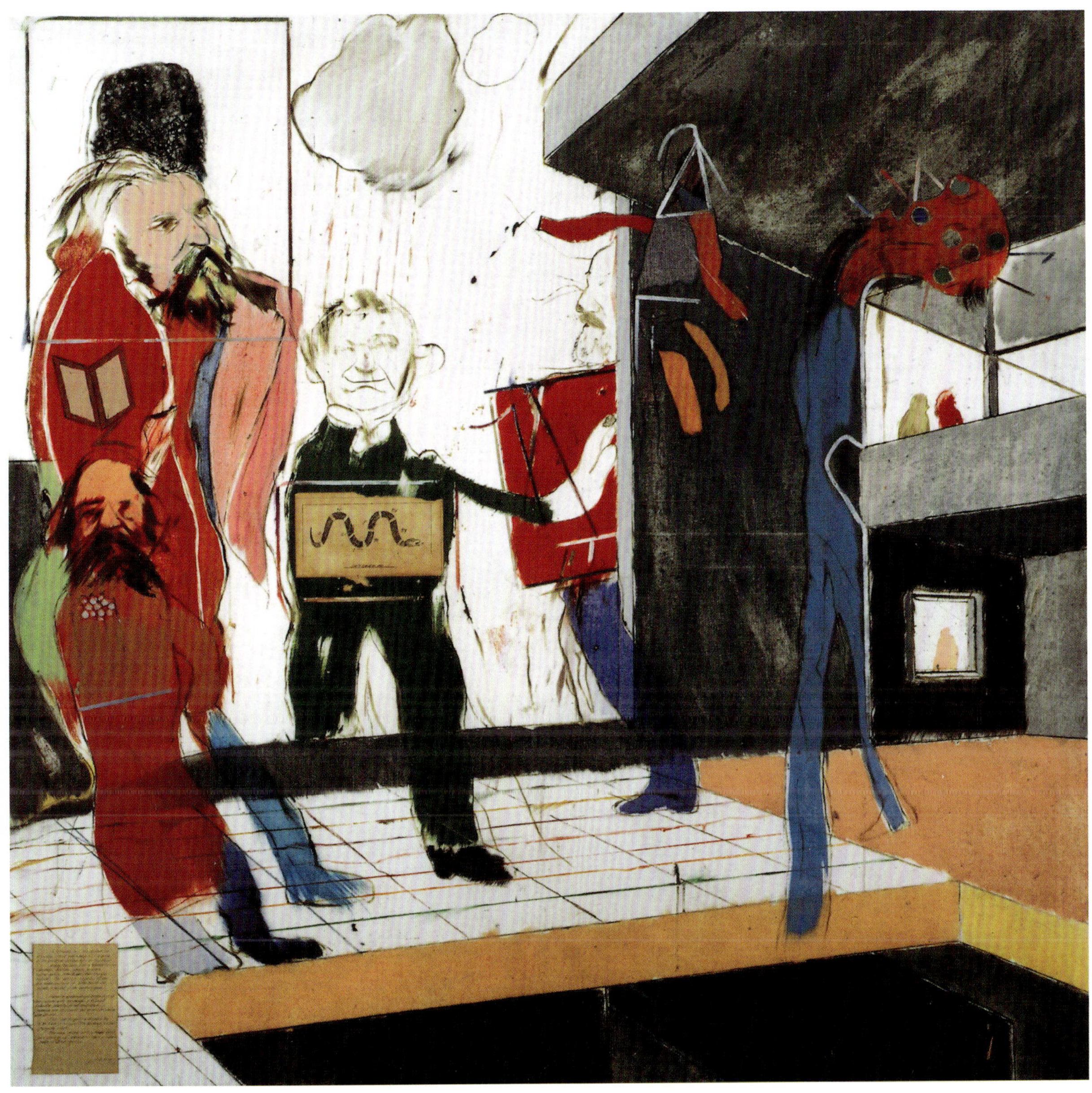

R. B. KITAJ

The Red Banquet

1960

The two bearded figures on the left are the Russian
revolutionary writers Aleksandr Herzen and Mikhail Bakunin.
According to Kitaj's note, 'In February 1854, Mr Saunders,
the American Consul, gave a banquet to a dozen of the
principal refugees in London'. One visual source is a
photograph of Le Corbusier's Villa Stein (1928), reproduced
in a book by the Warburg Institute's director, Fritz Saxl.

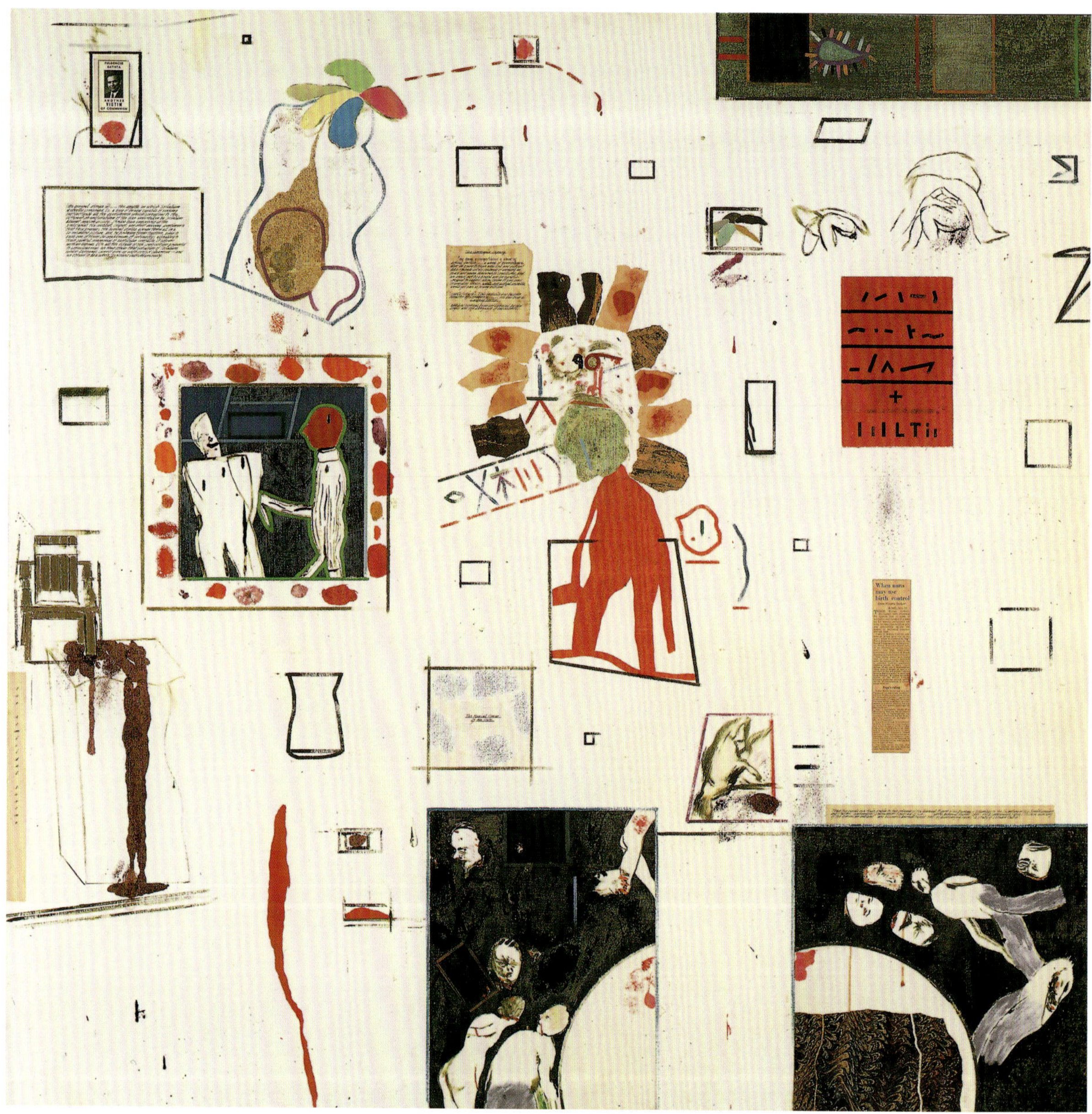

R. B. KITAJ

Reflections on Violence

1962

The 'pictographs and 'ideograms' of this painting
were triggered by his reading of Georges Sorel's
1908 revolutionary syndicalist tract, *Reflections on
Violence*, translated by T. E. Hulme.

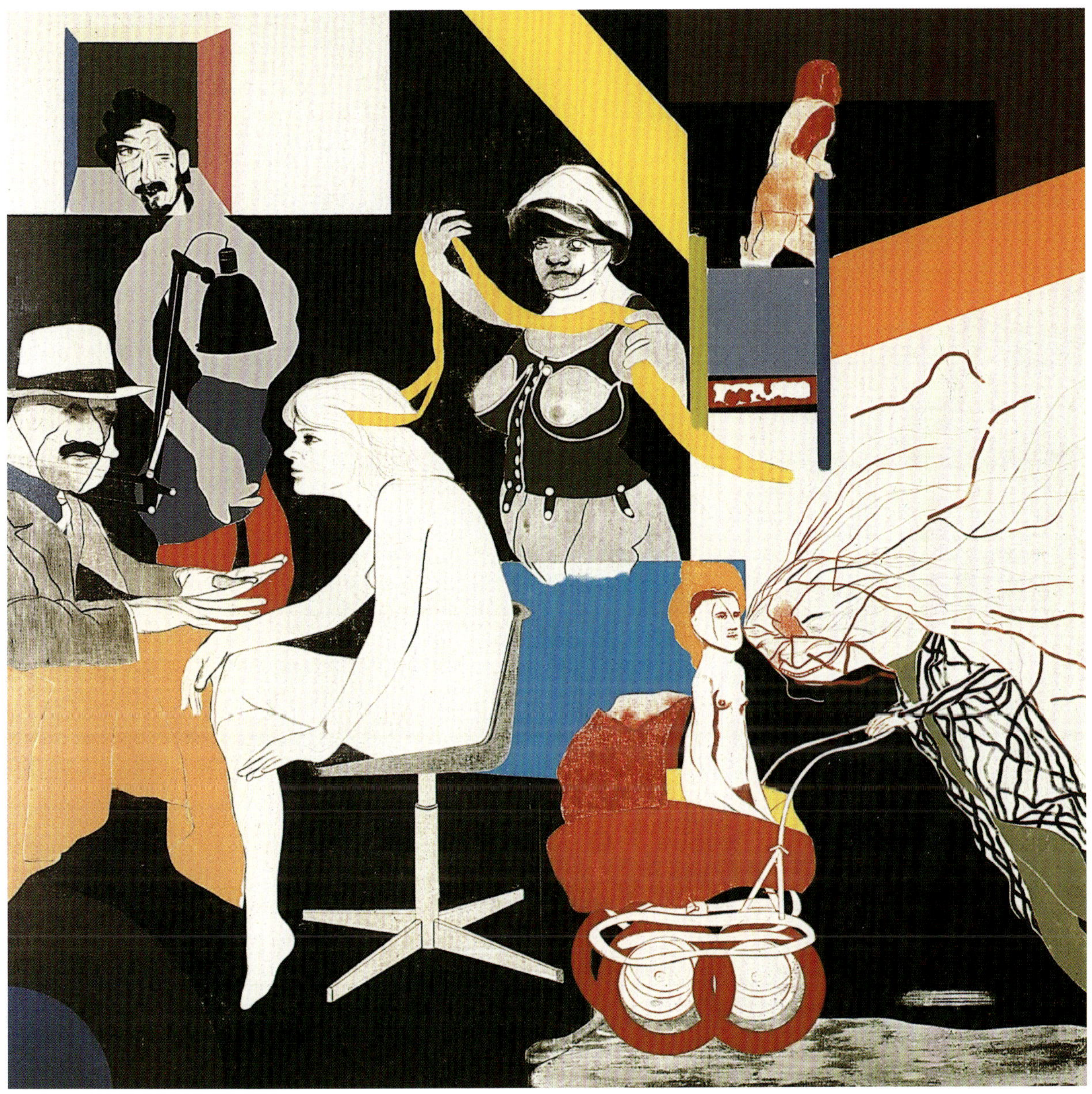

R. B. KITAJ

The Ohio Gang

1964

Kitaj's own 1994 note begins, 'This (very) late Surrealist picture was a freely associated depictive abstraction…'. Ezra Pound, a huge influence on Kitaj, was from Ohio, though the standing figure portrays Kitaj's Poundian poet-friend Robert Creeley. 'I was still under the Warburg spell in those early sixties…. There was no rational plan for this picture, no programme to speak of…'.

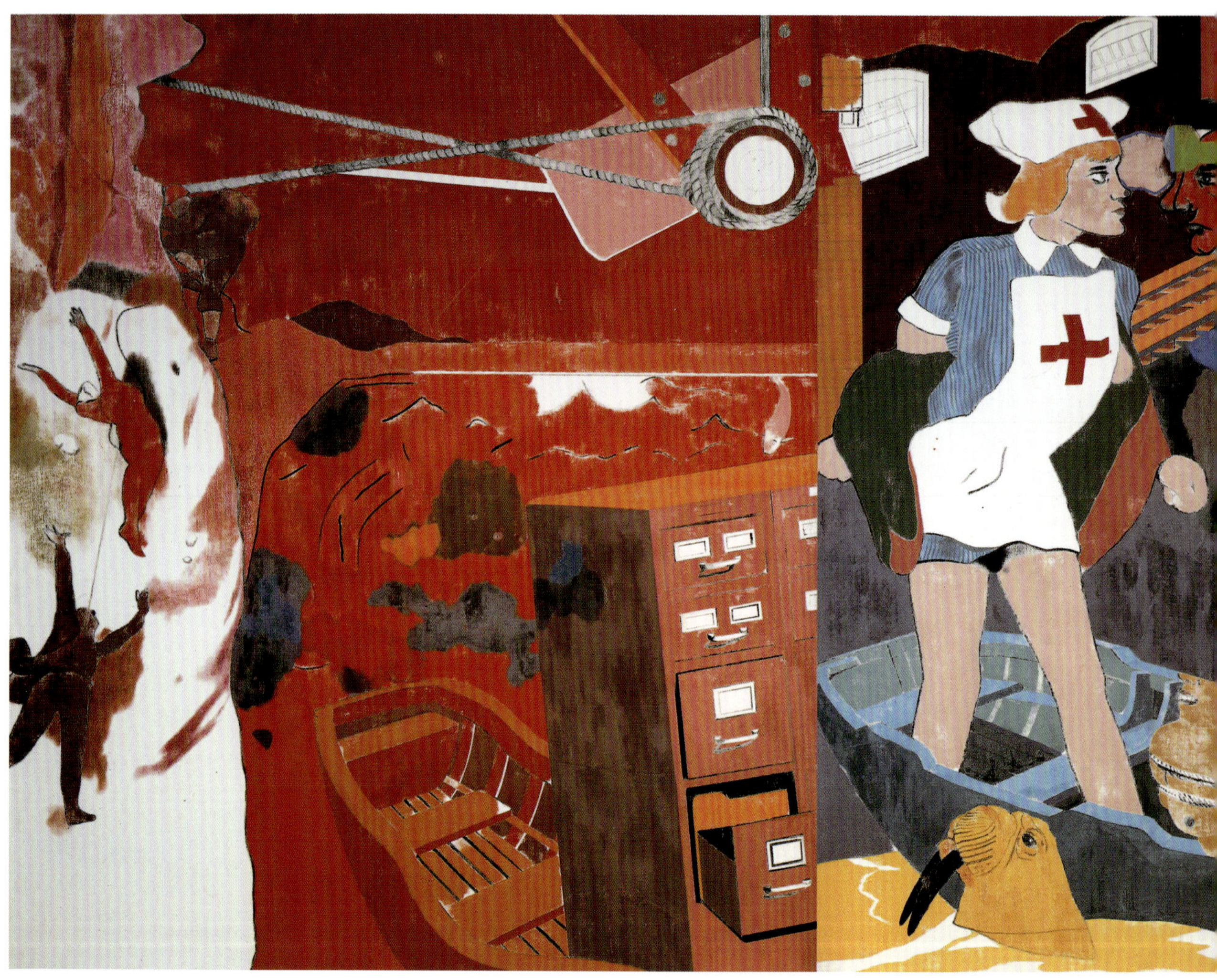

R. B. KITAJ
Erie Shore
1966

as moved by Rembrandt as I was by Pound'. It is fascinating to observe how Pound, looking at Cubist and Futurist painting, adopted the same fragmentation in words, to build up a collage of lyrical passages, and to create in *The Cantos* a sense of ideas unfolding in world history; and how Kitaj in turn rendered Pound – with all his exasperating tendentiousness and mystification – back into the visual realm. The overriding thrust towards inclusivity, the juxtaposition of multiple languages, the quixotic attempt to revive the epic (even if it meant an epic of fragmentation, even if the lyrical impulse was thereby constantly jarred and thwarted) – these are just some of the ways in which Pound 'translated' into Kitaj.

In an era dominated by formalist abstraction, Kitaj's insistence on literary subject matter was bound to provoke. His riposte to one such attack has become famous: 'Some books have pictures, and some pictures have books'. Nevertheless, what raised Kitaj's painting into art of lasting value was not so much intellectuality as grace: beauty of touch, a surprising intensity of colour and a wonderful rhythmic fluidity of design.

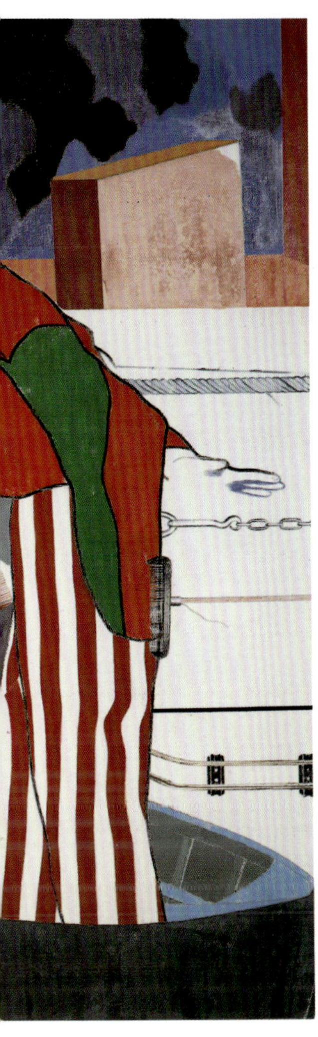

In *The Ohio Gang* (1964) [illustration p. 201] and *Erie Shore* (1966) [illustration left] he brings together diverse imagery without compartmentalization, as a kind of dream montage or flux, with larger, more monumental figures, morphing one into another. Kitaj develops a style that suggests the interpenetration of material things – usually based on photographs – and mental entities. His conjunction of these floating thought-forms owes much to the way Max Ernst and other Surrealists represented the metamorphoses that occur in dream. *The Ohio Gang* is an 'association of ideas'. It conveys a sense of the mind roving and creates a language partly freed from representation, where limbs, objects and unnameable devices float about with independent life.

The monumental diptych *Erie Shore* (each panel nearly six by five feet), with its blaze of red and orange, and its marvellously fluid space, is Kitaj's masterpiece. The ostensible subject is the pollution of Cleveland's lake, where the artist had grown up. The underwater filing cabinet is thereby explained (but not, to its left, the falling mountaineers). In the right-hand panel, the corruption seems to be ethical: a doctor in striped pyjamas (he may be Kitaj's first concentration-camp figure) is 'examining' a nurse: her skirt rides up to expose her crotch, while at the bottom of the boat is a miniaturized and bound female nude.

I don't think anyone before Kitaj had made such convincing pictures of *ideas*, images of sufficiently complex incongruity that we could recognize them as looking like the inside of our own minds. This euphoric flow might seem a wonderful compositional possibility that could go on forever. Yet in 1964, in the midst of completing these much-imitated works, Kitaj set out on a self-condemnatory lecture-tour. In anguished tones, with the perspiring delivery of a Baptist preacher, he spoke of the failure of contemporary art to grapple with contemporary life, of his own shame and guilt. All considerable recent painting seemed to him fatally distanced – through formalism in the case of the abstract, through irony in the figurative. We had come to a desperate impasse, in which all of modernism was implicated. Against a Frank Stella or a Jasper Johns, he contrasted the urgency of news photographs; but he also threw in, by way of suggestion, Balthus's then little-known *The Lesson* (1934) [illustration p. 96], proposing that it might be 'closer to the art of the twenty-first century' than any image he'd so far shown.

Kitaj's self-criticism deepened over the following decades. He came to detest the bright, comic-crass, designer-graphic look of his early paintings and screen prints:

> Collage emphasizes *arrangement*, an aesthetic of conjoining, at the expense of depicting, picturing people and aspects of their time on[this] scorched earth, which was what I always wanted to represent.

The suicide of his first wife in 1969 paralysed his painting for several years. When Kitaj surfaced again, he was in his forties. *If Not, Not* [illustration p. 204] preserves the same dry-brush surface – which, as the art historian Michael Podro observed, conveys simultaneously 'both materiality and elusiveness' – allowing Kitaj to move between phantasm and fact; but sadness now predominates over wit, and the graininess has taken on an aura of rain, or tears. At first glance we might suppose

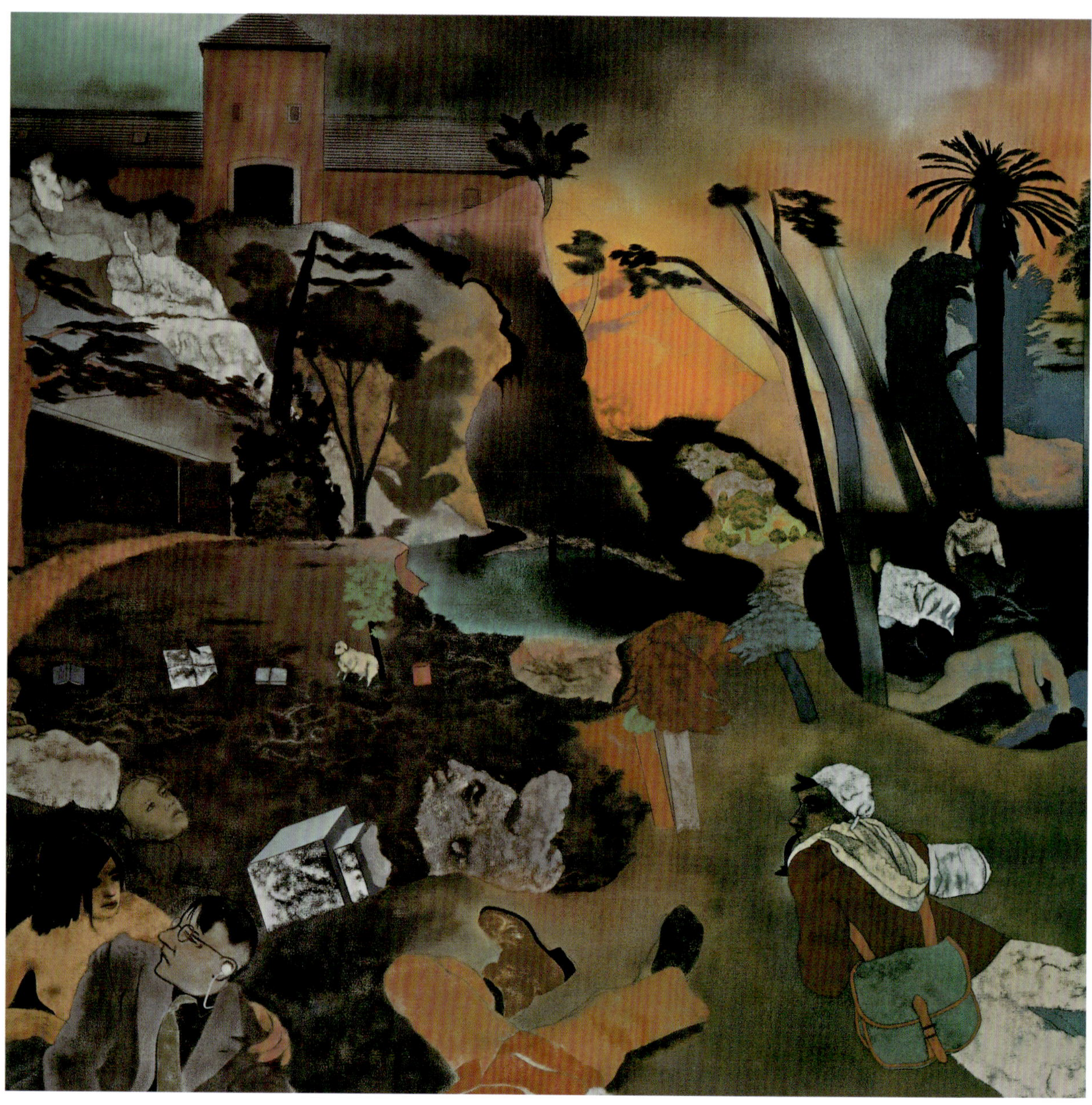

R B KITAJ

If Not, Not

1975–76

In response to a commission for the
entrance hall of the new British Library,
Kitaj conjures imagery for T. S. Eliot's
great poem *The Waste Land* (1922).
Hence the corpses that 'sprout' the 'stony
rubbish', and the 'heap of broken images'.

this a Golden Age idyll, part of that lineage stretching from Giorgione to Gauguin to the Matisse of *Le Bonheur de vivre* (see Introduction p. 8): figures lolling about in a tropical landscape, a Venetian farmhouse high on the hill. Then the double-take strikes home. Everything festers. The terrain creeps with fragmentary, apparitional figures, drowning in a kind of swamp. That 'farmhouse' is suddenly recognized, horrifyingly, as the gate to Auschwitz.

The image was partly a response to *The Waste Land*. ('Some pictures have books....') In his homage, Kitaj has created a microcosm: 'These fragments I have shored against my ruins.' No contemporary was so equipped as Kitaj to create an equivalence to Eliot's poem – a great classical composition 'gone wrong'. Kitaj's nostalgia for some earlier condition of painting is here *taken care of* by the choice of Eliot's persona through which to dramatize his own dilemma.

The first stimulus for his 1964 lectures was an evening of conversation with Clement Greenberg and the abstract painter Kenneth Noland. From the mid-1970s, he expended much energy in polemic, always with a penitential subtext, whether as inadequate painter or inadequate Jew. Kitaj ridiculed the new dominance of conceptual art (likening it to an imagined situation in which the experimental filmmaker Stan Brakhage had become the mainstream of cinema). Together with Hockney, he embarked on a crusade to reinstate life drawing in art schools. He selected a touring exhibition of contemporary drawings of the single figure, 'The Human Clay'. He spent a year in Paris, drawing from the model, in order to 'reform' his art.

Kitaj had been constantly reinventing himself. Unable to touch centre, his best work had been about that very absence of centre. Now he took as his exemplars artists working from direct observation, especially those he nominated 'The School of London' (including Frank Auerbach, Lucian Freud and Leon Kossoff). A conflict arose between the irrepressible 'craziness' of his ideated figures – dislocated limbs for dislocated protagonists – and the beefy solidity and firm contour he now imposed on those phantoms. His art lost its verve. Rueful comic absurdity remained one mainspring – writing his manifestos in a Poundean persona, he mythologized himself as a 'Diasporist', or as a paranoid 'Solitary Walker'. His best late paintings are still peopled by the comic ghosts of history: in Kitaj's imagery (as in Gillray's at the end of his own century) history painting becomes burlesque. He had started out as a dream-artist, his sense of displacement fulfilled in the restless motion of his earliest figures. Turning to The Real was a violation. He tried to follow the straight path, but the crooked paths were for him the true ones.

DAVID HOCKNEY'S *THE SECOND MARRIAGE* (1963)

The one student I kept talking to a lot was Ron Kitaj…I was a keen vegetarian then, and interested in politics a bit, and he'd say to me, why don't you paint those subjects?… So that was the way I broke it…. And I thought, well, it's better; I feel better; you feel as if something's coming out.

DAVID HOCKNEY, 1976

DAVID HOCKNEY

The Second Marriage
1963

In this three-canvas construction, the segment on the right is collaged with wallpaper.

Five years younger than Kitaj, David Hockney (b. 1937) arrived at the Royal College of Art in 1959 and like nearly all his contemporaries followed the path towards formal abstraction. In Hockney's own vivid account, even after that 1961 breakthrough conversation with Kitaj, 'I didn't have the courage to paint a real figure'; that would still have seemed 'too anti-modern':

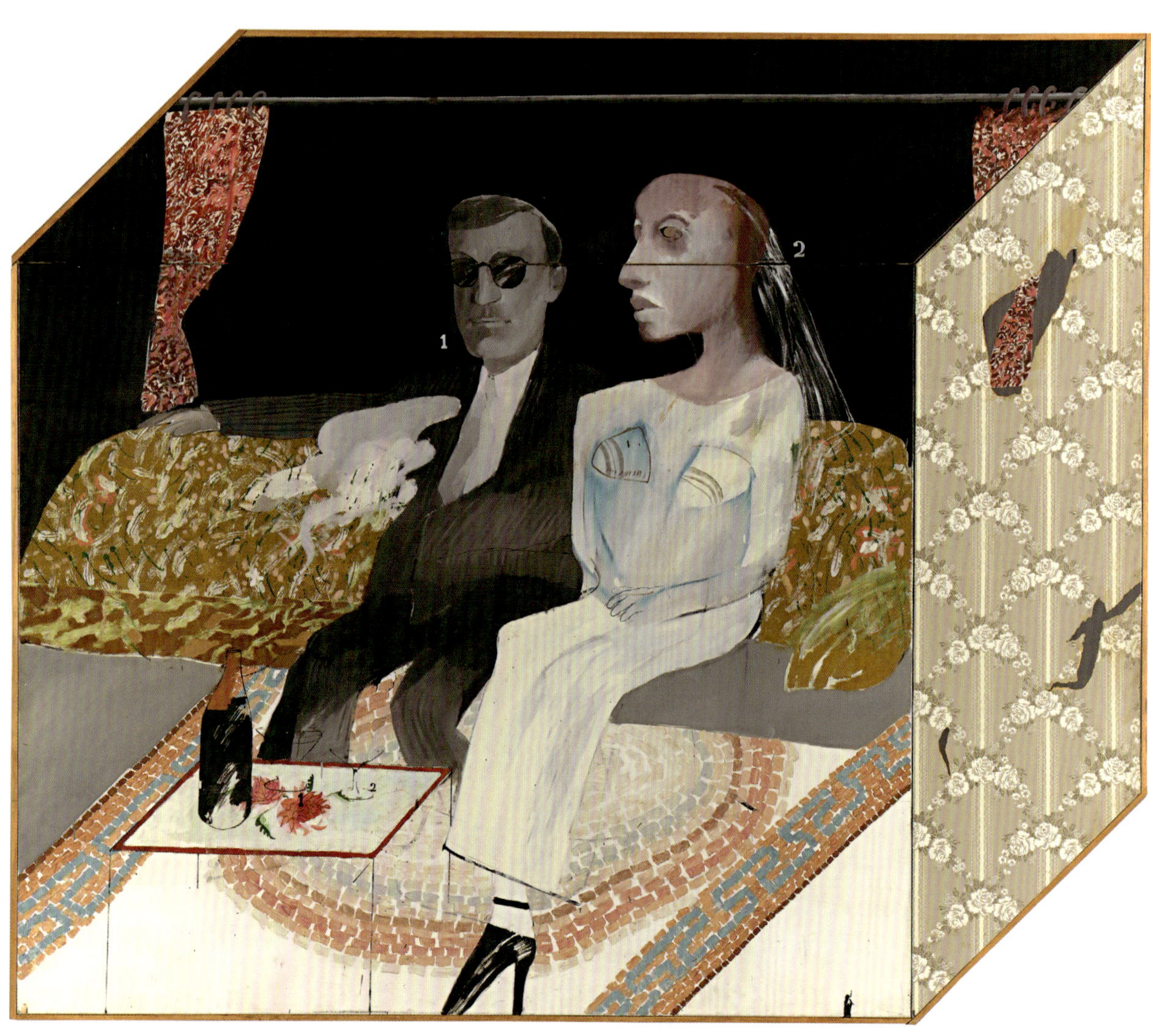

> In the 1960s the subject had been completely played down; abstraction
> had begun to dominate everything and people firmly believed that this was
> the way painting had to go. There was no other way out...I think I felt that
> even as late as 1966.

The graphic directness of Hockney's new imagery was a liberation for all contemporary painters. Suddenly everything was permitted again: to draw figures, to make jokes, to tell stories.... Less esoteric than Kitaj's, Hockney's work always received a warmer public reception. The scale and boldness came partly from advertising; the mood was closer to the hedonism of the new youth culture. In all his early pictures, especially in *The Second Marriage* (1963) [illustration opposite], there is an edge of satirical comedy. This odd couple – the Ancient Egyptian girl wedded to the distinctly unreliable spiv in dark glasses – seem already boxed-in. He is number one, she number two; this marriage doesn't bode well.

Shortly after completing this image, Hockney painted a sequence of 'Domestic Scenes', in which the potentially transgressive subject – two pink men in the shower together – was rendered inoffensive, not only by the wit of composition, but by its formalism. His dealer, Kasmin, was showing a mostly abstract stable, and Hockney's human narrative was bolted on to a formalist armature, creating an inherently humorous tension in the pictorial language. The young painter saw himself as ambassador for a way of life that would remain illegal in Britain until 1967; these paintings were 'partly propaganda of something I felt hadn't been propagandized, especially among students, as a subject: homosexuality. I felt it should be done.'

Thus Hockney's early pictures wedded formal and sexual emancipation. In his subsequent work, both tensions would be lost, though his many varieties of representation became all the more popular even as their intensity and significance diminished. Looking at Kitaj and Hockney fifty years later, I think of the Pound/Eliot double-act, which Pound imaged as a house-breaking team; 'I'm the one who puts the brick through the window; you escape through the back with the loot.' At this distance, Kitaj's 'failure' might appear more exemplary than Hockney's 'success'.

ALEX KATZ: THE EARLY CUT-OUTS AND THEIR MILIEU (1959-62)

Katz's people simply existed somewhere. They stayed
in the picture as solutions of a formal problem, neither
existential nor lost, neither deprived nor dismayed.

FRANK O'HARA, 1966

When Alex Katz (b. 1927) chose 1958 as the starting point for his first retrospective, he was marking the 'breakthrough' he made that year in his paintings of figures; but also perhaps the crystallization of a particular New York milieu, which would provide a stance distinct from that of both the Abstract Expressionists and Pop. Within that alternative subculture the poet Frank O'Hara, who worked as a curator for the Museum of Modern Art, is now perhaps the most celebrated. Their wise elder, something of a mentor to Katz, was the dance critic Edwin Denby, whose writing – like O'Hara's New York street poems – reflected a conscious interplay of art and everyday life. Denby, wrote O'Hara, was 'as attentive to people walking in the streets or leaning against a corner...as he is to the more formal and exacting occasions of art.' Denby's younger life-partner was the Swiss-born photographer and filmmaker Rudy Burckhardt; an elusive and anti-careerist artist, he helped Joseph Cornell with his films and made some delightful ones of his own, both non-narrative and spoof-narrative. (*Money*, of 1967, has Katz in a small role alongside the poet John Ashbery, with Denby leading as The-Richest-Man-in-the-World, 'Hemlock Stinge', and Red Grooms as a bank robber.) Katz appreciated Burckhardt's poise, too warm to be characterized as 'cool', and wrote of him in 1963: 'The art is classic, precise in proportion, natural, worldly and contained.' Today that reads as a kind of manifesto for his own painting.

In Katz's early portraits, each individual sitter was suspended in what O'Hara called 'a void of smoothly painted colour.' But in 1959, 'Katz then proceeded to remove even the void', literally cutting out the silhouette and sticking it on to wood to form a free-standing figure. The 'flat statues' of Katz's 1962 exhibition at the artists' co-op Tanager Gallery on Tenth Street were painted directly on wood from small studies and drawings. The invitation to that show [illustration opposite] is a photograph of Katz's studio by Burckhardt: a casual assembly of cut-outs of all scales and types, most of them double-sided. O'Hara is the second from the left. There are also front and back images of Ada, who Katz first met in 1957; she has been a constant muse for his art ever since. When Katz's friends entered the room for the opening party, they saw a reconstruction of their own milieu – a conversation piece that had burst out of painting into the world.

The cut-outs resist the high-style formality of Katz's canvases, which he sees as very much about 'elegance and beauty' rather than 'social messages, suffering, inner expression, all of those things I'm not interested in.' He cites Egyptian art and Piero della Francesca, but can't stand Rembrandt. While Katz has written admiringly of, for example, Marsden Hartley, Max Beckmann and the early works of Francis Bacon, he wants his own art free from both narrative and fantasy. 'I'd like to have style take the place of content, or the style be the content.'

In 1954, Greenberg had declared that figuration could 'yield only minor art'; Katz set out to prove his paintings – in scale, in sheer authority – the equal of any formalism. 'I was hostile, I was tired of being patronized.... I wanted to kick machos on their asses.' Sharply observant of sartorial fashion, Katz rendered his choreography of daily life on ever more enormous canvases, up to thirty foot wide. These pictures could be seen as emulating billboard and cinema screen, but they eschew the irony and consumer-critique associated with Pop. Each comes out of a seen moment, real figures in real light, seized first in small, quasi-naturalistic studies, to be enlarged and redrawn over several weeks, in preparation for that

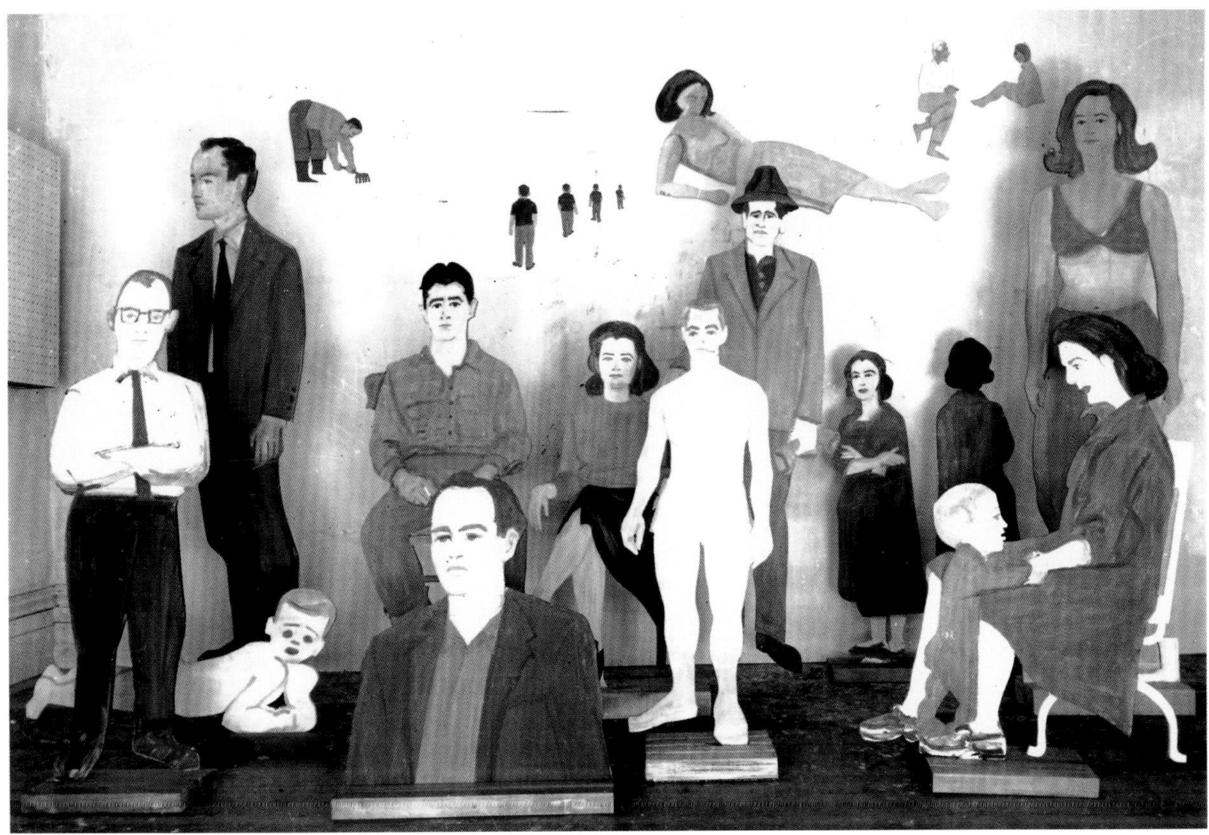

single day in which he completes each vast canvas – and of which he speaks as a performative feat of technique.

Others were painting 'post-abstract' realism (for example David Park and Richard Diebenkorn in California) but only Katz pushed scale and surface to such a pitch of visionary vacancy. He acknowledges the blankness of his figures; from childhood, he says, 'I never responded emotionally.' If those first flat statues had been intimate, each portraying a particular friend, the figures of his later canvases tend to be more generic: Ada apart, they are nameless thirty-somethings, so blandly affluent and unblemished as to make any true bohemian bridle. Grounding them again upon a single flat hue – that Void which expands into the room – Katz compounds the legacy of Matisse's *The Dance* [illustration pp. 8–9] with that of Colour Field.

Immaculate, neutral, withholding as much as they give, the big canvases of Alex Katz do offer one recipe for achieving viable and very grand figure painting into the twenty-first century. The plotless is raised to the hieratic; and something that resembles history painting does result. In 1959, cutting around the figure, Katz had returned painting to its primal origin, the shadow outlines traced on walls, as in the myth of the Corinthian Maid. He has continued to exhibit new cut-outs, in many inventive formats – segments, close-ups, slices-of-life. When installed in combination with his massive paintings, they can appear almost a reproach.

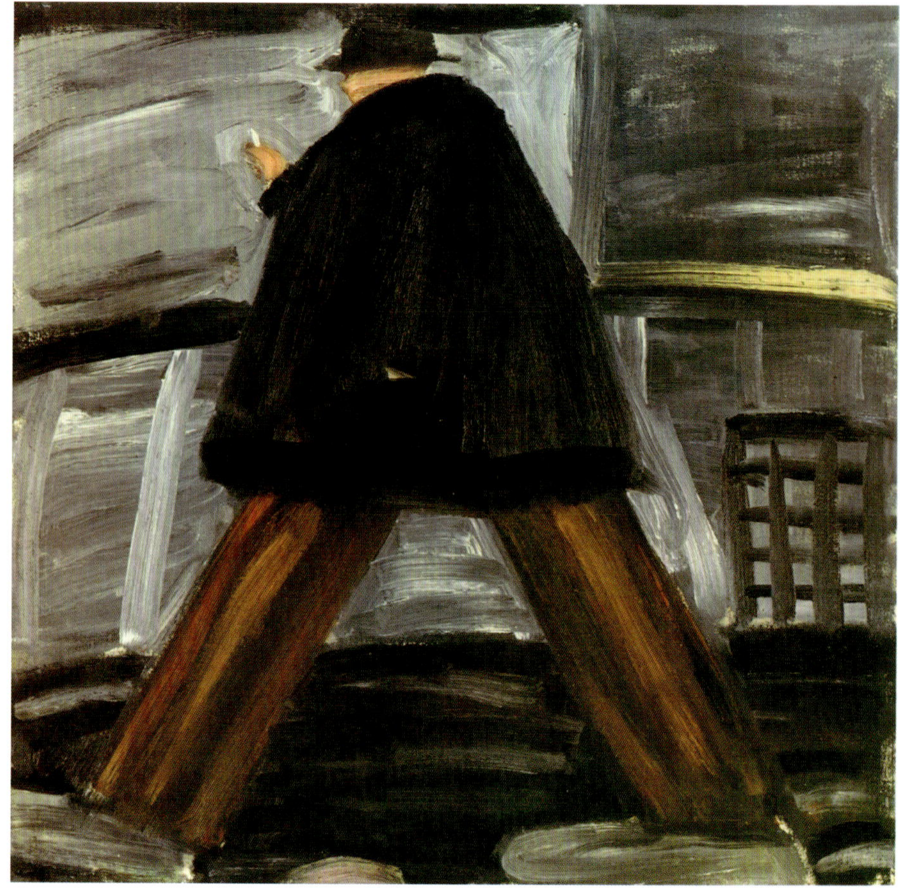

RED GROOMS AND THE SCULPTO-PICTORAMA (1962-76)

*When I first came to New York I was kind of horrified, because
it's on top of you…everything was junked up, jangled-up.
The 'bad taste' of the place…. All that has influenced my work.*

RED GROOMS, 2002

In 1956, at the high point of AbEx, Red Grooms (b. 1937) arrived in New York
from Nashville via Chicago; almost immediately, in images such as *Walking Man*
(1957) [illustration above], he began to subvert the visceral impasto of Franz
Kline into an infantile icon. The city – and, specifically, the most disorderly and
broken-down areas of Lower Manhattan – became his subject matter, embraced
with a carnival euphoria, a manic zest. In his early twenties, Grooms became
famous as the most energetic pioneer of Happenings – those performances and
installations which at the very end of the 1950s cut a navigable passage through
the iced-up aesthetic of abstract painting. Often staged in studio lofts (Grooms
called his The Delancey Street Museum) or derelict shops, Happenings spurned
art as commercial product. Grooms also linked up in 1958 with the young Claes

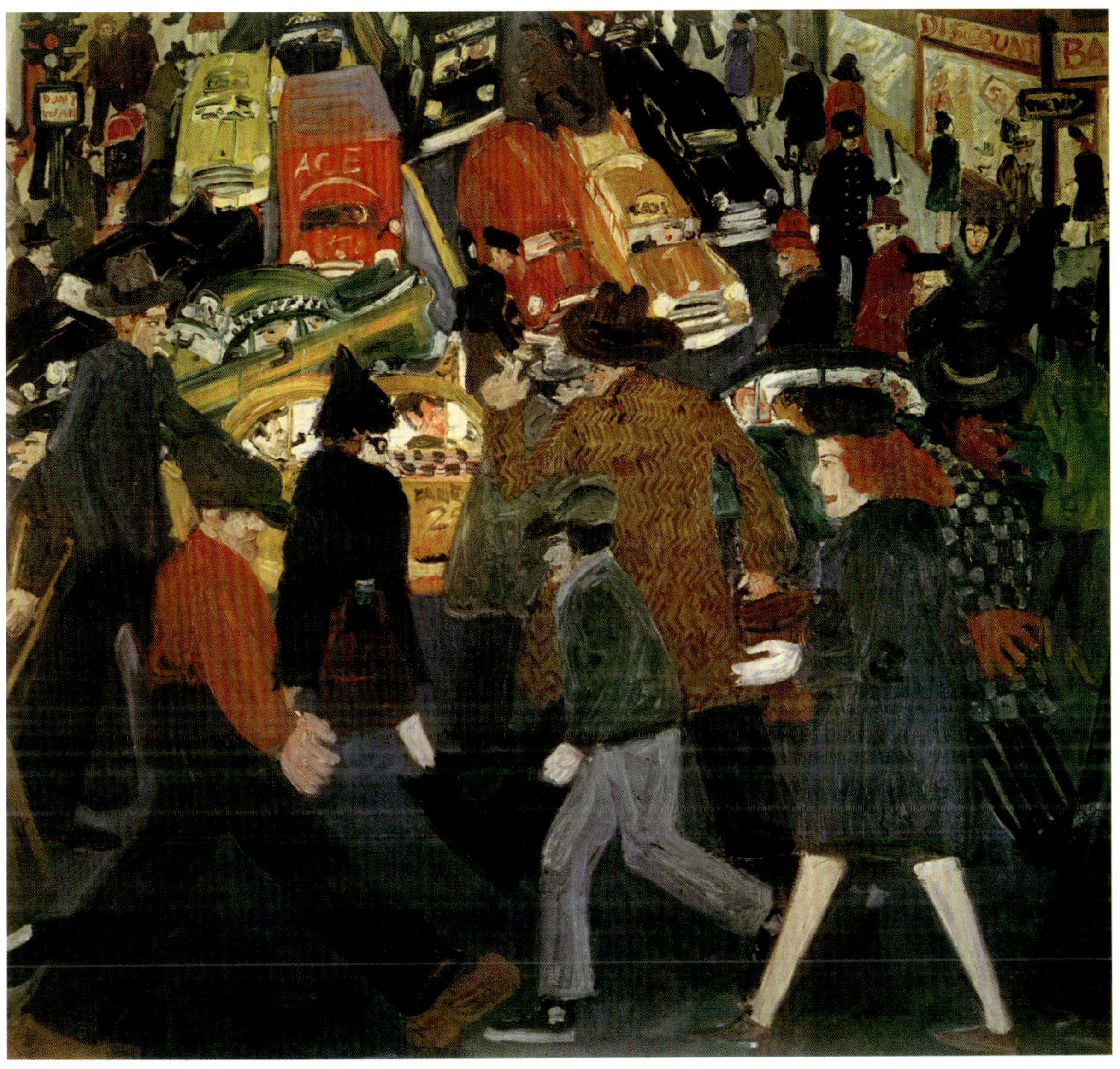

RED GROOMS

Don't Walk

1963

Grooms countered the exalted sublimities
of AbEx with a 'Low' vernacular of the
populist street; very much in contrast to
his mentor Alex Katz, who moved away
from the candour of the cut-outs towards
his own highly formalized figuration.

Oldenburg (b. 1929), the two of them producing primitive props in painted
plaster – shoes, sandwiches, supermarket assemblages – to recreate the urban
everyday as a monstrous apparition.

Grooms admired the delicate collages of Alex Katz, and became part of the
same dissident subculture. He had a long-standing interest in the achievements
of 'Outsiders', and he shared with Rudy Burckhardt a love for the primitive
cinema of Georges Méliès. His collaboration with Burckhardt on the 1962 film
Shoot The Moon, their homage to Méliès, culminates in a splendid sequence
where the returned astronauts are paraded through The City – for which, in the
spirit of Facteur Cheval constructing his *Palais Idéal* (Ideal Palace), Grooms set
out to rebuild Manhattan as a handmade, carnivalesque world. (Frank O'Hara,
in his beautiful, moonstruck street poem, *Avenue A,* refers to 'Red Grooms'
locomotive landscapes'.)

When, in 1960, he had decamped to Italy for eighteen months, he painted
fresh, entertaining images in Florence, and with his partner Mimi, travelled
from town to town in a horse-drawn cart, on which they mounted puppet-plays.
On his return to New York, he had found his former comrades, now labelled 'Pop',
strangely altered. His art, like theirs, alluded to popular imagery,

> but I liked it to have a warmness to it. I didn't grasp giving it a sterile look.
> Pop was all about cool, and I knew I didn't fit in with that.

It was just at this point he saw Alex Katz's cut-out show [illustration p. 209]. Katz
had admired *The Burning Building* and other Happenings by Grooms, and had
taken a role in *Shoot The Moon.* Both artists shared a sense of the constraints
imposed by the painted rectangle; Grooms had already added bits of cardboard to
several of his own canvases, calling them *Stick-outs.* But for Grooms, Katz's cut-outs
meant 'a bad blockage':

> He kind of owned a territory that was very appealing.... He liked folk art a lot;
> he worked in a framing shop, and he made a carved wooden chest with a folk
> feeling to it. Soon after that, I remember him telling me, he made a conscious
> decision to take the High Road, instead of the Low Road.

Grooms himself committed steadfastly to 'the Low Road'. *Don't Walk* [illustration
p. 211] makes an almost defiant embrace of the chaotic, gridlocked street and
its disorderly populace, who disobey all traffic signals and just keep on walking.
Across this big canvas a childlike energy and vitality carries an heroic affirmation
of the everyday.

Partly on Katz's advice, Grooms steered away from easel painting towards
more hybrid media. He has spoken of his childhood enchantment with theatre
and cinema, of his 'vision of doing clownlike magic things'. In 1966 *Fat Feet,*
his nineteen-minute masterpiece of animation and live action, fulfilled that
potential. Alongside Mimi Gross and close friends, Grooms recreates elements of
urban experience – a panorama of smoking chimneys, a garbage lorry, a revolving
door – improvised anew. The live actors clunk about the set, transformed by

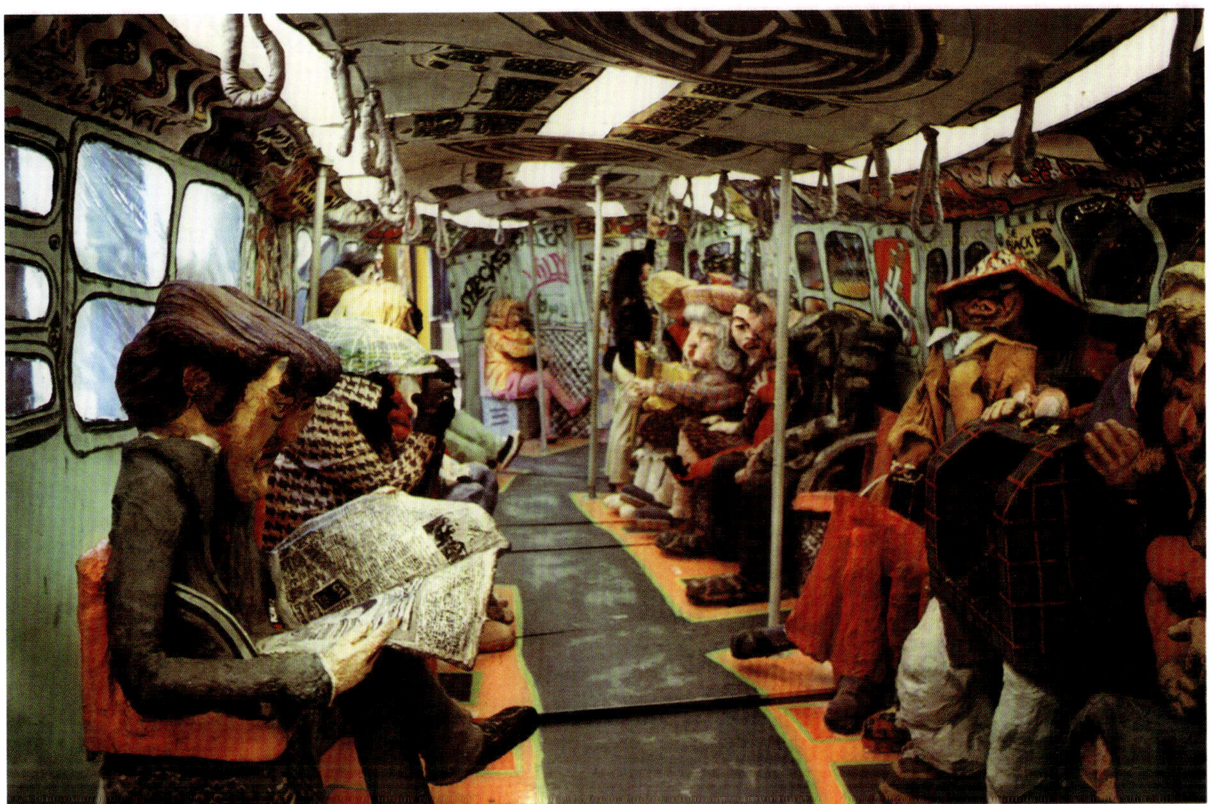

enormous foot extensions into comic archetypes: Cop, Hoodlum, Hooker, Witch, Hobo....

A decade later, Grooms and Mimi Gross assembled a much larger team to build together the vast and astounding sculpto-pictorama *Ruckus Manhattan*. He saw it as 'something to do with *The Cabinet of Dr Caligari*': Expressionist film-set combined with cartoon-cliché, installation crossed with fairground ride. You entered 'Manhattan' by lurching through a thirty-seven-foot subway car, past an array of over life-size sculptural grotesques, who jolted and heaved to either side as you trod across the sprung floor [illustration above]. You could take the ferry, walk down Wall Street, cross a phantasmagoric Brooklyn Bridge. Grooms's imagery is always based on first-hand experience – on rapid drawings made whilst standing in the street.

> When I draw in the city, it's great fun, and it's frustrating too – because
> there's so much going on, you're always so far behind. I find that while you're
> out there, you feel almost ludicrously helpless. But when you get back to the
> studio you hang on to it for all your life is worth.

Ruckus made Grooms a household name in the United States, and his achievement was recognized by several sophisticated commentators – the poet John Ashbery, the critic Peter Schjeldahl, the philosopher Arthur Danto. Aiming for what he called a 'proletarian' or 'Discount Store' style, Grooms had retrieved a kind of innocence from popular culture without irony, reaching out to an audience far wider than the art world. Bob Dylan, who'd first encountered Grooms's work in the early 1960s, 'marvelled at his ability to create excitement out of mundanity'. Grooms was his 'favourite artist': 'I loved the way Grooms used laughter as a diabolical weapon. Subconsciously, I was wondering if it was possible to write songs like that.' Danto saw *Ruckus* as 'a healing work', through which New Yorkers apprehensive about their city 'coming undone' would find courage, would feel more able to join the new society that was emerging: hybrid, mixed-up, multi-everything.

Grooms's contemporaries were at work on multi-media installations – Ed Kienholz (1927–94), for instance (who he dubbed 'Kinda the Hell's Angels side of the operation'); but none could rival Grooms's generosity of spirit, his acceptance of the city as passing show, as carnival procession. Asserting the freedom of foolishness, *Fat Feet* and *Ruckus Manhattan* enact a loss of control – a 'bursting into laughter' that releases and restores.

GEORG BASELITZ: *BIG NIGHT DOWN THE DRAIN* (1962–63)

At that time there were very few possible ways of making pictures at all....
All the things I painted up to 1968 have to be seen as provocations.

GEORG BASELITZ, 1981

In divided post-war Germany, two opposed styles of painting soon prevailed: Socialist realism in the GDR, abstraction in the West. For Hans-Georg Kern, born in Saxony in 1938, son of a Nazi-party member, the constraints of academic training in East Berlin proved unbearable. He was expelled at eighteen for 'social and political immaturity'. Moving to West Berlin in 1958 (the Wall went up three years later, in 1961), he adopted a new identity as 'Georg Baselitz'. The self-consciously sanitized varieties of abstraction that emerged from the rubble in West Germany owed more to the purist design-aesthetic of the Bauhaus than to any metaphysical quest for the absolute. Although excited the following year by the new American abstraction (and especially by Guston's tender touch in, for example, the 1958 canvas *To Fellini*), Baselitz found himself wanting to establish a relationship with German painting pre-dating the Nazis' rise to power in 1933.

> What no-one can escape, what I could never escape, was Germany,
> and being German…something that lingers on most unpleasantly…
> I stopped trying to disown it and instead completely threw myself into
> this business of being German.

The figure in *Big Night Down the Drain* [illustration opposite] retains that 'unpleasantness', that ugly and disquieting character Baselitz associated with all true German painting. He worked on the seven-foot canvas for over two months; his starting point was in Munch's confrontational figures, though this 'masturbating

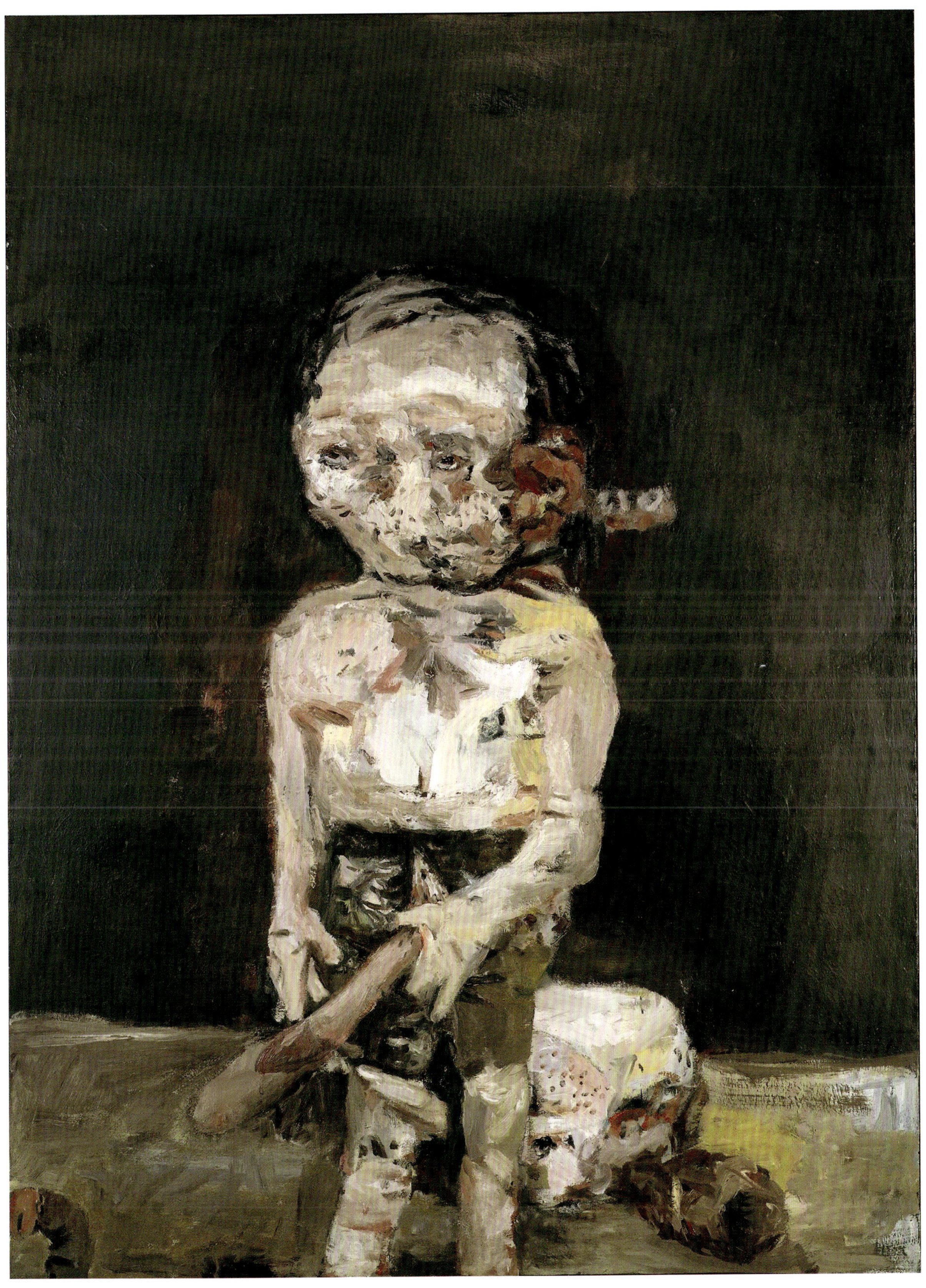

midget' is far more abject. The enormous head and short trousers suggest a child–
puppet protagonist, a variant of Pinocchio, whose monstrously expanded organ
isn't his nose but his penis. Like the monstrous little Oskar, the anti-hero of Günter
Grass's novel *The Tin Drum* (1959), this figure embodies all that had been repressed
in the post-war German psyche. And at some level it is also unmistakably *Selbst-
Kunst*, a self-image, wrenched out of the Void.

PHILIP GUSTON'S RENEWAL-BY-DRAWING (1965–67)

So, I'll draw. And they're goofy drawings. I mean,
just searching, searching, searching, and they're germinating.
My painting comes out of drawing. I couldn't live without drawing.

PHILIP GUSTON, 1974

For an eighteen-month period in the mid-1960s, Philip Guston (1913–80) found
himself unable to paint and worked only in line (see pp. 197–98). Although it
began with extreme reduction – 'I'm down to one line', he told his close friend, the
composer Morton Feldman – the drawing episode ended by supplying the imagery
for the outpouring of his final decade [illustrations pp. 218–19]. It was through
drawing that Guston renewed his art and accomplished his transition from AbEx to
narrative, producing canvases such as *Painting, Smoking, Eating* (1973) [illustration
p. 196]; images that would make him, in Sanford Schwartz's phrase, 'the cornerstone
of recent painting.' The publication in 2010 of Guston's *Collected Writings, Lectures
and Conversations* has made that episode far more vivid. As early as 1958, Guston
had written:

> I do not see why the loss of faith in the known image and symbol in our time
> should be celebrated as a freedom. It is a loss from which we suffer, and this
> pathos motivates modern painting and poetry at its heart.

Guston had long admired the bareness of Mondrian's drawings, and when in 1965
he began to make long sequences of ink-and-brush images, he envisaged them as
similarly skeletal abstract signs. Drawing for him would be a kind of *tabula rasa*.
He wrote of 'a feeling of needing to start again, with the simplest means. I wanted
to clear the decks'. The idea of the primal artist had been part of the mythology
of American abstraction. Guston repeatedly quoted the French poet Stéphane
Mallarmé's summation of the paradoxical condition of the modern artist –
'*un civilisé Édenien*' (one who has the freshness of Eden but is also sophisticated):

> I think we are primitive, really, in spite of our knowing.
> It's a long, long preparation for a few moments of innocence.

At fifty-three, increasingly in retreat from the New York art world, living upstate
in Woodstock, he was making hundreds upon hundreds of abstract drawings,

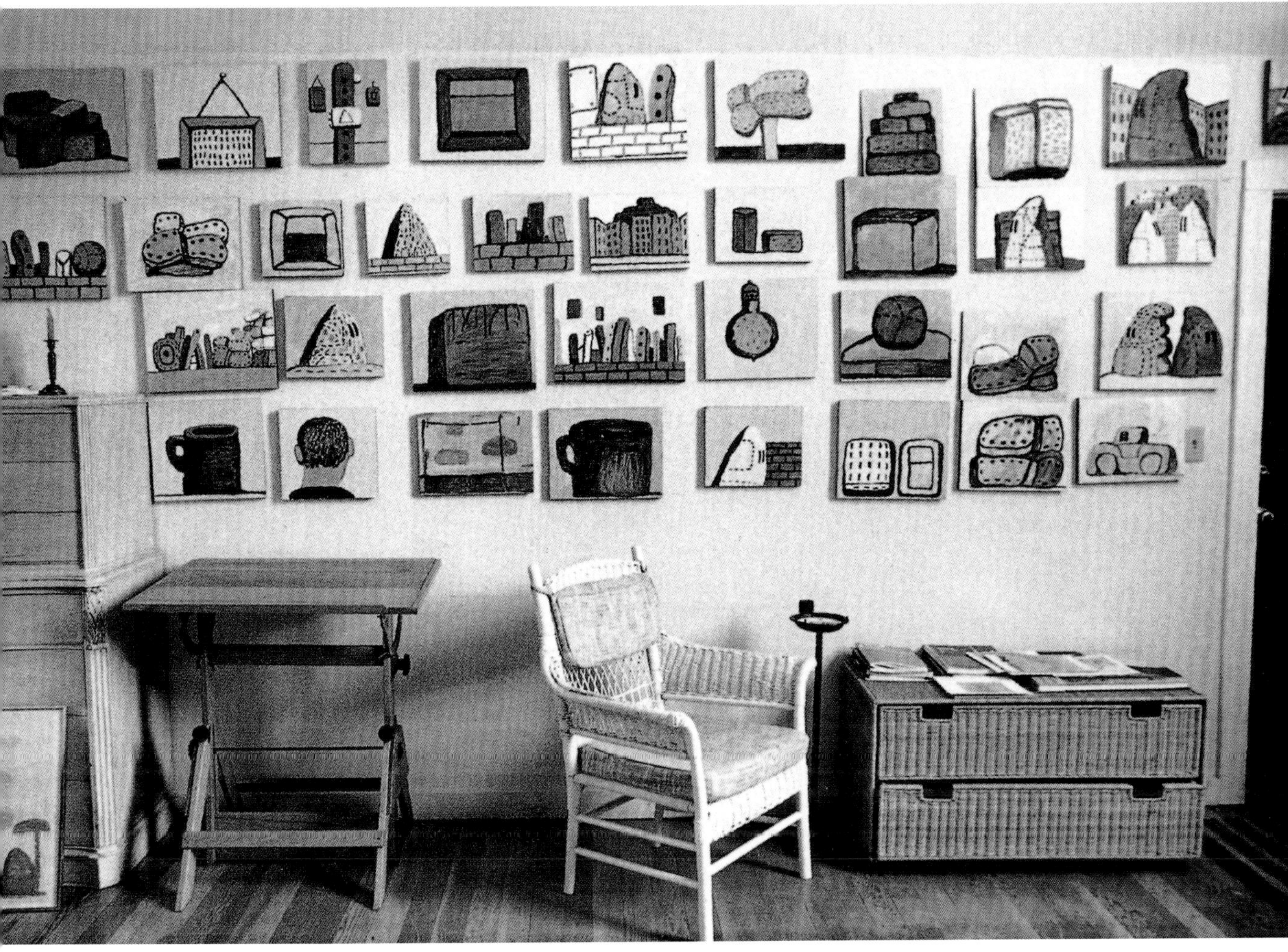

as a helplessly obsessional activity. Painters have often turned to drawing as a relief from crisis. I'm thinking especially of Bonnard in 1916–17, shortly after completing *Dining Room in the Country* [see Ch 3 pp. 116–17, illustration p. 116], when he almost ceased to paint, setting aside his camera and instead drawing every day; 'I have returned to school. I need to start all over again, from ABC...'. Yet Guston, unlike Bonnard, was not drawing from observation, and was perhaps all the more surprised when his own new alphabet began to emerge as a visual syntax made up not of abstract forms, but of real-life objects.

Guston's painting crisis coincided with a personal crisis: he abandoned his wife after almost thirty years and moved to Florida with a much younger woman. He entered a different mind-set. 'Drawing is everything. It's the core, the bones of it, the line. Why do I need colour?' But as he explained to the writer Dore Ashton, after some months, a 'tug-of-war' developed.

> It was two equally powerful impulses at loggerheads. I would one day
> tack up in the house a bunch of pure drawings, feel good about them....
> And that night go out to the studio to the drawings of objects – books,

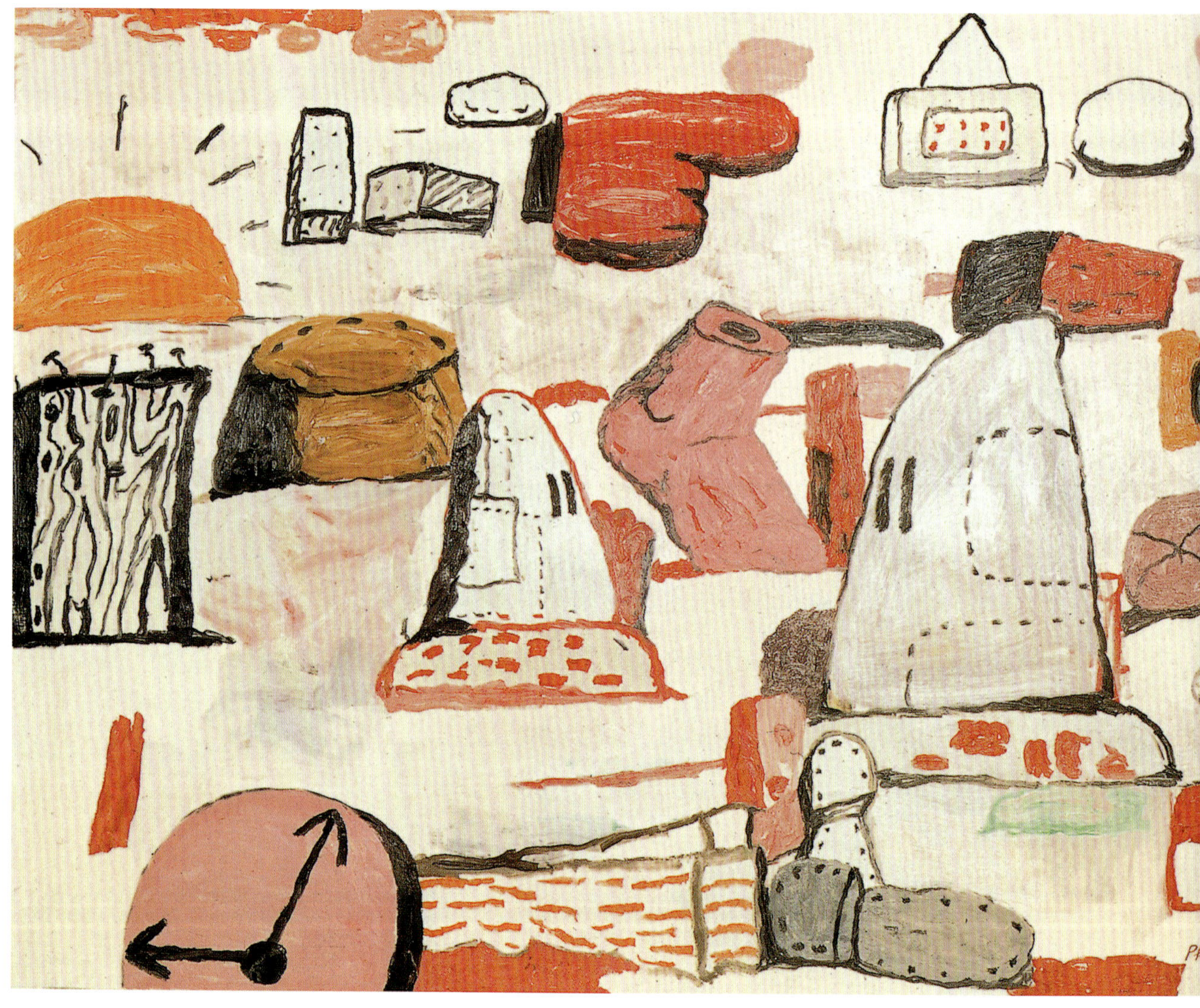

PHILIP GUSTON

Flatlands

1970

The half-buried forms that rise from the mud include a sculpted foot, as well as shoes with legs attached; a clock as well as a dial; a smoking brick chimney, a picture hung with a string, a plank with nails; a disembodied paw, a sun, and two Klansmen – all of them lost in their separateness.

shoes, buildings, hands – feeling *relief* and a strong need to cope with tangible things.

When Guston extends that list – 'rusted iron, mended rags, brick walls, cigarette butts, empty booze bottles, the hands of clocks' – we realize this alphabet-of-the-world has thrown up a narrative, and its function is to reconnect his art with the 'suppressed realities' of a catastrophic childhood.

Born in Montreal, he grew up as Philip Goldstein, the youngest of seven children whose parents had fled from the 1905 pogroms in Odessa. In Los Angeles, where the family settled, his father drove a rag-and-bone cart; when he hanged himself, it was the ten-year-old Philip who found the body. He witnessed the accident in which his beloved brother's legs were crushed; gangrene set in, leading to amputation, and death. In 1935, when he was twenty-two, he changed his name and had almost no further contact with his family.

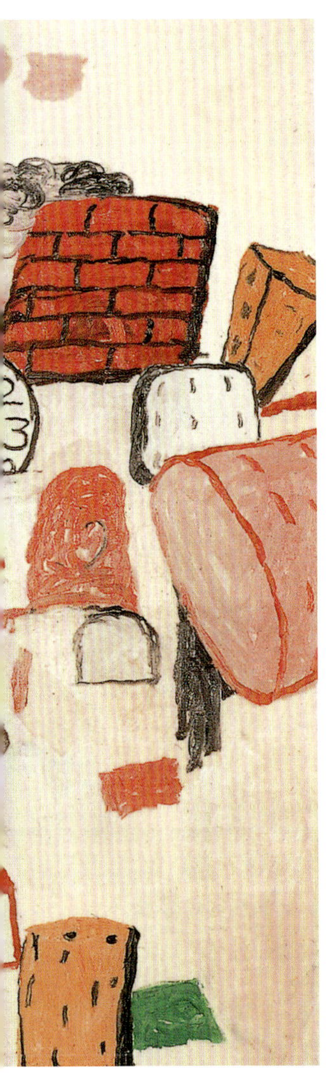

The drawings that surfaced in the reinvented 'Philip Guston' thirty years later echo the comic-strips he'd drawn from obsessively as a child (in a cupboard lit by a naked bulb), as well as the contemporary narratives drawn by the young Robert Crumb. Like them, he 'wanted to tell stories'. Bringing together all those base objects on one wall, he re-entered a lost core of identity – in W. B. Yeats's lines, 'I must lie down where all the ladders start/ In the foul rag and bone shop of the heart.' Guston could not, in any normal parlance, be termed a realist. Yet in his deepest impulse, he was turning away from the dematerialized, to assert The Real, and his medium was line; that over-emphatic black line we've already encountered in Léger, Beckmann, Hartley. For fifteen years Guston had painted within an ideology centred on that which could not be delineated. As he'd said to the writer Bill Berkson in 1964, 'Doubt itself becomes a form'. But by 1966, he had 'discovered that as I'm going to move forward into what obviously is a figuration, I don't have the illusion that I know what I'm going to do. I mean, there's even more ambiguity and complication.'

When Guston glued one of those drawings to a board, it became a 'painting'. Soon his studio was full of small masonite panels depicting single objects [illustration p. 217]. He had meanwhile returned to Woodstock and to his marriage. Full-scale paintings began to take shape. 'There is nothing to do now but paint my life.' His new imagery exposed the intimate self-revelation of a distressed, middle-aged painter who was drinking, smoking, eating far too much; admissions of folly and bad faith, subject to surfacings of Buchenwald corpse-heaps and amputated limbs, all wrapped in a slapstick gallows humour. By 1970, in *Flatlands* [illustration left] part-objects were scattered across a canvas of AbEx dimensions. 'At one point,' Guston said of that painting, 'I sort of sank the whole world, like it was doomed…. It's what's left.' That flotsam is the litter and debris of catastrophe. He had carried over from his abstract work his beautiful pinks and whites – the nacreous palette of James Ensor [see Ch 4 pp. 163–65, illustration pp. 164–65] – together with his tenderness of painterly touch. But it was through line, through its script-like potential to communicate, to grasp and to metamorphose, that Guston had been able to create his parallel world.

'TO BRING BACK THE LOST REALITY OF THE WORLD': BHUPEN KHAKHAR AND INDIAN EXPERIENCE (1975-87)

An artist must be vulnerable.
His paintings must reflect all his weak points.

BHUPEN KHAKHAR, 1978

Much of the history of twentieth-century painting could be retold as a narrative of artists who, having long since ruled out the option of naturalism, were nevertheless impelled to create a world of figures, to reconstitute the world

anew. That was the dilemma facing Bhupen Khakhar (1934–2003) – as it had
been for Guston, Carrà and Léger before him – when, at the end of the 1960s, he
tested one mode after another. Could he shape a figurative idiom equivalent to
his experience? Around 1972, Khakhar's pictorial language gelled; all its hybrid
elements fell into place. It was as though a door suddenly opened, onto a vista no
painter had penetrated before: the vast terrain of half-Westernized modern India.

The Indian art world then numbered at most a few hundred 'professional'
painters, set apart from the traditional arts in which millions remained active.
Two successive generations had been instrumental in shaping a lively art
climate: in pre-Independence Bengal, centred on Tagore's forest university at
Santiniketan (see Ch 1 pp. 45–47 and Ch 4 pp. 171–73); and in the 1940s, a more
urbane and international-minded grouping, known as the Bombay Progressives,
looking especially to post-war Paris. Khakhar grew up in Bombay, qualifying
as a chartered accountant. In 1962, at twenty-eight, he took the momentous
step of enrolling in the Fine Arts faculty at Baroda (founded in 1950, following
India's Independence in 1947, and embracing modernism, in contrast to the
academicism of the colonial art schools). The outstanding teacher there was
K. G. Subramanyan, who assisted Binode Behari Muhkerjee on his great mural
[see Ch 1 pp.45–47, illustration p. 44]. But for Khakhar the most important
input came from a contemporary of Hockney and Kitaj at the Royal College of
Art in London (see pp. 198–207) – Jim Donovan, who arrived in Baroda in 1962.
Khakhar recalled the dose of Pop he then received as 'the foundation'. It helped
him recognize the beauty and vitality of the contemporary Indian street, to
become attentive to Indian popular imagery – oleographs, film posters and all
the 'debased' genres that were, like himself, 'on the margins of art'.

In the mid-1960s, exhibiting half-abstracted collages that incorporate kitsch
imagery from contemporary Indian temples, Khakhar had got off to a false
start, and there had followed several years of stylistic floundering. In parallel,
he was writing short stories, phrased in the half-Anglicized Gujarati of the
lower-middle-class business community; he was still working each morning as a
salaried accountant, in a small Baroda factory, which kept him in daily contact
with ordinary life, while leaving the afternoons free for painting. The focus of
his beautiful early oil paintings of the 1970s was The Insignificant Man – Watch-
repairer, Barber, Factory Accountant – rendered in a crisp vernacular; resembling
signboards, the separate objects and attributes that made up reality itemized
with an accountant's precision.

Khakhar spoke of how, in an actual room, he would scrutinize each object –
how best to render it, whether as a Vuillard, a Léger or a Rousseau. In *Man Eating
Jalebee* (1974) [illustration opposite] we can work our way across the foreground
in terms of a series of surface decisions: spatters for the marble-chip table-top;
diagonal strokes for the plastic strings of the chair-back; Léger-like precision for
the red rail of the terrace; ribbons of shot colour to make palpable the rayon-
sheen of his shirt. A poetic relation is established between the foreground figure,
whose huge hand reaches out so awkwardly, and the world beyond him: the car

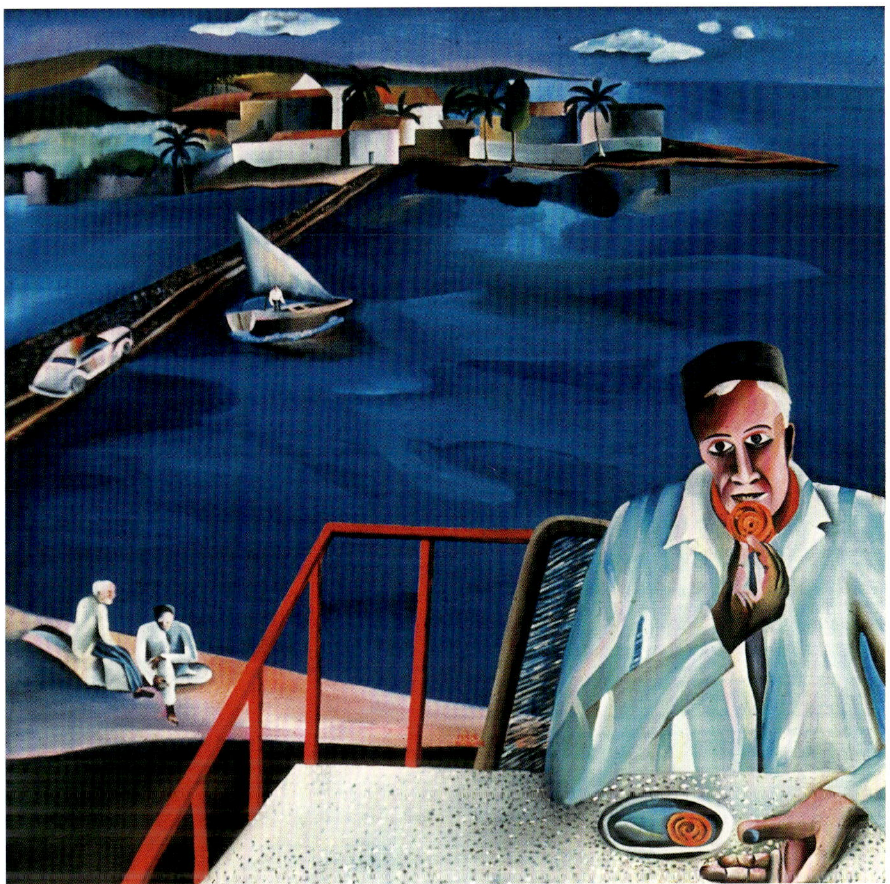

on the causeway, the boat setting out with its lone sailor. Is this reality or fantasy? Are we witness only to his dream of escape, a new voyage-of-life?

By the early 1970s Khakhar was seen, together with others of his 'Baroda generation', as an *indigenist*. India's leading young critic, Geeta Kapur, was questioning the relevance of internationalism to the needs of Indian painters:

> Internationalism and Formalism have accompanied each other and have, for all the claims of avant-gardism, made art conformist and conventional.... My point of view is that internationalism as a cult imposes upon the individual artist, and especially outside the Western metropolis, a set of false imperatives that need to be examined.

Khakhar would need to jettison the tyranny of internationalist aesthetics, to unlearn received ideas of good taste, if he was to enter into the reality of that class he wanted not only to depict but to *represent*. The over life-size effigy in *Man with Bouquet of Plastic Flowers* from 1976 [illustration p. 222 and detail p. 192] is funereal – a messenger from the grave, zombie eyes in a darkened face. This painting is about a milieu and an absence: an icon and altarpiece to a life misspent, to a death-in-life. The double-scale relates both to Indian 'uplift' posters – for example, of Gandhi amid his deeds – and to the Italian *Vita-Icon*, where the saint stands among his miracles. Later that year, visiting Europe for the

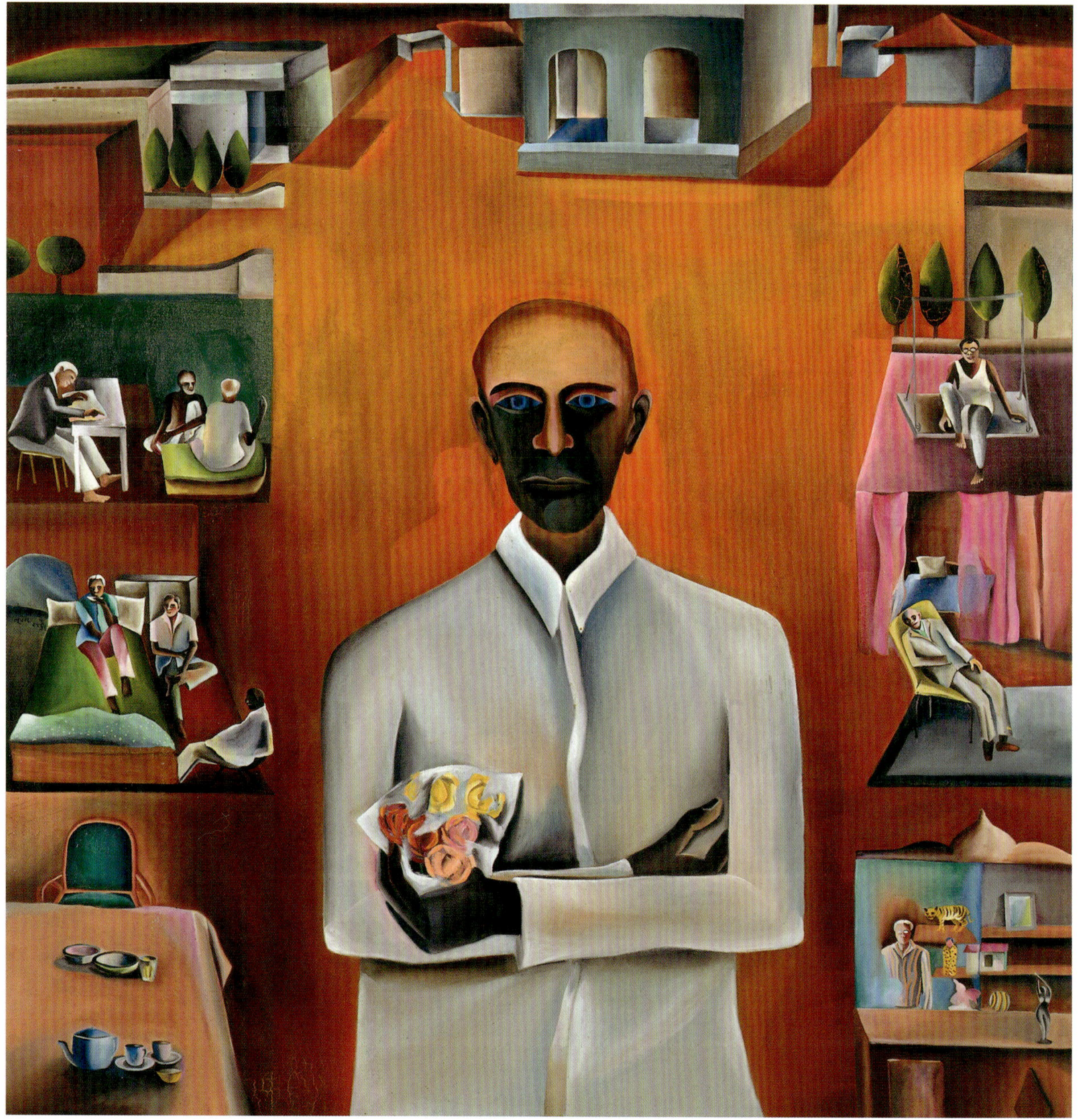

BHUPEN KHAKHAR

Man with Bouquet of Plastic Flowers

1976

The death's head protagonist is set against the orange
Void of his burnt-earth compound, amid vignettes of
reading a newspaper, napping, at the teashop, on the
swing, lounging with business friends – and, most tellingly,
a table and empty chair stretching into the foreground
(see also detail p. 192).

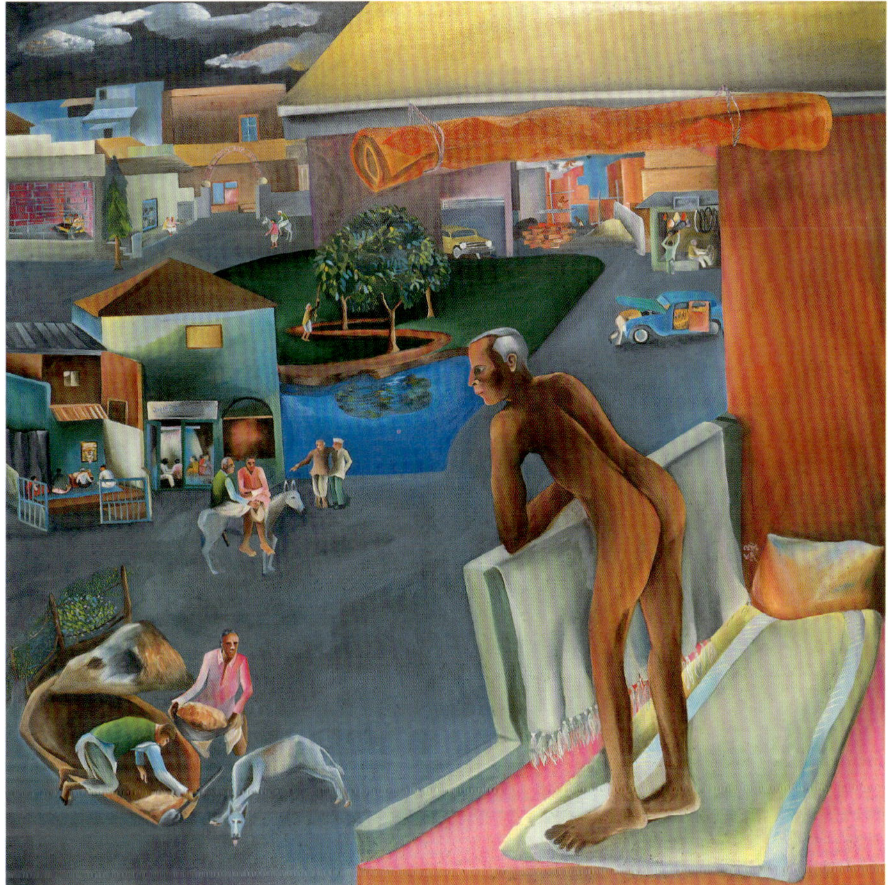

first time, Khakhar identified most with the fourteenth-century Sienese painters. 'The early Italians faced certain problems which I face also as a painter: how to include the narrative elements in a painting without destroying its structure.' He loved their ' diffidence', a 'timidness in their work. They are trying to evolve a language for the first time…a kind of meekness.'

In Italy again, in 1979, his travel companion was Howard Hodgkin (see Epilogue pp. 239–41); they stood together in Mantegna's frescoed *Camera degli Sposi* (Bridal Chamber), and challenged one another to enlarge their scale. Two years later, the panoramic townscape of *You Can't Please All* [illustration above] is at once an homage to Ambrogio Lorenzetti – the retelling of an ancient fable, employing the 'continuous narration' of the Sienese – and a far more urgent and personal theme, which is embodied in the watcher, who has come out onto the balcony and sees the fable unfolding below him. At forty-seven, Khakhar painted himself 'just standing naked before everyone'. This *coming out* is still half-covert, though there are other clues. Why, when the donkey makes its second appearance, is it sporting an enormous erection? The artist's sly response: 'Because he is carrying two men.'

Khakhar's gradual pictorial coming-out over the course of the 1980s may have been the most courageous act of his life. 'Up to 1975, I felt that if my friends knew I am gay, I was prepared to commit suicide.' Homosexuality had remained invisible in Indian culture, unrepresented even in novels and films. Khakhar found himself,

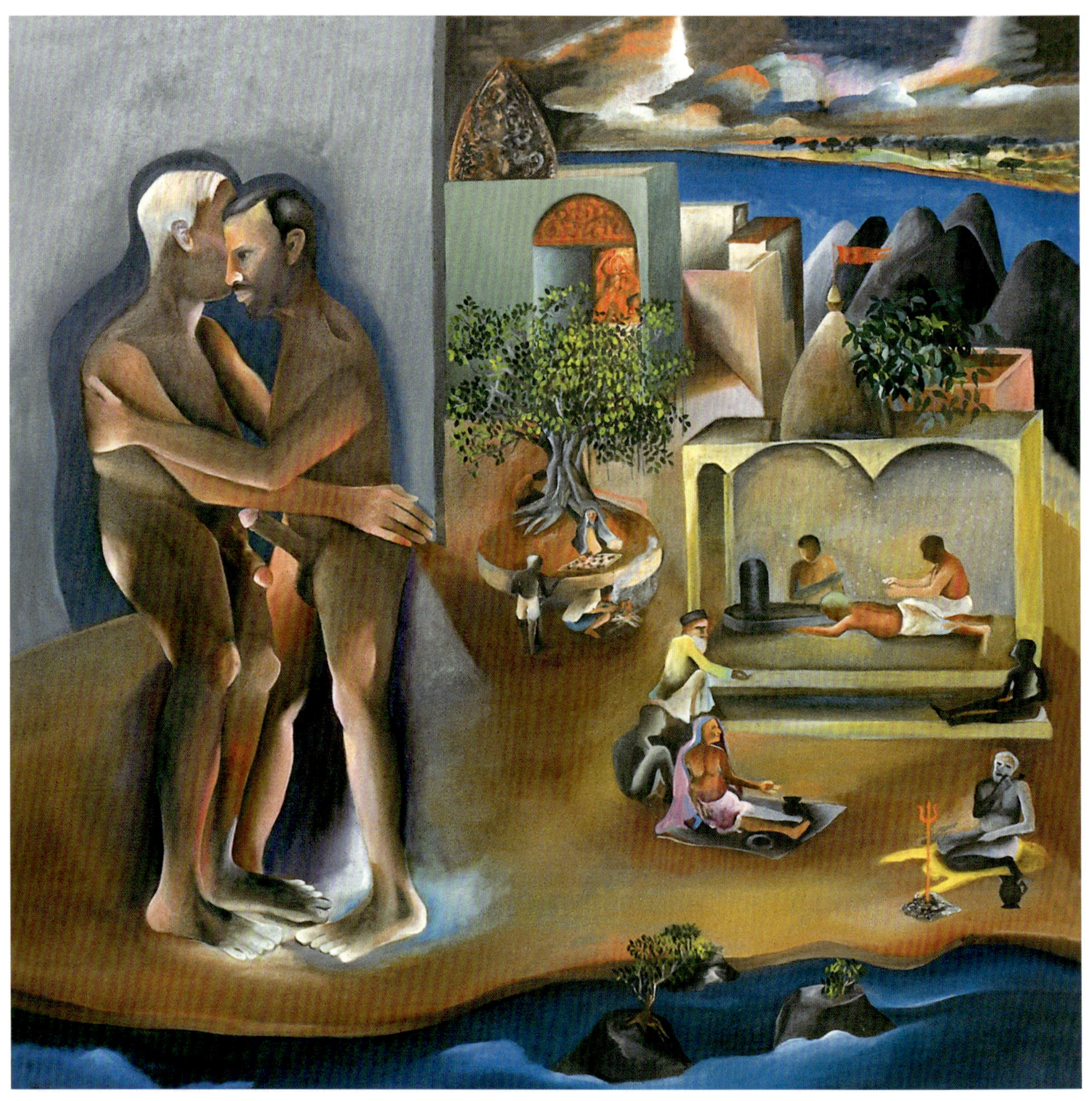

BHUPEN KHAKHAR

Two Men in Banaras

1982

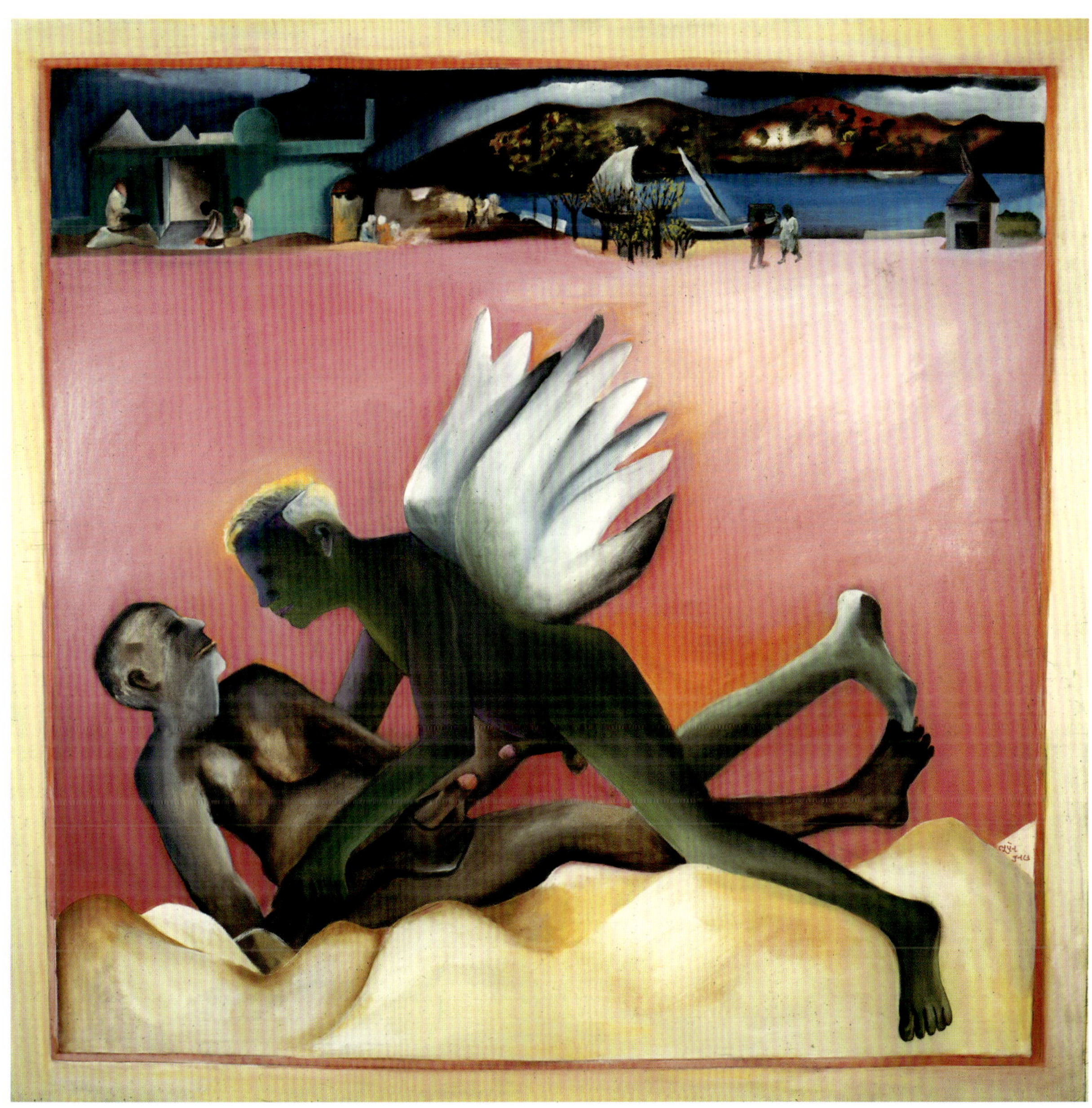

BHUPEN KHAKHAR

Yayati

1987

once again, painting on behalf of a constituency hitherto unregarded, unrecorded. His art became explicitly confessional, though the self is always juxtaposed to some larger context. At the end of the 1970s, Geeta Kapur was writing of a new generation of Indian painters, who sought 'to bring back the lost reality of the world'; moving away from the painting-as-autonomous-object, towards a more societal art. *Two Men in Banaras* (1982) [illustration p. 224] is another divided and double-scale image. A lyrical golden landscape, with sadhus and small shrines among trees, is set against Khakhar's naked embrace of a bearded stranger: the sexual is located in the sacred.

Throughout his adult life, Khakhar, whose father died when he was four, devoted himself to a succession of elderly men. In *Yayati* [illustration p. 225] he takes an episode from *The Mahabharata* in which the king, who grows old and impotent, asks his son to give him his youth. The first impact of *Yayati* is of an enormous vertical plane of flat pink (which turns out to be constantly modulated, from alizarin to orange to purest rose). That intensity of saturated colour makes the winged figure's green-and-purple seem credible, even inevitable. The sudden shift of scale into the landscape-strip at the top of the canvas locks the image into place. Held within that tension, a self-portrait as white-haired angel glides erect into an old man almost dead.

Those three images – *You Can't Please All*, *Two Men in Banaras* and *Yayati* – were, in Khakhar's words, 'efforts to come out in-open', and to create a homoerotic iconography very different from David Hockney's:

> Hockney is concerned with physical beauty. I am much more concerned with
> other aspects, like warmth, pity, vulnerability, touch.

Khakhar's celebrations of the energies and illuminations detonated in sexual intimacy extend beyond the couple themselves. According to Julian Bell, writing of *Two Men in Banaras* in 2007, Khakhar was accessing Ambrogio Lorenzetti 'for his vision of the flow of humanity and landscape behind the lovers.' The fourteenth-century Sienese artist in whose microcosm of *The Well-Governed City* 'painting [had] made the World known to itself' was a model for post-formalist painters, 'for returning to their one-time role, as creators of communal imaginative space.'

Bell is right to point to the 'communal' dimension in Khakhar's art; the painter was a lifelong Gandhian. His work as a whole points to a renewal of the local against the international, but a local stripped of traditional divisions of caste and hierarchy. He embraces a 'reality' multiple, diffuse and hybrid, very much in parallel with the vision of Salman Rushdie. (Khakhar painted a memorable portrait of Rushdie, while the artist himself had a cameo role as The Accountant in Rushdie's 1996 novel *The Moor's Last Sigh*.) Of all the 'history painters' in this chapter, it may be Khakhar who most convincingly affirms painting's continuing function.

ANSELM KIEFER: *OPERATION SEA LION* (1975–84)

At the core of Kiefer's painting – supplying both subject matter and language – is *hubris*, with all the heroic, tragic and catastrophic overtones that implies. Born in West Germany in 1945, seven years younger than Baselitz, he grew up not under Nazism but in its defeat. His earliest experience was of a ruined world, and rubble became an essential constituent of his art. Hubristic inflation and its consequence, utter devastation, gave Kiefer's first mature paintings their burnt-out grandiloquence.

Kiefer enacted, in Léger's prescription, a 'Return to Great Subjects' (see Ch 1 pp. 20–26). In content and in scale his early canvases were evidently modern history paintings, yet from the Italians to Géricault, from Balthus to Kitaj, that aspiration had always implied a complex, many-figured composition; whereas Kiefer's worlds were without people. *Operation Sea Lion* [illustration below] is twelve by eighteen feet. A wartime episode – Hitler's abortive plan for an invasion of southern England – is transformed into a mighty emblem of power and folly. The foreground toy battleships in the bathtub create a dreamlike uncertainty of scale, reinforced by the vast wave of ploughed plain (a photographic projection) that rears up behind.

Entering art school at the end of the 1960s, only after training as a lawyer, Kiefer had experienced the stylistic hegemony of American abstraction, but also painting's eclipse by conceptual austerities; most potently, at the Kunstakademie in Düsseldorf, by the charismatic gospel of Joseph Beuys (1921–86), who he came to know well. In *Operation Sea Lion* the AbEx sublime is conjoined to Beuys's historical consciousness, his fetishization of materials, his shamanic – and hubristic – persona.

ANSELM KIEFER
Operation Sea Lion
1983–84

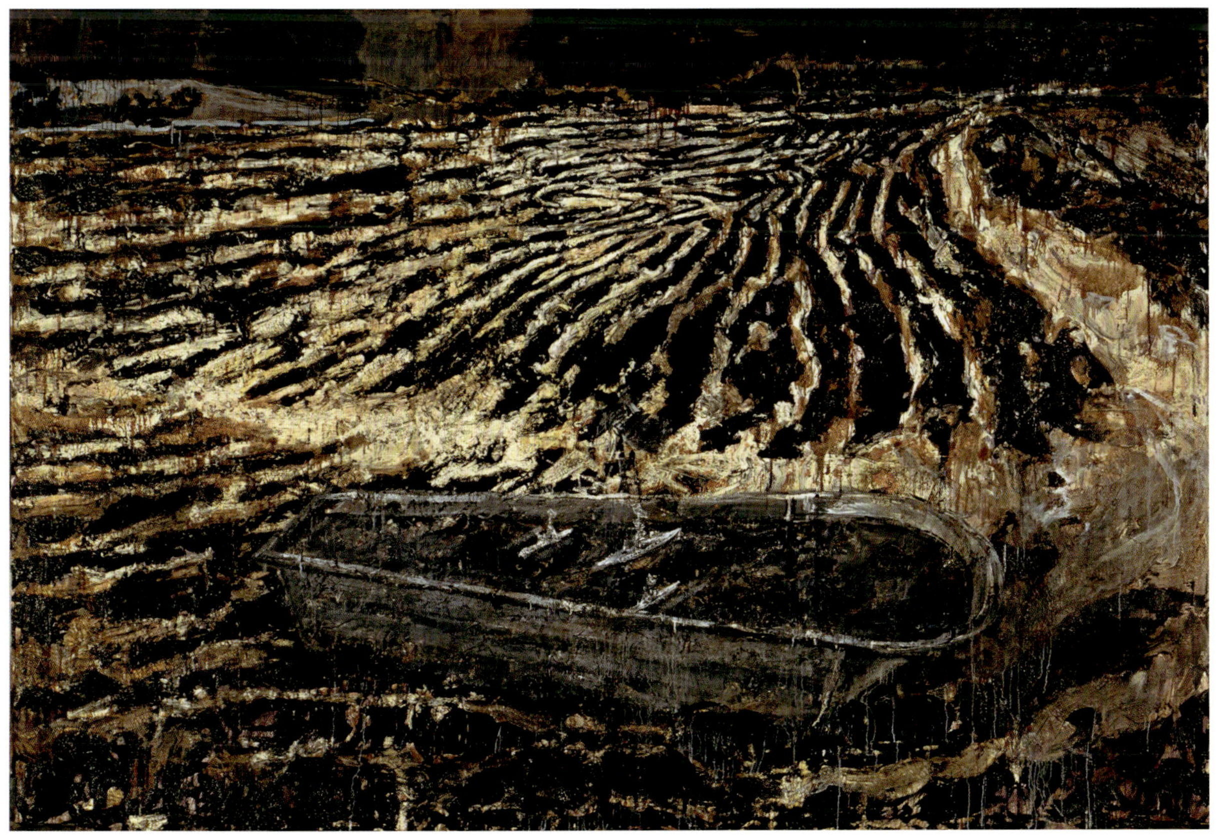

'The subjective, the visionary, the mythical have been brought back from exile,' announced the triumphalist catalogue to 'Zeitgeist', the huge international painting show mounted in Berlin in 1982, in which both Baselitz and Kiefer had starring roles. It followed London's 'A New Spirit in Painting' at the Royal Academy the previous year, which presented thirty-eight painters, all of them male, embedding masters of an earlier generation, such as Bacon and Guston, within the current painting mode. Almost instantaneously the liberation of painting had turned into another stylistic tyranny. Painters such as Julian Schnabel (b. 1951) adopted all the marks of extreme emotion, of an expressionistic assertion of subjectivity, even though their exaggerated 'painterliness' signified no more than a strategy for picture-making, for product. A new postmodern criticism justified the inauthentic as the 'true' mode of the times: whether we call it New Image or Neo-Expressionism or *Transavantguardia*, this international style took over the Western art market for several years. Well before the end of the century, this spurious 'movement' had burnt itself out, having discredited painting in the eyes of most young artists.

Kiefer's art could appear tainted with that same intimidatory rhetoric. Yet there remained a poetic core – some of his finest images are dedicated to, or inscribed with a quotation from, the great Austrian poet Ingeborg Bachmann. Even into the twenty-first century, several Kiefer masterpieces have vindicated painting as a contemporary medium of prophecy.

IDA APPLEBROOG'S POLYPTYCHS (1986-89)

The idea of a painting that can incorporate several separate parts, each panel performing a different role – monumental icon juxtaposed to intimate narrative, the metaphysical alongside the 'real' – goes back beyond the time of Duccio and Giotto. Discarded in the centuries after the Renaissance, the polyptych remained mostly without heirs among modern painters, whether figurative or abstract. Ida Applebroog's strange image-assemblies were conceived not to celebrate multiplicity – as a polyptych might have been by Max Beckmann or Stanley Spencer or R. B. Kitaj – but, she says, 'to keep things from falling apart'. Yet while her own patchworks may have been first generated by her personal testament as a woman and as a feminist, they can also be seen as opening another way by which future history painters might break out of their over-formalized, rectangular mindsets.

Brought up in a Yiddish-speaking, Orthodox Jewish family in the Bronx, Ida Applebaum (b. 1929) trained as a graphic designer, developing into a sculptor and video artist, as well as a maker of books (which she calls 'performances'). But as Faye Hirsch wrote in *Art in America* in 2012, the artist had

> long been fascinated with the broken language associated with mental
> breakdown – including asyndetic speech, in which conjunctions are left out.
> She herself, when admitted to the hospital in San Diego, found it nearly

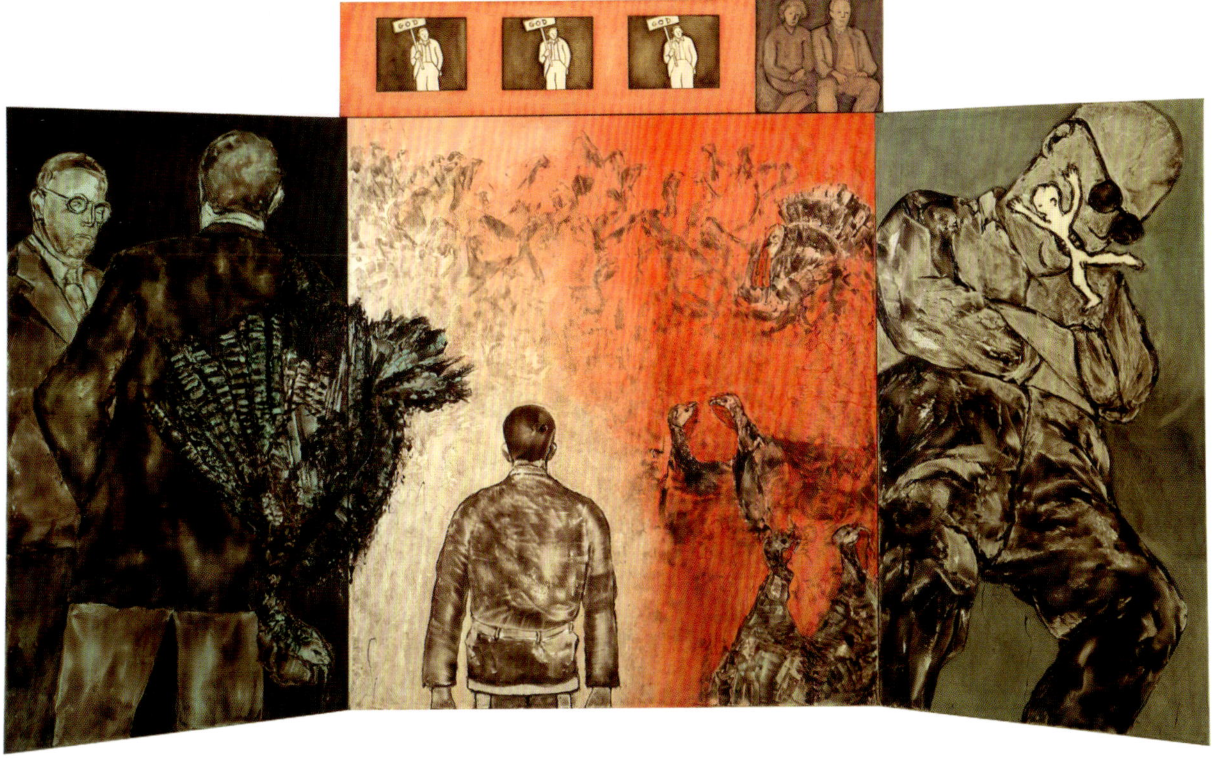

impossible to form coherent sentences, and when asked her name, replied,
'Applebrrr, brrr, brrrgh,' as she tells it. Her maiden name was Appelbaum,
but in 1975 she took the name Applebroog, honouring the most vulnerable
moment of her life, when speech failed her.

In 1971 Applebroog visited the house in Mexico Frida Kahlo had shared with Diego
Rivera (see Ch 3 pp. 136–38). She too was impelled to tackle real-life subject matter
– marital and medical, sexual and political – but like many of her contemporaries
in the burgeoning feminist movement, she spurned painting – especially American
abstraction – as a male-dominated preserve. Only in her fifties, in large-scale image-
assemblies such as *Camp Compazine* (1988) [illustration above] did she begin to
discover in painting a medium that could embody feminist discourse. Compazine
is a medication that suppresses vomiting; other titles reference lithium, and the
suburban hospitals (*Hillcrest State* and *Riverdale Home for the Aged*) where helpless,
stupefied patients are incarcerated.

Her canvas constructions when encountered in the life prove far more awkward,
more primitive and *misfitting* than they appear in reproduction. Applebroog's
montage evades that potential 'boredom' which Francis Bacon saw as inherent in
narrative imagery (see Ch 1 pp. 54–55). In Bhupen Khakhar's version of a polyptych,
Man with Bouquet of Plastic Flowers [illustration p. 222] the protagonist and the
scenes from his life are connected, but in *Camp Compazine* the narrative is rendered
elliptical, dysfunctional. Is the little man with his insistent 'GOD' placard the same
who is seated inert beside his spouse; and does he become that slumped – perhaps
straitjacketed – grey figure on the right? This whole circuit of imagery might be

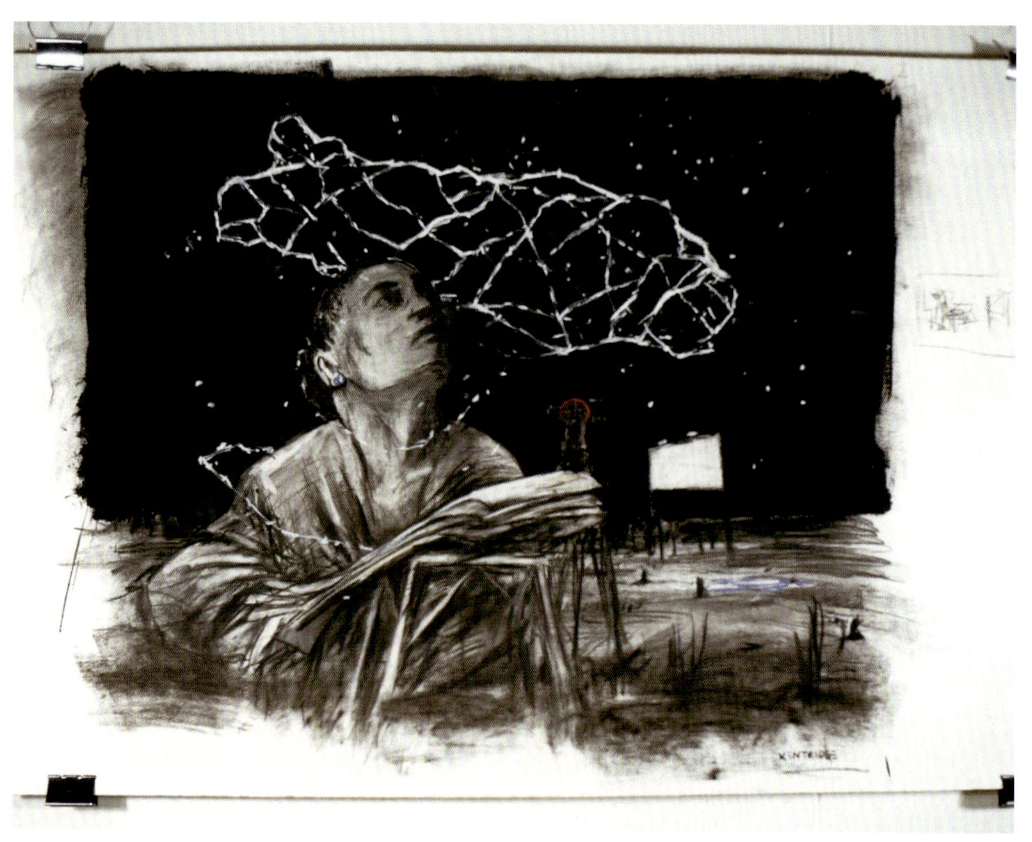

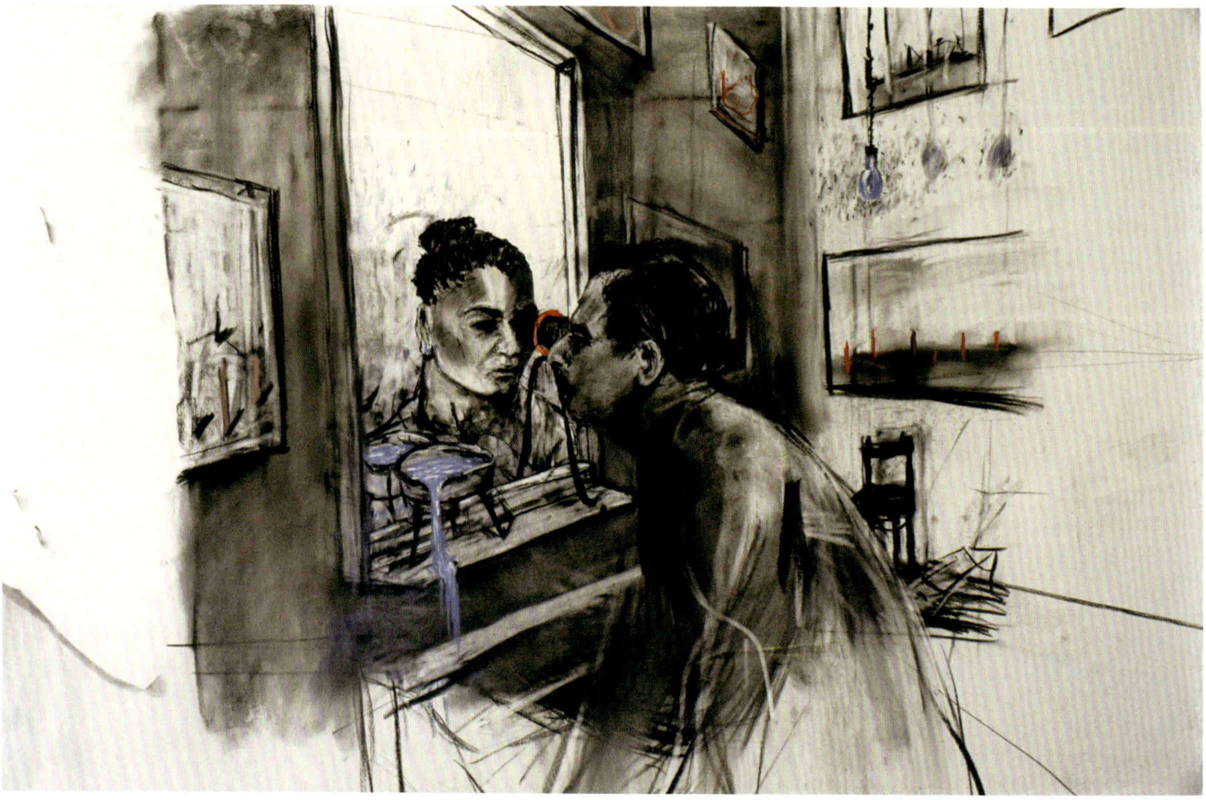

understood as a 'herstory' of Males, the vision of a sixty-year-old female: those two sober-suits on the left (psychiatrists? administrators?); the enigmatically illuminated central panel, with an everyman moving into a field of turkeycock with turkeyhens. The damped-down neutrality of Applebroog's depiction, stripped of consolation or affect, is at one with her medicated world.

WILLIAM KENTRIDGE'S *FELIX* NARRATIVES (1989–2003)

A drawing is started on the paper, I walk across to the camera,
shoot one or two frames, walk back to the paper, change the
drawing (marginally) walk back to the camera, and so on.
It is more like making a drawing than making a film.

WILLIAM KENTRIDGE, 1993

When viewed in sequence, William Kentridge's 9 *Drawings for Projection* (2005) unfold a localized history – South Africa during the apartheid years – while making us participants in a more universal experience: the slow, painful passage of time, the endurance by which an image, an individual or a society grows and is changed. He began his fifth film, *Felix in Exile* [illustrations opposite and pp. 232–33], in Johannesburg just before the April 1993 elections that marked the end of apartheid and continued to work on it all through the summer; the finished projection lasts under nine minutes. (Kentridge reckons one week of drawing yields about forty seconds.) As always, he proceeded in his 'stone-age filmmaking' without script or storyboard, trusting only to intuition, though he was finding it 'harder to reclaim each time the space of not knowing what I was doing'. But he held fast to Uncertainty:

> I believe that in the *indeterminacy* of drawing – the contingent way that images
> arrive in the world – lies some kind of model of how we live our lives.

His two archetypal alter egos – stripe-suited tycoon Soho Eckstein and naked intellectual Felix Teitelbaum – are, like Kentridge himself, of Lithuanian-Jewish origin. Both carry the guilt of the settler, and those uncertain narratives that gather around each in their polarity convey above all a shared shame. Holed up in Paris among his drawings, Felix yearns for Soho's wife...until the apparition of Nandi (surveyor and emancipator, African Cassandra) floods his hotel room.... Eventually we see Nandi's corpse lying out in the mine-scarred veld, becoming covered in newspapers, then dissolving. Finally, fat Felix stands naked in a flooded mine shaft.... No synopsis will be adequate to convey that visceral morphing of black charcoal (the lines emphatic, but easily erased and remade). Nor will any reproduction show how those residual drawings, with their generic, slightly stodgy 1950s look, are brought magically to life, not least through the plangent musical soundtrack by Philip Miller.

WILLIAM KENTRIDGE
Stills from *Felix in Exile*
1994

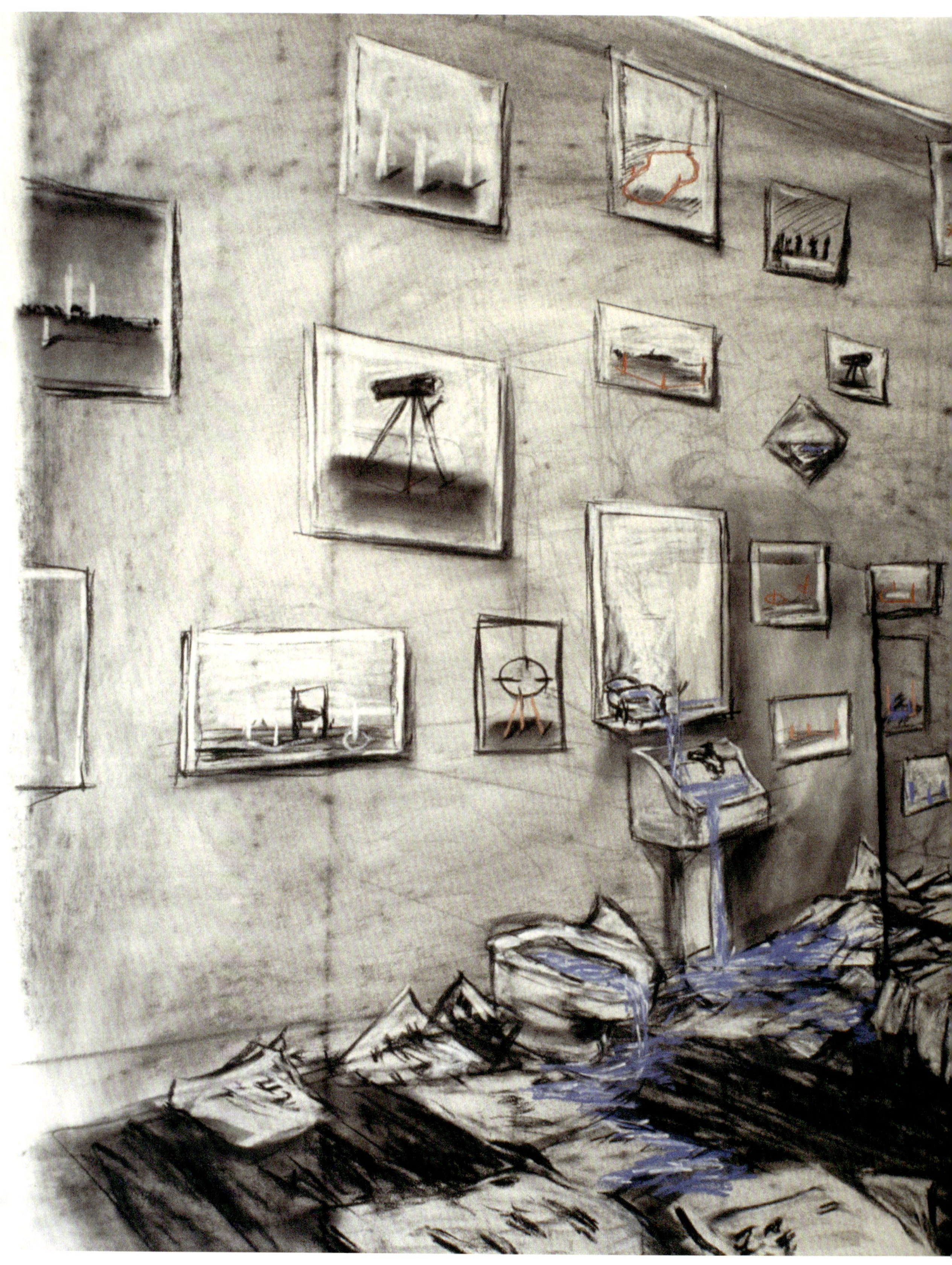

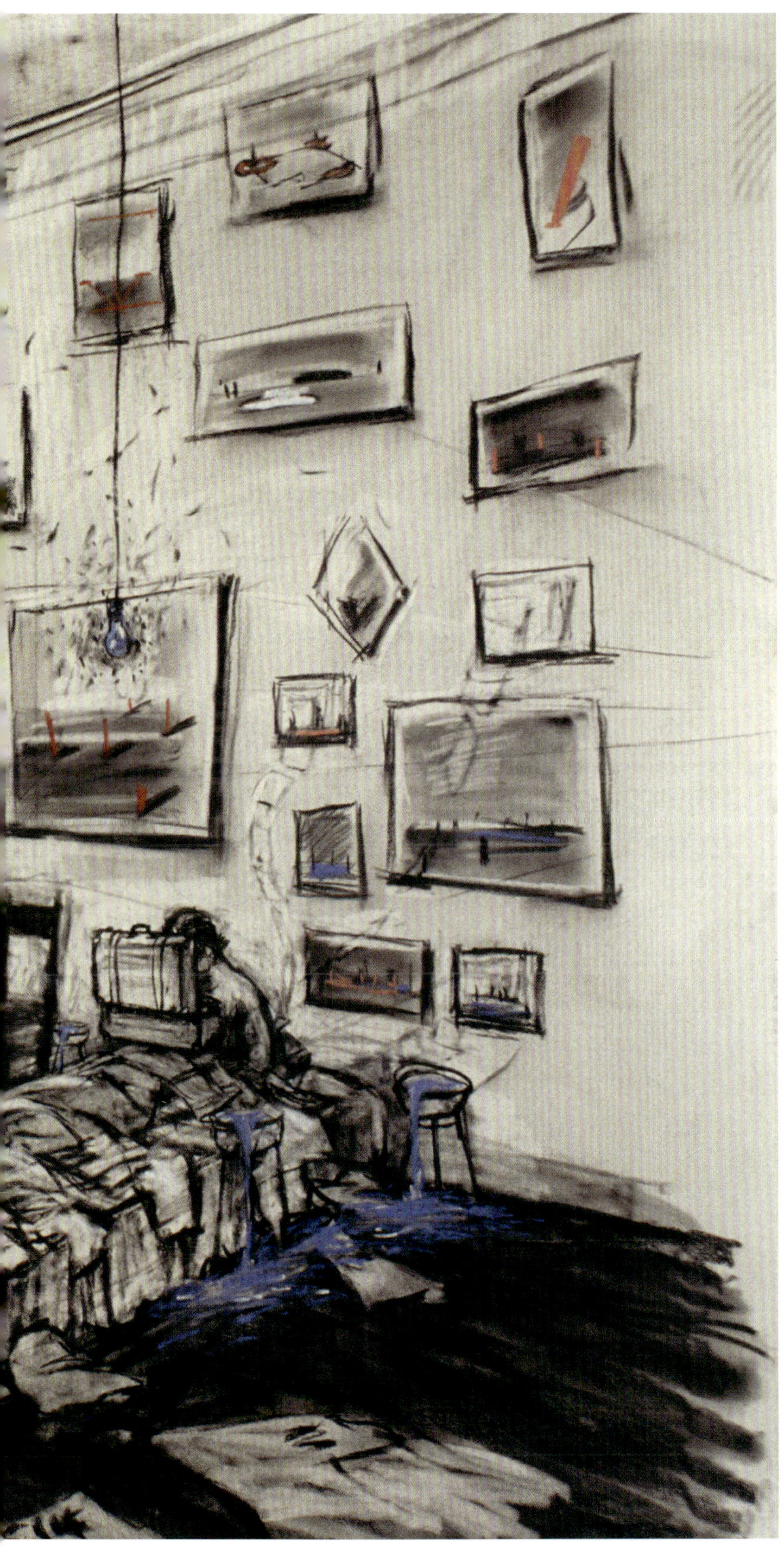

WILLIAM KENTRIDGE
Felix in Exile
1994

Having read Politics alongside Art at
university (his father was a QC and
celebrated defence lawyer at several
ANC trials), Kentridge ventured into
puppetry and acting, before returning
to drawing in 1985. The first 'drawing
for projection' was not shown until
the early 1990s; by the time he had
completed the fifth, *Felix in Exile*, he
was almost forty.

For a young artist growing up in South Africa, William Kentridge (b. 1955) later recalled:

> Much of what was contemporary in Europe and America during the 1960s and 1970s seemed distant and incomprehensible.... The art that seemed most immediate and local dated from the early twentieth century, when there still seemed to be hope for political struggle rather than a world exhausted by war and failure. [...] I remember thinking that one had to look backwards...

His creation of narrative out of 'not knowing', his 'seeing into a blank sheet of paper', aligned him with all those other so-called figurative painters of the early twentieth century, from Picasso to Beckmann, whose starting-point was the Void. Six years before *Felix in Exile* he'd written of Beckmann's *Death* [see Ch 3 p. 154, illustration p. 153] as 'a beacon for endangered souls. It accepts the existence of a compromised society and yet does not rule out all meaning and value, nor pretend those compromises should be ignored'.

Kentridge's 2008 multi-media masterpiece, *I am not me, the horse is not mine*, moved away from South Africa, and from drawing. The Gogol/Shostakovich opera, *The Nose* (1837/1928), was dissolved into an eight-screen installation formed around the legacy of the Russian Revolution, combining narration, stop-motion animation and instrumental soundtrack. When staged underground in the Tanks at Tate Modern, it re-enacted Plato's Cave (see discussion of William Roberts, Ch 2 pp. 80–83, illustration p. 84) – that myth of Enlightenment insistently retold by Kentridge. (He returned to the same theme in 2015 in his magisterial shadow procession, *More Sweetly Play the Dance.*) The artist's role is not as philosopher or truth-enforcer, but to seat himself alongside those other prisoners, enthralled by illusions and projections, by shadows. 'The pleasure accompanying self-deception, seems to me fundamental in what it is to be a visual being.' This book has focused on 'illusionistic' painting and drawing. But our twenty-first century may be a time when divisions of media and genre – along with those wider *apartheids* of race and gender – dissolve, become 'mixed'.

NEO RAUCH AND LEIPZIG FIGURATION (1999-2005)

It is not the task of painting to be an instrument of Enlightenment.

NEO RAUCH, 2015

In East Germany Neo Rauch (b. 1960) served out a full academic training in Leipzig under Bernard Heisig (the painter to whom Beckmann's unused canvases had been given after his death) and emerged just after reunification as a *Meister* (master), a far more technically accomplished painter than his de-skilled contemporaries in the West. By 1990, both Heisig's social realist version of Expressionism, and that of the 'Zeitgeist' revivalists (p. 228), had come to appear crass. Rauch's graphic linearity was, he said, 'a conscious draining dry of my former effervescent style of painting'. Those first, very beautiful and elegant canvases created a post-Communist iconography, in which 'workers' and engineering diagrams were deployed together in a collage-space that often recalled the puzzle-pictures [illustration p. 200] of early Kitaj.

Alter (Elder, 2001) [illustration p. 236] marks his transition towards a more naturalistic idiom, yet one in which realism is rendered absurd: a wry fairy tale, with a shiny mould-made 'elder' in attendance, as well as empty speech-bubbles. Many of Rauch's contemporaries had abandoned painting – 'an art form', explained Lynne Cooke that same year, 'now widely regarded as marginal, if not simply moribund'. The installation-maker Ilya Kabakov (b. 1933) likened painters to senile tenants inherited by the House of Art, smelly and messy; Rosalind Krauss, speaking in London at the National Gallery in a Thames and Hudson lecture, referred to painting as 'that etiolated pursuit'. The internal criticism administered by conceptual art from the 1970s onwards had left institutions confused; the very same museum directors, curators and international art diplomatic who had embraced so much postmodern figuration in the 1980s swung into a general shunning of painting *per se* that has lasted almost until the present day.

In *Alter*, and in his subsequent ever-larger pictures, Rauch retrieves an idea, of painting-as-dream, of magic realism, that had hung in the air ever since the Romantic era; surfacing in Chagall and Beckmann and the Surrealists; later in Kitaj; and plentifully in the 1980s, as in the early Glasgow pictures of Steven Campbell. 'For me,' wrote Rauch, 'painting means the continuation of a dream through other means.' His extraordinary skills reaffirm the painter's potential to realize alternative or parallel intersecting worlds, more freely than film-maker or photographer – to create 'plausible monsters', in the phrase Baudelaire found for Goya's aquatints; and, like the latter's *Disparates* (see Ch 4 p. 168) these are allegories without any key. Rauch's later big productions, some of them twelve or fifteen feet wide, assemble with all the virtuosic resources of academic illusionism whole casts of life-size characters in a fully elaborated space. 'I understand myself', he says, 'to be a director of plays.' These sleepwalkers (I think of the actors in Werner Herzog's 1976 film *Heart of Glass* who played their parts under hypnosis) enact dysfunctional narratives, sudden morphings of human into animal or insect, of contemporary dress into Biedermeyer costume drama – louche and overripe, though always oddly non-sexual.

Rauch has been recognized as a twenty-first-century phenomenon, and around him and his painter-wife Rosa Loy a painting community has taken shape, with young artists from all over the world attracted to Leipzig – who return to their own cultures as missionaries, with renewed belief in painting's future. Placed beside Léger's *The Campers* [see Ch 1 pp. 13 and 25–26, illustration p. 15], Rauch's equally huge easel pictures a century later make evident the continuing failure of painting to find a function in society, in the world – that is, other than to produce trophies for oligarchs (although Rauch himself laments the commercialization of The New Leipzig Painting as a genre). Nevertheless, his art has been one factor in reopening the possibility of a contemporary history painting.

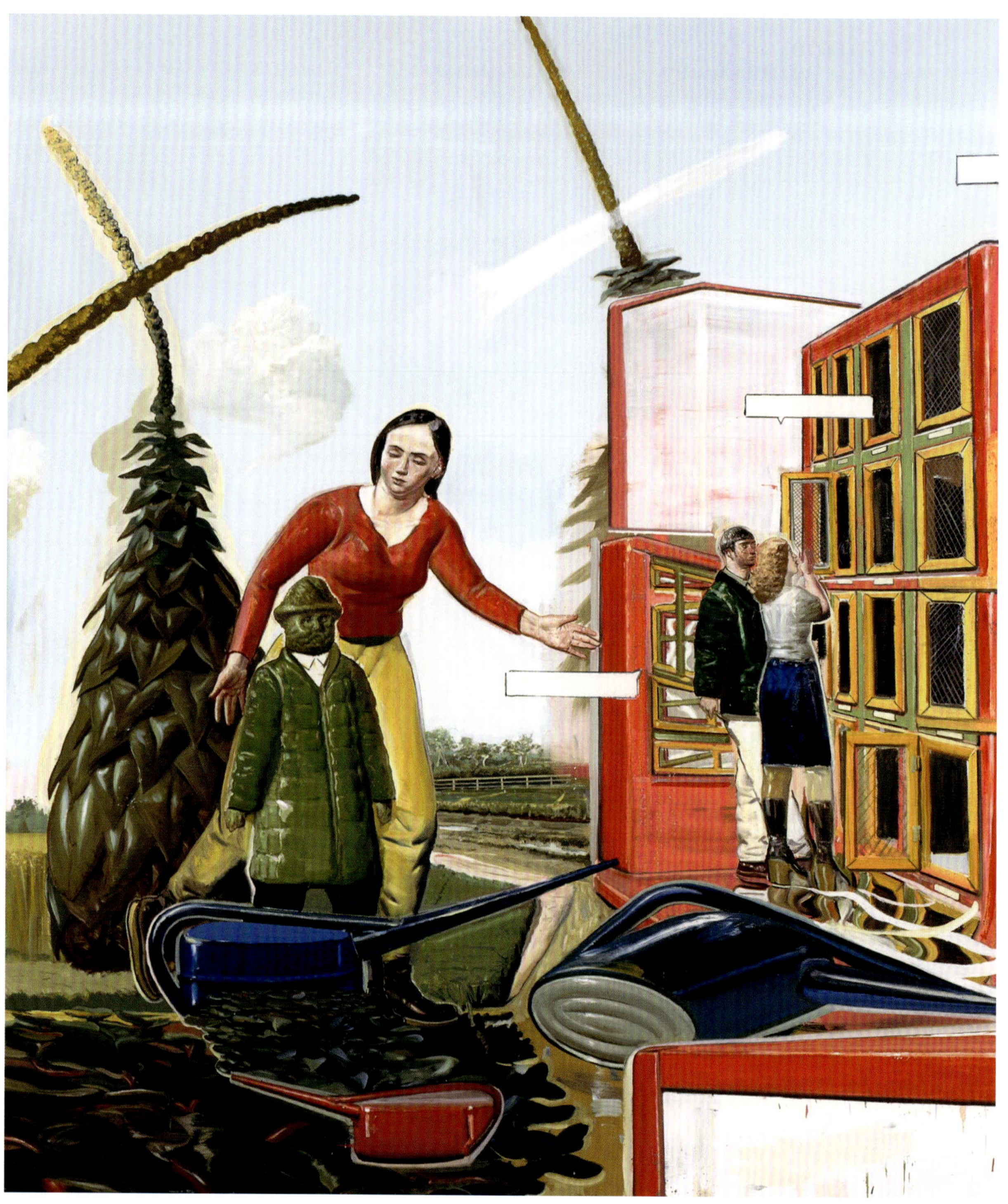

NEO RAUCH

Alter (Elder)

2001

LEON GOLUB'S FINAL PAINTINGS (1999–2002)

I think of the work as history painting, and I think
of history painting as being public. But it's ambiguously
public because it's modernist history painting.

LEON GOLUB, 1984

Early in the year 2000 I listened in New York to a succession of art-related persons –
dealer, critic, museum curator, art historian, computer-programmer – each delivering
their prognostication as to what the new millennium might hold. A future dominated
by digital art seemed generally agreed; painting was barely mentioned. The final
speaker was a small, gnome-like presence: the seventy-eight-year-old painter Leon
Golub (1922–2004). He began rather slowly. He'd been researching the equivalent
predictions published by the Parisian art world in 1900. He read extracts, showing that
every one had, in its different way, proved utterly mistaken. In a lulling, incantatory
sing-song, Golub's voice flowed onwards until, with a shock, I realized the discourse
had switched seamlessly into an entirely different mode. It went something like this:

> So there are two metaphors for the contemporary painter. First, the sewer rat.
> There are so many of them, they're below the system, they're running around
> under the city, sometimes they surface, you're never far from them…. Second,
> the cockroach. They're almost indestructible, scientists tell us they'll survive
> even the nuclear holocaust, they're very hard to tread on, they keep coming
> back…

The voice ended abruptly. There was neither laughter nor applause. Golub died four
years later.

Ever since he emerged in Chicago in the 1950s, Golub had been a fringe figure,
conducting together with his lifelong studio companion and wife, Nancy Spero
(1926–2009), a critical commentary on both political and art-world follies. Nine years
younger than Philip Guston, he too had wanted to refute abstract painters' 'contempt
for figuration',

> [their] deeply held belief system that representation had failed the world
> and the world can only be saved in a spiritual, even a physical sense through
> abstraction…. For me, figuration is a way into the world.

Golub spent twenty years without a New York gallery and remained unrepresented
in key 1980s surveys such as 'Zeitgeist' and 'A New Spirit in Painting'. The pictures
he worked on during that time, now known as *Mercenaries* – shock-images of
contemporary abuses committed somewhere unspecified in America's imperial
reach – did begin to feature widely in exhibitions. Their over-life-size figures
(sourced from Golub's extensive photographic archive) were subjected to a process
of brutalization: laid on the floor, scraped with meat-cleavers, the paint surface
flayed and degraded.

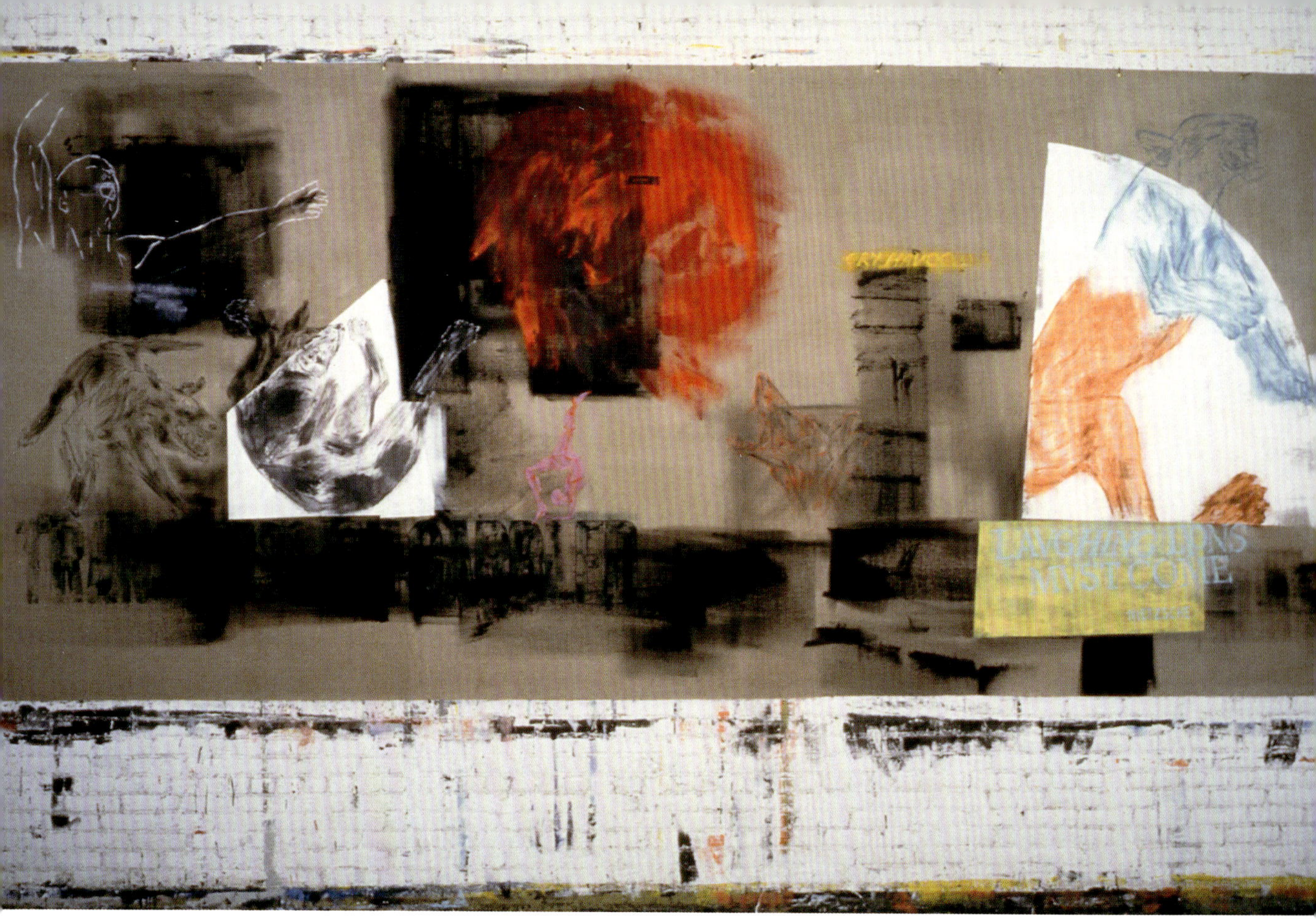

But *Laughing Lions* [illustration above] evidenced a very different spirit, which Golub himself characterized as 'gallows humour' or 'Endgame'. At sixteen feet, it retains that intimidatory scale of his youth – which Spero critiqued as masculinist – yet its grandiosity is undermined by Golub's self-mocking consciousness of mortality. He takes us into a dangerous neighbourhood, filthy and feral, a night town defaced by graffiti. Like Kentridge and Rauch, he sets out without any scenario: these late pictures accrete imagery 'piecemeal'. 'I start with a dog, then what? I deliberately don't know.' In a filmed interview of 2004, he spoke about these works as 'sort of… political, sort of…metaphysical, and sort of…bullshit.'

In the best of this final imagery, out of Golub's limbo zone, emerges yet another mode of history painting to nourish the painters – those 'cockroaches', or 'sewer rats' – of the future. Ten years later it seems clear that ambitious and significant figurative painting does continue to flourish all over the world; and in each painting culture, several of its leading protagonists are female. Yet the overall vision of society that this contemporary painting suggests to me is one where gender has become as fluid as other traditional markers of identity. In the painting of Beckmann and Khakhar, Kitaj and Salomon, a fully human pictorial language has surfaced, well equipped to mirror this new transitional world taking shape around us.

Continuous Narratives

For any aspiring figurative painter of the last fifty years the most pressing problem has been that modern art has seemed so barren of helpful examples. The canonical modern masters – Matisse and Picasso among them – were appropriated long ago as stepping-stones to abstraction; a formalist education rendered young artists not just ignorant of recent human-centred painting, but predisposed to reject all such projects as retrograde, provincial, reactionary. Almost by a sleight of hand, twentieth-century figuration had been made to appear a desert landscape. Only when those empty regions are re-excavated, when artists who have been 'disappeared' stand visible again as significant presences – Beckmann and Spencer, Hartley and Salomon, Kahlo and Balthus, Carrà and Neel – can the true history of twentieth-century painting be told, in such a way as to provide a resource for the twenty-first.

The great multiplicity of figurative 'vernaculars' that burgeoned in Europe after Cubism, created alongside their abstract counterparts – one of the most fertile eras in the entire history of Western art. Yet in the mid-1960s, when I entered art school as a young painting student, most of that cast-list had been forgotten. It was the high-water mark of New York's imperium: not long after, Barnett Newman was photographed in front of *Who's Afraid of Red Yellow and Blue*; Rothko and Pollock were already canonized – but Warhol was waiting in the wings, and the Duchampian critique of painting was about to move from marginal to mainstream. Like many others of my generation, potential painters of narrative and confession, fantasy and history, I was often paralysed by the fear that the kind of art I aspired to create was a lost cause. In order to continue painting in the subsequent decade, we needed to construct an alternative lineage that challenged the formalist canon.

Howard Hodgkin: 'The Elusiveness of Reality'

I have felt extraordinarily isolated in the area of feeling I was working about.
When everything was abstract painting, of the kind which often seemed
to me rather rhetorical, I was trying to celebrate moments of the greatest
possible intimacy.

HOWARD HODGKIN, 1978

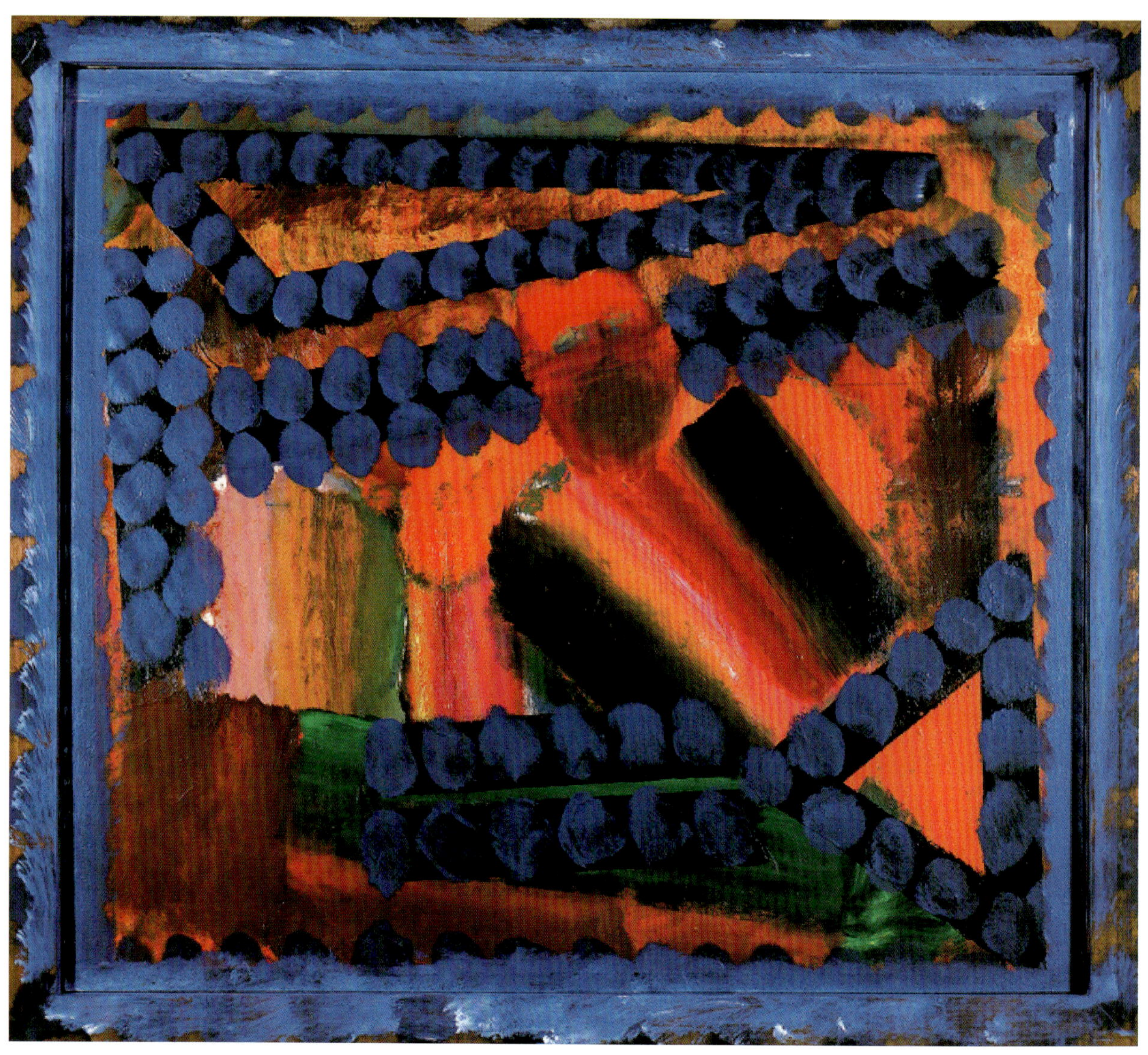

HOWARD HODGKIN

First Portrait of Terence McInerney

1981

The sitter was a close friend, and a dealer in
the Indian album paintings of which Hodgkin
has been a passionate collector all his life.

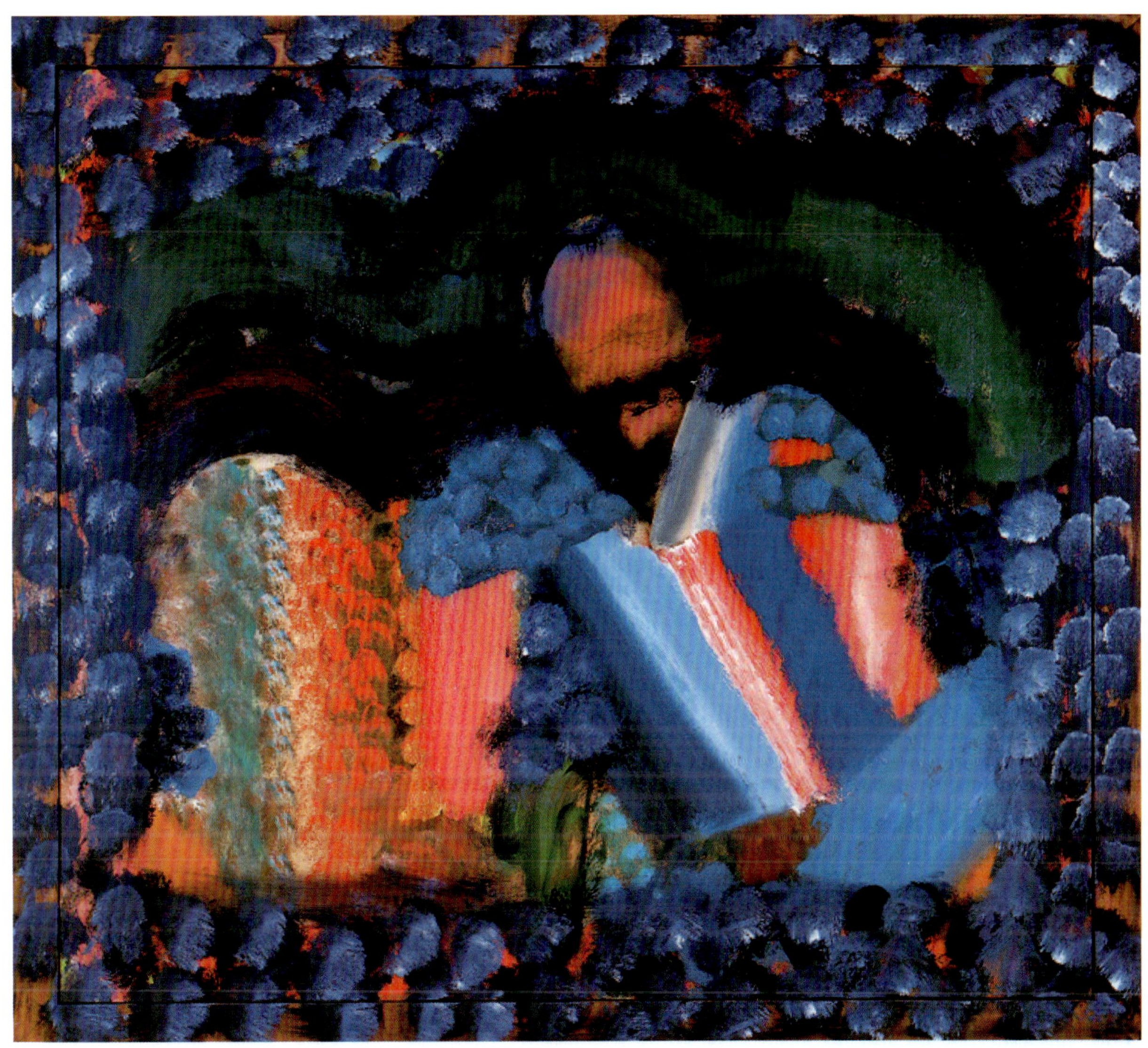

HOWARD HODGKIN

Second Portrait of Terence McInerney

1981

Both portraits were initially, in the artist's own
account, 'incredibly representational, and I was
very proud of the way I was able to remember
and make a coherent almost life-size figure'.
However, he went on to overlay each image with
very assertive marks.

In 1975 I felt impelled to publish – and that first essay was on the paintings of Howard Hodgkin (b. 1932). Hodgkin's two *Portraits of Terence McInerney* [illustrations pp. 240 and 241], both completed in 1981, are the culmination of a twenty-year development. In 1972 he'd identified his work as 'narrative paintings which describe specific moments and very definite people'. He continues: 'I have made several portraits in which I have tried to create an amalgam between the individuals and their surroundings as well as between one another'. The word 'amalgam' here is interesting – as though the artist hoped to meld together all these elements and to seal them within the image, like a fossil in amber. The figures would need to emerge from, be embedded in, the very matrix of the picture, even if that meant reducing them to the most vestigial stick or sign.

When I first encountered Hodgkin's work, in the late 1960s, I felt he was addressing fundamental questions of depiction. How, for instance, to represent the experience of *being with* another person? Hodgkin several times declared that he couldn't imagine 'anything less like visual or physical reality than the traditional portrait.' The riddling dimension in his work, the camouflage, came partly from that conviction: that there was no truth to be found in straight representation. Hodgkin's work seemed to point the way to a new language that could take account instead of what he called 'the elusiveness of reality' – a figuration employing abstract colour and gestural mark as resources. Such a language might convey the thickening atmosphere that exists between two people in a room: hence those aerated blobs and splodges that overlay and invade each canvas, resetting Vuillard's patterned intimacy to a wilder rhythm.

Those two *Portraits* still seem to me a visionary quintessence of the way we experience the friend, or beloved, rearing up aslant and dominant in the mind's eye, into the centre of our field of vision. In both pictures Hodgkin found quite primitive devices to signify the foreground self, that bearded other. But the paintings diverge. In the first, the blue marks gather into an almost aggressive geometry, like DNA molecules, against an infernal light. In the second, they grow liquid, and we see the image as if through tears. The shift of syntax ends by invoking two entirely different possibilities within the same human relationship.

Across all Hodgkin's imagery is the aspiration to make paint and brush mark summon a world knocked off balance, where particular forms are overwhelmed by emotion. Those marks might equally stand for points of light hitting the eye, stabs of pleasure or chunks of conversation. (In much the same way, Bonnard had earlier exploited the approximate quality of Impressionist mark-making, in order to stress subjectivity – objects subsumed in the intensity of seeing.) In Hodgkin's art the frame that grasps the image is the rim of the eye, of the self. Colour, liberated from representation, can regain its full amoral and euphoric power. As Gilles Deleuze proposed in 1981 (writing *à propos* of Francis Bacon): 'The extraordinary work of abstract painting was necessary in order to tear modern art away from figuration. But is there not another path...?'

Hodgkin belongs to a generation whose maturity coincided with the dominance of formal abstraction. His own pictorial language was always under severe formal strain, its promise of representation withheld, and that tension part of its meaning. By contrast, painters twenty years younger were already finding it possible to delineate, say, the features of a face. As more imagery from the earlier twentieth century became known, there was a relaxation and dissolution of formalist embargoes against representation.

The Human Image

The seam never really gave out…. It's not as if an instinct which lies
in the race of men from way before Sassetta and Giotto has run its course.
It won't. Don't listen to the fools who say that pictures of people can be
of no consequence….. There is much to be done.

R. B. KITAJ, 1976

The imagery assembled in this book sets in question any narrowly formalist account of art's development over the past century. Digging up those lost eras has provided a newly exhumed range of painters in whom young artists can recognize their own present-day concerns. This expanded cast grapples with a much wider range of subject-matter than we'd become accustomed to in 'Modern Art'. Instead of a reductive simplicity of image, a many-figured complexity; instead of a solemn impersonality, first-person confessions, tilted towards comedy; instead of a prohibition against illustration, pictorial narratives crowded with historical and literary allusion.

Painting is revealed as no longer an evasion of the political and sexual substance of our lives, but as an historical witness, a reimagining. These artists have responded to the great alterations and ruptures in social mores over these decades, and their imagery reflects a society radically different from that of our starting point in 1910. Cumulatively they reclaim the libertarian dimension that was modern painting's impetus – in Matisse's *Dance*, or Léger's *The Campers*. Individually, each of these painters experiences the uncertainty of their time and discovers in the face of the Void, a new authenticity of representation. Each can be seen as having contributed to the shared quest for a new visual language through which to describe a new world.

On the monochrome foundation of Cubism, formalists erected the great grey house of modern art. Here I have tried to expose our wider, more irregular foundations: the anarchic, many-coloured, multi-gendered and multi-figured painting of the twentieth century, upon which I hope a new art – whether a sprawl of settlement or a People's Palace – will now be built.

BIBLIOGRAPHY, SOURCES, FURTHER READING

This book comes out of more than thirty years of looking and note-taking; I cannot list every source but what follows gives some indication of the reading I've most valued.

INTRODUCTION

One of the most rewarding of all monographs – and an education in painting in itself – is Pierre Schneider's monumental *Matisse* (Thames & Hudson, 1984, revised 2002). The quotation 'When the means of expression...' is from his 'Statement to Tériade' of 1936, reprinted in *Matisse on Art* (ed. Jack D. Flam, University of California, revised 1995). Clement Greenberg's *Art and Culture: Critical Essays* (Beacon Press, Boston, 1961) was by far the most influential critical text of its time, presenting a very clear lineage in which New York abstract painting was both the heir to Cubism and the culmination of a century's development. As Irving Sandler reminisces in *A Sweeper-Up After Artists* (Thames & Hudson, 2009, reprint), 'Figurative art as a whole was suspect in the 1950s.' Herbert Read wrote of 'the new classless society' in 'What is Revolutionary Art?', an essay published in *5 on Revolutionary Art* (Artists International Association, London, 1935). The Nietzsche quotation is my own translation from *Zur Genealogie der Moral* (On the Genealogy of Morals), 1887. Picasso spoke of the Void to Christian Zervos, in *Cahiers d'art* X, nos 7–10 (Paris, 1935). For 'this infinite space...' see *Max Beckmann*, ed. Peter Selz (MoMA, New York, 1964). Fernand Léger's 'It was the Impressionists...', is from 'The New Realism Goes On', *Art Front*, 3:1 (New York, February 1937), reprinted in *Functions of Painting* (Thames & Hudson, 1973). 'I hardly need to abstract things...' – see 'On My Painting', in *Max Beckmann: Self-Portrait in Words: Collected Writings and Statements, 1903–1950*, ed. and trans. Barbara Copeland Buenger (Chicago, 1997).

Chapter One
AFTER CUBISM: REINVENTING THE LANGUAGE OF REPRESENTATION

John Golding's *Cubism* (Harvard, 1988, 3rd edition) remains a helpful and non-doctrinaire account. I recommend Monica Bohm-Duchen's *Chagall* (Phaidon, 1998); Jackie Wullschlager's biography of Chagall (Allen Lane, 2008) is comprehensive. Chagall's *My Life* (English version translated by Dorothy Williams for Peter Owen, London, 1965) was written first in Yiddish then in Russian, 1921–22. 'Beyond all Cubist stylization...' see discussion of *Dead Souls*, etc., later in this chapter. In 1944, interviewed by James Johnson Sweeney, Chagall explained: 'I have admired the great Cubists and have profited from Cubism. But...I felt painting needed a greater freedom than Cubism permitted.' Matisse, 'The period when Cubism...', is from an interview with André Verdet, *Verve*, nos 27–28 (Paris, 7 December 1952).

Peter de Francia's monograph *Fernand Léger* (Yale, 1983) and the anthology of writings listed above, *Functions of Painting*, are my principal sources on that artist. The original publications: 'During those four war years...', Léger interviewed in *Arts*, no. 205 (Paris, March 1949); 'I was attracted to Romanesque...', Léger, 'Correspondence', *Bulletin de l'effort moderne*, no. 4 (Paris, April 1924); 'I came straight...' *Fernand Léger* by André Verdet (Pierre Cailler, Geneva, 1955). Léger wrote to Eisenstein in June 1932. 'My architect friends...' is from Léger's key statement 'The Wall, the Architect, the Painter' (1933), in *Functions of Painting*. Versions of my essay on Léger first came out in *London Magazine* (December 1977) and appeared in *Artscribe* (January 1978).

'The dissolving forces...', Carlo Carrà, 'Misticità e ironia nella pittura moderna' (Mysticism and Irony in Contemporary Painting), *Valori Plastici* II, nos vii–viii (Rome, 1920). When *Valori Plastici* was republished in its French edition, it became *Le Neoclassicisme dans l'art contemporain.* 'The artist whose forms...', Carrà of Giotto (caption p. 26), is quoted from *On Classic Ground: Picasso, Léger, de Chirico and the New Classicism, 1910–1930*, Elisabeth Cowling and Jennifer Mundy, exh. cat. (Tate Gallery, London, 1990). Wilhelm Worringer's essay on Carlo Carrà's *Il Pino sul Mare* came out in *Wissen und Leben* (Zurich, 10 November 1925). 'Easel painting is too weak...' – Sironi first wrote this in 'Pittura murale' (Mural Painting), *L'Arca* (Rome, April 1932). Bakhtin's essay 'Verbal Language and the Folk Culture of Laughter' is included in the Norton Critical Edition of *Dead Souls* (New York, 1985), as is Herzen's commentary. Eisenstein 'a strange provincial town' (1940), quoted in *Mikhail Bakhtin*, Clark and Holquist (Harvard, 1984, p. 48); for Chagall in Vitebsk see Aleksandra Shatskikh, *Vitebsk: The Life of Art* (Yale, 2008). 'Painting was done for long ago' – this and other Malevich quotations from exhibition captions and catalogue, *Malevich* (Tate Modern, London, 2014, especially p. 152). Chagall's letter to Lunacharsky, summer 1921, is printed in Benjamin Harshav's revelatory *Marc Chagall and His Times: A Documentary Narrative* (Stanford, 2004). *Dead Souls*, translated by Donald Rayfield, is now available with Chagall's illustrations (The Garnett Press, London, 2008). Nabokov's *Nikolai Gogol* was published by Editions Poetry (London, 1947). *Clarté*'s attack is quoted from Richard Sonn's *Jews, Expatriate Artists, and Political Radicalism in Interwar France*, proceedings of the Western Society for French History, vol. 37 (Michigan, 2009).

Diego Rivera: A Retrospective, exh. cat. (Detroit Institute of Arts, 1986) is a useful overview. Matisse's condemnation of 'Propaganda' comes from Patrick Marnham's *Dreaming with His Eyes Open: A Life of Diego Rivera* (University of California, 2000). The superb monograph *Benodebehari Mukherjee*, exh. cat. (National Gallery of Modern Art, New Delhi, 2006) includes the artist's 'My Experiments with Murals' (1969) and G. M. Sheikh's 'Ruminating on *Life of the Medieval Saints*'. 'The most noble and effective work...', is from Satyajit Ray's commentary to *The Inner Eye*, 1972 (currently available free online). K. G. Subramanyan's essay is in *Moving Focus: Essays on Indian Art* (Lalit Kala Akademi, Delhi, 1978).

The most comprehensive Hartley monograph is *Marsden Hartley* (Yale, 2002) but the compilation *Marsden Hartley and Nova Scotia* (Halifax, 1987) includes much essential material, including the artist's text *Cleophas and His Own: A North Atlantic Tragedy* (I am grateful to Peter Doig for alerting me to this). Hartley's autobiography, *Somehow a Past* (MIT Press, 1997), is another key source. 'Late courage' appears in an unpublished review written in 1940 by William Carlos Williams (Smithsonian Archives, reel 1368, frames 548–49). Ryder's 'Paragraphs from the Studio of a Recluse' was published in *Broadway Magazine*, XIV, no. 6 (New York, September 1905). Jonathan Weinberg wrote on Hartley in *Speaking for Vice* (Yale, 1995). Greenberg's 1950 review is in *Collected Essays and Criticism*, vol.3 (Chicago, 1993). Hartley's epitaph is from *Marsden Hartley*, Bruce Robertson (Abrams/Smithsonian, New York, 1995). My essay on Hartley came out in *The Sienese Shredder*, no.3, ed. Brice Brown and Trevor Winkfield (New York, 2009).

David Sylvester's *Interviews with Francis Bacon* (Thames & Hudson, 1975) is an essential text, while Michael Peppiatt's *Francis Bacon: Anatomy of an Enigma* (Constable, London, 1996) remains the most reliable biography.

I strongly recommend John McEwan's monograph, *Paula Rego* (Phaidon, 2006, 3rd edition).

Chapter Two
AFTER EXPRESSIONISM: THE NEW THINGNESS

G. F. Hartlaub's definition of *Neue Sachlichkeit* appeared in a circular of May 1923. (A touring exhibition he organized, 'Die Neue Sachlichkeit', would open in Mannheim in 1925.) The most comprehensive recent survey is *New Objectivity: Modern German Art in the Weimar Republic 1919–33*, which accompanied a show at LACMA (Prestel, 2015). Wieland Schmied's version comes from his essay 'De Chirico, Metaphysical Painting and the International Avant-Garde: Twelve Theses', in *Italian Art in the Twentieth*

Century: Painting and Sculpture 1900–1988, exh. cat. Royal Academy, London (Prestel, 1989); Elias Cannetti's, from *The Torch in My Ear* (Granta, London, 1982). Roger Fry's *Letters* were edited by Denys Sutton (see vol. 2, Chatto and Windus, London, 1972), pp. 502 and 625–27. Emil Nolde's *Letters* (Briefe) were published in Berlin, 1927; 'Our task...' is from 20 March 1908. The Beckmann quotation is from 'Schöpferische Konfession', written in 1918 and leter published in *Tribüne der Kunst und Zeit* 13 (Berlin, 1920); a version of the full text in translation appears as 'Creative Credo' in *Max Beckmann, Self-Portrait in Words*, op. cit. (intro). Fritz Löffler's *Otto Dix: Life and Work* (Holmes and Meier, New York, 1982) is a primary monograph. Eva Karcher's *Otto Dix* (Taschen, 1988) is a well-illustrated, inexpensive overview. The 1992 Tate Gallery/Galerie der Stadt Stuttgart catalogue *Otto Dix* includes several worthwhile essays. Dix's important statement 'Das Objekt ist das Primäre' (The Object is Primary) came out in *Berliner Nachtausgabe* (3 December 1927); Carl Einstein had written on Dix in *Das Kunstblatt* in March 1923. *The Berlin of George Grosz: Drawings, Watercolours and Prints, 1912–1930*, exh. cat. Royal Academy, London (Yale, 1997), and Grosz's 1955 autobiography in English translation, *A Small Yes and a Big No* (Allison and Busby, London, 1982), are my main sources. Paul Klee's 1919 letter to Alfred Kubin is quoted in *The Romantic Spirit in German Art 1790–1990*, exh. cat. Hayward Gallery, London (Thames & Hudson, 1994). Grosz wrote 'Meinen neuen Bildern' (On My New Paintings) in *Das Kunstblatt* 5, no. 1 (Berlin, 1921); complete text in *Art in Theory* (Blackwell, 1992, see further reading). The Grosz and Herzfelde text, 'Die Kunst ist in Gefahr' (Art is in Danger), was published by Malik Verlag (Berlin, 1925); complete text in English is in *Art in Theory*, op. cit. Nietzsche's *Die Geburt der Tragödie aus dem Geiste der Musik* (The Birth of Tragedy) was published in 1872; I have used Francis Golffing's translation (Doubleday, 1956), pp. 33–34. Brecht, already in exile, wrote 'Solely because of the increasing disorder...' in 1934: it appears in *Bertolt Brecht Poems 1913–1956* (Eyre Methuen, London, 1976). I first published on Beckmann in *London Magazine* (November, 1978).

This section on 'A New Sort of Realism' is partly drawn from my own catalogue introduction to Tate Britain's 2001 *Stanley Spencer* retrospective, which has full references to the gallery's archive of Spencer's writings. Paul Nash's letter of November 1917 was printed in *Outline* (Faber and Faber, 1949). Marsden Hartley's letter is from *My Dear Stieglitz* (University of South Carolina, 2002). The 1914 critique of William Roberts is quoted in Lisa Tickner's *Modern Life and Modern Subjects: British Art in the Early Twentieth Century* (Yale, 2000), p. 224, note 32. Roger Fry wrote on 'The esthetic emotion...' in *The Artist and Psychoanalysis* (London, 1924), reprinted in *A Roger Fry Reader,* ed. Christopher Reed (Chicago, 1996); his condemnation of Spencer is from Patricia Preece's diary, 24 February 1932. Paul Nash's disenchantment with Spencer is in a letter to Gordon Bottomley, November 1922, in *Poet and Painter* (OUP, 1955). 'It's as if a pre-Raphaelite...', is an anonymous review from *The Times*, 1927, quoted by Fiona McCarthy in *Stanley Spencer: An English Vision*, exh. cat. Hirshhorn, Washington, DC, et al. (Yale, 1997). 'I no longer have...' – Spencer in *Modern English Painters: Lewis to Moore*, John Rothenstein (Eyre & Spottiswoode, London, 1956). Burra's letter to Nash, 19 May 1931 (Tate Archive, 795.2), is quoted in *Edward Burra: Twentieth Century Eye*, by Jane Stevenson (Cape, London, 2007). Spencer's 'I feel, really, that everything...' is from a letter to Desmond Chute, 17 November 1926, printed in *Stanley Spencer: The Man: Correspondence and Reminiscences*, ed. John Rothenstein (Harper Collins, 1979).

Balthus, ed. Jean Clair, exh. cat. Palazzo Grassi, Venice (Thames & Hudson, 2001) is the outstanding monograph on Balthus in English; it includes some of his correspondence with Antoinette. Giorgio de Chirico wrote about 'perspective and metaphysics' in *Courbet* (Valori Plastici, Rome, 1926). On 18 January 1934 Balthus wrote to Antoinette, referring to 'the boy trying to rape the little girl'. Rilke's *Marionetten-Theater* (The Puppet Theatre) was written in Paris, 20 July 1907. The full text of Antonin Artaud's *The Theatre of Cruelty: First Manifesto*, 1932, is translated in *Antonin Artaud: Selected Writings*, ed. Susan Sontag (Farrar, Straus and Giroux, 1976). 'What was important to me...' is from *Balthus the Painter* (film directed by Mark Kidel, Rosetta Pictures, 1996). Pierre Klossowski wrote on his brother in 'Balthus: Beyond Realism', *ARTNews*, vol. 55, no. 8 (New York, 1956). I published on Balthus in *London Magazine* (July, 1980).

Edward Hopper, ed. Sheena Wagstaff, exh. cat. (Tate, London, 2004) assembles several excellent essays. *George Bellows*, exh. cat. (NGA Washington, DC/The Metropolitan Museum of Art, New York/Royal Academy, London, 2012) is a superbly illustrated survey. 'It seemed awfully crude...' – Hopper to Brian O'Doherty, *Art in America*, vol. 52, no. 6 (December 1964); 'It had a sociological trend...', Hopper to Katherine Kuh, *The Artist's Voice* (Harper & Row, New York, 1962). 'The reproduction of the world...' – Goethe to Jacobi, 21 August 1774, quoted by Sheena Wagstaff in *Edward Hopper*, op. cit. Hopper, 'photography is so light...' to Raphael Soyer, 1963, ibid.

Alice Neel: Painted Truths, exh. cat. (MFA Houston, 2010) includes several revelatory texts, by Tamar Garb, Frank Auerbach, Marlene Dumas and others. 'Art is two things...' – Alice Neel to Patricia Hills, *Alice Neel* (Abrams, 1983). 'Poor art...' – Arshile Gorky, quoted in Phoebe Hoban's biography, *Alice Neel: The Art of Not Sitting Pretty* (Saint Martin's Press, New York, 2010). 'The Havana Manifesto', May 1927, is quoted by Hoban, op. cit. Joseph Mitchell wrote on Joe Gould in *Up in the Old Hotel* (Vintage, New York, 1993). Peter Schjeldahl wrote on Neel in *The Village Voice*, 31 March 1988. Alice Neel's famous self-identification as a 'collector of souls' first appeared in *The Hasty Papers,* ed. Alfred Leslie (New York, 1960). I recommend the excellent film *Alice Neel* (dir. Andrew Neel, 2009), available on DVD.

For Lucian Freud's early work, see David Sylvester in *About Modern Art* (Chatto and Windus, 1996, see further reading) and Helen Lessore in *A Partial Testament: Essays on Some Moderns in the Great Tradidion* (Tate, London, 1987).

Chapter Three
FIRST-PERSON PAINTING

The catalogue of *Identity and Alterity*, ed. Jean Clair (Venice Biennale, 1995), and Hans Belting's 1984 discussion of the Narrator-Self in *Max Beckmann*, translated by Peter Wortsman for Timken (New York 1989), are two starting-points for this chapter. Paul Westheim (editor of the leading German art journal *Das Kunstblatt*) wrote of 'self-art' in *Für und Wider* (Potsdam, 1923). Christa Wolf's 1976 conversation with Hans Kaufmann is in *The Fourth Dimension: Interviews with Christa Wolf* (Verso, London 1988), p. 22. I recommend Elizabeth Wynn Easton's *The Intimate Interiors of Edouard Vuillard*, exh. cat. MFA Houston (Thames & Hudson, 1989).The correspondence between Vuillard and Denis is quoted extensively in another exhibition catalogue: *Edouard Vuillard* (Art Gallery of Ontario, Toronto and Art Institute of Chicago, 1971), pp. 62–65. My monograph *Bonnard* (Thames & Hudson, 1998) is the basis for both this and the later Bonnard section.

Paula Modersohn-Becker: The Letters and Journals, first published in German in 1979 (available in translation from Northwestern University Press, 1998, 2nd edition) is a foundation text. *Paula Modersohn-Becker: The First Modern Woman Artist*, Diane Radycki (Yale, 2013), is a tendentious but revealing monograph. Rilke's *Requiem* (known in English as *for a Woman Friend*) was written in 1908; he wrote of a 'great renewal of the world...' from Worpswede on 16 July 1903, published in *Letters to a Young Poet*, ed. and trans. Charlie Louth (Penguin, 2012). Clara Rilke's letter to Rainer Maria was suppressed in the standard *Letters and Journals* and first published in 1982.

Magdalena M. Moeller's *Ernst Ludwig Kirchner: Die Strassenszene 1913–15* (Hirmer, Munich, 1993) reproduces many of the street drawings. Jill Lloyd writes well on Kirchner's drawings in *German Expressionism: Primitivism and Modernity* (Yale, 1991). The fine catalogue of the Royal Academy's 'Kirchner: the Dresden and Berlin Years' (London, 2003) includes Kirchner's writing as 'L. de Marsalle'; I reviewed the exhibition in the *TLS* (25 July 2003).

I recommend Jean Clair's writings on Bonnard, especially in the catalogue of the exhibition he curated, *Bonnard* (Centre Pompidou, Paris, and The Phillips Collection, Washington, DC, 1984); this includes the artist's *Notes of a Painter*. Charles Terrasse's 1927 monograph (Paris) includes the passage on 'the eye of the painter'. For Bonnard's 1930 letter to Georges Besson, see Sarah Whitfield, *Bonnard*, exh. cat. (Tate Gallery, London, 1998), p. 27. Picasso's aversion to Bonnard appears both in John Richardson's writings and, extensively, in Françoise Gilot, *Life with Picasso* (Penguin, 1964). *Bonnard/Matisse: Letters Between Friends* was published by Abrams in 1992.

Maurice Tuchman's *Chaim Soutine: Catalogue Raisonne* was published by Taschen in 1993 and contains much material unavailable elsewhere. D. H. Lawrence's 1929 essay *Cézanne* can be read online; Clement Greenberg wrote on Soutine in *Art and Culture,* op. cit. (intro), p. 117.

For Frida Kahlo, I can strongly recommend the 2005 Tate retrospective catalogue. The full text of the 1938 *Manifesto* by Rivera, Trotsky and Breton is in *Art in Theory*, op. cit.

The basis of my section here on Spencer is my 2001 introduction, 'Angels and Dirt', for the Tate's retrospective. His lecture at the Ruskin School, Oxford, was transcribed by Richard Carline, see *Stanley Spencer*, exh. cat. (Royal Academy, London, 1980), p. 12. 'It would be better and truer…' – Spencer, from *Essay 2: On Distortion* (Tate Archive 733.3.2). 'During the war…', see *Stanley Spencer*, Maurice Collis (Harvill, London, 1962), pp. 138–39. 'I love myself…' – Spencer, letter to Hilda, June 1923, from *Stanley Spencer: The Man,* Rothenstein, op. cit., p. 26. Mikhail Bakhtin, 'disclosing the potentiality…', is quoted in *Rabelais and His World* (MIT Press, 1968), p. 48; Merlin James, 'a literary artist…', from the *TLS* (1 February 1991).

In numbering Charlotte Salomon's *Life? Or Theatre?*, I have referred to *Charlotte* (Allen Lane, 1981) rather than the Royal Academy's 1998 edition. I recommend *Reading Charlotte Salomon* (Cornell, 2006) edited by Michael P. Steinberg and Monica Bohm-Duchen; Griselda Pollock's essay is especially powerful and challenging. Mary Lowenthal Felstiner's biography, *To Paint Her Life: Charlotte Salomon in the Nazi Era* (Harper Collins, 1994) is an important source. (I have left aside some recently discovered indications – not as yet fully sifted – that Salomon may have hastened her grandfather's death.) Frans Masereel's *Mein Stundenbook*, 1919, was republished with an introduction by Thomas

Mann in 1926; translated as *Passionate Journey* (Penguin, 1987).

Stefan Lackner's *Max Beckmann: Memories of a Friendship* (University of Miami, 1969) contains much important material not available elsewhere. I recommend the catalogue of the Tate's retrospective *Max Beckmann* (London, 2003), which includes essays by Kentridge and Golub. Carl Einstein wrote on Beckmann in 1931, translated in *Max Beckmann,* Belting, op. cit., p. 81. Beckmann's 1938 lecture *On My Painting* exists in several translations; it is included, along with Eric Fischl on 'Max Beckmann's *Departure*', in exh. cat. *Max Beckmann in Exile* (Guggenheim, New York, 1996). 'The world is rather *kaput*…' – Beckmann, 27 August 1945, letter to Lackner, in *Memories of a Friendship*, op. cit., p. 90.

'The second half of my life…', *Munch By Himself*, exh. cat. (Royal Academy, London, 2005), p. 153.

Chapter Four
BEYOND THE FORMALIST CANON: VISIONARIES, DREAMERS, OUTSIDERS

A lucid and well-illustrated book on the intersection between outsiders and contemporary mainstream painting is *Parallel Visions: Modern Artists and Outsider Art*, exh. cat. (LACMA and Princeton, 1992). *The Discovery of the Art of the Insane* is an early text, of 1978, by the most eminent writer on outsider artists, John M. MacGregor (Princeton, 1989 and 1992). For recent writing on James Ensor see the 2009 MoMA New York/ Musée d'Orsay, Paris, retrospective catalogue; *Hareng Saur: Ensor and Contemporary Art*, exh. cat. (S.M.A.K. and MSK Ghent, 2009) has many responses to Ensor's work by contemporary artists. In 1997 I contributed an essay to the catalogue *James Ensor: Theatre of Masks* (Barbican Art Gallery, London); it also includes Susan Canning's 'Visionary Politics'. Golub's advocacy of Ensor as 'Modernist' was relayed to me by Max Kozloff; it is a recurrent theme in his writings.

For Ken Kiff the best source remains Andrew Lambirth's monograph *Ken Kiff* (Thames & Hudson, 2001). Alfred Kubin's dream-novel *The Other Side* (1909) was republished by Penguin Modern Classics, together with his autobiography, in 1973. Among many Kubin volumes, the most accessible in English may be Kubin's *Dance of Death and Other Drawings* (Dover Publications, New York, 1973); *The Scorpion* is on p. 34. Odilon Redon's journal, *A Soi-même* was translated as *To Myself: Notes on Life, Art, and Artists* (G. Braziller, New York, 1986). For Klee and Kubin at the Prinzhorn Collection see MacGregor, op. cit.

In 2011 Rabrindranath Tagore's complete paintings were published in four large volumes under the title *Rabindra Chitravali,* edited by R. Siva Kumar (Pratikshan Books,

Kolkata); the same author selected some two hundred works by Tagore for the catalogue *Last Harvest* (Mapin, Ahmedabad and National Gallery of Modern Art, New Delhi, 2012), which accompanied three simultaneous travelling exhibitions. I published on Tagore's paintings in *London Magazine* (July 1979 and October 1986). The two-volume catalogue raisonné of Jack Yeats's paintings came out in 1992 (Deutsch), while Bruce Arnold's biography was published by Yale in 1998. The catalogue of the Whitechapel Art Gallery's exhibition 'Jack B. Yeats: The Late Paintings' can be recommended (London, 1991); it includes a note by Frank Auerbach. (I reviewed the exhibition in the *TLS*, 19 April 1991.)

Henry Darger: In The Realms of The Unreal by John M. MacGregor (Delano Greenidge, New York, 2002) is by far the best of several monographs. In 1998 MacGregor published 'Why Darger?' in *The Outsider* vol. 2, issue 2 (The Center for Intuitive and Outsider Art, Chicago). For Grayson Perry on Darger see *Grayson Perry: A Portrait of the Artist as a Young Girl* (2006) by Wendy Jones (Vintage, 2007). I published on Darger in the *TLS* (30 October 1998).

Jacob Lawrence: *The Migration Series*, ed. Elizabeth Hutton Turner, exh. cat. (The Phillips Collection, Washington, DC, 1993) is an important source; MoMA has published a further book of the same title (New York, 2015). *Over The Line: The Art and Life of Jacob Lawrence* (University of Washington, Seattle, 2001) is a fascinating overview.

Ken Kiff's Sequence by Iain Biggs (Making Space, Bristol, 1999) has useful reproductions in black and white and in colour. Kiff's 1979 dialogue with Wynn Jones came out in *Artscribe*. I wrote in the Serpentine Gallery catalogue *Ken Kiff* (Arts Council, London, 1985). Yves Bonnefoy's essay 'What is Poetry?' was published in the *TLS* (12 August 2005).

Chapter Five
AFTER ABSTRACT EXPRESSIONISM: TOWARDS A NEW HISTORY PAINTING

Jed Perl's anthology *Art in America, 1945– 1970* (Library of America, 2014), is helpful in locating painters such as de Kooning and Guston within a literary context; the poet Frank O'Hara and the dance critic Edwin Denby provide especially interesting commentary. The anthology includes de Kooning's 'What Abstract Art Means to Me', first published in *Museum of Modern Art Bulletin* XVIII, no.3 (New York, Spring 1951). In 1990, Robert Hughes referred to AbEx as 'thirty years ago, pretty well a mandatory world-style'; see Hughes, *Nothing If Not Critical* (Knopf/Collins Harvill), see further reading. Balzac's short story *The Unknown Masterpiece* has been a key text for many twentieth-century artists; it has been translated often, but one useful version is Anthony Rudolf's *Gillette or*

The Unknown Masterpiece (Menard, London, 1988). *Philip Guston: Collected Writings, Lectures and Conversations* (University of California Press, 2010) is a compelling and rewarding volume. In 2004 Red Grooms wrote on de Kooning in *The New York Times Book Review* (12 December). Irving Sandler's memoir, op. cit. (intro) conveys a vivid sense of the AbEx period from a standpoint often opposed to Clement Greenberg. The history of the CIA's involvement in AbEx has been explored most fully so far by Frances Stonor Saunders; her film *Hidden Hands* (1995) interviewed several of the agents involved, while her two books, *Who Paid The Piper* (Granta, 1999) and *The Cultural Cold War: The CIA and the World of Arts and Letters* (New Press, London, 2013, reprint) reveal much fascinating material. Robert Crumb is quoted from exh. cat. *High and Low: Modern Art and Popular Culture*, ed. Kirk Varnedoe (MoMA, New York, 1990), p. 226; the catalogue also includes a penetrating essay by Robert Storr.

The essays in *R. B. Kitaj: Obsessions*, exh. cat. (Jewish Museum, Berlin, 2012) are of exceptional quality; 'Warburgian Artist' by Edward Cheney is particularly illuminating. (I reviewed the Berlin exhibition in *The Burlington Magazine* (May 2013). Richard Morphet's long interview with Kitaj for the Tate's retrospective (*R. B. Kitaj*, exh. cat., London, 1994) and my own interview 'A Return to London' (*London Magazine*, February 1980, reprinted Washington 1982, and in *R. B. Kitaj*, Thames & Hudson, 1983) are primary sources. Kitaj's own texts include *The Human Clay*, exh. cat. (Arts Council, London, 1976) and *First Diasporist Manifesto* (Thames & Hudson, 1989).

David Hockney by David Hockney (Thames & Hudson, 1977) includes a vivid account of what it meant to paint figuratively in the 1960s.

Jed Perl wrote on Katz's cut-outs in *New Art City* (Knopf, 2005). Katz's own mordant commentaries can be enjoyed in the expanded edition of *Alex Katz* by Carter Ratcliffe, Robert Storr and Iwona Blazwick (Phaidon, 2014).

Red Grooms: A Retrospective, ed. Judith Stein, exh. cat. Pennsylvania Academy of Fine Arts/ Denver Art Museum/MoCA LA/Tennessee State Museum, Nashville (Philadelphia, 1985) is a well-selected monograph with excellent plates, and includes a warm essay by John Ashbery. Judd Tully's *Red Grooms and Ruckus Manhattan* (G. Braziller, New York, 1977) is a compact study of this key work. *Red Grooms* (Rizzoli, 2004) includes an essay by Arthur C. Danto, and my 2002 interview with the artist.

Franz Dahlem's *Georg Baselitz* (Taschen, 1990) has good illustrations of his early paintings, and includes many extracts from the artist's texts, including his 1960 'Pandemonium'.

My account of Guston's transformation is drawn chiefly from his *Collected Writings* (see above), and from *Night Studio*, Musa Mayer's moving memoir of her father (Knopf, 1988). *Yes, But...* was the title of Dore Ashton's pioneering 1976 monograph, later republished as *A Critical Study of Philip Guston* (University of California, 1990). For Bonnard's 'drawing crisis' see *Bonnard*, Timothy Hyman (Thames & Hudson, 1998), pp. 97–98. I recommend Sanford Schwartz on Guston in *Artists and Writers* (Yarrow Press, New York, 1990), especially p. 200.

My 1998 monograph *Bhupen Khakhar* (Mapin, Ahmedabad) and the catalogue of his Reina Sofía retrospective (Madrid, 2002) remain at present the two most substantial publications; though by the time this book appears, Khakhar's Tate retrospective catalogue will be out (London, 2016). An early text by Geeta Kapur, 'View from the Teashop', in *Contemporary Indian Painters* (Vikas, New Delhi, 1978) is a very enjoyable account of Khakhar's beginnings. Julian Bell writes on Khakhar in *Mirror of the World* (Thames & Hudson, 2007), pp. 248–49; Salmon Rushdie's memoir *Joseph Anton* (Cape, London, 2012) includes a description of his experience of sitting for Khakhar.

In *The New Subjectivism* (UMI, 1988), Donald Kuspit writes interestingly about Kiefer's early work, as does Thomas McEvilley in *The Exile's Return* (Cambridge University Press, 1994), see further reading. The catalogue to 'Zeitgeist' at Martin-Gropius-Bau was published by Frölich and Kauffmann (Berlin, 1982).

Ida Applebroog: Happy Families, exh. cat. (Contemporary Arts Museum Huston, 1990), is an informative survey focusing mainly on the multi-canvas constructions. See also Mira Schor, 'Medusa Redux', *Artforum* xxviii (March 1990), and Faye Hirsch in *Art in America* (1 June 2012).

William Kentridge, exh. cat. Hirshhorn, Washington, DC, et al. (Abrams, 2001) is a helpful overview. The artist's statement of 1993, 'Stone-Age Film-Making', is frequently quoted. Carolyn Christov-Bakargiev's *William Kentridge*, exh. cat. (Palais de Beaux-Arts, Brussels, 1999), is illuminating. *Six Drawing Lessons* (Harvard, 2014) is based on Kentridge's 2012 Norton Lectures, some of which are available free online.

Neo Rauch (Hatje Cantz, 2002) includes a brief essay by Lynne Cooke. The enormous double-tome published by Hatje Cantz in 2010 provides an overview through exhibitions in Leipzig (Museum der Bildendern Künste) and Munich (Pinakothek der Moderne). *Neo Rauch, Schilfland* (Reed Fen), (Prestel, 2009) is an anthology of works on paper 2005–8, with an interview and text by Wolfgang Büscher. Peter Schjeldahl's *Let's See* (Thames & Hudson, 2008, see further reading) includes his brilliant 2007 essay 'Paintings for Now: Neo Rauch'.

Jon Bird's *Leon Golub: Echoes of The Real* (Reaktion, London, revised edition 2011) is the definitive monograph, while *Leon Golub: Bite Your Tongue*, is the interesting catalogue to the Serpentine Gallery's exhibition in 2015. *Leon Golub: Do Paintings Bite?* (Hatje Cantz, 1997) collects together many of the artist's writings. The fascinating DVD *Golub/Spero* (Kartemquin, Chicago) includes *Golub: Late Works are the Catastrophes* (2004, 80 mins).

EPILOGUE

My 1975 essay on Howard Hodgkin's paintings came out in *Studio International* vol. 198, no. 975 (May/June), and I interviewed Hodgkin for *Artscribe* (December 1978). *Howard Hodgkin: The Complete Paintings*, ed. Marla Price (Thames & Hudson, 2006), includes a helpful anthology of critical commentary.

Suggested further reading on painting in the twentieth century
Among the most readable volumes of essays on twentieth-century artists, are: John Berger's *Permanent Red: Essays in Seeing* (Methuen, London, 1960); Jed Perl's *Paris Without End: On French Art Since World War I* (North Point Press, San Francisco 1988); and, as noted above, Robert Hughes's *Nothing if Not Critical: Selected Essays on Art and Artists* (Collins Harvill, London, and Knopf, New York, 1990); David Sylvester's *About Modern Art: Critical Essays, 1948–96* (Chatto and Windus, London, 1996); and Peter Schjeldahl's *Let's See: Writings on Art from The New Yorker* (Thames & Hudson, 2008). For discussion of later 20th-century figuration, both Donald Kuspit's *The New Subjectivism: Art in the 1980s* (UMI Research Press, Ann Arbor 1988) and Thomas McEvilley's *The Exile's Return: Towards a Redefinition of Painting for the Postmodern Era* (Cambridge University Press, 1994) are rewarding. *Art in Theory, 1900–1990: An Anthology of Changing Ideas*, edited by Charles Harrison and Paul Wood (Blackwell, Oxford, 1992), assembles an unrivalled collection of artists' texts and manifestos, as well as extracts from critical essays, but with a conceptual and theoretical bias. The seven-hundred-page *Art Since 1900: Modernism, Antimodernism, Postmodernism* (Thames & Hudson, 2004, 3rd edition 2016), written collaboratively by Rosalind Krauss, Yve Alain Bois, Benjamin Buchloh and Hal Foster, is a committed, conceptually based account in which painting is edged out and makes no appearance at all after 1980; I reviewed it in the *TLS* (28 October 2005). Brendan Prendeville's *Realism in 20th Century Painting* (Thames & Hudson, 2000), is a wide-ranging survey, moving swiftly across a crowded field. In an accessible and superbly illustrated overview, Jon Thompson's *How to Read a Modern Painting: Understanding and Enjoying the Modern Masters* (Thames & Hudson, 2006) places abstract and figurative pictures together within the spectrum of twentieth-century achievement.

LIST OF ILLUSTRATIONS

Dimensions of works are given in centimetres and inches, height before width.

Cover: detail of page 48
Frontispiece: detail of page 155

INTRODUCTION

8: Henri Matisse, *The Dance*, 1909–10. Oil on canvas, 260 × 391 (102 ½ × 154). The Hermitage, St Petersburg. © Succession H. Matisse/DACS 2016

1 AFTER CUBISM

12 detail of page 38–39

14 Pablo Picasso, *Seated Man with Glass*, 1914. Oil on canvas, 236 × 167.5 (93 × 66). Private collection. © Succession Picasso/DACS, London 2016

15 Fernand Léger, *The Campers*, 1954. Oil on canvas, 300 × 245 (118 × 96 ½) Musée national Fernand Léger, Biot, France. © ADAGP, Paris and DACS, London 2016

16 Marc Chagall, *Half Past Three (The Poet)*, 1911–12. Oil on canvas, 196 × 145 (77 × 57) Philadelphia Museum of Art (Arensberg Collection). Chagall ®/© ADAGP, Paris and DACS, London 2016

19 Henri Matisse, *View of Nôtre Dame*, 1914. Oil on canvas, 147 × 94 (58 × 37). Museum of Modern Art, New York. © Succession H. Matisse/DACS 2016

21 Fernand Léger, *The Mechanic*, 1920. Oil on canvas, 115 × 88 (45 × 35). National Gallery of Canada, Ottawa. © ADAGP, Paris and DACS, London 2016

22: Henri Rousseau, *Child with Doll*, 1904–5. Oil on canvas, 67 × 52 (26 ½ × 20 ½). Musée de l'Orangerie, Paris

25l Fernand Léger, *The Syphon*, 1924. Oil on canvas, 91 × 60 (36 × 23 ½). Collection Rafael Tudela Reverter, Caracas. © ADAGP, Paris and DACS, London 2016

25r Fernand Léger, *Nude on a Red Background*, 1927. Oil on canvas, 130 × 81 (51 × 32). Hirshhorn Museum and Sculpture Garden, Washington, DC. © ADAGP, Paris and DACS, London 2016

27 Carlo Carrà, *The Pine Tree by the Sea*, 1921. Oil on canvas, 68 × 52.5 (27 × 20 ½). Private collection. © DACS 2016

28 Carlo Carrà, *The House of Love*, 1922. Oil on canvas, 90 × 70 (35½ × 27 ½). Pinacoteca di Brera, Milan (Gift of Emilio and Maria Tesi). © DACS 2016

29 Mario Sironi, *Urban Landscape with Chimneys*, 1921. Oil on canvas, 49 × 67 (19 ½ × 26 ½). Pinacoteca di Brera, Milan. © DACS 2016

30–31 Mario Sironi, Study for *Italy Between the Arts and the Sciences*, 1935. Tempera on paper on canvas, 370 × 475 (145 ½ × 187). Location unknown. © DACS 2016

34 Marc Chagall, *Sobakevich in front of the Armchair* (illustration to Gogol's *Dead Souls*), 1924–25. Etching and drypoint with aquatint, 27 × 21 (10 ½ × 8 ½). Private collection. Chagall ®/© ADAGP, Paris and DACS, London 2016

34 Marc Chagall, *The Volga Barge-Haulers* (illustration to Gogol's *Dead Souls*), 1924–25. Etching and drypoint with aquatint, 21 × 27 (10 ½ × 8 ½). Private collection. Chagall ®/© ADAGP, Paris and DACS, London 2016

35 Marc Chagall, *The Garden Beyond Plyushkin's House* (illustration to Gogol's *Dead Souls*), 1924–25. Etching and drypoint with aquatint, 27 × 21 (10 ½ × 8 ½). Private collection. Chagall ®/© ADAGP, Paris and DACS, London 2016

38–39 (detail p. 12) Marc Chagall, *Introduction to the Yiddish Theatre*, 1920. Tempera, gouache and opaque white on canvas, 284 × 787 (112 × 310). Tretyakov State Gallery, Moscow. Chagall ®/© ADAGP, Paris and DACS, London 2016

43 Diego Rivera, *The Day of The Dead: City Fiesta*, 1923–24. Fresco, 417 × 375 (164 × 148). Ministry of Education, Mexico City. © 2016 Banco de México Diego Rivera Frida Kahlo Museums Trust, Mexico, DF/DACS

44 Benode Behari Mukherjee, *The Lives of the Medieval Indian Saints*, 1946–47. Fresco, south wall, 244 × 865 (96 × 341), total length of mural 244 × 2,307 (96 × 908). Hindi Bhavan. Courtesy Visva Bharati University, Santiniketan, Bengal, India

48 Marsden Hartley, *Adelard the Drowned, Master of 'The Phantom'*, 1938–39. Oil on board, 71 × 56 (28 × 22). The Frederick R. Weisman Art Museum, University of Minnesota, MN. Bequest of Hudson D. Walker from the Ione and Hudson D. Walker Collection

49 Marsden Hartley, *Fishermen's Last Supper*, 1938. Oil on board, 56 × 71 (22 × 28). Private collection

50 Marsden Hartley, *Sustained Comedy: Portrait of an Object*, 1939. Oil on board, 71 × 56 (28 × 22). Carnegie Museum of Art, Pittsburgh

51 Marsden Hartley, *Portrait of Albert Pinkham Ryder*, 1938. Oil on masonite, 71 × 56 (28 × 22). The Metropolitan Museum of Art, New York

54 Francis Bacon, *Three Studies for a Crucifixion*, 1962. Oil on canvas, three panels each 198 × 145 (78 × 57). Solomon R. Guggenheim Museum, New York. © The Estate of Francis Bacon. All rights reserved. © DACS 2016

57 Paula Rego, *The Barn*, 1994. Acrylic on canvas, 270 × 190 (106 × 75). Museu Coleção Berardo, Lisbon. © Paula Rego. Courtesy Marlborough Fine Art, London

2 AFTER EXPRESSIONISM

61 Emil Nolde, *Excited People*, 1913. Oil on canvas, 102 × 76 (40 × 30). Nolde Foundation Seebüll, Germany. © Nolde Stiftung Seebül

62 Max Beckmann, *The Night*, 1918–19. Oil on canvas, 133 × 153 (52 × 60). Kunstsammlung Nordrhein-Westfalen, Düsseldorf. © DACS 2016

64 Otto Dix, *The Trench*, 1920–23. Oil on canvas, 227 × 250 (89 ½ × 98 ½). Lost, presumed destroyed. © DACS 2016

65 Otto Dix, *Pragerstrasse* (Prague Street: Dedicated to My Contemporaries), 1920. Oil and collage on canvas, 101 × 81 cm (40 × 32). Kunstmuseum, Stuttgart. © DACS 2016

66 Otto Dix, *The Barricade*, 1920. Oil and collage/mixed media on canvas, dimensions uncertain. Lost, presumed destroyed. © DACS 2016

67 Otto Dix, *The Artist's Parents I*, 1921. Oil on canvas, 99 × 113 (39 × 44 ½). Kunstmuseum, Basel. © DACS 2016

68 Otto Dix, *Portrait of the Journalist Sylvia von Harden*, 1926. Oil on wood, 120 × 88 (47 × 34 ½). Centre Pompidou, Paris. © DACS 2016

69 (detail p. 58) Otto Dix, *To Beauty*, 1922. Oil on canvas, 144 × 122 (56 ½ × 48). Von der Heydt Museum, Wuppertal, Germany. © DACS 2016

71 George Grosz, *The Funeral (Dedicated to Oskar Panizza)*, 1917–18. Oil on canvas, 140 × 110 (55 × 43). Staatsgalerie, Stuttgart. © Estate of George Grosz, Princeton, NJ/DACS 2016

72 George Grosz, *The Seated Toads*, c. 1920–21. Ink (reed pen and brush) on paper, 53 × 41 (21 × 16). Scottish National Gallery of Modern Art, Edinburgh. © Estate of George Grosz, Princeton, NJ/DACS 2016

75a Max Beckmann, *The Synagogue*, 1919. Oil on canvas, 90 × 140 (35 ½ × 55). Städel Museum, Frankfurt. © DACS 2016

75b Max Beckmann, *Landscape near Frankfurt with Factory*, 1922. Oil on canvas, 66 × 101 (26 × 40). Rose Art Museum, Brandeis University, Waltham, MA. © DACS 2016

76 Otto Dix, *Grossstadt* (Big City), 1927–28. Oil on wood, 181 × 404 (71 × 159). Kunstmuseum, Stuttgart. © DACS 2016

77 Max Beckmann, *Chinese Fireworks; Small Dream*, 1927. Oil on canvas, 55.5 × 62.5 (22 × 24 ½). Pinakothek der Moderne, Munich. © DACS 2016

78–79 Max Beckmann, *Departure*, 1932 and 1933–35. Oil on canvas, side panels each 215 × 100 (84 ½ × 39), central panel 215 × 115 (85 × 45). Museum of Modern Art, New York. © DACS 2016

81 Stanley Spencer, *Zacharias and Elizabeth*, 1913–14. Oil on canvas, 143 × 143 (56 × 56). Tate, London. © Estate of Stanley Spencer. All Rights Reserved 2016/Bridgeman Images

83 Paul Nash, *The Menin Road*, 1919. Oil on canvas, 183 × 318 (72 × 125). Imperial War Museum, London. © IWM (Art. IWM ART 2242)

84 William Roberts, *The Cinema*, 1920. Oil on canvas, 91 × 76 (36 × 30). Tate, London. The Estate of John David Roberts

85 Stanley Spencer, *The Sandham Memorial Chapel, Burghclere*, 1926–32. Oil on canvas glued to wall, Burghclere, Hampshire, UK. National Trust Photographic Library/A. C. Cooper/Bridgeman Images. © Estate of Stanley Spencer. All Rights Reserved 2016/Bridgeman Images

87 Edward Burra, *Minuit Chanson* (Midnight Song), 1931. Watercolour and gouache on paper, 54 × 73 (21 × 28 ½). Private

collection. © Estate of Edward Burra, c/o Lefevre Fine Art Ltd, London

88 Edward Burra, *Harlem*, 1934. Watercolour, ink and gouache on paper, 79 × 57 (31 × 23). Tate London. © Estate of Edward Burra, c/o Lefevre Fine Art Ltd, London

89 William Roberts, *The Vorticists at the Restaurant de la Tour Eiffel: Spring, 1915*, 1961–62. Oil on canvas, 202 × 233 (79 ½ × 91 ½). Tate London. The Estate of John David Roberts

90 Stanley Spencer, *The Leg of Mutton Nude (Double Portrait of the Artist and His Second Wife)*, 1937. Oil on canvas, 84 × 94 (33 × 37). Tate, London. Photo Bridgeman Images. © Estate of Stanley Spencer. All Rights Reserved 2016/ Bridgeman Images

91 Christian Schad, *Self-Portrait with Model*, 1927. Oil on wood, 76 × 62 (29 × 24). Private collection. © Christian Schad Stiftung Aschaffenburg/VG Bild-Kunst, Bonn and DACS, London 2016

94 Balthus, *La Rue* (The Street), 1933. Oil on canvas, 195 × 240 (77 × 94 ½). Museum of Modern Art, New York. © Balthus

95a Balthus, *Drawings to Wuthering Heights: 'You needn't have touched me'*, 1933. India ink on paper, 39.4 × 30.9 (15 ½ × 12). Private collection. © Balthus

95b Balthus, *Drawings to Wuthering Heights: 'Pull his hair when you go by'*, 1933. India ink on paper, 38.5 × 31 (15 × 12). Private collection. © Balthus

96 Balthus, *La leçon de guitare* (The Lesson), 1934. Oil on canvas, 161 × 138.5 (63 ½ × 54 ½). Private collection. © Balthus

98 Balthus, *Joan Miró and His Daughter Dolorès*, 1937–38. Oil on canvas, 130.2 × 88.9 (51 ¼ × 35). Museum of Modern Art, New York. © Balthus

99a Balthus, *La Chambre* (The Room), 1952–54. Oil on canvas, 270.5 × 335 (108 ½ × 132). Private collection. © Balthus

99b Balthus, *Le Passage du Commerce-Saint-André* (Commerce-St-Andrew Passage), 1952–54. Oil on canvas, 294 × 330 (115 ½ × 130). Private collection. © Balthus

102 Edward Hopper, *Nighthawks*, 1942. Oil on canvas, 84 × 152 (33 × 60). Art Institute of Chicago

105 Alice Neel, *Joe Gould*, 1933. Oil on canvas, 99 × 79 (39 × 31). Private collection. Courtesy David Zwirner, New York/London. © The Estate of Alice Neel

106 Alice Neel, *Andy Warhol*, 1970. Oil on canvas, 152 × 102 (60 × 40). Whitney Museum of American Art, New York. Courtesy David Zwirner, New York/London. © The Estate of Alice Neel

107 Alice Neel, *The Soyer Brothers*, 1973. Oil on canvas, 152 × 117 (60 × 46). Whitney Museum of American Art, New York. Courtesy David Zwirner, New York/London. © The Estate of Alice Neel

108 Alice Neel, *Self-Portrait*, 1980. Oil on canvas, 137 × 102 (54 × 40). National Portrait Gallery, Smithsonian, Washington, DC. Courtesy David Zwirner, New York/ London. © The Estate of Alice Neel

p111 Lucian Freud, *Interior at Paddington*, 1951. Oil on canvas, 152 × 114 (60 × 45). Walker Art Gallery, Liverpool. © Walker Art Gallery, National Museums Liverpool/© The Lucian Freud Archive/Bridgeman Images

3 FIRST-PERSON PAINTING

115 Edouard Vuillard, *Married Life*, 1900. Oil on cardboard, 51 × 57 (20 × 22 ½). Private collection

116 Pierre Bonnard, *Dining Room in the Country*, 1913. Oil on canvas, 164.5 × 206 (65 × 81). The Minneapolis Institute of Art. © ADAGP, Paris and DACS, London 2016

118l Paula Modersohn-Becker, *Self-Portrait in Paris*, 1900. Oil on paper, 38 × 26 (15 × 10). Private collection

118r Paula Modersohn-Becker, *Self-Portrait with Necklace*, 1903. Oil on paper, 38 × 26 (15 × 10). Kunsthalle, Bremen

119 Paula Modersohn-Becker, *Standing Nude Self-Portrait*, 1906. Oil on canvas, 170 × 70 (67 × 27 ½). Galerie Neue Meister, Dresden, on loan from a private collection

120 Paula Modersohn-Becker, *Self-Portrait with Lemon*, 1906. Oil on cardboard, 50 × 28 (20 × 11). Private collection

122 Paula Modersohn-Becker, *Mother and Child*, 1906. Oil with tempera (and wax?) on canvas, 82.5 × 124.5 (32 ½ × 49). Museen Böttcherstrasse, Ludwig Roselius Collection, Bremen

123 Paula Modersohn-Becker, *Self-Portrait on My Sixth Wedding Anniversary*, 1906. Oil with tempera (and wax?) on cardboard, 102 × 70 (40 × 27 ½). Museen Böttcherstrasse, Ludwig Roselius Collection, Bremen

125 Ernst Ludwig Kirchner, *Berlin Street Scene*, 1913. Sketchbook page, pencil on paper, 21 × 17 (8 × 6 ½). Courtesy Galerie Kornfeld Auktionen AG, Bern

127 Ernst Ludwig Kirchner, *Potsdamer Platz*, 1914. Oil on canvas, 200 × 150 (78 ½ × 59). Neue Nationalgalerie Berlin

129 Pierre Bonnard, *Large Blue Nude*, 1924. Oil on canvas, 101 × 73 (40 × 28 ½). Private collection. © ADAGP, Paris and DACS, London 2016

130 Pierre Bonnard, *Nude in the Bath with Small Dog*, 1941–46. Oil on canvas, 73 × 100 (28 ½ × 39 ½). Carnegie Museum of Art, Pittsburgh. © ADAGP, Paris and DACS, London 2016

131 Pierre Bonnard, *The Boxer*, 1931. Oil on canvas, 54 × 74 (21 × 29). Private collection. © ADAGP, Paris and DACS, London 2016

132 Pierre Bonnard, *Self-Portrait*, *c*. 1938–40. Oil on canvas, 76 × 61 (30 × 24). Art Gallery of New South Wales, Sydney. © ADAGP, Paris and DACS, London 2016

133 Pierre Bonnard, *Self-Portrait*, 1945. Oil on canvas, 56 × 46 (22 × 18). Collection Fondation Bemberg, Toulouse. © ADAGP, Paris and DACS, London 2016

135 Chaim Soutine, *Le Pâtissier* (The Baker's Boy, The Little Pastry Cook) *c*. 1919. Oil on canvas, 66 × 51 (26 × 20). Photo The Barnes Foundation, Philadelphia. The Barnes Foundation, Philadelphia, PA/Bridgeman Images

136 (detail p. 112) Frida Kahlo, *What the Water Gave Me*, 1938. Oil on canvas, 91 × 71 (36 × 28). Collection of Daniel Filipacchi, Paris. © 2016 Banco de México Diego Rivera Frida Kahlo Museums Trust, Mexico, DF/DACS

137 Max Beckmann, *Feet in the Bath*, 1931–50. Oil on canvas, 66 × 26 (26 × 10). Michael Werner Gallery, New York. © DACS 2016

140 Stanley Spencer, *The Beatitudes of Love: Toasting*, 1937–38. Oil on canvas, 76 × 51 (30 × 20). Private collection. Photo © Agnew's, London/Bridgeman Images. © Estate of Stanley

Spencer. All Rights Reserved 2016/ Bridgeman Images

141 Stanley Spencer, *The Beatitudes of Love: Consciousness*, *c*. 1938. Oil on canvas, 76 × 56 (30 × 22). Private collection. © Estate of Stanley Spencer. All Rights Reserved 2016/Bridgeman Images

142 Stanley Spencer, *Sunflower and Dog Worship*, 1937. Oil on canvas, 71 × 108 (28 × 42 ½). Private collection. © Estate of Stanley Spencer. All Rights Reserved 2016/ Bridgeman Images

143 Stanley Spencer, *Love Letters*, 1950. Oil on canvas, 86 × 117 (34 × 46). Private collection/Bridgeman Images. © Estate of Stanley Spencer. All Rights Reserved 2016/ Bridgeman Images

144 Stanley Spencer, *Self-Portrait*, 1959. Oil on canvas, 51 × 40 (20 × 15 ½). Tate, London. © Estate of Stanley Spencer. All Rights Reserved 2016/Bridgeman Images

146–49 Charlotte Salomon, Pages from *Life? Or Theatre?*, 1940–42. Watercolour and gouache on paper, 33 × 25 (13 × 10). Collection Jewish Historical Museum, Amsterdam. Charlotte Salomon ®/© Charlotte Salomon Foundation

152 Max Beckmann, *The Liberated*, 1937. Oil on canvas, 60 × 40 (24 × 15 ½). Private collection. © DACS 2016

153 Max Beckmann, *Death*, 1938. Oil on canvas, 121 × 177 (47 ½ × 69 ½). Nationalgalerie, Berlin. © DACS 2016

155 (detail frontispiece) Max Beckmann, *Acrobats*, 1937–39. Oil on canvas, side panels 200 × 91 (78 ½ × 36), centre panel 201 × 168 (79 × 66). Saint Louis Art Museum, MO. Bequest of Morton D. May/ Bridgeman Images © DACS 2016

156–57 Max Beckmann, *Blindman's Buff*, 1944–45. Oil on canvas, side panels 191 × 110 (75 × 43 ½), centre panel 205 × 230 (80 ½ × 90 ½). The Minneapolis Institute of Art, MN. © DACS 2016

158 Max Beckmann, *Self-Portrait in Black*, 1944. Oil on canvas, 95 × 60 (37 ½ × 23 ½). Pinakothek der Moderne, Munich. © DACS 2016

159 Max Beckmann, *The Cabins*, 1947–48. Oil on canvas, 141 × 191 (55 ½ × 75). Kunstsammlung Nordrhein-Westfalen, Düsseldorf. © DACS 2016

160 Edvard Munch, *Self-Portrait: Between Clock and Bed*, 1940–43.

Oil on canvas, 150 × 121 (59 × 47 ½). Munch Museet, Oslo

4 BEYOND THE FORMALIST CANON

164 James Ensor, *Tribulations of Saint Anthony*, 1887. Oil on canvas, 118 × 168 (46 ½ × 66). Museum of Modern Art, New York. © DACS 2016

166–67 Ken Kiff, from *The Sequence*, number 113, *Talking with a Psychoanalyst: Night Sky*, 1975–79. Acrylic on paper, 81 × 137 (32 × 54). Private collection. © Estate of Ken Kiff

169 Alfred Kubin, *The Scorpion, c.* 1922. Ink on paper, dimensions and location unknown. © Eberhard Spangenberg/DACS, 2015

172 Rabindranath Tagore, *Untitled, c.* 1935. Ink on paper, 27 × 37.5 (10 ½ × 15). National Gallery of Modern Art, New Delhi

174 Jack Yeats, *The Clown Among the People*, 1932. Oil on canvas, 46 × 61 (18 × 24). Private collection. © Estate of Jack B. Yeats. All rights reserved, DACS 2016

175 Jack Yeats, *The Expected*, 1948. Oil on canvas, 61 × 91 (24 × 36). Private collection. © Estate of Jack B. Yeats. All rights reserved, DACS 2016

178–79 Henry Darger, *[Storm] Brewing, 1930–72.* Tracing, watercolour and collage on paper, 77 × 317 (30 × 125). Collection de l'Art Brut, Lausanne. © ARS, New York and DACS, London 2016

180–81 Henry Darger, *The Massacre at Norma Catherine*, 1930–72. Three-panel tracing, watercolour and collage on paper, 56 × 226 (22 × 89). Kyoko Lerner, Chicago. © ARS, NY and DACS, London 2016

183a Jacob Lawrence, from *The Migration of the Negro*, number 15, *'Another cause was lynching. It was found that where there had been a lynching, the people who were reluctant to leave at first left immediately after this.'*, 1940–41. Casein tempera on masonite, 31 × 46 (12 × 18). The Phillips Collection, Washington, DC. © Estate of Jacob Lawrence. ARS, NY and DACS, London 2016.

183b Jacob Lawrence, from *The Migration of the Negro*, number 30, *'In every home people who had not gone North met and tried to decide if they should go North or not.'*, 1940–41. Casein tempera on masonite, 31 × 46 (12 × 18). Museum of Modern Art, New York. © Estate of Jacob Lawrence. ARS, NY and DACS, London 2016

186 Ken Kiff, from *The Sequence*, number 1, *Something Unknown Has to Be Eaten or Drunk*, 1971. Acrylic on paper, 25 × 25 (10 × 10). Private collection. © Estate of Ken Kiff

187 Ken Kiff, *Person Cutting an Image*, 1965–71. Tempera on board, 61 × 61 (24 × 24). Tate, London. © Estate of Ken Kiff

188 Ken Kiff, from *The Sequence*, number 35, *Walking (The Dead Father)*, 1972. Acrylic on paper, 58 × 46 (23 × 18). Private collection. © Estate of Ken Kiff

189 (detail p. 162) Ken Kiff, from *The Sequence*, number 97, *Writing*, 1977–79. Acrylic on paper, 72 × 58 (28 × 23). Private collection. © Estate of Ken Kiff

191 Ken Kiff, from *The Sequence*, number 91, *Earth Face, c.* 1978. Acrylic on paper 58 × 39 (23 × 15 ½). Private collection. © Estate of Ken Kiff

5 AFTER ABSTRACT EXPRESSIONISM

193 detail of page 193

195 Willem de Kooning, *Woman I*, 1950–52. Oil on canvas, 193 × 147 (76 × 58). Museum of Modern Art, New York. © The Willem de Kooning Foundation, New York/ARS, New York and DACS, London 2016

196 Philip Guston, *Painting, Smoking, Eating*, 1973. Oil on canvas, 196 × 262 (77 × 103). Stedelijk Museum, Amsterdam. © The Estate of Philip Guston

199 R. B. Kitaj, *The Red Banquet*, 1960. Oil and collage on canvas, 152 × 152 (60 × 60). Walker Art Gallery, Liverpool. © R. B. Kitaj Estate

200 R. B. Kitaj, *Reflections on Violence*, 1962. Oil and collage on canvas, 152 × 152 (60 × 60). Kunsthalle, Hamburg. © R.B. Kitaj Estate

201 R. B. Kitaj, *The Ohio Gang*, 1964. Oil on canvas, 183 × 183 (72 × 72). Museum of Modern Art, New York. © R. B. Kitaj Estate

202 R. B. Kitaj, *Erie Shore*, 1966. Oil on canvas, diptych, each section 183 × 152 (72 × 60). Nationalgalerie, Berlin. © R. B. Kitaj Estate

204 R. B. Kitaj, *If Not, Not*, 1975–76. Oil on canvas, 152 × 152 (60 × 60). Scottish National Gallery of Modern Art, Edinburgh. © R. B. Kitaj Estate

206 David Hockney, *The Second Marriage*, 1963. Oil on canvas, 198 × 228 (78 × 90). National Gallery of Victoria, Melbourne. Photo National Gallery of Victoria, Melbourne. © David Hockney

209 Invitation to 'Alex Katz: Flat Statues', Tanager Gallery, New York, 1962. Studio photograph by Rudy Burckhardt. © Alex Katz, DACS, London/VAGA, New York 2016; Burckhardt © ARS, NY and DACS, London 2016

210 Red Grooms, *Walking Man*, 1957. Oil on canvas, 64 × 64 (25 × 25). Collection Dominic Falcone and Yvonne Andersen, Lexington, MA. © ARS, NY and DACS, London 2016

211 Red Grooms, *Don't Walk* 1963. Oil on canvas, 183 × 196 (72 × 77). Private collection. © ARS, NY and DACS, London 2016

213 Red Grooms with Mimi Gross, *Subway from Ruckus Manhattan*, 1976. Mixed media, 274 × 566 × 1,133 (108 × 223 × 446). Kunsthalle, Bremen. Red Grooms © ARS, NY and DACS, London 2016. © Mimi Gross

215 Georg Baselitz, *Big Night Down the Drain*, 1962–63. Oil on canvas, 250 × 180 (98 ½ × 71). Museum Ludwig, Cologne. © Georg Baselitz 2016

217 A wall in Philip Guston's Woodstock studio hung with several small panels, 1968. Black and white photograph by Denise Hare. © Denise Hare 1989. © The Estate of Philip Guston

218 Philip Guston, *Flatlands*, 1970. Oil on canvas, 178 × 291 (70 × 114 ½). Promised Gift to the San Francisco Museum of Modern Art, CA. © The Estate of Philip Guston

221 Bhupen Khakhar, *Man Eating Jalebee*, 1974. Oil on canvas, 119 × 119 (47 × 47). Collection Mr and Mrs James Kirkman, England. Courtesy Chemould Prescott Road Archives, Bombay, India

222 Bhupen Khakhar, *Man with Bouquet of Plastic Flowers*, 1976. Oil on canvas, 145 × 140 (57 × 55). National Gallery of Modern Art, New Delhi. Courtesy Chemould Prescott Road Archives, Bombay, India

223 Bhupen Khakhar, *You Can't Please All*, 1981. Oil on canvas, 167 × 167 (65 ½ × 65 ½). Tate, London. Courtesy Chemould Prescott Road Archives, Bombay, India

224 Bhupen Khakhar, *Two Men in Banaras*, 1982. Oil on canvas, 175 × 175 (69 × 69). Private collection. Courtesy Chemould Prescott Road Archives, Bombay, India

225 Bhupen Khakhar, *Yayati*, 1987. Oil on canvas, 91 × 122 (36 × 48). Private collection. Courtesy Chemould Prescott Road Archives, Bombay, India

227 Anselm Kiefer, *Operation Sea Lion*, 1983–84. Oil, emulsion, shellac, acrylic, straw and photograph (on projection paper) on canvas, 380 × 555 (150 × 218 ½). Private collection. Photo Atelier Anselm Kiefer © Anselm Kiefer

229 Ida Applebroog, *Camp Compazine*, 1988. Oil on canvas, four panels, 218 × 356 overall (86 × 140). Private collection. Courtesy of the artist and Hauser & Wirth. © Ida Applebroog

230, 232–33: William Kentridge, *Felix in Exile*, 1994. Frames from animation (drawn in charcoal). Courtesy William Kentridge and Goodman Gallery, Johannesburg and Cape Town

236 Neo Rauch, *Alter* (Elder), 2001. Oil on canvas, 250 × 210 (98 ½ × 82 ½). Sammlung Rudolf & Ute Scharpff, Stuttgart. Photo Uwe Walter, Berlin, courtesy Galerie EIGEN + ART Leipzig/Berlin and David Zwirner, New York/London. © Neo Rauch courtesy Galerie EIGEN+ART Leipzig/Berlin/DACS 2016

238 Leon Golub, *Laughing Lions*, 1995. Acrylic on raw linen without stretcher, 234 × 514 (92 × 202 ½). Ulrich and Harriet Meyer Collection, Chicago. Photo David Reynolds. Courtesy Ronald Feldman Fine Arts, New York

EPILOGUE

240: Howard Hodgkin, *First Portrait of Terence McInerney*, 1981. Oil on wood, 127 × 140 (50 × 55). Private collection. © Howard Hodgkin

241: Howard Hodgkin, *Second Portrait of Terence McInerney*, 1981. Oil on wood, 127 × 140 (50 × 55). Private collection © Howard Hodgkin

ACKNOWLEDGMENTS

Immediately after art school I was hired to deliver thirty talks on 'modern artists' at the venerable Working Men's College in north London. At first my list conformed, culminating in American Abstraction. But in the course of the 1970s, partly through looking and reading, but also through conversations with fellow painters of several generations in Britain, that cast changed. My first thanks goes to those artists, each of them helping to reshape my view of the twentieth century: Ken Kiff and Andrzej Jackowski; Peter Darach and Alexander Moffat; Howard Hodgkin and R. B. Kitaj; Jeffery Camp and Anthony Green; Josef Herman and Peter de Francia. I'd begun in the same years an often stormy, but lifelong, dialogue with the critic Geeta Kapur, and I owe a debt both to her and to a group of Indian artists, including Gulammohammed Sheikh, Bhupen Khakhar, Vivan Sundaram, Gieve Patel, K. G. Subramanyan and Sudhir Patwardhan, all of them debating Western art from a fresh angle. In 1979 I curated the exhibition 'Narrative Paintings', which toured to the ICA in London; for a few years in the 1980s a group of disparate painters met informally, dubbed by Dexter Dalwood 'The Narrative Nobodies'. In addition to Dalwood and myself they included Darach, Camp and de Francia, as well as Leonard McComb, Manuel Botelho, Marjan Hormozi, Francis West, Tracey Emin and Neil Jeffries. Those meetings helped to shape this book. Also formative was itinerant teaching; my painting students, especially at Saint Martin's School of Art, The Slade, Glasgow School of Art and the Royal College of Art, were instrumental in alerting me to a changing climate.

My first published essays were on cinema, and a long friendship with Derek Jarman nourished that parallel interest. But there was also a literary component, and I was fortunate to be befriended in my early twenties by G. Wilson Knight; we'd met through our shared passion for the fiction of John Cowper Powys. I owe much to friends in The Powys Society (especially Dr David Goodway, Louise de Bruin, Dr Richard Maxwell and Professor Charles Lock). Alan Ross was an encouraging editor and mentor at London Magazine. My most sustained dialogue has been with Gabriel Josipovici, and I am grateful to him for commenting on this book at a late stage. I have learnt much from friends in the Department of Art History at University College, London, especially Professor David Bindman and Professor Tamar Garb; both generously read the book, as did Professor Linda Nochlin in New York. The beautiful library at the Royal Academy proved a wonderful resource, and among the library staff I want particularly to thank Adam Waterton.

In the twenty-first century my fiercest conversations have been with Paul Gopal-Chowdhury; I've valued discussion with artists of many persuasions (especially Merlin James, Nurit David, Tess Jaray and John Davies) and I've enjoyed critical exchanges with Julian Bell, Itamar Levi, Jed Perl and the late Tom Lubbock. Several younger artists have commented helpfully on sections of this book, including Alexandra Blum, Liza Dimbleby, Heidrun Rathgeb, Eleanor Ray and Perienne Christian. Friends in New York – including Trevor Winkfield, David Carbone, Gabriel Laderman, Joyce and Max Kozloff – all helped thicken the brew. I'm grateful to many who've assisted in various ways over the years, among them Janet Atkinson, John Austin, Gillian Barlow, Professor Jon Bird, Dr Susan Canning, Dinah Casson, Jean Clair, Peter Doig, Roger Farrington, David Gervais, Sir Lawrence Gowing, Sandro Graziani, Charles Hewlings, Robert Hoozee, David Fraser Jenkins, Anna Kiff, Richard Lannoy, Jeremy Lewison, Roger Malbert, John MacGregor, Lino Mannocci, Miranda Miller, Richard Morphet, Jacqueline Morreau, Sir Alan Moses, Mrinalini Mukherjee, Roy Oxlade, Martin Perks, Oliver Probyn, Meg Rosoff, Noah Saterstrom, John Spencer, Andrew Spira, Louis Spitalnick, Jean Pierre Tison, John Toft, Vitek Tracz, Rose Wylie and Richard Zimler. I want to thank my patient editors at Thames & Hudson: Andrew Brown, who first commissioned the book; Jacky Klein, who whipped it into shape; and Roger Thorp, Sarah Hull and Tamsin Perrett, as well as Sophy Thompson. Wonderful support through all these years has come from Judith Ravenscroft: partner, soulmate, wife. Finally, almost every word from synopsis to final text has been typed by, and talked enjoyably through with, Richard Burton – a gifted painter and a marvellous studio assistant who was willingly dragged into the project; without his unflagging aid, it perhaps would never have been completed.